Expert Witnesses in Child Abuse Cases

Expert Witnesses in Child Abuse Cases

What Can and Should Be Said in Court

Edited by
Stephen J. Ceci and Helene Hembrooke

AMERICAN PSYCHOLOGICAL ASSOCIATION
WASHINGTON, DC

Published by
American Psychological Association
750 First Street, NE
Washington, DC 20002

Copies may be ordered from
APA Order Department
P.O. Box 92984
Washington, DC 20090-2984

In the U.K., Europe, Africa, and the Middle East, copies may be ordered from
American Psychological Association
3 Henrietta Street, Covent Garden
London WC2E 8LU, England

Typeset in Goudy by EPS Group Inc., Easton, MD

Printer: Braun-Brumfield, Inc., Ann Arbor, MI
Dust Jacket Designer: Design Concepts, San Diego, CA
Technical/Production Editor: Amy J. Clarke

Library of Congress Cataloging-in-Publication Data
Expert witnesses in child abuse cases : what can and should be said in court /
     edited by Stephen J. Ceci, Helene Hembrooke.—1st ed.
          p.   cm.
     Includes bibliographical references and index.
     ISBN 1-55798-515-4 (acid-free paper)
     1. Child abuse—Law and legislation—United States.   2. Evidence, Expert—
United States.   I. Ceci, Stephen J.   II. Hembrooke, Helene.
KF9323.E96   1998
345.73′025554—dc21   98-13683
                                                                            CIP

British Library Cataloguing-in-Publication Data
A CIP record is available from the British Library.

Printed in the United States of America
First Edition

CONTENTS

CONTRIBUTORS

Ronald J. Allen, JD, School of Law, Northwestern University

Lucy Berliner, MSW, Harborview Center for Sexual Abuse and Traumatic Stress, University of Washington

Eugene Borgida, PhD, Department of Psychology, University of Minnesota

Maggie Bruck, PhD, Department of Psychology, McGill University, Montreal, Quebec, Canada

Stephen J. Ceci, PhD, Department of Human Development and Family Studies, Cornell University

Celia B. Fisher, PhD, Applied Developmental Psychology, Fordham University

Betty N. Gordon, PhD, Department of Psychology, University of North Carolina

Helene Hembrooke, PhD, Department of Human Development and Family Studies, Cornell University

Jonathan J. Koehler, PhD, Graduate School of Business and Law School, University of Texas at Austin

Margaret Bull Kovera, PhD, Department of Psychology, Florida International University

Michael Lavin, PhD, Department of Psychology, University of Arizona

Richard J. Lawlor, JD, PhD, James Whitcomb Riley Hospital for Children, Indianapolis, IN

Thomas D. Lyon, JD, PhD, Law School, University of Southern California

Mary Ann Mason, JD, PhD, School of Social Welfare, University of California, Berkeley

Lucy McGough, JD, LLM, Paul M. Herbert Law Center, Louisiana State University

Joseph S. Miller, MS, JD, Sidley and Austin, Chicago, IL

Peter A. Ornstein, PhD, Department of Psychology, University of North Carolina, Chapel Hill
Kyle D. Pruett, MD, Yale Child Study Center, Yale University
Bruce D. Sales, JD, PhD, Department of Psychology, University of Arizona
Albert J. Solnit, MD, Yale Child Study Center, Yale University
John R. Spencer, MA, LLD, The Law Faculty, Selwyn College, Cambridge University, Cambridge, England
Katherine A. Whiting, MA, Departmett of Psychology, Fordham University

Expert Witnesses in Child Abuse Cases

INTRODUCTION

STEPHEN J. CECI AND HELENE HEMBROOKE

"Ethics in the courtroom," to the less cynical among us, may seem redundant, nouns that are the embodiment of each other. Granted that occasionally someone is called to testify even though he or she has a vested financial or professional interest that interferes with his or her objectivity and perhaps even renders such testimony fraudulent, but this is the rare exception, not the rule. Each day thousands of decent, knowledgeable experts ascend the stand to provide fact finders with information that can be expected to improve their decision making. Most of these experts do not enjoy testifying, and many abide by a set of practices established to ensure the integrity of their testimony. They are conscientious about avoiding real and perceived conflicts of interests, and they take great pains to be balanced in their testimony—even to the point of providing ammunition to the other side when the situation warrants it. Without such testimony, the quality of justice would be diminished. Without such input into their decisions, thousands of family court judges would be left to their surmises to make custody and support decisions.

To some, however, the phrase ethics in the courtroom evokes a sardonic smirk, even the suggestion of an oxymoron. After all, expert witnesses have been held in the lowest regard by jurists almost from the very beginning of the adversarial system. As Justice John Pitt Taylor noted in 1858 (as cited in Gross, 1991),

> Perhaps the testimony which least deserves credit with a jury is that of skilled witnesses ... It is often quite surprising to see with what

facility, and to what extent, their views can be made to correspond with the wishes and interests of the parties who call them. (p. 1114)

Such jaundiced views of the expert's ethics continue to be expressed by current American jurists as well as British jurists:

To put it bluntly, in many professions service as an expert witness is not generally considered honest work. . . . Experts in fields see lawyers as unprincipled manipulators of their disciplines, and lawyers and experts alike see expert witnesses—those members of the learned professions who will consort with lawyers—as whores. (Gross, 1991, p. 1115)

Expert evidence is sometimes given by people whose level of knowledge seems lamentably low. A number of the recent, and best-known scandals show this. . . . How does this come about? In the first place, I think it is because our present system provides no systematic quality control. Broadly speaking, anyone can be an expert witness, provided they have some relevant knowledge, and nothing whatever is done to see that only the best people are used. To be allowed to give expert evidence, witnesses must satisfy the judge that they have some practical experience, or some professional qualifications; but that is all. No minimum standards are laid down. The only test is opposing counsel's cross-examination; and, in a jury trial, this may be designed to score clever points, rather than to test whether they (i.e., the experts) are really good at their job. (Spencer, 1992, pp. 216–217)

Perhaps nowhere is the issue of expert testimony more relevant than in the arena of child abuse and custody determinations because it is in this arena that psychologists are increasingly being called on to testify. Social workers, clinicians, and researchers are being asked to testify about such issues as the behavioral and psychological markers of sexual abuse, the credibility of a child's statements, the malleability of a young child's memory, the ability to sway or influence the child's statements, the interpretation of the child's drawings and dreams, projective tests and behaviors, and the child's best interests in acrimonious custody disputes. What undoubtedly began with good intentions to help inform the court and protect the rights and safety of children has become for some, wittingly or otherwise, a venue for advocacy and supplemental income.

Although we have been privy to the breakdown in this process in the trial transcripts that we were asked to review, we are not alone in this regard. In this volume and elsewhere, Mary Ann Mason (chapter 10, this volume; 1991) provides us with the numbers to support our subjective impressions. Mason's analysis of appellate court decisions and the expert testimony provided in those cases brings to light some stark realities regarding the qualifications of experts, the contradictions within and between the testimony of experts, the dual role played by many experts as forensic interviewer as well as therapist to the child, and the court's willingness to accept expert testimony, regardless of the expert's scientific training or the empirical basis for his or her testimony.

The time is right to open a dialogue between professionals from different walks and exposures to childhood sexual abuse to illuminate exactly what the issues are. As researchers, we recognize all too well that the problem is much larger than the relative validity of the statements that experts make in court. To this end, we have gathered together in this volume professionals whose perspectives and proximity to the problems are different from our own. Such diversity, it is hoped, will leave the reader with a more informed, coherent, and comprehensive understanding of the issues and of where the problems arise. In addition, we feel that with this new insight comes a responsibility for professionals in these diverse roles to work together toward developing a consensus on their ethical responsibilities in the courtroom.

CONTENT AND CONTROVERSIES

Each chapter in this book depicts one or more current problem areas associated with expert testimony in cases of child abuse. The controversies fall within three basic categories: (a) those that describe personal pitfalls, such as remaining objective, presenting evidence in a fair and equitable manner, and competency issues; (b) the role of the expert, what the boundaries of his or her testimony should be, and how the role of an expert differs as a function of the system; and (c) the distinction between what is legally permissible and acceptable and what we in our respective professions find morally and ethically justifiable.

The book is divided into four sections. In the first section, authors provide an overview and comparative view of the uses of expert testimony both here and abroad as well as the moral and ethical standards to which psychologists serving as experts should adhere. Berliner's chapter provides an excellent introduction to the types of testimony that may be offered on direct and cross, where the legal and professional disputes arise with reference to these various testimonies and why, and what the expert needs to do before and during a testimony. Spencer takes us inside the courtrooms in other countries and provides a depiction of how experts are used, the limitations of their testimony, and the problems encountered in using court-appointed experts. Such a comparison between civilian and common law allows for a greater depth of understanding and appreciation of the shortcomings as well as the merits of the different systems of justice. In the last chapter in this section, Lavin and Sales outline three moral perspectives and the American Psychological Association's (APA) Ethical Principles of Psychologists and Code of Conduct in terms of expert testimony and analyze the coincidence between and among these principles with respect to limitations of expert testimony. Despite the diversity among different moral perspectives and the lack of overlap among ethics, morals, and the law, both popular moral theory and APA's ethics code suggests certain limitations to the issues experts should testify to.

In the next section, authors focus on the experience of providing expert testimony and how the uniquely human qualities that compel us to want to help are the very qualities that can make us poor experts. Bruck provides a personal glimpse into her first few experiences as an expert witness and the changes that accompany experience and reflection. Lawlor (chapter 5) and Pruett and Solnit (chapter 6) outline the professional and ethical dos and don'ts. These two chapters formalize the more personal account provided by the earlier chapter of Bruck and set the stage for Miller and Allen's chapter, which completes this second section. This last chapter very clearly enunciates the guidelines for helping experts to maintain their own personal and professional integrity as well as the integrity of the adversarial process.

The next section is devoted to the kinds of evidence most often offered in cases of suspected child abuse, the admissibility of such evidence, and the effects of this information on juror decisions. Fisher and Whiting provide a thorough review of the most common sexual abuse validation instruments and criteria used today: None deserve a ringing endorsement, and as these authors rightfully warn, all possess questionable validity. In the next chapter, Kovera and Borgida remind us of changes in the rules regarding the admissibility of the evidence provided by an expert. These changes make it more likely that less reliable forms of testimony will be heard by a jury (although see also McGough, chapter 13, this volume). Kovera and Borgida investigate the relative probative value of such evidence and whether traditional judicial safeguards can mitigate potentially prejudicial effects. In the final chapter in this section, Mason gives us a clearer picture of exactly who is providing expert testimony, the nature of the testimony allowed, and the range of sexual abuse criteria cited by the experts. Mason's chapter reveals some of the glaring inconsistencies in such testimony and the sometimes convoluted logic of the courts' decisions to accept it under different conditions.

The final section of this book brings together lawyers and psychologists who have read the earlier content of the book and offer their comments and insights. These works extend, challenge, and add yet another dimension to the previous chapters by widening the porthole through which they are viewed. Each takes one or more issues raised in the preceding chapters and discusses at length the implications and needs that remain. Ornstein and Gordon go beyond the advice offered in other chapters regarding the limitations that experts should impose on themselves and in clear and certain language delineate what experts should do, what is considered "scientific," and what the boundaries of expertise should encompass. They call for training programs for would-be experts to clarify such issues from the outset. Lyon and Koehler discuss at length an issue alluded to in several chapters, base rates, and show the importance of this information in decision making and how the relative significance of a particular behavior changes as a function of its prevalence among abused and nonabused children. Lyon and Koehler frame their description of base rates of behavioral indicators of abuse within the larger discussion of interpretive differences among researchers. The juxtaposition of these two issues reminds all of us of the tenuousness of our objectivity. Finally, McGough discusses the evidence most commonly offered in child sexual abuse cases and how it measures up against the admissibility constraints of the *Daubert v. Merrell Dow Pharmaceuticals, Inc.* (1993) ruling. With respect to this realm of evidence at least, *Daubert* allow the court to hear a body of data that is continously growing and becoming ever refined. Thus, the jury may evaluate the evidence "in the best light possible." Presumably that beacon will only become brighter and more focused with continued advancements in research on children, their abilities and dispositions, and the conditions that foster accuracy in their reporting.

THE NEED FOR GUIDANCE

Although the chapters vary greatly on their "take" concerning what it means to provide ethical expert testimony, all of the authors speak eloquently to the issue of the chasm that often seems to exist between the ethical and legal needs, on the one hand, and scientific values, on the other. On one side of the chasm are the lawyers whose profession has comparatively clear rules regarding what the expert "can" tell the court. Several hundred years of legal precedent and case law have honed the expectations, so that courts have clear rules for various types of opinion testimony. On the other side of the chasm are the psychologists and researchers, relatively new to this forum, who must grapple with issues that are only vaguely addressed by their professional codes of ethics.

In addition to these more extrinsic or codified issues, we can find ourselves struggling with our own internal tendencies, which, if unguarded, can easily draw us into the adversarial process as "partisans." The result is an expert who has become personally invested in the outcome of a case. After this occurs, the expert's status becomes that of an advocate, a lay witness with a title or degree whose testimony may be slanted toward achieving a partisan victory even at the cost of full disclosure of scientific or mental health considerations. When this occurs, the damage may or may not be undone by cross-examination.

A theme that resounds throughout the pages of this volume is that as researchers and psychologists serving as experts, we must concern ourselves with what we "should" be telling the court as opposed to what we "can" tell it. However, a global admonition without explicit guidelines too easily lends itself to individual interpretation, situational decision making, and justifications motivated by extrinsic forces. Just as the legal profession has standards that evidence must meet before it can be considered admissible, so must our profession develop clear guidelines for what it considers "admissible behavior" for psychologists serving as experts. Such guidelines would help to define our role in the courtroom and facilitate our ability to assume and maintain nonpartisan involvement. Having said this, all commentators in this volume recognize the difficulty inherent in codifying such guidelines.

Some might argue that the development of specific guidelines for psychologists serving as experts is redundant and, therefore, unnecessary. Although APA's ethics code does address the psychologist's role in forensic activities in a number of sections, these sections are too few in number to adequately encompass the myriad of ethical issues psychologists as experts must confront. As a result, the delineated sections of the APA ethics code are nonspecific and relatively obvious. Although other standards throughout the ethics code are also applicable (i.e., Standards 1.06, 1.15, 2.01, and 2.05), these standards are far too general to be of much use. Again, although the reader is alerted to these sections as relevant to the expectations for psychologists involved in forensic activities, they seem either only remotely related or so obvious as to render them nearly useless (e.g., avoiding conflicts of interest, being knowledgeable about the topic of one's testimony).

To a certain extent, the ambiguity and incompleteness of the current standards is understandable because it was impossible to anticipate the present social and judicial situation when the ethics code was first drafted. For example, no one could have anticipated the reverse trend for children's custody, which throughout most of the 19th century was routinely awarded to fathers as part of their paternal property rights. No one could have also anticipated that the child's own voice would be so evident in criminal proceedings, when only a few decades ago this was exceedingly rare. However, not all of the ethics code's lack of specificity stems from such unanticipated trends. Some of it is the result of an apparent lack of willingness to take a stand on thorny issues, particularly when "guild" interests are involved. Given the influence, impact, and potential consequences of expert testimony, it seems imperative that we now attempt to do so—even if the consequence of being more explicit about the ethical responsibilities of an expert means that psychologists restrict their role and possibly their earnings and influence.

Designed with greater specificity in mind, in 1991 Division 41 (Psychology and Law) of APA outlined Specialty Guidelines for the Forensic

Psychologist. Albeit the guidelines' primary audience is a restricted one, a few principles are clearly relevant for any expert, especially those who address issues of competence. Given the willingness of courts to receive expert psychological testimony, psychologists in nearly every subdiscipline, including forensic psychology, have found themselves testifying about a range of issues. Thus, a code is needed that is, on the one hand, broad enough to include a wider range of professional audiences (i.e., clinicians, social workers, child interview specialists, researchers from all disciplines as well as forensic psychologists) and yet specific enough to encompass the unique responsibilities of these different expert roles, both for the parties involved and for the court.

Ambiguity, relevancy, and completeness aside, APA's ethics code, as well as the guidelines of Division 41, lacks any discussion concerning the gap between what the court considers expert behavior (i.e., that which is legally permissible) and the rules that govern our profession's decisions regarding scientific expertise and moral appropriateness. That psychologists in the past have been willing, for example, to provide testimony that speaks to the "ultimate issue" illustrates poignantly that there exists a breakdown between what guidance our profession has attempted to provide and our own interpretation and understanding of that guidance. Even in this cleverly disguised form (e.g., by posing ultimate issues as hypotheticals or asking whether such behavior is consistent with a syndrome or abuse status), to provide such testimony can violate principles of ethical conduct. Such distinctions, when they occur, must be expressed in clear, unequivocal language.

An expanded version of the current APA principles regarding psychologists involved in forensic activities, one that includes the applicable standards from the Specialty Guidelines for Forensic Psychologists (e.g., those involving competency and methods), could provide the foundation for such an undertaking, thus rectifying this sad state of affairs. Many of the chapters in this volume could help inform this process further, if for no other reason than by illuminating the issues that have heretofore not been adequately addressed by professional societies or the courts (i.e., speaking to the ultimate issue, self-scrutiny regarding competence and expertise, the inherently conflicting nature of the dual role played by many therapists—experts, opinion-based testimony vs. scientifically informed testimony, to name but a few).

The chapters in this volume are successful in addressing what the issues are. The next logical, moral, and ethical step is to address them formally in a manner that is complete and unambiguous. The duality of the question "What can (and should) an expert tell the court?" will always exist in theory, given the differences between the legal and psychological forums. This book is a first step toward eradicating this duality in practice.

Our hope is that professionals serving as experts will concern themselves with the *should.*

REFERENCES

Daubert v. Merrell Dow Pharmaceuticals, Inc., 509 U.S., 113 S. Ct. 2786 (1993).

Gross, S. R. (1991). Expert evidence. *Wisconsin Law Review, 1113*, 1113–1231.

Mason, M. A. (1991, Fall–Winter). A judicial dilemma: Expert witness testimony in child sex abuse cases. *Psychiatry and Law,* 185–219.

Spencer, J. R. (1992). Court experts and expert witnesses. In R. W. Rideout & B. Hepple (Eds.), *Current legal problems* (Vol. 45, pp. 214–236). London: Oxford University Press.

I

LEGAL STRUCTURE AND PROFESSIONAL ETHICS

1

THE USE OF EXPERT TESTIMONY IN CHILD SEXUAL ABUSE CASES

LUCY BERLINER

Expert social science testimony has come to play an important role in child abuse litigation. It may be offered in civil and criminal proceedings and on a variety of topics. Numerous trial courts have permitted such testimony, and a large number of appellate decisions have been rendered on the admissibility of this testimony (Myers, 1992). In recent years, as many more children reporting sexual abuse have become participants in legal proceedings, particularly the criminal justice system, the number of court decisions concerned with sexual abuse expert testimony has increased. The legitimacy and permissible scope of this testimony have been debated by social scientists (e.g., Melton, 1994; Sagatun, 1991) and by lawyers (e.g., Mosteller, 1989; Myers et al., 1989).

Testimony offered in child abuse cases is subject to the same legal rules as other forms of expert testimony. It must be relevant, not common knowledge; its value in helping prove the case cannot be outweighed by the potential for creating unfair prejudice; and it must be helpful to the trier of fact (*Federal Rules of Evidence* Rule 702). The state may not offer such testimony that because a defendant shares characteristics of a group, he or she is more likely to be a member of the group [*Federal Rules of*

Evidence Rule 404(a)]. Furthermore, if the testimony is challenged or consists of novel scientific evidence, the court may hold a hearing and use either the general acceptance or the relevance standard to determine if it will be admitted (Black, Ayala, & Saffron-Brinks, 1994).

It is worth noting that in some child abuse situations, testimony by social science or clinical experts is not particularly controversial. For example, in a civil damage suit, the introduction of expert testimony describing the psychological status of the plaintiff and the expert's opinion about the relationship of a child abuse history to the actual and potential psychological damage suffered by the child is an essential ingredient. The defense might submit expert testimony disputing the conclusions of the plaintiff's expert. But an opinion about psychological outcomes, based on familiarity with a specialized body of knowledge, is central to the facts at issue. Similarly, expert testimony regarding the psychological impact of separation from an abusive parent or amenability of an admitting sex offender to treatment falls in a realm that draws on the expertise of mental health or social science experts. Critics, however, argue that virtually any testimony based on clinical judgments fails to meet the necessary legal standard of reasonable certainty and of assistance to the trier of fact (Faust & Ziskin, 1988).

The major legal and social science disagreements have been about testimony designed to assist the trier of fact in determining whether child sexual abuse took place. There are a variety of forms this testimony can take. Courts and experts remain divided, although there is a greater consensus on some points than others. Professionals seeking to serve as experts in sexual abuse cases should be familiar with the general nature of the disputes as well as the current status of the relevant knowledge.

THE NEED FOR EXPERT TESTIMONY

The reason the introduction of expert testimony is considered necessary is because until quite recently, it could be assumed that fact finders had little knowledge about the nature of child abuse situations or held prejudicial views about children who claimed to have been abused. These concerns were particularly relevant in sexual abuse cases where a long history of societal skepticism had existed and, unlike cases of physical abuse, supportive evidence was often lacking. In both social science and legal treatises, the prevailing norm was reflected in explicitly negative positions regarding the credibility of child witnesses (Goodman, 1984).

It can now be argued that most people are probably aware that sexual abuse is not rare and that children making such claims should not automatically be viewed with suspicion, because people have been exposed to a large amount of information in the popular media about sexual abuse

(Finkelhor, 1984). However, as a recent content analysis of major national publications revealed (Beckett, 1996), following a brief period in the early 1980s where the dominant theme was about children as victims of a long-hidden crime, current portrayals of child witnesses emphasize the weaknesses of children's memories as well as concerns about "false memories" of sexual abuse reported by adults. Media stories about a few extraordinary cases involving young children in day-care settings, making accusations often of a bizarre nature, far surpass stories about the much more common, garden-variety cases heard in courtrooms every day.

In addition to general concerns about public recognition of the social problem of sexual abuse and negative bias toward child witnesses, there is the question of whether jurors are familiar with the nature of sexual abuse situations, characteristics of offenders, and patterns of reporting. Morison and Greene (1992) directly addressed this question with potential jurors and found significant disagreement between experts and the jurors on many items in a questionnaire designed to tap knowledge regarding sexual abuse.

TYPES OF TESTIMONY

The usual form social science testimony takes in sexual abuse cases is known as *social frameworks* testimony (Walker & Monahan, 1987) or "the use of general conclusions from social science research in determining factual issues in a specific case" (p. 570). It serves the purpose of providing a framework or background context for evaluating the evidence presented in the case; it can "tell jurors something they do not already know or disabuse them of common but erroneous misconceptions" (p. 583). Testimony about the nature of child sexual abuse, reactions of victims, and the memory and suggestibility of children (Myers et al., 1989) would fall into this category.

In decisions upholding the admission of certain types of expert testimony, courts have usually asserted that there are characteristics of sexual abuse situations that unless explained might interfere with jurors' fair evaluation of the evidence or testimony. As the Minnesota Supreme Court stated in *State v. Myers* (1984), "background data providing relevant insight into the puzzling aspects of the child's conduct and demeanor which the jury could not otherwise bring to its evaluation of her credibility is helpful and appropriate" (p. 610). For this reason, testimony introduced for the general purpose of educating jurors or correcting misapprehensions has been most widely accepted.

A more specific form of expert testimony is when an expert gives an opinion that a child has been abused or that the child witness exhibits the characteristics commonly found in sexually abused children. Although the expert may rely on general social science knowledge, the opinion is specifically linked to the child witness. As one commentator noted, courts have seemed more willing to allow testimony of this sort in child sexual abuse cases than in adult rape cases, although the testimony is not substantively different (Mosteller, 1989). Mosteller suggested, as a possible explanation, a more favorable judicial disposition toward child victims because of increased awareness that sexual abuse is a serious social problem. An analysis of appellate decisions concluding that courts did not always rigorously examine the scientific basis for the expert testimony they allowed (Mason, 1991) lends support to this interpretation.

One kind of testimony—opinions rendered about the credibility of a particular witness—has been soundly rejected by the courts. As one court stated,

> we have said it before, and we will say it again, but this time with emphasis—we really mean it—no psychotherapist may render an opinion on whether a witness is credible in any trial conducted in this state. The assessment of credibility is for the trier of fact and not for therapists. (*State v. Milbradt*, 1988, p. 624)

This prohibition often extends to more general testimony that children, as a group, rarely lie about sexual abuse.

EXPERT TESTIMONY AS SUBSTANTIVE EVIDENCE

Testimony offered as *substantive evidence*—opinions that a child was abused or shares characteristics of abused children—has been challenged by both legal and social science commentators. Opinions that a child has been abused have been criticized by courts as being nothing more than thinly disguised opinions of belief in the child's statements and therefore a direct comment on credibility (*United States v. Whitted*, 1993). Similarly, Melton and Limber (1989) have taken the position that giving an opinion that a child has been abused is the same as opining that the child is telling the truth. These authors asserted that because mental health professionals have no special ability to determine whether someone is telling the truth, such an opinion is improper under all circumstances.

However, the social science literature describing the process of forming a clinical opinion in sexual abuse cases makes clear that much more is involved in the determination than simply believing or not believing what the child says (Berliner & Conte, 1993; Conte, 1992; Heiman, 1992) and that stating an opinion or making a diagnosis is the accepted standard of practice (American Academy of Child and Adolescent Psychiatry, 1990; American Professional Society on the Abuse of Children, 1997). There is agreement among professionals about the criteria they weigh (Conte, Sorenson, Fogarty, & Rosa, 1991), and a majority believe that results of an evaluation can establish abuse (Oberlander, 1995). In spite of this, there is currently no empirical evidence that clinicians reliably arrive at the same conclusions from comparable clinical information. For these reasons, some commentators have taken the position that the scientific basis for expert opinion about sexual abuse may not be sufficiently valid and reliable for admission in court (McAnulty, 1993). Some have gone even further and asserted that "psychologists, in the role of expert witness, should not be asked to tell the police, the Child Protection Service worker or the court whether or not the abuse actually occurred as alleged" (Hall, 1989, p. 453).

Myers (1992) has argued that a distinction can be made between testifying to the ultimate *legal* issue, which is prohibited, and to the ultimate *factual* issue, which may be permitted. Some courts have agreed. For example, an Idaho court ruled that "if a proper foundation has been laid, it is proper for the expert to testify regarding whether a person has been sexually abused" (*State v. Lewis*, 1993, p. 409). However, an affirmation of the use of this testimony, especially in criminal proceedings, is a minority view among legal decisions.

Although the rules governing admissibility of expert testimony apply equally to criminal and civil settings, courts may be more willing to grant latitude in child protection proceedings. In part, this is because the fact finder is usually the judge, not the jury; therefore, the risk of the fact finder being overawed by expert testimony or ceding the legal determination is reduced. Because the best interests of the child rather than criminal responsibility of the adult are at issue, courts may find testimony about the results of clinical evaluations or clinical opinions particularly helpful. In addition, because the standard of proof in civil proceedings is lower, the courts may consider this standard to be more comparable with the criteria used in clinical decision making. Of course, opposing lawyers are free to challenge the basis for the opinion, argue for alternative explanations, or point out the limitations of clinical determinations.

Testimony about emotional and behavioral reactions of sexually abused children generally involves a clinical expert testifying that certain behaviors are typical of abused children. Early on, clinical experience served as the basis for these general conclusions, and there was an impression that a cluster of symptoms that accurately discriminated abused from nonabused children could be identified. As an empirical body of knowledge was accumulated, scientific support for the notion of a unique or universal response to sexual abuse has not been forthcoming. In a review of this literature, Kendall-Tackett, Williams, and Finkelhor (1993) found that no symptom was reported to be present in more than half of sexually abused children. Even the presence of age-inappropriate or aggressive sexual behavior in young children cannot be definitively linked to a history of sexual abuse. Although certain sexual behaviors are extremely uncommon in children who have not been sexually abused, they do occur (Friedrich et al.,

1992). Emotional disturbances, such as anxiety, depression, or low self-esteem, which are relatively common in abused children, could clearly have etiologies other than a history of child abuse.

Melton (1994) has pointed out that because of the relatively low base rate of child abuse in the general population, even the presence of emotional or behavioral reactions, which occur in a high percentage of abused children and a very small percentage of nonabused children, indicates that in absolute numbers, many more nonabused children have the symptoms often viewed as specific to sexual abuse. He concluded that testimony about psychological consequences is misleading because fact finders, and even some experts, are unlikely to understand the importance of base rates in weighing the significance of such testimony.

In addition to scientific reasons for excluding this testimony, some courts and legal commentators have argued against its admission, as the New Hampshire Supreme Court did in *State v. Cressey* (1993): "We see no appreciable difference between [a statement that the children exhibited symptoms consistent with those of sexually abused children] and a statement that, in her opinion, the children were sexually abused" (p. 699). Bulkley (1992) asserted that the presence of psychological reactions is highly consistent with a history of abuse and would be easily recognized as such by fact finders. Therefore, there is no need to educate jurors that children might be upset or disturbed by having been abused, and expert testimony is unnecessary.

However, testimony about emotional and behavioral reactions is not ordinarily offered as stand-alone proof of sexual abuse but rather either because a general discussion about the range of possible outcomes for sexually abused children provides a context or framework for understanding the complaining witness or because the particular behaviors of the child are probative of the allegations. For example, the sudden onset of sexually aggressive behavior or offense-specific fears does tend to support the conclusion that the child was abused. Just as a clinician would consider such reactions relevant and helpful in forming an opinion, so may a fact finder.

EXPERT TESTIMONY AS REHABILITATIVE EVIDENCE

Although there is less consensus about the introduction of expert testimony as substantive evidence, most courts have ruled that testimony designed for rehabilitative purposes is permissible, at least in some cases (Myers, 1993). There are circumstances when a child's credibility is challenged because of his or her emotional or behavioral responses, even though the reactions might be consistent with a history of abuse. For example, if a child had exhibited reactions that were very unusual, such as severe dissociative symptoms, and these reactions were used to discredit the child, an expert might properly explain the nature of dissociation and its possible association with a traumatic history (American Psychiatric Association, 1994). In contrast, the defense might argue that a child who has no apparent psychological problems could not have been abused. In this case, an expert could provide relevant information based on the scientific literature that some abused children are asymptomatic (Kendall-Tackett et al., 1993). As the court in *State v. Jones* (1993) put it, "we agree with the current trend of authority that such testimony may be used to rebut allegations by the defendant that the victim's behavior is inconsistent with abuse" (p. 819).

Testimony about delayed or piecemeal reporting and recantation has almost always been allowed. Data from numerous scientific studies as well as clinical experience provide a sound basis for this testimony. Most adults in general population studies did not report the abuse in childhood (e.g., Finkelhor, Hotaling, Lewis, & Smith, 1990); among children who come to the attention of authorities, many do not spontaneously tell, delay in reporting, or make gradual disclosures (e.g., Sauzier, 1989; Sorensen & Snow, 1991); some recant actual abuse (e.g., Jones & McGraw, 1987) or refuse to report actual abuse when directly asked (e.g., Elliott & Briere, 1994; Lawson & Chaffin, 1992). Some psychological and environmental forces inhibit reporting or lead some children to adapt and go along with abusive situations (Summit, 1992). This testimony is relevant and helpful in cases when the child witness's testimony is discredited or challenged as being inconsistent with the expected responses if abuse had actually occurred.

One form that this type of testimony has taken is the introduction of the child sexual abuse accommodation syndrome (CSAAS; Summit, 1983). Summit described and named elements of sexual abuse situations and the accompanying psychological dynamics that could produce delayed, unconvincing disclosure and retraction. Unfortunately, in some cases, prosecutors offered and clinical experts testified that this syndrome was akin to a diagnosis and its presence was proof of a sexual abuse history. In part, the use of the term *syndrome* contributed to the confusion, especially because "battered child syndrome" is a diagnosis and testimony regarding this syndrome is permitted to prove physical abuse. It is also likely that some experts misunderstood the meaning intended by the author. As Summit (1992) has clarified, the term was never meant to be a device for establishing the truth of a child's statements. However, as a result of the misapplication of the term and the failure of some courts to distinguish proper and improper use of the syndrome, testimony that relies on or refers to CSAAS has been virtually banned in some jurisdictions (*Hellstrom v. Commonwealth*, 1992).

Another type of rebuttal testimony is about characteristics of sexual offenders. This testimony can only be introduced if the defendant raises his or her character as evidence by asserting that he or she does not fit the profile of an offender. The state could properly introduce expert testimony to refute the impression that a certain set of characteristics or psychological qualities discriminate offenders from nonoffenders. For example, numerous investigations have demonstrated that there is no specific psychological profile found on personality tests of offenders and that, in fact, most offenders have normal profiles (e.g., Murphy & Peters, 1992; Williams & Finkelhor, 1990).

TESTIMONY OFFERED BY THE DEFENSE

Even though most of the expert testimony in child sexual abuse cases has been offered by the state, increasingly the defense has argued for the admission of expert testimony. The proffered testimony has primarily been about the suggestibility of children. The purpose is to impeach the credibility of the complaining witness by providing information about the weaknesses or vulnerabilities of memory itself. The testimony usually consists of identifying those aspects of the disclosure or investigative process that might be implicated in memory distortion. The circumstances under which the original report was elicited and the interviewing methods of investigators or other involved professionals are the usual targets of critique. Experts rely on the scientific literature that shows that the memory of children can be quite vulnerable to influence under certain circumstances (e.g., Ceci & Bruck, 1993). Many studies demonstrate that when children, especially young children, are repeatedly interviewed about possible abuse or questioned in a suggestive or coercive fashion by an interviewer seeking to confirm a preexisting belief about what happened, there is a significant increase in the potential for errors.

THE IMPACT OF EXPERT TESTIMONY

Little is known about the usefulness of social framework evidence in child sexual abuse cases. Crowley, O'Callaghan, and Ball (1994) used a videotaped simulation of a criminal trial involving child witnesses of various ages. In some conditions, a psychological expert testified regarding delayed disclosure, memory, suggestibility, and reality monitoring. The jurors who heard the expert testimony rated the child witness significantly higher on memory expertise, reality monitoring, and resistance to suggestion, but there was no significant relationship to guilty–not guilty verdicts. Jurors who heard expert testimony generally gave high ratings on impartiality and helpfulness, although jurors who voted to convict gave significantly higher ratings on helpfulness. Even jurors who were not exposed to expert testimony indicated, in response to a hypothetical question, that they would have found it helpful. Using simulated trials, Gabora, Spanos, and Joab (1993) compared the effects of "specific" expert testimony, which included an opinion by the expert that the complaining child had been abused, general social framework testimony, and no-expert testimony. Expert testimony was significantly related to the verdict only in the specific expert condition, although both expert conditions resulted in changes with regard to common misconceptions as compared with the no-expert trial. These studies support the idea that juror knowledge improves and that they do find such testimony helpful but that expert testimony may not directly affect verdicts (Crowley et al., 1994; Gabora et al., 1993).

Lawyers seeking to use experts should address the question of usefulness as well as admissibility of the testimony. Just because a trial court can be persuaded to admit testimony does not mean that the testimony is helpful or will withstand appellate scrutiny. The history of appellate decision making reveals that overreaching can result in the reversal of convictions and the barring of whole classes of testimony. Social framework evidence for the general purpose of educating the fact finder or correcting misapprehensions is only necessary to the extent that fact finders are uninformed or when opposing lawyers intend to exploit a lack of knowledge or misunderstanding.

DISPUTED ISSUES ABOUT EXPERT TESTIMONY

In most jurisdictions, the disputes have essentially been settled as a matter of law. The most conservative position, taken by a minority of courts, is that expert testimony offered during legal proceedings to determine whether abuse occurred should rarely, if ever, be permitted as substantive evidence. Many of these courts have ruled that an opinion that a child has been sexually abused is not admissible (e.g., *Jenkins v. Commonwealth*, 1996). Others have also disallowed testimony about emotional and behavior reactions (e.g., "child sexual abuse may not be proven by evidence that the victim exhibited residual characteristics or behavioral traits similar to other victims of such abuse"; *State v. Anderson*, 1994, p. 730). A few have taken the position that even rebuttal testimony is impermissible (e.g., *Commonwealth v. Dunkle*, 1992). The bases for these decisions encompass a range of interpretations, including the following: Opinions about abuse are simply a proxy for a comment on credibility, information about characteristics of sexually abused children is misleading or is unnecessary because of a changed societal awareness, and common sense can be applied to the facts.

The majority of courts continue to affirm that there are circumstances when both the legal and scientific justifications are present for expert testimony (Myers, 1993). Depending on the type of evidence offered and the accumulated case law of the jurisdiction, courts are more or less willing to allow versions of expert testimony. For example, a few appellate courts have recently upheld the admission of expert opinion that a child was sexually abused (e.g., *State v. Figured*, 1994). Many courts have ruled that a qualified expert can inform the jury about general characteristics of sexually abused children. In some jurisdictions, experts can relate these characteristics to the child but may not state an opinion that abuse occurred (e.g., *United States v. Johns*, 1994); whereas in others, they may not refer specifically to the child witness in the case (e.g., *Commonwealth v. Trowbridge*, 1995). The large majority of courts approve rehabilitation testimony when a proper foundation is laid.

The courts have scrutinized expert testimony more carefully in recent years; cases remain divided into three approaches: (a) some forms of expert testimony is permitted, (b) most or all such testimony is barred, and (c) psychological testimony as substantive evidence is treated as novel scientific evidence (J. E. B. Myers, personal communication, March 30, 1998). A certain amount of correction is necessary. Some experts did overstep in their testimony. Initially, the primitive state of knowledge and concerns on the part of both experts and the courts about the plight of abuse victims created an environment where assertions were made and accepted, which are no longer considered supportable. Testimony that the CSAAS is proof of an abuse history, that an abused child will react in a certain typical way, or that an offender profile exists would fall in this category. It is also likely that some clinical experts, because they lacked rigorous scientific training, were simply unfamiliar with important scientific principles, such as the base-rate phenomenon, or relied excessively on skewed anecdotal evidence to make general statements. As the courts and experts have become more sophisticated, testimony that does not have adequate scientific support will presumably be less often offered or allowed.

In the more controversial areas, such as the introduction of expert testimony in the form of an opinion about whether a child was abused or of emotional and behavioral reactions as substantive evidence, courts that have not yet resolved the issue may consider the testimony a form of novel scientific evidence subject to the *Frye v. United States* (1923) or *Daubert v. Merrell Dow Pharmaceuticals, Inc.* (1993) hearings. For example, some courts that have rejected testimony giving an opinion that a child was abused have ruled that it might be admissible in the future if such opinions could be shown to be reliable (*State v. Rimmasch*, 1989).

Courts are in the process of establishing the parameters for defense expert testimony describing children's suggestibility or criticizing interviews. They are currently divided on the question of whether trial courts can exclude the testimony. Some courts have held that it can be properly rejected (e.g., *State v. Ellis*, 1996) and is not ineffective assistance of counsel to fail to present such testimony (e.g., *Commonwealth v. Clements*,

1994). Others have found trial court exclusion of testimony to be reversible error (e.g., *United States v. Rouse*, 1997). The most celebrated case addressing this form of testimony is *State v. Michaels* (1994). Not only did the court rule that the prosecution expert testimony was improper, but also the court explicitly approved of the admission of expert testimony on interviewing. The court went even further to recommend that the defense be permitted to request a special hearing involving expert testimony if a showing of interviewing errors could be made.

It is clear that states have arrived at different positions on the question of admissibility of expert testimony in child sexual abuse cases. Whether experts can testify and on what topics is determined by the applicable case law in the jurisdiction, regardless of the state of scientific or clinical knowledge. Courts may bar expert testimony even when there is an established or undisputed body of knowledge or when experts believe that the testimony would be helpful. Experts should be familiar with the relevant court rulings before providing testimony.

WHAT EXPERTS CAN DO

Professional societies, such as the American Psychological Association (1992), have established ethical codes for professionals serving as expert witnesses. Experts are expected to present scientific knowledge in a complete and accurate fashion, prevent the misuse of research findings, not testify beyond their expertise, and resist the pressures to become partisans. Adhering to these standards can be exceedingly difficult in an adversarial context when lawyers are always and properly seeking to advance their version of the facts; experts may find that codes of ethics conflict with the real-life pressures to become advocates instead of witnesses (Saks, 1990). Experts can avoid many of the pitfalls of participation in an adversarial process by clearly establishing their role in a particular case, insisting on full disclosure of information, and restricting their involvement to providing scientific information (Saunders, 1997).

Those who would be experts in child sexual abuse cases, as a first step, have a duty to be certain that what they testify to is consistent with a growing and changing body of knowledge. This presents some difficulties for the purely clinical expert. Although they may meet the legal criteria for being an expert by virtue of their extensive experience, this does not always mean they are familiar with the published literature. These experts may increasingly find themselves faced with lawyers who will challenge them on cross-examination to provide the basis for their opinions or to respond to questions about specific research findings.

It is currently considered appropriate for professionals to form an opinion that abuse occurred; in one small survey, a majority of experts agreed that it is acceptable to testify to such an opinion (Oberlander, 1995). Although commentators have written extensively on the evaluation process (e.g., Faller, 1996), the scientific and clinical communities have yet to agree on exactly what factors should be considered and how they should be weighed when forming an opinion in a specific case. In the meantime, experts who are asked to give this type of testimony should be very cautious and should only make statements that can be fully supported and adequately qualified. They may even want to refrain from explicitly testifying to the opinion in court, instead taking the approach of providing an indication of the weight to be accorded and the various possible explanations for a child's statements and behaviors (Wood, 1996).

Testimony about emotional and behavioral reactions requires greater precision than has often been the case. Only unusual sexual behavior and posttraumatic stress symptoms have been specifically correlated with sexual abuse. It is possible to provide testimony about the probability that these responses have their origin in sexual abuse experiences (e.g., Freidrich et al., 1992; McNally, 1993). However, all other symptoms and behaviors are nonspecific and, at most, are indications that the child is suffering from some untoward or disturbing life experience. Responsible experts must make clear that such reactions are consistent with a variety of stressors.

Experts who testify for rehabilitation purposes have a substantially more straightforward task than those who give substantive evidence. If a party argues that certain reactions or behaviors are inconsistent with abuse and there is clinical or empirical data to refute the assertion, such testimony is quite legitimate and most often going to be permitted. Testimony about delayed or piecemeal reporting and recantation is also frequently allowed because there is a substantial supporting clinical and scientific body of knowledge. However, experts should be careful not to overstate the prevalence of these phenomena or to imply that their presence can only be explained by sexual abuse. For example, recantation is relatively rare (e.g., Bradley & Wood, 1996) and could be a truthful correction of a prior false allegation.

Defense experts, similarly, should exercise caution and properly qualify their testimony. Data on children's suggestibility are primarily derived from laboratory or analogue studies. It cannot be assumed that findings regarding staged or relatively innocuous or commonplace events are generalizable to the experience of sexual abuse. For example, experts should take care not to create an impression that because children were first questioned by their upset parents, had talked to their friends, and had therapy or were interviewed imperfectly, they should be considered unreliable witnesses. Research does not support the premise that children whose memory is consolidated and accurate in the first place will become inaccurate reporters simply because they have been interviewed repeatedly (e.g., Fivush & Schwarzmueller, 1995). Researchers have consistently found that children, especially older children, are able to resist suggestive or leading questions much of the time (e.g., Myers, Goodman, & Saywitz, 1996).

Every trial involves testimony about events, and it is true that memory of both adults and children is fallible. This should not mean that experts are called to trials to discuss the reconstructive nature of memory. A situation might be created where jurors are unfairly prejudiced against any testimony from children because it will virtually never be the case that abused children's first statements are elicited during a formal investigative interview conducted by a trained professional. There is the possibility that exaggerated concern about suggestibility might lead to a social policy that discouraged children from talking about their experiences or isolated them from support. This would have very real and harmful consequences for abused children. However, when there is evidence in a particular case that significant factors are present that have been shown to adversely affect the accuracy of statements and that jurors might need assistance in understanding, the introduction of this kind of testimony is helpful and relevant.

In addition to what the law allows and science says, there is still the question about the proper role of an expert in a given case. Unlike fact witnesses, experts choose to participate. It is disingenuous for experts to fail to acknowledge that in an adversarial process, their testimony is introduced for the purpose of advancing a particular version of the facts. Experts may want to make it a practice to determine, in each case, whether social science testimony is really necessary to assist the trier of fact. Are there reactions in the child that are very specific to victimization? Is the defense going to try to impeach the child witness on the basis of a delay in reporting? Was the child interviewed in an egregiously improper way? Conversations with lawyers can help clarify what the facts are and what arguments are anticipated. Alternative avenues for making the points can be explored, such as addressing a lack of awareness among jurors during the *voir dire* (the examination of a prospective jury) process or having a teacher testify about behavior or the child testify about his or her reasons for not telling. In other words, testifying just because it is possible risks being a form of advocacy, regardless of what might be permitted on behalf of the prosecution or the defense.

CONCLUSION

It is important to keep in mind that in the long run, the expertise of experts is most useful outside of a courtroom. Social scientists make their best contributions when they expand knowledge and clinicians when they apply their clinical skills. Experts can be helpful to the legal process in a variety of ways without testifying. They can provide education about the current state of knowledge, so lawyers are better able to evaluate the meaning and strength of the evidence. Clinical experts can prepare children to testify. They can also inform courts of the impact of victimization and make dispositional recommendations after the legal determination has been made. Finally, what experts know can be more widely disseminated to promote an informed public, so that experts will be less necessary in the courtroom.

REFERENCES

American Academy of Child and Adolescent Psychiatry. (1990). *Guidelines for the clinical evaluation of child and adolescent abuse.* Washington, DC: Author.

American Professional Society on the Abuse of Children. (1997). *Guidelines for psychosocial evaluation of suspected sexual abuse in children.* Chicago: Author.

American Psychiatric Association. (1994). *Diagnostic and statistical manual of mental disorders* (4th ed.). Washington, DC: Author.

American Psychological Association. (1992). Ethical principles of psychologists and code of conduct. *American Psychologist, 47,* 1597–1611.

Beckett, K. (1996). Culture and the politics of signification: The case of child sexual abuse. *Social Problems, 43,* 57–76.

Berliner, L., & Conte, J. (1993). Sexual abuse evaluations: Conceptual and empirical obstacles. *Child Abuse & Neglect, 17,* 111–125.

Black, B., Ayala, F. J., & Saffran-Brinks, C. (1994). Science and the law in the wake of *Daubert*: A new search for scientific knowledge. *Texas Law Review, 72,* 715–802.

Bradley, A. R., & Wood, J. M. (1996). How do children tell? The disclosure process in child sexual abuse. *Child Abuse & Neglect, 20,* 881–891.

Bulkley, J. A. (1992). The prosecution's use of social science expert testimony in child sexual abuse cases: National trends and recommendations. *Journal of Child Sexual Abuse, 1*(2), 73–93.

Ceci, S. J., & Bruck, M. (1993). Suggestibility of the child witness: A historical review and synthesis. *Psychological Bulletin, 113,* 403–439.

Commonwealth v. Clements, 36 Mass. App. 205, 629 N.E.2d 361, 364 (1994).

Commonwealth v. Dunkle, 602 A.2d 830 (Penn. 1992).

Commonwealth v. Trowbridge, 419 Mass. 750, 647 N.E.2d 413, 420 (1995).

Conte, J. R. (1992). Has this child been sexually abused? Dilemmas for the mental health professional who seeks the answer. *Criminal Justice and Behavior, 19,* 54–73.

Conte, J. R., Sorenson, E., Fogarty, L., & Rosa, J. (1991). Evaluating children's reports of sexual abuse: A survey of professionals. *American Journal of Orthopsychiatry, 61,* 428–437.

Crowley, M. J., O'Callaghan, M. G., & Ball, P. J. (1994). The juridical impact of psychological expert testimony in a simulated child sexual abuse trial. *Law and Human Behavior, 18,* 89–105.

Daubert v. Merrell Dow Pharmaceuticals, Inc., 113 S. Ct. 2786 (1993).

Elliott, D. M., & Briere, J. (1994). Forensic sexual abuse evaluations of older children: Disclosures and symptomatology. *Behavioral Sciences and the Law, 12,* 261–277.

Faller, K. C. (1996). *Evaluating children suspected of having been sexually abused: APSAC Study Guide 2.* Thousand Oaks, CA: Sage.

Faust, D., & Ziskin, J. (1988). The expert witness in psychology and psychiatry. *Science, 214,* 31–35.

Federal rules of evidence, 28 U.S.C. (1974).

Finkelhor, D. (1984). What the public knows about sexual abuse. In D. Finkelhor (Ed.), *Abuse: New theory and research* (pp. 87–106). Free Press: New York.

Finkelhor, D., Hotaling, G., Lewis, I. A., & Smith, C. (1990). Sexual abuse in a national survey of adult men and women: Prevalence, characteristics, and risk factors. *Child Abuse & Neglect, 14,* 19–28.

Fivush, R., & Schwarzmueller, A. (1995). Say it once again: The effects of repeated questions on children's event recall. *Journal of Traumatic Stress, 8,* 555–580.

Friedrich, W. N., Grambsch, P., Damon, L., Hewitt, S. K., Koverola, C., Lang, R. A., Wolfe, V., & Broughton, D. (1992). Child Sexual Behavior Inventory: Normative and clinical comparisons. *Psychological Assessment, 4,* 303–311.

Frye v. United States, 293 F.1013 (D.C. Cir. 1923).

Gabora, N. J., Spanos, N. P., & Joab, A. (1993). The effects of complainant age and expert psychological testimony in a simulated child sexual abuse trial. *Law and Human Behavior, 17,* 103–119.

Goodman, G. S. (1984). Children's testimony in historical perspective. *Journal of Social Issues, 40,* 9–31.

Hall, M. D. (1989). The role of psychologists as experts in cases involving allegations of child sexual abuse. *Family Law Quarterly, 23,* 451–464.

Heiman, M. L. (1992). Putting the puzzle together: Validating allegations of child sexual abuse. *Journal of Child Psychology and Psychiatry, 33,* 311–329.

Hellstrom v. Commonwealth, 825 S.W.2d 612 (Ky. 1992).

Jenkins v. Commonwealth, 22 Va. App. 508, 471 S.E.2d 785, 789 (1996).

Jones, D. P. H., & McGraw, J. M. (1987). Reliable and fictitious accounts of sexual abuse to children. *Journal of Interpersonal Violence, 2,* 27–45.

Kendall-Tackett, K. A., Williams, L. M., & Finkelhor, D. (1993). Impact of sexual abuse on children: A review and synthesis of recent empirical studies. *Psychological Bulletin, 113,* 164–180.

Lawson, L., & Chaffin, M. (1992). False negatives in sexual abuse disclosure interviews: Incidence and influence of caretaker's belief in abuse in cases of accidental abuse discovery by diagnosis of STD. *Journal of Interpersonal Violence, 7,* 532–542.

Mason, M. A. (1991). A judicial dilemma: Expert witness testimony in child sexual abuse cases. *Journal of Psychiatry and the Law, 19,* 185–219.

McAnulty, R. D. (1993). Expert psychological testimony in cases of alleged child sexual abuse. *Archives of Sexual Behavior, 22,* 311–324.

McNally, R. J. (1993). Stressors that produce PTSD in children. In J. T. Davidson & E. B. Foa (Eds.), *Posttraumatic stress disorder: DSM-IV and beyond* (pp. 57–74). Washington, DC: American Psychiatric Press.

Melton, G. B. (1994). Doing justice and doing good: Conflicts for mental health professionals. *The Future of Children, 4,* 102–118.

Melton, G. B., & Limber, S. (1989). Psychologists' involvement in cases of child maltreatment. *American Psychologist, 44,* 1225–1233.

Morison, S., & Greene, E. (1992). Juror and expert knowledge of child sexual abuse. *Child Abuse & Neglect, 16,* 595–613.

Mosteller, R. P. (1989). Legal doctrines governing the admissibility of expert testimony concerning social framework evidence. *Law & Contemporary Problems, 52,* 85–132.

Murphy, W. D., & Peters, J. M. (1992). Profiling child sexual abusers: Psychological considerations. *Criminal Justice & Behavior, 19,* 24–37.

Myers, J. E. B. (1992). *Legal issues in child abuse and neglect.* Newbury Park, CA: Sage.

Myers, J. E. B. (1993). Expert testimony regarding child sexual abuse. *Child Abuse & Neglect, 17,* 175–185.

Myers, J. E. B., Bays, J., Becker, J., Berliner, L., Corwin, D. L., & Saywitz, K. J. (1989). Expert testimony in child sexual abuse litigation. *Nebraska Law Review, 68,* 1–145.

Myers, J. E. B., Goodman, G. S., & Saywitz, K. J. (1996). Psychological research on children as witnesses: Practical implications for forensic interviews and courtroom testimony. *Pacific Law Journal, 27,* 1–82.

Oberlander, L. (1995). Psychological issues in child sexual abuse evaluation: A survey of forsenic mental health professionals. *Child Abuse & Neglect, 19,* 475–490.

Sagatun, I. (1991). Expert witnesses in child abuse cases. *Behavioral Sciences and the Law, 9,* 201–215.

Saks, M. J. (1990). Expert witnesses, nonexpert witnesses, and nonwitness experts. *Law & Human Behavior, 14,* 291–313.

Saunders, B. E. (1997). Medical and mental health professionals as experts in legal cases. In P. Stern (Ed.), *Preparing and presenting expert testimony in child abuse cases* (pp. 116–154). Thousand Oaks, CA: Sage.

Sauzier, M. (1989). Disclosure of child sexual abuse: For better or worse. *Psychiatric Clinics of North America, 12,* 455–469.

Sorensen, T., & Snow, B. (1991). How children tell: The process of disclosure in child sexual abuse. *Child Welfare, 70,* 3–15.

State v. Anderson, 880 S.W.2d 720 (Tenn. Criminal App. 1994).

State v. Cressey, 628 A.2d 696 (N.H. 1993).

State v. Ellis, 669 A.2d 752 (Me. 1996).

State v. Figured, 116 N.C. App. 1, 446 S.E.2d 838, 842 (1994).

State v. Jones, 71 Wn. App. 798 (Wash. 1993).

State v. Lewis, 848 P.2d 394, 409 (Idaho 1993).

State v. Michaels, 136 N.J. 299, 642 A.2d 1372 (1994).

State v. Milbradt, 756 P.2d 620 (Ore. 1988).

State v. Myers, 359 N.W.2d 604 (Minn. 1984).

State v. Rimmasch, 775 P.2d 388 (Utah 1989).

Summit, R. C. (1983). The child sexual abuse accommodation syndrome. *Child Abuse & Neglect, 7*, 177–193.

Summit, R. C. (1992). Abuse of the child sexual abuse accommodation syndrome. *Journal of Child Sexual Abuse, 1*(4), 153–163.

United States v. Johns, 15 F.3d 740, 730 (8th Cir. 1994).

United States v. Rouse, 111 F.3d 561 (8th Cir. 1997).

United States v. Whitted, 994 F.2d 444 (8th Cir. 1993).

Walker, L., & Monahan, J. (1987). Social frameworks: A new use of social science in law. *Virginia Law Review, 73*, 559–598.

Williams, L. M., & Finkelhor, D. (1990). The characteristics of incestuous fathers: A review of recent studies. In W. L. Marshall, D. R. Laws, & H. E. Barbaree (Eds.), *Handbook of sexual assault: Issues, theories, & treatment of the offender* (pp. 231–255). New York: Plenum Press.

Wood, J. M. (1996). Weighing evidence in sexual abuse evaluations: An introduction to Bayes' theorem. *Child Maltreatment, 1*, 25–36.

2

THE ROLE OF EXPERTS IN THE COMMON LAW AND THE CIVIL LAW: A COMPARISON

JOHN R. SPENCER

A popular view of the role of experts in the different types of legal system goes like this: There are two systems of justice in the Western world, the common law systems and the civilian systems.[1] The common law countries have the accusatorial (alias adversarial) system, whereas the civilian countries have the inquisitorial system. In the *accusatorial* system, the parties put their rival versions of the case before an impartial court, the job of which is limited to deciding who wins. In the *inquisitorial* system, however, the court has an active duty to seek the truth; to this end, the court carries out its own inquiries. As far as experts are concerned, this means that in the common law countries, their role is, and can only be, that of expert witnesses called adversarially by the parties, whereas in the civilian countries, their role is, and can only be, that of helpers brought in by the judge. Whichever system is inherently better, this much is clear: Expert witnesses must remain the rule in the common law world because it uses the accusatorial system. Accusatorial and inquisitorial are like oil and water: There is no way in which you can blend or mix the two.[2]

Although there are elements of truth in this, I think it is a serious oversimplification. There is nowadays no clear-cut distinction between accusatorial and inquisitorial systems. In so far as the distinction is still valid, it does not conclusively determine the status of experts because the so-called accusatorial systems already make some use of court experts and expert witnesses called adversarially are also found in the so-called inquisitorial systems. I therefore think that the wider use of court experts is a feasible option in the world of common law and that it is not a waste of time to think seriously about the possible advantages and disadvantages.

In the first part of this chapter, I explain the current meaning of the terms *inquisitorial* and *accusatorial* and the relationship between the two systems. In the second part, I explain how the role of the expert differs in the two systems. In the third part, I assess the relative advantages and disadvantages of court experts and expert witnesses.

Before going any further, I must issue a disclaimer and make a confession of ignorance. My knowledge of the common law world is mainly based on what I know of England and Scotland; my knowledge of the civilian systems consists largely of what I know about France.[3] In each case, my knowledge is mainly about criminal rather than civil procedure. I have, however, drawn on what I know about civil procedure in these jurisdictions and such information as I have about Holland, Germany, Italy, and Portugal[4] as well as the United States and other jurisdictions in the common law world.

INQUISITORIAL AND ACCUSATORIAL: A TRUE OR FALSE DICHOTOMY?

When people talk about the difference between accusatorial and inquisitorial procedure, they usually refer to criminal procedure; within this context, the history of the distinction is most easily explained.[5] Until the early 13th century, criminal procedure was similar on both sides of the English Channel. Person A accused Person B; if B denied the accusation, then the court invited God to tell it whether B had committed the crime by making B undergo some kind of ordeal. In a society where nearly everyone believed that ordeals really worked, this was the logical method. Nobody complained about it, except perhaps those whom the ordeal falsely condemned, whom nobody believed.[6] In 1215, however, the Lateran Council of the Church condemned ordeals and forbade priests to take part in them and, thereby, caused a problem. If God cannot be made to give the answer, how can mere mortal men resolve the question of guilt or innocence in disputed cases?

In England, the problem was resolved by the judge's summoning a jury of 12 citizens and compulsorily requiring them instead of God to say if Person A's accusation was true. By this means, the accusatorial nature of the trial was preserved. In France and other parts of continental Europe, however, a different system evolved. Copying the sort of procedure the Church used when investigating alleged wrongdoing by priests, the kings would commission a trusted official to inquire into the matter. This official would question the suspect, the accusers, and anyone else who seemed to have relevant information to give and would decide whether the suspect was guilty or not on the basis of the information collected. This was the beginning of the inquisitorial system of criminal procedure.

At first, it was the inquisitorial procedure that was rational and civilized and the English jury trial that was crude and harsh. The continental inquisitor judged by applying reason to the evidence. In the early jury trial, however, there was no evidence: The jury was supposed to decide the question of guilt or innocence on the basis of their own knowledge, if they had any[7]—and if they did not know anything about the case, they still had to produce a verdict because the law refused to take "We don't know" for an answer. So instead of being convicted on evidence, the English defendant risked being convicted on gossip, a hunch, or simply because the jury wanted to go home.

In the course of several centuries, however, the common law accusatorial jury trial improved and the continental inquisitorial trial worsened. The common law judges started to allow the parties to call witnesses to tell the jury what had happened when the jury did not know the case themselves. The jury gradually assumed its modern role as a body of independent citizens who decide on the defendant's guilt according to the evidence of witnesses called for by the prosecution and defense.[8] Meanwhile, the inquisitorial procedure adopted the systematic use of torture.[9] To protect defendants against being wrongly convicted on insufficient evidence and to ensure that the decision was as reliable as the one that was formerly thought to come from God, the courts decided early on that the defendant who did not confess could only be condemned on the evidence of two eyewitnesses. This created an obvious impediment to justice in many cases, which the system then avoided by allowing defendants against whom there was a certain minimum quantity of evidence to be tortured as an encouragement to confess.

From the end of the 17th century onward, enlightened thinkers in the civilian world began to attack torture as both cruel and likely to lead to the conviction of the innocent.[10] As the critics of torture gained ground, so did admiration for English criminal procedure. The critics pointed to it as a system that—officially at least[11]—managed to operate without suspects being tortured. As the 18th century progressed, the debate about criminal procedure on the Continent got intertwined with the debate about constitutional reform. The focal point of the debate was the jury. Although originally an exercise in royal power,[12] by the 18th century juries had emerged as an important limit on this power, thanks to their habit of acquitting the king's political enemies when he tried to use the criminal courts to crush them. From foreign admiration for English criminal justice during this period probably comes the idea—still firmly held by many common lawyers—that common law procedure is somehow morally superior to other systems and the idea—still sometimes expressed by English lawyers—that English criminal procedure is "the envy of the world."

One of the first things the French revolutionaries did was to abolish the traditional criminal procedure and replace it with what they believed was a copy of English criminal procedure.[13] The change, however, proved to be a disaster. The new procedure turned out to be grossly inefficient and quite unable to deal with the crime wave that swept through France (like the crime wave sweeping through Russia today) following the breakdown of the previous social order. Frenchmen—Napoleon among them—began to see the virtues of the authoritarian system that had been abolished. In 1808 when Napoleon become emperor, a new system of criminal procedure was devised with the intention of combining the advantages of the new system with some of the advantages of the old.

Napoleon's *Code d'instruction criminelle* of 1808 introduced a cleaned-up version of the old inquisitorial procedure—shorn, of course, of torture—for use in serious cases as a preliminary stage in the criminal process.[14] A new judicial officer, the *juge d'instruction*, interrogated the defendant and the witnesses in private, recorded their statements in writing, and prepared a dossier, which then formed the basis of the case against the defendant. Unlike in the old procedure, however, the judge did not carry out the initial investigation and then make the final decision on guilt or innocence. This was now done at a public trial, before new judges, sitting (in serious cases) with a jury. To the French, this was not a return to the old inquisitorial system but a new system, which they called (and still call) neither accusatorial nor inquisitorial but *mixed*.[15] This is still the basic shape of French criminal procedure today—although Napoleon's code was replaced by a new *Code de procédure pénale* in 1958. In a serious criminal case, there is still a pretrial instruction over which a *juge d'instruction* presides. One of the duties of this judicial figure is to call in experts when necessary, define their tasks, and supervise their work.[16]

Napoleon's *Code d'instruction criminelle* was imposed on most of continental Europe during the French occupation. When the French left, it was the model the liberated countries used when drawing up their own procedural codes. In doing so, they all departed from the French model in various ways—and have continued to do so over the intervening years. Thus, not only is criminal procedure in civilian countries no longer strictly inquisitorial, but also there is no longer any single "system." Juries, for example, continue to exist in France, but in Germany, they have been replaced by lay assessors.[17] In Holland, they abolished them altogether.[18]

In Germany, too, the *juge d'instruction* has been abolished, with most of the powers of inquiry transferred to the public prosecutor.[19]

If criminal procedure in the civilian countries is now mixed rather than inquisitorial, criminal procedure in the common law world has also become mixed as well. English criminal procedure, for example, has absorbed a number of the ideas that have long been current in the continental procedures. It was once supposed to be a distinguishing feature of common law criminal procedure that the suspect could not be detained for interrogation, whereas this could be done in France, for example. In 1984, however, the English police were given an express power to hold suspects for the purpose of interrogation.[20] Another important change concerns the pretrial disclosure of evidence. At one time, the common law saw the "surprise witness" as a legitimate weapon for both the prosecution and the defense. This is in sharp contrast to the position in the civilian jurisdictions where each side was expected to reveal its hand ahead of trial. But in the common law world today, duties of advance disclosure are increasingly more common—even ones that force the defense to reveal their evidence.[21] The world is no longer divided into two camps, the accusatorial and the inquisitorial. All systems are mixed, with a flavor that differs from one place to another depending on how the ingredients are blended.[22]

One of these ingredients is the duty (if any) of the court to take active steps to see that the truth comes out. In civilian jurisdictions—and particularly in criminal procedure—this duty figures prominently and is stated in a number of codes of criminal procedure.[23] It is sometimes thought that in the common law systems, the court is under no such duty. However, this is not completely true. In England, for example, the court is expected to take active steps to get to the truth in civil proceedings to decide questions about the welfare and upbringing of children.[24] It is even present, to some degree, in criminal proceedings. In a contested criminal case, the trial judge, at least in England, has a residual power to call a witness whom neither side has called (although these days it is rarely exercised).[25] Once the defendant's guilt has been established, the English criminal court regularly takes the initiative in discovering the facts it needs to know to decide the sentence. The idea that the court has an active duty to establish the truth is thus known in the common law, although it is less pervasive than it is in civilian jurisdictions.

In recent years, the common law world has seen the reverse of the public debate that took place in 18th-century France. A number of influential commentators in the common law world have pointed out the defects and inefficiencies of the English accusatorial criminal procedure and have held up the civilian systems as the place to look for answers.[26] In the civilian world, however, criminal procedure still has its vigorous critics, some of whom praise the accusatorial system as it supposedly exists in England and North America, and these critics want to make yet more borrowings from it. For example, a body of opinion in the civil law jurisdictions thinks that the *juge d'instruction*—recently much admired by certain would-be English reformers[27]—confuses functions that ought to be kept separate and wants the office to be abolished.[28] In Italy, these ideas have prevailed. In 1988, Italy repealed its existing French-based code of criminal procedure and replaced it with a new one, which is usually described as Anglo-Saxon and accusatorial.[29] Under this new code, the Italian *juge d'instruction* has disappeared; during the pretrial phase, Italian judges play a passive and reactive role, as they do in common law jurisdictions.

It is interesting to note, however, that the reformers in continental Europe do not seem keen to dislodge one feature of the existing systems: the general rule that experts are neutral figures, whose help is invoked by the court, rather than expert witnesses after the fashion of the common law. This is the position in Italy under the new code of criminal procedure.[30] It was also recommended by an official committee in France, which made otherwise radical proposals to change French criminal procedure.[31]

THE POSITION OF THE EXPERT

Court Experts in France

As an example of how the system of court-appointed experts works in the civil law systems, let us look at how it operates in criminal proceedings in France.[32] The present rules in this regard date from 1958 and were laid down to answer a number of criticisms as it operated before. The old system was attacked for many reasons; for example, it was insufficient to make sure that the court received experts' help of a sufficiently high standard.[33]

The way court experts are appointed is laid down in a series of detailed provisions of the *Code de procédure pénale*. The first of these provides that any court may have recourse to an expert if the court is confronted with a "technical question"; the court may do so either on the application of the parties or on its own motion.[34] Although the judge at the trial court has the power to appoint an expert, in practice it is usually the *juge d'instruction* who appoints an expert during the pretrial phase (or *instruction*). In France (although not generally in the other civilian countries), the expert usually must be chosen from an official list,[35] to which entry is strictly controlled. Those who have gained admission to the list have taken an oath that they will lend their help to justice *"en leur honneur et en leur conscience"*[36] and are thereafter obliged to act when called on for the fees prescribed by the State.

The *juge d'instruction* has a discretion over the number of experts he or she calls in. In a simple case, a single expert is nominated; in a difficult case, there are two experts—or even a group of them.[37] The *juge d'instruc-tion* defines the questions the expert must address and lays down a time limit within which the job must be done.[38] There are rules about the people whom the expert is permitted to question; in particular, one rule normally requires any interview between the expert and the defendant to take place in the presence of the *juge d'instruction*.[39] The parties, if they wish, may request the *juge d'instruction* to require the expert to "carry out certain researches or listen to any designated person who is said to be able to give them technical information."[40] When the expert (or experts) has produced the report, the *juge d'instruction* communicates the report to the parties, who can then offer comments on it and can request the *juge d'instruction* to get a second opinion (*contre expertise*). The *juge d'instruction* is not bound to agree to this; but if he or she refuses, reasons must be given.[41] At trial, the experts appear to speak to their report "if there is occasion for this"[42]; in practice, they always do so in a serious case. An expert who appears at trial is liable to be questioned in the same way as a witness. The rules that apply to experts in French civil proceedings differ in detail, but the position is similar to the extent that the expert is nominated by the court.[43]

Although the official court-appointed expert usually delivers techni-cal information to the courts in the civilian countries, it is not the exclu-sive method; expert witnesses sometimes present information. It is open to the parties (in particular, to the defense in a criminal case) to call their own expert as a witness. Although this occasionally happens, it does not happen very frequently. It is partly a question of money and the availability (or nonavailability) of legal aid. But it is also due to the fact that other opportunities are provided to challenge the official expert's opinion apart from calling expert witnesses in contradiction; thus, most lawyers normally use these opportunities.[44] There is also a general feeling that an expert who is called by one of the parties to the case is less likely to be neutral and objective and, therefore, less worthy of belief.[45] When the parties do call their own experts as witnesses at trial to contradict the official one, the French *Code de procédure pénale* contains a provision designed to head off a "battle of the experts." Article 169 gives the presiding judge the power, in such a case, to adjourn "while any measure which he considers useful in relation to the expert opinion is taken." Thus, the judge could require the official expert to consult with the parties' expert witnesses, to produce a further report commenting on what they have said, or to seek the opinion of a further expert or—more probably—a group of experts.[46]

Court Experts in the Common Law World

In the common law world, experts are predominantly expert wit-nesses. However, just as expert witnesses are used to some extent in the civilian systems, so court-appointed experts are used to some extent in the common law jurisdictions—indeed, the extent of their use is probably wider than many people realize. In both England and Scotland, the civil courts that deal with maritime matters, such as collisions at sea, always use *nautical assessors*, people experienced in nautical matters who do not merely provide the court with a report but actually sit throughout the case as advisors to the judge. In England and Scotland, the judge in any civil case has the general power to appoint an independent expert if the parties ask for this (but they usually do not).[47] In English civil proceedings brought to determine the future of a child, the court often appoints a *guardian ad litem* to safeguard the interests of the child; this guardian may then commission an expert report. If an export report is commissioned, then the court receives the advice of an expert who is independent of the two parties in the case—although the court does not appoint the neutral expert itself.[48]

In criminal cases, less use is made of court-appointed experts in the common law world. However, the criminal courts in England (if not elsewhere) have the power to call for expert reports when sentencing convicted offenders, and they make great use of them.[49] In some common law jurisdictions, the judge has the power to appoint on his or her motion a neutral expert at the earlier stage of a criminal trial when the court has to decide whether the defendant is guilty or innocent. In the United States, for example, it is expressly conferred by Rule 706 of the *Federal Rules of Evidence* (although this power is rarely used).[50]

What Are Experts Allowed to Speak On?

There is an interesting difference between the common law and the civilian jurisdictions over the range of matters on which the courts are willing to listen to experts. In the civilian jurisdictions, the range of subjects is considerably wider. In particular, the courts in the civilian jurisdictions are generally willing to receive expert evidence bearing on the credibility of witnesses.

In the common law world, there is widespread reluctance to allow this sort of evidence and the courts have built various rules to avoid it. One of these, well known in the United States, is the Frye test, a rule that forbids the use of expert testimony that is based on any new scientific principle except where it has "gained general acceptance in the particular field to which it belongs." This was first laid down when a federal court refused to accept evidence of how a particular person had performed on a polygraph (lie detector) test.[51] In England and other parts of the common law world where the Frye test has never been accepted,[52] other basic principles of the law of evidence have been invoked—or possibly invented—as reasons why expert evidence about credibility must be rejected. One such principle is the "ultimate issue" rule,[53] which prohibits any witness from giving his or her opinion about a matter if it is the very question on which the court is called to determine—or at any rate, the question is one that the court is at least theoretically capable of answering for itself.

Even in jurisdictions where the ultimate issue rule has been formally abolished or has fallen into judicial disfavor, the judges are prone to reject this sort of evidence for other reasons. In England, the courts seem at present to be particularly reluctant to accept it. At one time, they would not even hear psychiatric evidence that the credibility of witness was undermined by his or her mentally abnormal state. Having accepted this,[54] they are still extremely suspicious of evidence from psychologists that bears on the credibility of people who are not "mentally abnormal." They have, in recent years, gone as far as allowing the defense to call psychologists to show that a given defendant is suggestible and hence more likely—as is claimed—to have made a false confession to the police.[55] But until now, the courts have refused to allow psychological evidence that suggests that a given witness is likely to tell lies.[56] In a recent case, the English Court of Appeal condemned the prosecution for calling an educational psychologist to inform the court about the mental abilities of a mentally handicapped teenager, allegedly the victim of a sexual assault, and in particular to say that she was not highly suggestible.[57] Such evidence was to be rejected, said the court, because the common law does not allow "oath helping," that is, evidence that merely asserts that a witness is worthy of belief.[58]

Elsewhere in the common law world, expert evidence about the credibility of witnesses seems to be a matter of controversy and dispute. In the United States, the position is confused. Some jurisdictions generally allow it, some generally ban it, and others have taken up a compromise position. This position is that such evidence is not generally permitted, but the prosecution may call it in rebuttal for a case where the defense tries to claim that a particular prosecution witness is not worthy of belief. In reality, the dispute is largely about expert evidence in child abuse cases: evidence about the mental age and development of particular children, evidence about the way in which sexually abused children typically behave, and evidence from various types of experts who have examined the child in question and claim that in their opinion, the child has or has not been abused.[59] In some parts of the common law world, it has been necessary to enact legislation to resolve this matter. In 1989, for example, the New Zealand Evidence Act was amended to specify, in some detail, what type of expert can give what kind of expert evidence in a prosecution for a sexual offense against a child.[60]

In the civilian jurisdictions, however, the courts are very ready to seek expert help about the credibility of witnesses and defendants and—by comparison with what has been going on in the common law world—

this has given rise to little legal controversy. A French psychiatrist, for example, has written that

> where the testimony of the victim supports the accusation, an expert opinion on this victim may be asked for. This is frequently the case with sex offence victims, and a fortiori when it is a case of a child or an adolescent.[61] (translated from French)

A French prosecutor described a recourse to a psychological expert as one of the "classic procedures . . . long used in cases which call minors into question."[62] Expert evidence of this sort is also regularly used in Germany. There, the use of psychological experts to pronounce on the credibility of children who are allegedly the victims of sexual offenses is virtually routine and dates back to the early 20th century and the general fear of false accusations in sexual abuse cases. At first, the experts seem to have concentrated on general statements about the risk of errors and lies in children's testimony and on assessments of the child's background and character. Subsequently, however, German psychologists devised the procedure now usually called in English the statement validity analysis (SVA)—the theory of which is that truthful accounts by children typically show certain characteristics that untruthful accounts do not and vice versa.[63] An Italian judge, too, may seek an expert opinion on the credibility of a problematic witness in a criminal case,[64] as may a judge in Portugal.[65]

As far as I am aware, most of the criticism that has been made of the use of experts in this type of case has not come, as it would probably come in the common law world, from those who say that this sort of expert evidence is inherently unreliable or that if it is reliable, such evidence usurps the proper function of the court. Such complaints as are made seem to be voiced on behalf of the victims. It is sometimes said to demean the victims to put them through a psychological examination before the court accepts their word, or it is sometimes said that the practice has the effect of reinforcing outdated ideas about the credibility of certain types of people.[66] French and German colleagues with whom I have discussed the matter tell me that no one really questions the idea that such evidence is in principle proper and in practice often helpful. In Germany, indeed, a judge who did not appoint an expert to advise the court on the credibility of a problematic witness could find the verdict appealed because he or she had failed in the duty to take all proper measures to establish the truth.[67]

In Holland, however, there has been some public disquiet about the use of credibility experts. The Dutch courts, like the French and German ones, also use experts in prosecutions for child abuse. In some cases, the expert has questioned the children during play interviews using anatomically correct dolls; the courts have then founded their conviction on the expert's opinion based on this interview that the child was abused by the defendant. This has led to some public criticism.[68] In 1989, the Dutch

Supreme Court reacted to this criticism by ruling that a court should not convict on the basis of a single expert's report if the defense could show that the methods used by the expert were controversial. Either the court should have done what the defense wanted and adjourned the case for further investigations; or if it was not prepared to do this, it should at least have given reasons for its refusal.[69]

Psychiatric Experts on the Continent: A Particular Complaint

However, there is one aspect of the role of experts that has certainly given rise to widespread controversy in the civilian systems, namely, the psychiatric evidence about the mental state of a defendant. To some extent, the debate is, as it is in the common law world, about the competency of psychiatrists to pronounce whether the defendant is responsible for his or her acts—arguably a legal rather than a strictly psychiatric matter. But in the civilian systems, there is another and peculiar problem, which arises from the way in which criminal trials are conducted. In most of the civilian systems, there is no such thing as a guilty plea. In a case where the defendant denies guilt, there is no clear division (as there is in the common law world) between the part of the trial when guilt is established and the part when the sentence is decided. At trial, therefore, evidence that is relevant to guilt and evidence that (in common law terms) is relevant to sentencing only come out all jumbled up together. When a defendant strenuously denies guilt and is possibly suffering from mental problems, this can cause particular problems. With a view to deciding what to do with the defendant if convicted, the court usually obtains a psychiatric opinion on the defendant's mental state. The court hears this opinion before it formally decides whether the offense was committed, an order of events that creates the risk of an innocent defendant being convicted partly on the basis of a psychiatric opinion that was built on the hypothesis that he or she is guilty and that he or she is dangerous and likely to reoffend.[70]

In Italy, concerns of this sort have led to a section of the *Codice di procedure penale* being enacted that prohibits expert opinions on the defendant's "tendency to offend, his general character and his psychic qualities independent of any pathological cause"—except when the court is considering the execution of the sentence.[71] In France and Germany, proposals are sometimes made to divide the trial of defendants who contest their guilt into two phases: a first one where the court hears only evidence that is strictly relevant to guilt or innocence, on the basis of which it decides to acquit or convict; and if it convicts, then a second phase in which it pronounces the sentence after hearing evidence relevant to the sentence.[72] Surprisingly, such proposals never seem to come to anything.

COURT EXPERTS AND EXPERT WITNESSES:
THE ADVANTAGES AND DISADVANTAGES

Broadly speaking, a system of adversarially appointed expert witnesses is said to give rise to four problems: (a) incompetence because it encourages the use of experts whose technical abilities are poor; (b) bias because it leads to expert evidence that is unreliable when the expert, consciously or otherwise, is prejudiced to the favor of the side that calls and pays him or her; (c) unfairness because in practice, if not in theory, one side will be able to afford more and better experts than the other; and (d) ineptitude because it causes a "battle of experts" that generates more heat than light. To what extent are these problems real ones in the common law world, and would a system of court-appointed experts enable the courts to avoid them?

Incompetence

Expert evidence of poor scientific quality has certainly been a major problem in Britain, if not elsewhere in the common law world. In recent years, it has been at the center of a number of celebrated miscarriages of justice.[73] In theory, the expert's poor technical skills are supposed to be detected by counsel for the other side in a cross-examination. So strong is the common lawyer's faith in this method that English law has never imposed any rules limiting who may or may not act as an expert witness: Anyone who claims to have relevant knowledge is free to "have a go" if he or she has the courage to face a cross-examination. Alas, a string of wrongful convictions in England shows that cross-examination is not the certain protection against incompetent expert evidence that it has been traditionally thought to be.[74]

Is this problem automatically solved by a system of court-appointed experts? The honest answer to this question must be "No—not automatically." In principle, the fact that an expert is appointed by the court rather than chosen by one of the parties does not guarantee that the expert knows the job. In England, those who are skeptical about court-appointed experts oppose the idea by saying that if we had such experts, the same incompetent people would give the same misleading evidence but from a more elevated position where they could less easily be attacked.[75] The view that court appointment of experts is no guarantee of quality is supported to the extent that there is public criticism of the quality of official experts in some of the jurisdictions that use them.[76]

I think, however, that a system of court-appointed experts is more likely to provide consistently competent expert advice than a system of expert witnesses called and examined adversarially. In the common law world, experts frequently express the bitterest criticism of the system under which they appear as witnesses for one side or the other. A common reason they give for disliking this system is that it inhibits them from presenting their scientific knowledge to the court fairly and accurately.[77] The fact that they are adversarially examined, they say, tends to prevent them from saying exactly what they want to say; each advocate will try to make them say what suits the case, no less and definitely no more. The experts dislike the fact that however honestly and fairly they have done their job, the other side is likely in cross-examination to accuse them of being biased in favor of the party that called them.[78]

The result, I believe, is that many of the better scientists prefer not to get involved as expert witnesses; in consequence, the courts are deprived of the services of some of those who are the most competent in their field. This is in contrast to the position in France, where admission to the official list of court experts is seen as a professional honor, to which, on the whole, the best scientists and professionals aspire. Furthermore, a system of expert witnesses not only discourages good scientists and professionals from getting involved but also positively encourages the selection of bad ones. From the parties' point of view, the ideal expert witness is one who is confident and certain and will concede nothing under cross-examination. Because the essence of good science is open-mindedness, the less a scientist is willing to admit to the possibility of a qualification or error, the worse he or she is likely to be as a scientist. In addition, the ability to stand up to an advocate under cross-examination is to a large extent a test of wit and presence, qualities not of the scientist but of the entertainer.[79]

The French system of court-appointed experts, furthermore, provides a system of quality control in the form of an official list of experts, to which a person must normally belong before he or she may be nominated to act as an expert in a case. There are local lists and a national list. The French courts are organized regionally under local courts of appeal, and the local lists are drawn up by each of these courts. A person who wishes to be put on the list submits an application. The public prosecutor checks that the applicant is formally eligible and passes the file to an independent advisory committee, which interviews the candidate, obtains a view of the candidate's standing among his or her professional colleagues, and passes the file along with its views on the candidate to the president of the local court of appeal. A committee of judges makes the final decision. In practice, it is difficult to get on the list because the courts operate an unofficial quota system, with the view of keeping the standard high. The national list is drawn up in the same sort of way, except that it largely consists of people who have already been inscribed on a local one.[80] From the judgment of my French colleagues, the French system of official lists has largely disposed of the problem of experts who simply do not know their job as well as the "professional expert witness."[81] However, it has caused certain other problems, in particular, delays where the official experts have too much work to do.

On balance, however, it looks as if the system of official lists has much to commend it. Although it was invented in a system where experts are predominantly appointed by the court, it could theoretically be adopted in a system where the parties appoint them.

Bias

There are undoubtedly serious problems in the common law world with expert evidence that is unreliable through bias. In the United States, complaints are heard about "hired guns"—experts of doubtful quality and even more dubious ethical standards who charge high fees and never appear except for the defense.[82] A spectacular example of this type of evidence was seen in the trial of John Demjanjuk in Israel. A defense handwriting expert who testified that a signature on a particular document was probably not Demjanjuk's was confronted with his earlier public statement to the contrary. The expert refused to explain further on the grounds that he had a "contractual relationship" with the Demjanjuk Defense Fund, and they would sue him if he did.[83] In England, even more worryingly, it seems that several of the more spectacular wrongful convictions that occurred in trials for terrorist outrages were partly due to bias by prosecution expert witnesses, for example, forensic chemists who deliberately concealed scientific information that supported the case for the defense.[84]

Part of the reason for biased expert evidence is that the expert is often chosen, not because he or she is widely respected in the profession, but because he or she is willing to tell the court what the party in question wants the court to hear. Prosecutors are generally under certain ethical restraints, but defendants in criminal cases, and both parties in civil litigation, are usually free to "shop around." This shopping around consists of tearing up one "unhelpful" expert report after another until they find an expert who will take the line they want.[85] This expert may be a reputable and honest expert but may equally be the one person in the profession incompetent enough to hold the view in question or the only one corrupt enough to take a fee for falsely claiming to do so. Even if the expert tries to be fair and objective, there is the further problem of unconscious bias; even honest experts will feel the need to side with the people who have invoked their help.[86] Even if the honest expert surmounts the problem of unconscious bias, there are two additional problems. One problem is that the expert who is called by one of the parties to a case usually depends on that party for information and may not be given all the information that is relevant.[87] Another is that the expert will often not be allowed to "tell the tale" in his or her own way but will be examined adversarially by opposing advocates, each of whom is anxious to get the expert to say what suits the client's case. Even if the expert's evidence is given (as it sometimes is) in the form of a written report, this may well be a redraft of the original report, containing modifications that the lawyers for the party calling the expert have pressed him or her to make.[88]

To what extent does a system of court-appointed experts avoid the difficulties of bias? In principle, I believe such a system can avoid these difficulties; but an important qualification is that much depends on who it is that actually nominates the expert and how far the nominator exercises an independent judgment. In French criminal proceedings, the expert is usually nominated by the *juge d'instruction*, a judge who has the official duty of investigating the case with an even hand as between the prosecution and defense. Appointed under this arrangement, French court experts, as far as I can gather, do largely escape criticism on the ground of bias.[89] In German criminal procedure, where the *juge d'instruction* no longer exists, the expert is often nominated by the public prosecutor, whose nominee is then taken over by the court. This understandably leads to criticism.[90]

In addition to this particular problem in Germany, it seems that in all the systems that use court-appointed experts, a problem sometimes arises with psychiatric experts who are called in to evaluate the criminal responsibility of the defendant. In this area there are wide differences of opinion, and it is sometimes easy to predict what the opinion of a particular expert will be. If this is the case, then there is sometimes said to be bias in the court, in the expert, or both: People say "the judge chose X because he [or she] knew what X would say."[91]

There seems to be no doubt, however, that the use of court-appointed experts gets around the problem of the expert being given only half the evidence. Indeed, one sometimes hears the criticism that the court experts are too active in seeking information, to the extent of usurping the functions of the court.[92] It also seems that when experts are appointed by and report directly to the court, this solves the related problem of the expert being unable to express a scientific opinion in his or her own words because it is extracted by an adversarial examination.

Unfairness—Inequality of Arms

Although a system under which each side appoints its own expert gives an impression of equality, often this is only an impression. In the first place, expert witnesses usually have to be paid, and often one side is better able to afford their fees than the other. Even if both sides are equally rich, there is still a problem when the number of competent experts is limited and all the most convincing ones in some way "belong" to one side or the other. This was the case in England until recently. All the best-equipped forensic science laboratories were run by the State; in criminal cases, these experts would work for the prosecution but not for the defense.[93] Even when both sides have equal access to good experts, there is also the problem that certain types of test can only be done early or only done once. In a criminal case, the prosecution expert may have performed the tests already by the time the defense expert is appointed.[94]

Child abuse cases sometimes raise this difficulty; obviously, there is a limit to the number of times the child in question can be made to undergo a psychiatric or psychological examination.[95] Where tests are not easily repeatable, the fact that experts are appointed by the parties rather than the court can mean, in practice, that the court is presented with the evidence of the prosecution expert, take it or leave it. All the defense expert can then do, if anything, is comment on the way the prosecution expert did the job. If this is what equality of arms between the prosecution and defense can mean in practice, it is surely fairer as between the parties for there to be a neutral expert or experts nominated by the court.

Ineptitude

As a means of putting the work of scientists before the court and genuinely testing its validity, letting each side call their own experts at the trial and publicly cross-examine their opponents' is a bad one. The most truth-producing way to get a scientist or other professional to adjust his or her view is to arrange a meeting to discuss the matter calmly with another scientist who holds a different view and to give the first scientist the chance to reflect on a second scientist's view before giving a reply. Waiting until the expert commits himself publicly to a particular view in the witness box and then publicly confronting the expert with a contrary view tends to make the arrogant scientist refuse to budge for fear of looking stupid;[96] conversely, a timid scientist might concede a point that he or she would not have conceded if there had been time to reflect.[97] The civil law systems work to avoid this problem by encouraging the different experts to discuss their conclusions early and in private. As a French book on criminal procedure explains,

> the Code de procédure pénale has tried to avoid the inadequacies of the expertise being challenged and discussed at trial, in public and in conditions harmful to the good name of science—eminent workers being called on to expose in the witness-box differences that may arise from a simple misunderstanding—and also harmful to the good name of justice. It takes the position that attacks upon the work of experts should be presented more discreetly, and also while there is still time for gaps or imperfections to be put right.[98]

Thus, as explained above, French criminal procedure has a number of rules designed to encourage the parties to challenge the official expert's view in private, before the expert has taken a public stand on the matter and there is still time for reflection. If a battle of experts does break out at trial, the judge can impose a cease-fire for negotiations.

It is obviously possible to introduce pretrial negotiations between experts in a system that uses expert witnesses called adversarially. Indeed, a number of changes of this sort have been made in recent years in England.[99] But even if the common law system of expert witnesses is modified in this way, there is still the risk that it will mask the area of agreement that in truth exists between all the serious experts in the field and will present the court with a conflict of views that looks more serious than it is. When each side is free to present more or less anyone (however bizarre or disreputable) as an expert worthy of belief, it can always find someone who will flatly contradict what the expert for the other side has said. When confronted with a head-on collision between two rival expert opinions, a court of law without its own independent expert to turn to is often left with no real basis on which to decide which expert is talking scientific sense. Sometimes the result is that what started out as a battle of experts ends up as a beauty contest.[100] Sometimes it leaves the court without any guidance at all. As a famous American lawyer, Learned Hand, said nearly a century ago,

> one thing is certain, [the jury] will do no better with the so-called testimony of experts than without, except where it is unanimous. If the jury must decide between such they are as badly off as if they had no one to help. The present system in the vast majority of cases— there being some dispute upon almost all subjects of human inquiry— is a practical closing of the doors of justice upon the use of specialized and scientific knowledge.[101]

From this, Hand concluded that the only sensible solution was "a board of experts or a single expert, not called by either side, who shall advise the jury of the general propositions applicable to the case which lie within his province."[102]

Does a system of court-appointed experts create any new problems that do not arise with expert witnesses? There are said to be two problems. First, it makes the expert's conclusions harder to attack if they are wrong.[103] Second, it makes the courts more reliant on the expert than they should be.

Impregnability: The Expert on a Pedestal

The argument that the official expert is immune from attack is sometimes made by people who assume that in a system with official experts, the parties to the case have no official opportunity to challenge the experts' conclusions.[104] This is completely false: The parties can contest the conclusions of the official expert in some way or other in all the civilian systems on which I have any information. The complaint that official experts are impregnable to attack is true only to the extent that in some of the civilian systems, the means of challenging the official expert's opinion is insufficient.

In French criminal procedure, as seen earlier, the parties are given not one but a series of chances to challenge the court expert's opinion. First, they can request the *juge d'instruction* to instruct the expert to discuss the matter with another expert. Second, when they receive the court expert's report, they can criticize it and ask the *juge d'instruction* to ask the expert to carry out further tests or ask the *juge d'instruction* to get a second opinion.[105] Third, in a serious case, they are able to put questions to the expert in person at the trial. Fourth, they can, if need be, call their own expert as an expert witness. In France, furthermore, the risk that the court will be swayed by the view of a single expert who has "got it wrong" is further reduced by the tradition, in a difficult case, of nominating not one single expert but a panel of them.[106]

In Italian criminal procedure, the parties have an additional possibility. The new code of criminal procedure, although it is said to be Anglo-Saxon, retains the rule that experts are appointed by the court. But both prosecution and defense have the right to nominate "technical consultants," whose job it is to work alongside the official expert.[107] Similar provisions were included in the new Portuguese Codigo de Processo Penal of 1987.[108]

In German criminal procedure, however, the parties are in a much worse place to challenge the official expert. Article 244(4) of the German Code of criminal procedure provides that

> a motion to take evidence by examining an expert can, except where otherwise provided, be refused if the court itself possesses the necessary expertise. The hearing of an additional expert can also be refused if through the earlier expert opinion the opposite of the relevant fact has already been established; but this does not apply if the competence of the original expert is in doubt, if his opinion is based on an incorrect view of the facts, if his opinion contains contradictions, or if the new expert has methods of research available which seem superior to those of the original expert. (translated from German)

In consequence of this provision, it is said to be difficult to persuade a German criminal court to seek a second opinion[109] or to hear expert evidence that goes against the view expressed by the original court expert.

Overinvolvement With Experts

There seems to be more truth in the criticism that a system of official experts sometimes causes judges to get too closely involved with the experts. At any rate, this is one complaint about official experts that is regularly made by lawyers who operate within the civilian jurisdictions (as against by common lawyers from a position of relative ignorance).

The complaint takes several forms. One complaint is that particular judges make excessive use of particular experts, and these experts are not always the most competent ones.

> The selection of experts does not rest on competence alone. . . . It is clear that judges favour selecting 'comfortable' experts. An expert is comfortable in this sense when one generally knows beforehand what he will say. Surprises are always uncomfortable. . . . Experts are chosen like restaurants: one prefers to return to places where one has eaten well in the past.[110]

Another complaint is that some judges are said to be too willing to hand over to experts difficult questions that they really should answer for themselves. A French writer dealing with the problems that arise with experts in civil proceedings in France has written that

> a first complaint, of a fairly general sort, is tied to the fact that the courts too frequently have recourse to this way of getting information. They are said often to order an expert opinion in situations where the judge could, in reality, inform himself on the subject.[111]

Similarly, some Dutch writers, having criticized the overuse of experts in child abuse cases, have said that

> the judge who looks for support for a piece of witness evidence he is doubtful about would do better to work in the classic manner: does the witness's statement fit in with information which is established by other means? But that is burdensome, because it forces him to take risky decisions for himself. It would be nice if experts could share that responsibility with him, or even take it over. But the world is not so simple as that.[112]

Another form of this complaint is that some judges accept too readily what the expert says. In the civilian systems, the judge is not bound to accept the opinion of the expert; as in the common law system, the court is not theoretically obliged to believe the expert evidence, even if it is uncontradicted. But in practice, it is said that judges in the civil law systems sometimes defer to court-appointed experts to the extent of failing to look at the experts' reports with a properly critical eye.[113] It looks as if overinvolvement of court-appointed experts is a real risk, and one that any legal system that uses court-appointed experts needs to guard against.

The obvious point must still be made, however, that there is no such thing as legal procedure that works perfectly. The best system lawyers can ever aspire to is one that is least bad. The problem of excessive influence by experts is the negative aspect of something that on balance is surely good rather than bad: the fact that in jurisdictions where they use court-appointed experts, the judges trust them. Unlike in the common law world, the judges in these jurisdictions assume that experts will be unbiased, and they are confident that the experts have the skills to do the job. I suspect that this is the reason why, in the civilian jurisdictions, the courts are ready and willing (as seen earlier) to seek expert help about a number of matters on which, in the common law world, expert evidence is banned.[114] The real question, then, is whether the judges in the civilian jurisdictions are right in their assumption that their court-appointed experts are likely to be both independent and appropriately skilled. If they are, the question one has to ask oneself is this: Which is worse (a) for the courts to be overinfluenced by experts who are competent and neutral or (b) for them to refuse to hear experts or to ignore their conclusions, for fear that they are not competent and neutral?

CONCLUSION

What I have been able to learn about the system of court-appointed experts makes me think that it is inherently sounder than the rival method of expert witnesses who are adversarially called. However, like every other scheme, it has its inherent problems; so some checks and balances are needed. An obvious example appears to be the system introduced in criminal proceedings in Italy and Portugal, under which the parties can appoint their own "technical consultants" to collaborate with the official expert and to oversee the work that he or she does.

If such a scheme would be too fundamental a change for a common law jurisdiction to adopt, then, surely, the traditional system of expert witnesses would be improved by a different compromise, under which the court would invoke the help of official experts to resolve an otherwise insoluble conflict between the expert witnesses called by each side. Indeed, in some common law jurisdictions, as seen earlier, this is possible already.[115] However, in the cradle of the common law—England—the idea has not been well received. In 1993, the Royal Commission on Criminal Justice rejected it out of hand. After saying that court experts would be as unreliable as expert witnesses but harder to attack, the commission said "to have a court expert in addition to the experts for the parties would greatly extend the amount of time spent in examination and cross-examination of all three experts without making discovery of the truth any more certain."[116] But this is weak.[117] The point, surely, is that with the possibility of appointing its own expert, the court would have the means of resolving conflicts of expert evidence that it is not competent to resolve for itself and that if left unresolved, deprive the court of the help that science could otherwise provide. Even in England, however, there are signs that the tide of opinion is turning. In 1996, an official study on improving access to civil justice came out in favor of the idea of court-appointed experts in certain types of cases, at least.[118]

For those who are interested in comparative law, however, what is really interesting in views like those expressed by the Royal Commission on Criminal Justice is the attitude toward experts that underlies them. If civilian jurisdictions trust experts and want to make maximum use of them, the common law ones do not. To common lawyers, experts are basically untrustworthy, and the less you have to do with them the better.

NOTES

1. The "civilian systems" were developed in Western Europe in the countries that rose from the ruins of the western Roman Empire and the parts of the world that were later colonized by their inhabitants; the concepts and principles of such a system are largely drawn from Roman law. The term comes from *ius civile*, a Latin term often used to mean Roman law.

2. One English writer said that the idea of court-appointed experts "puts in issue the fundamental assumptions on which English criminal procedure is built" (P. Roberts, "Forensic science evidence after Runciman" [1994] *Criminal Law Review*, pp. 780, 790). (He therefore applauded the decision of the English Royal Commission on Criminal Justice to reject the idea—which it did very summarily in the space of a single paragraph (Report [1993], cm. 2263, para. 74). Less temperate, another English writer called the idea of court-appointed experts "totalitarian." (M. Howard, see note 75, p. 101). An American writer said that with court experts "trial by jury then becomes no more than an empty illusion" and that it "destroys fundamental rights" (Levy, see note 103).

3. For a fuller account of the position in France, see J. R. Spencer, "Court experts and expert witnesses—Have we a lesson to learn from the French?" (1992), *45 Current Legal Problems*, pp. 213–236.

4. When it comes to looking at original sources, I am limited, unfortunately, to those in the languages I can read: French, Dutch, and a little German. (For Germany, I have had to rely almost entirely on materials in English.) For a survey of the rules about experts in civil proceedings in a range of European countries, see M. F. Terré, "*L'expertise dans les principaux systèmes juridiques d'Europe, Institut de Droit Comparé de l'Université de Paris*" (1969), *Travaux et Recherches*, p. 32.

5. See A. Esmein, *A history of continental criminal procedure* (Boston, 1913); J. H. Langbein, *Prosecuting crime in the Renaissance* (Cambridge, MA, 1974).

6. R. C. Van Caenegem, *The birth of the English common law* (2nd ed., Cambridge, England, 1988), pp. 62–73.

7. It seems that the jury was encouraged to make their own inquiries before the trial (F. Pollock and F. W. Maitland, *History of English law*, S. F. C. Milsom, Ed., 2nd ed., Cambridge, England, 1968, pp. 622, 625).

8. T. Plucknett, *A concise history of the common law* (5th ed., London, 1956), pp. 127–129.

9. J. H. Langbein, *Torture and the law of proof* (Chicago, 1976).

10. Esmein, see note 5, p. 351 et seq.

11. For many years, it was used sparingly but unofficially in cases when the king gave his permission (see Langbein, note 9).

12. Because it was the method by which the king forced his unwilling subjects to give him an answer to a question—frequently one relating to royal revenues—that they would have preferred not to answer (Van Caenegem, see note 6, p. 73).

13. Esmein, see note 5, p. 446 et seq.

14. Ibid., p. 462 et seq.

15. See the report of the *Commission justice pénale et droits de l'homme, la mise en état des affaires pénales* (*La Documentation Française*, 1991), p. 19.

16. For an account of the French system in English, see J. Hatchard, B. Huber, and R. Vogler, *Comparative criminal procedure* (British Institution of International and Comparative Law, London, 1996). For experts in French criminal procedure, see Spencer, note 3.

17. J. H. Langbein, *Comparative criminal procedure: Germany* (St. Paul, MN, 1977), p. 63.

18. G. J. M. Corstens, *Het Nederlandse strafprocesrecht* (2nd ed., Arnhem, The Netherlands, 1995), p. 37.

19. O. Triffterer, "The pre-trial phase," in *The criminal justice system of the Federal Republic of Germany* (Association Internationale de Droit Pénal, Nouvelles études pénales 2, 1981), pp. 29, 46.

20. Police and Criminal Evidence Act 1984 §37(2); M. Zander, *The Police and Criminal Evidence Act 1984* (3rd ed., 1995, Pt. 4).

21. For the duty of the prosecution in England to give the defense advance notice of the evidence it intends to call, see Blackstone's *Criminal practice* (London, 1997), para. D12.16 et seq. In England, in cases tried on indictment, the defense must now give advance notice to the prosecution of the broad lines of its intended defense plus details of alibis and of expert evidence.

22. There is much more to the matter than the skeletal account I have given here. See M. Damaska, *The faces of justice and state authority* (New Haven, CT, 1986).

23. *Strafprozeßordnung* (Germany) article 244(2): "In order to search out the truth the court shall on its own motion extend the taking of evidence to all facts and means of proof that are important for the decision." *Code de procédure pénale* (France) article 310(1): "The president is invested with a discretionary power by virtue of which he may, in honour and good conscience, take any measure which he considers useful to discover the truth."

24. See, e.g., *R. v. Birmingham Juvenile Court ex parte G.* (1990), 2 *Queen's Bench*, 573.

25. The Royal Commission on Criminal Justice (1993, cm. 2263) acknowledged this power and said that it should be more widely used.

26. Much of the debate centers on the evils of plea bargaining in common law. See A. S. Goldstein and M. Marcus, "The myth of judicial supervision in three 'inquisitorial' systems: France, Italy and Germany" (1977), 87 *Yale Law Journal*, p. 240; reply by Langbein and Weinreb, ibid., p. 1549; reply by Goldstein and Marcus, ibid., p. 1570; J. H. Langbein, "Land without plea bargaining: How the Germans do it" (1979), 78 *Michigan Law Review*, p. 204. See also F. S. Frase, "Comparative criminal justice as a guide to American law reform: How do the French do it, how can we find out, and why should we care?" (1990), 78 *California Law Review*, p. 542.

27. For example, M. Mansfield, QC, *Presumed guilty—The British legal system exposed* (London, 1993).

28. This was the line taken in France by the *Comission justice pénale et droits de l'homme* (see note 15); see M. Delmas-Marty, "The *juge d'instruction*: Do the English really need him?," in (B. S. Markesinis, Ed.) *The gradual convergence* (Oxford, England, 1994). (The French government rejected the proposal.)

29. E. Amodio and E. Selvaggi, "An accusatorial system in a civil law country: The 1988 Italian Code of Criminal Procedure" (1989), 62 *Temple Law Review*, p. 1211.

30. *Codice di procedura penale* (1988), article 221.

31. See note 15, p. 197.

32. For a more detailed account, see Spencer, note 3.

33. A cataclysmic event was the trial of Marie Besnard, a *cause célèbre* that was dragged through the French courts from 1952 until 1961. It led, on the part of lawyers, to serious criticism of the standard of experts currently in use and, from the way experts were treated in that case, to fears that good experts would not wish to get involved. See M.-L. Rassat, "Forensic expertise and the law of evidence in France," in (J. F. Nijboer, C. R. Callen, and N. Kwak, Eds.) *Forensic expertise and the law of evidence* (Amsterdam, 1993), pp. 53, 58. There is an account of the case by the defendant, Marie Besnard (*The trial of Marie Besnard*, trans., D. Folliot, London, 1963).

34. *Code de procedure pénale*, article 156.

35. Ibid., article 157.

36. Article 160.

37. Article 159.

38. Article 161.

39. Article 164.

40. Article 165.

41. Article 167.

42. Article 168.

43. *Nouveau code de procédure civile*, articles 263–284–1; J. Vincent and S. Guinchard, *Procédure civile* (22nd ed., Paris, 1991), para. 1258 et seq.

44. "In certain rare cases—because this adversarial procedure certainly upsets the calmness of the discussion—the defence can bring forward experts on

their own account. . . . In general, however, the defence does not resort to this except in really difficult cases" (C. Bardet-Giraudon, "The place of the expert in the French legal system," in [J. R. Spencer, G. Nicholson, R. Flin, and R. Bull, Eds.] *Children's evidence in legal proceedings—An international perspective*, Cambridge Law Faculty, Cambridge, England, 1990, pp. 68, 69).

45. The point is made for Holland by H. F. M. Crombag, P. J. Van Koppen, and W. A. Wagenaar, *Dubieuze zaken—De psychologie van strafrechtelijk bewijs* (Amsterdam, 1992), pp. 303–317, 472. (A shorter version of this book appears in English by Wagenaar et al., *Anchored narratives* [New York, 1993].)

46. "As the defence can previously attack the expert report in the course of the *instruction*, the gain will be to exclude the production of unofficial experts at the trial, this possibility undermining the calm search for truth" (J. Pradel, *Procédure pénale* [9th ed., Paris, 1997], para. 295).

47. T. Hodgkinson, *Expert evidence, law and practice* (London, 1990), ch. 3. As a rule, the English court has no power to nominate an expert except when one of the parties requests it.

48. J. R. Spencer and R. Flin, *The evidence of children—The law and the psychology* (2nd ed., London, 1993), p. 250. This is particularly likely to happen in those difficult cases that are handled by the High Court and when the role of *guardian ad litem* is often carried out by the Official Solicitor, who "has access to the foremost forensic experts, especially child psychiatrists and pediatricians" (J. Thorpe, "Court intervention in child abuse" [1990] *Family Law*, p. 390).

49. The Criminal Justice Act 1991 actually requires the court to obtain various reports before imposing certain types of sentence.

50. *Federal criminal code and rules* (St. Paul, MN, 1994), p. 257: "While experience indicates that actual appointment is a relatively infrequent occurrence, the assumption may be made that the availability of the procedure in itself decreases the need for resorting to it. The ever-present possibility that the judge may appoint an expert in a given case must inevitably exert a sobering effect on the expert witness of a party and upon the person utilizing his services."

51. *Frye v. United States* (1923), 293 F 1013. Polygraph evidence is also rejected in France and Germany, although for different reasons; for France, see R. Merle and A. Vitu, *Traité de droit criminel. Tome II: Procédure pénale* (4th ed., Paris, 1989, p. 164); for Germany, see D. Frehsee, "Children's evidence within the German legal system," in (J. R. Spencer, G. Nicholson, R. Flin, and R. Bull, Eds.) *Children's evidence in legal proceedings—An international perspective* (Cambridge Law Faculty, Cambridge, England, 1990), pp. 28, 33. (In a context far removed from polygraph evidence, the U.S. Supreme Court disapproved of the Frye test in *Daubert v. Merrell Dow Pharmaceuticals, Inc.* [1993], 113 S. Ct 2786.)

52. *Robb* (1991), 93 *Criminal Appeal Reports*, p. 161.

53. J. D. Jackson, "The ultimate issue rule: One rule too many" (1984), *Criminal Law Review*, p. 75.

54. *Toohey v. Commissioner of Police for the Metropolis* [1965] Appeal Cases 595.

55. *Raghip, The Times*, 9 December 1991; *Ward* (1993) 96 *Criminal Appeal Reports*, p. 1.

56. *McKenney* (1983) 76 *Criminal Appeal Reports*, p. 271.

57. *Robinson* (1994) 98 *Criminal Appeal Reports*, p. 370. The English courts sometimes do allow experts to express opinions on the veracity of an informant in civil proceedings. See *Re M. and R.* [1996] 2 *Family Court Reporter*, p. 617.

58. Lord C. J. Taylor, who gave judgment in the Robinson case, is quoted as saying the following in a lecture to the British Academy of Forensic Science: "But even worse than impenetrable jargon was the nature of some of the evidence itself which was of dubious value: Questions of whether witnesses could realistically remember events included in their testimony; 'oath helping' evidence that a witness should be believed; evidence even of whether physical appearance or demeanour might affect a juror's perception of a witness's credibility" (1994), 158 *Justice of the Peace*, p. 768.

59. J. E. B. Myers, *Child witness law and practice* (New York, 1987), paras. 4.12–4.18; J. E. B. Myers, J. Bays, J. Becker, L. Berliner, D. L. Corwin, and K. J. Saywitz, "Expert testimony in child sexual abuse litigation" (1989), 68 *Nebraska Law Review*, pp. 1–145.

60. New Zealand Evidence Act 1908 (as amended by the Evidence Amendment Act 1989): "23G. Expert witnesses. (1) For the purposes of this section, a person is an expert witness if that person is—(a) A medical practitioner registered as a psychiatric specialist under regulations made pursuant to section 39 of the Medical Practitioners Act 1968, practising or having practised in the field of child psychiatry and with experience in the professional treatment of sexually abused children; or (b) A psychologist registered under the Psychologists Act 1981, practising or having practised in the field of child psychology and with experience in the professional treatment of sexually abused children. (2) In any case to which this section applies, an expert witness may give evidence on the following matters: (a) The intellectual attainment, mental capability, and emotional maturity of the complainant, the witness's assessment of the complaint being based on—(i) Examination of the complainant before the complainant gives evidence; or (ii) observation of the complainant giving evidence, whether directly or on videotape; (b) The general developmental level of children of the same age group as the complainant; (c) The question whether any evidence given during the proceedings by any person (other than the expert witness) relating to the complainant's behaviour is, from the expert witness's professional experience or from his or her knowledge of the professional literature, consistent or inconsistent with the behaviour of sexually abused children of the same age group as the complainant."

61. M. Godfryd, *Précis de psychiatrie légale* (Paris, 1987), p. 44.

62. T. Crétin, "*La preuve impossible? De la difficulté d'administrer la preuve des infractions dont sont victimes les mineurs: Attentats à la pudeur, violences et mauvais traitements*" (1992), *Revue de science criminelle et de droit pénal comparé*, pp. 53, 56.

63. A number of accounts of this procedure are available in English: H. Wegener, "The present state of statement analysis," in (J. Yuille, Ed.) *Credibility assessment* (Dordrecht, The Netherlands, 1989); M. Steller and T. Boychuk, "Children as witnesses in sexual abuse cases: Investigative interview and assessment techniques," in (H. Dent and R. Flin, Eds.) *Children as witnesses* (London, 1992); G. Kohnken, "The evaluation of statement credibility; social judgement and expert diagnostic approaches," in (J. R. Spencer, G. Nicholson, R. Flin, and R. Bull, Eds.) *Children's evidence in legal proceedings—An international perspective* (Cambridge Law Faculty, Cambridge, England, 1990).

64. *Codice di procedura penale*, article 196(2), which authorizes the judge to make inquiries about the physical or mental capacity of a witness.

65. *Codigo de processo penale*, article 131(3): "Concerning the evidence of a person under 16 years of age in proceedings for a sexual offence, an expert inquiry can be held into his or her personality."

66. For example, Crétin, see note 62.

67. D. Frehsee, see note 51, p. 32.

68. Crombag et al. (see note 45), ch. 14.

69. H.R. 28 February 1989, *Nederlandse Juristprudentie* 1989, p. 748. This was a departure from the normal rule, which is that the evaluation of expert opinions is left entirely up to the tribunal of fact.

70. K. Volk, "Forensic expertise and the law of evidence in Germany criminal cases," in (J. F. Nijboer, C. R. Callen, and N. Kwak, Eds.) *Forensic expertise and the law of evidence* (Amsterdam 1993), p. 37.

71. *Codici di procedura penale*, article 220(2).

72. Volk, see note 70; G. Stefani, G. Levasseur, and B. Bouloc, *Procedure pénale* (15th ed., 1993, Paris), para. 704.

73. Scandalously poor work by a forensic scientist was revealed in a case in 1981, after which a long series of cases on which the scientist had worked had to be referred to the Court of Appeal: *Preece v. H M Advocate* [1981] *Criminal Law Review*, p. 783; R. Smith, "Forensic pathology, scientific expertise, and criminal law," in (R. Smith and B. Wynne, Eds.) *Expert evidence* (London, 1990), p. 56, at 73ff. Bad quality work by prosecution forensic scientists— and in some cases, actual bias—was revealed in some of the cases in which the Court of Appeal quashed the convictions of a number of persons who had spent many years in prison for terrorist offenses: *McIlkenny et al.* (1991) *94 Criminal Appeal Reports*, p. 133; *Maguire et al.* (1991) *94 Criminal Appeal Reports*, p. 133; *Ward* (1993) *96 Criminal Appeal Reports*, p. 1. The cases are reviewed in C. Jones, *Expert witnesses: Science, medicine and the practice of law* (Oxford, England, 1994), ch. 10.

74. Ibid.

75. M. Howard, QC (Ed., *Phipson on evidence*), wrote that a system of court-appointed experts would be colonized by "the usual cabal of log-rollers, time-servers, self-publicists and people with friends" ("The neutral expert: A plausible threat to justice" [1991] *Criminal Law Review*, p. 98)—a remark that

also shows the contempt that many English lawyers feel toward expert witnesses.

76. Crombag et al. (see note 45) had very harsh words about psychiatric experts in Holland; Volk (see note 70) said that in Germany "public health doctors are often used for opinions concerning criminal responsibility (they produce over two-thirds of all opinions). The special expertise of these doctors in psycho-scientific questions is doubtful."

77. For example, D. J. Gee, "The expert witness in the criminal trial" [1987] *Criminal Law Review*, p. 307; L. Haward, *Forensic psychology* (London, 1981), p. 273; Professor K. Mant, as quoted in (T. Sargant and P. Hill, Eds.), *Criminal trials—The search for truth* (Fabian Research Series No. 38, 1986); J. D. J. Havard, "Expert scientific evidence under the adversarial system: A travesty of justice?" (1992), 32 *Journal of the Forensic Science Society*, p. 225.

78. As happened to the defense experts in the *Maguire* case—although it was really the prosecution experts who were guilty of this (May report, see note 84, para. 14.5).

79. Thus, Howard (see note 75) probably spoke more accurately than he realized when he referred to "organisations analogous to theatrical agents with experts in many fields on their books."

80. For further details, see Spencer, note 3.

81. Bardet-Giraudon (see note 44), referring to psychological experts, said that "the judges take care that those who act as experts do so in conjunction with normal professional practice, and make sure that no body of professional experts emerges consisting of people who have lost touch with clinical practice."

82. Such complaints are not a recent development. In 1936, an American writer said that "a serious abuse of expert testimony in personal injury actions is the role assumed by the expert as protagonist of the party who calls him and pays his fee" (B. L. Shientag, 22 *Cornell Law Quarterly*, p. 192).

83. *The Demjanjuk trial* (Israel Publishing House, Tel Aviv, 1991), pp. 321–323.

84. *Maguire* (1991) 94 *Criminal Appeal Reports*, p. 133; May Committee, *Interim report on the* Maguire *case*, HC 556 (12 July 1990); *Ward* (1993) 96 *Criminal Appeal Reports*, p. 1.

85. "The mode in which expert evidence is obtained is not such as to give the fair result of scientific information to the court. A man may go and does sometimes to half a dozen experts. . . . He takes their honest opinions, he finds three in his favour and three against him; he says to the three in his favour 'will you be kind enough to give evidence?' and he pays the three against him their fee and leaves them alone. . . . I am afraid the result is that the court does not get the assistance from the experts which, if they were unbiased and fairly chosen, it would have a right to expect" (Sir George Jessel, M.R., in *Thorn v. Worthing Skating Rink Co.*, 1876, *Law Reports 6 Chancery Division*, 415, 416n). In civil proceedings involving children, the English courts have now reacted against this by requiring one side to disclose

to the other expert reports they have obtained and decided not to use (*Oxfordshire County Council v. M.* [1994] *Family Court Reporter*, p. 151).

86. Both lawyers and psychologists have mentioned this. L. Haward (*Forensic psychology*, London, 1981, p. 177), noted the "conscious or unconscious identification on the part of the psychologist or psychiatrist with the party which employs him." In a wardship case, J. Cross said that "I have no doubt that the psychiatrists who give evidence in wardship cases are persons of the highest integrity, but if they are instructed on behalf of one party their views are bound to be coloured to some extent by that party's views. Further, if they are ordinary human beings, as I hope and believe that they are, they can hardly help having some faint desire that their side should win just because it is their side." (He therefore held that in such cases, the expert should be instructed by the Official Solicitor as *guardian ad litem*; see note 48.)

87. In *Turner* [1975] *Queen's Bench* 834, the English Court of Appeal was scathing about the report of a psychiatrist as instructed by the defense, which described the defendant, who had a record of offences of violence, as "a placid, rather quiet and passive person who is quite sensitive to the feelings of other people . . . even-tempered . . . not in any way aggressive . . . he seems to have displayed remarkably good impulse control." Would any psychiatrist have said this if he or she had known the defendant's background?

88. "A striking instance is the way in which Professor Tizard's [report] was 'doctored.' The lawyers blocked out a couple of lines in which he agreed with Professor Strang that there was no negligence" (Lord Denning, M.R., in *Whitehouse v. Jordan* [1980] *1 All England Law Reports*, 65).

89. This is not to say, of course, that no French expert has ever been accused of bias; for example, see the case of Buffet and Bonnetemps (see Spencer, note 3, p. 234, and note 49).

90. Volk, see note 70.

91. "It is clear that judges favor selecting 'comfortable' experts. An expert is comfortable in this sense when one generally knows beforehand what he will say" (Volk, see note 70, p. 45).

92. Volk (see note 70) in article 164 of the French *Code de procédure pénale* specified whom the French expert is allowed to interview and how.

93. In 1991, the six main forensic science laboratories in England, formerly run directly by the Home Office, were reorganized as an "executive agency." There are indications that this has made their services more available to the defense.

94. As in *DPP v. British Telecommunications Plc* (1991) *155 Justice of Peace Reports*, 869, for example: A vehicle examiner working for the police in the course of inspecting the vehicle's brakes adjusted them; the result was that no defense expert could then say how the brakes were at the time of the accident.

95. In England, the Rules of Court now require the consent of the court before any child who is the subject of civil proceedings can be medically or psy-

chiatrically examined; when giving one or the other party leave, the courts increasingly do so on terms that the report be disclosed to the other side.

96. As seems to have happened in the *Maguire* case, "the scientists had honestly reported positive results . . . on 4th December 1974. Once charges were laid and the defendants were committed for trial, there was no going back on what had been said" (May Committee, *Interim report on the* Maguire *case*, House of Commons 556 [12 July 1990], para. 11.33).

97. As in the trial of Frederick Henry Seddon, the defense counsel in a murder case nearly got his client acquitted by tripping up the prosecution expert in cross-examination; but the expert eventually thought of the answer, and thanks to the slow progress of the trial, the prosecution was able to recall him to give it (C. P. Harvey, *The advocate's devil*, London, 1958, p. 122 et seq.).

98. G. Stefani, G. Levasseur, and B. Bouloc, *Procédure pénale*, para. 602.

99. Under §84 of Police and Criminal Evidence Act 1984, and the rules made under it, both sides in a criminal case that is tried on indictment must disclose their expert evidence in advance. The Royal Commission on Criminal Justice (1993, cm. 2263) proposed a legal requirement that the experts for both sides should hold a meeting before the trial. Wider duties of mutual disclosure already exist in civil cases.

100. As the judge who presided at the trial of the Birmingham Six put it when he directed the jury on the conflicting expert evidence in that case, "members of the jury, the resolution of scientific argument of this sort is difficult, particularly for a jury of lay people. . . . The only way that you can resolve these difficulties is by your impression of the witnesses. Use any technical knowledge that you have, but I suspect that in the end you will judge primarily by your impression of the witnesses, and perhaps by a comparison of their relative experience" (quoted in the judgment of the Court of Appeal, *McIlkenny et al.* [1991] 93 *Criminal Appeal Reports*, pp. 287, 296).

101. "Historical and practical considerations regarding expert testimony" (1901), *15 Harvard Law Review*, p. 40.

102. Ibid.

103. "[B]y designating a medical witness as court appointed and 'impartial' the court has in effect cloaked him with a robe of infallibility" (E. S. Levy, 1961, *34 Temple Law Quarterly*, pp. 416, 424).

104. For example, see Howard, note 75.

105. French informants tell me that such requests are usually granted.

106. Prior to 1985, the court was obliged to nominate two experts. Now under article 159 of the *Code de procédure pénale*, the judge designates a single expert, but "if the circumstances justify it, he may designate several experts."

107. *Codice di procedure penale*, article 225; P. Corso on Italy, in *La preuve en procédure pénale comparée*, 63 *revue internationale de droit pénal*, pp. 205, 230.

108. Ibid., article 155A; see also Rodrigues on Portugal, in *La preuve en procédure pénale comparée*, pp. 289, 313.

109. Volk, see note 70.

110. Ibid., p. 45.

111. M. F. Terré, see note 4; cf. J. Pradel, *L'instruction préparatoire* (Paris, 1990), para. 468.

112. Crombag et al., see note 45, p. 394.

113. Ibid., especially the chapter on psychiatric evidence.

114. There is a parallel with the favorable attitude of English judges toward experts in child-care cases where the expert is neutral because he or she has been selected by the *guardian ad litem* (see note 48).

115. For example, the U.S. federal jurisdictions, see p. 36.

116. Royal Commission on Criminal Justice report (1993, cm. 2263), p. 160.

117. A committee of the organization JUSTICE, also hostile to the idea, gave an even weaker reason: "The appointment of such an expert would not be regarded with favour by the expert witnesses[!]" (JUSTICE, *Science and the administration of justice*, 1991, para. 7.15).

118. Access to Justice, *Final report to the Lord Chancellor on the civil justice system of England and Wales* (Lord Woolf, July 1996), ch. 13.

3

MORAL JUSTIFICATIONS FOR LIMITS ON EXPERT TESTIMONY

MICHAEL LAVIN AND BRUCE D. SALES

The tradition of courts allowing expert testimony is a venerable one. O'Connor, Sales, and Shuman (1996), citing the work of Learned Hand, noted that as far back as the 17th century, courts have allowed medical doctors to offer testimony on the sanity of a defendant. Even before then, courts had recognized that to help jurists and jurors know the facts beyond the ken of their ordinary experience, it is sometimes necessary to turn to the authority of experts. J. S. Mill (1960) explained the logic of relying on the knowledge of authorities well when he wrote that

> the mass of mankind, including even their rulers in the practical departments of life, must, from the necessity of the case, accept most of their opinions on political and social matters, as they do on physical, from the authority of those who have bestowed more study on those subjects than they generally have it in their power to do. (p. 148)

The lives of average persons afford them neither the time nor the opportunity to become knowledgeable about all matters. This limitation on what persons can reasonably come to know is all the more apparent in courts of law, where jurors may need the assistance of accountants, engineers, physicians, meteorologists, and the like to understand technical aspects of a case and reach a verdict on the matter.

That psychologists can and do serve as expert witnesses is uncontestable. Indeed, the frequency of expert witnessing and its financial significance to the lives of many psychologists partially led the American Psychological Association (APA) to add a section on forensic activities to its 1992 revision of the *Ethical Principles of Psychologists and Code of Conduct* (1992a). It states the following:

7. Forensic Activities

7.01 Professionalism

Psychologists who perform forensic functions, such as assessments, interviews, consultations, reports, or expert testimony, must comply with all other provisions of this Ethics Code to the extent that they apply to such activities. In addition, psychologists base their forensic work on appropriate knowledge of and competence in the areas underlying such work, including specialized knowledge concerning special populations. (See also Standards 1.06, Basis for Scientific and Professional Judgments; 1.08, Human Differences; 1.15, Misuse of Psychologists' Influence; and 1.23, Documentation of Professional and Scientific Work.)

7.02 Forensic Assessments

(a) Psychologists' forensic assessments, recommendations, and reports are based on information and techniques (including personal interviews of the individual, when appropriate) sufficient to provide appropriate substantiation for their findings. (See also Standards 1.03, Professional and Scientific Relationship; 1.23, Documentation of Professional and Scientific Work; 2.01, Evaluation, Diagnosis, and Interventions in Professional Context; and 2.05, Interpreting Assessment Results.) . . .[1]

7.03 Clarification of Role

In most circumstances, psychologists avoid performing multiple and potentially conflicting roles in forensic matters. When psychologists may be called on to serve in more than one role in a legal proceeding—for example, as consultant or expert for one party or for the court and as a fact witness—they clarify role expectations and the extent of confidentiality in advance to the extent feasible, and thereafter as changes occur, in order to avoid compromising their professional judgment and objectivity and in order to avoid misleading others regarding their role.

7.04 Truthfulness and Candor

(a) In forensic testimony and reports, psychologists testify truthfully, honestly, and candidly and, consistent with applicable legal procedures, describe fairly the bases for their testimony and conclusions.

---

[1]Sections b and c have been omitted from this excerpt because they are not relevant to the current discussion.

(b) Whenever necessary to avoid misleading, psychologists acknowledge the limits of their data or conclusions.

7.05 Prior Relationships

A prior professional relationship with a party does not preclude psychologists from testifying as fact witnesses or from testifying to their services to the extent permitted by applicable law. Psychologists appropriately take into account ways in which the prior relationship might affect their professional objectivity or opinions and disclose the potential conflict to the relevant parties.

7.06 Compliance With Law and Rules

In performing forensic roles, psychologists are reasonably familiar with the rules governing their roles. Psychologists are aware of the occasionally competing demands placed upon them by these principles and the requirements of the court system, and attempt to resolve these conflicts by making known their commitment to this Ethics Code and taking steps to resolve the conflict in a responsible manner (see also Standard 1.02, Relationship of Ethics and Law). (p. 14)[2]

Moreover, Section 7 of the code recognizes the importance of forensic activities in the same way that the code recognizes other major areas of psychological work (i.e., evaluation, assessment, or intervention; therapy; teaching, training supervision, research, and publishing), but it places no more stringent requirements on the delivery of expert testimony than on all of the other types of psychological activity (for detailed proof of this point, see Perrin & Sales, 1994). Thus, this may lead many psychologists to believe that they can ethically provide expert testimony almost with impunity.

The law provides no greater threshold or barrier for most expert testimony by psychologists. When it comes to the admissibility of clinical opinion testimony, for instance, the law relies on a broad relevancy approach (see generally Sales, Shuman, & O'Connor, 1994). If the preferred testimony is relevant to a factual issue in question in the litigation, the court will admit the testimony if its probative value is not substantially outweighed by the danger of prejudicing or confusing the jury. No special requirements are placed on the quality of the testimony, only on the qualifications of the person offered as an expert. Thus, if the court finds that the proffered expert has the requisite educational and experiential credentials and his or her opinions are relevant to the issue in question but are not unduly prejudicial, the expert will be admitted to testify. It is then up to the *trier of fact* (the jury if there is one or the judge) to decide on the credibility of the admitted testimony during jury deliberations. Thus, admissibility is no more difficult than offering one's services in the

---

[2]From *Ethical Principles of Psychologists and Code of Conduct* (p. 14) by the American Psychological Association, 1992a, Washington, DC: Author. Copyright 1992 by the American Psychological Association. Reprinted with permission.

community—once licensed to practice, it is permissible to serve as an expert and present testimony.

When the testimony is based on scientific knowledge, depending on the jurisdiction in question, the law relies on the decisions in *Frye v. United States* (1923), *Daubert v. Merrell Dow Pharmaceuticals, Inc.* (1993), or a variant of the standards presented in these cases. The opinion in *Frye* requires general acceptance in the relevant scientific community as a prerequisite to the admissibility of scientific evidence. Interpreting the *Federal Rules of Evidence* Rule 7.02, *Daubert* instructs federal courts to be concerned with the (evidentiary) reliability of the scientific evidence and considers general acceptance within the relevant field of science as only one pragmatic consideration in ascertaining reliability. Other considerations include but are not limited to the following: Is the theory or technique testable, and has it been tested? Has the theory or technique been subjected to peer review and publication? What is the known or potential error rate for the scientific technique, and are there standards controlling the technique's operation? Whatever the approach used by individual jurisdictions, the standard for admissibility is no more stringent than scientists face in their normal activities (e.g., subjecting their work to peer review).

Although there is no current serious doubt about the ethical and legal ability of psychologists to serve as expert witnesses, doubts still remain about what their role as expert witnesses ought to be. To address this issue, we need to distinguish the legal requirements for admissibility and the ethical obligations in the provision of expert testimony from the moral requirements, proscriptions, and permissions. If distinguishing the legal and ethical from the moral seems odd to some readers, an example may make our distinction clear.

It was once legally permissible in the United States to own slaves. During this period, it is imaginable that there could have existed an association of slave owners who promulgated a code of ethics on the treatment of slaves. Perhaps this hypothetical code would have required slave owners to provide adequate housing and food to slaves, prohibited the killing or raping of slaves, but permitted the selling of slave children without an accompanying sale of a parent. Morality's standing on slavery, however, is and was at odds with the 19th-century law in the United States. Slavery is and was morally prohibited. Furthermore, even though it was ethical to sell a child under terms of the hypothetical code, it was morally wrong to do so. No stand needs be taken on the precise nature of the moral principles used to reach our conclusions for the purposes of this chapter. The point is obvious. There are differences between the legal, ethical, and moral bases for behavior. Moreover, these differences play a substantial part in our analysis of what the role of psychologists as expert witnesses ought to be.

To address what ought to be in expert psychological testimony, we first consider the question of who is an expert. What, precisely, is involved in the claim that a psychologist is an expert and has an expertise that is worth sharing in court? Second, we consider whether what the law allows psychologists to do is too lenient to match the constraints that morality places on expert testimony. Our analysis does not depend on any particular understanding of morality. Instead, we use the most prevalent approaches to morality—consequentialist, deontological, and Aristotelian virtue moralities. Third, we reconsider whether APA's ethics code can be interpreted to coincide with our conclusions about the restrictions that morality places on expert testimony by psychologists in the courts. Finally, we briefly explore the practical implications of our analyses. Because of the title and topic of this volume, we use examples from the recovered-memory controversy and controversies in expert testimony regarding allegations of child molestation to illustrate our central point when examples are needed, although our analysis raises issues far beyond the confines of these specific issues.

BEING AN EXPERT

On the one hand, experts come to court because they can offer knowledge that will assist the court in its fact-finding mission. Neither judges nor jurors have the kind of detailed knowledge about such matters as ballistics, DNA assays, meteorology, police methods, medicine, blacksmithing, or psychology. On these topics, as well as many others, jurists and jurors may need the advice and opinion of experts to assist them in determining the facts of a case.

Nonexpert testimony, on the other hand, typically operates under a set of constraints designed to have the witness serve as a surrogate sensory organ for the fact finder. A nonexpert witness may say, for example, that he heard Smith yell at Jones and then saw Jones hit Smith in the face. Likewise, a nonexpert witness might testify that Maurice told him or her of recently remembering being sexually molested as a child. A nonexpert witness may not testify that Maurice, in his or her opinion, has had a true recovered memory of being molested by his father. A judgment such that a person has had a true recovered memory or that a child recounted an actual occurrence of sexual abuse rather than a suggested memory of such an event is beyond the knowledge of nonexpert witnesses. Moreover, without the assistance of an expert, neither ordinary jurists nor jurors will be able to differentiate true recovered memories and false accounts from lies, confabulations, or misremembrances. These are subjects beyond the knowledge of ordinary persons.

Unfortunately, courts are not citadels of science, and no jurist could possibly have the knowledge necessary to distinguish bogus from real expertise across the full range of topics that could come before a court. So courts have had to rely on admissibility rules to determine who is recognizable as an expert, rules that focus on the person's qualifications (e.g., Does the person possess an advanced degree, a state license to practice, publications in learned journals, and the like?). Likewise, a field of knowledge is an area of expertise if it is generally recognized as an area of real knowledge. The idea is to banish junk science, not just phony experts, from the courts. So it is not enough for a person to be recognized as an expert, for example, by his fellow astrologers because astrology is not an area that the courts are prepared to recognize as a source of expert knowledge.

Given that the credentials of psychology are not in question, the issue of expertise within the field is a question of What psychologists qua psychologists can have expert opinions about, keeping in mind that no psychologist has expertise in all areas of psychology.

EXPERT TESTIMONY AND MORAL THEORIES

With the variety of moral theories, the controversies surrounding them, and the absence of any consensus on even which form of moral theory is correct, the value of moral theories might plausibly be thought of as limited in discerning what psychologists should or should not do in regard to expert testimony. However, skepticism about the value of moral theory for discerning moral obligation in relation to testimony is misplaced.

First, even without trying to harmonize what competing moral theories imply about expert testimony, it is possible to do what is sometimes done in public policy by policy analysts. We can ask, What is known? How did it come to be known? and In light of our theoretical and empirical knowledge, how would we evaluate the proposed policies? We are not proposing, however, a policy analysis of expert witness testimony. Rather, we content ourselves with describing what we think major moral theories are likely to imply about experts prepared to testify on the basis of personal knowledge but in the absence of sound science.

Second, moral theories often agree about moral principles, even when they disagree about the rational grounding of those principles. For example, Beauchamp and Childress's (1994) standard biomedical ethics text is written by two philosophers who disagreed on the rationale for the four principles they used to analyze medical ethics cases. Beauchamp is a consequentialist; Childress is a deontologist. All the same, they were able to reach agreement on the formulation of four moral principles—autonomy, beneficence, nonmaleficence, and justice. In *The Belmont Report* (National Commission for the Protection of Human Subjects of Biomedical and Behavioral Research, 1978), ethicists managed to achieve a consensus on the relevant moral principles governing human subjects research, despite their failing to achieve a consensus on the reasons for their principles. So although moral theorists of different camps often disagree on the grounds for their opinions, they may nevertheless concur about particular cases.

With these admonitions in mind, we consider the three types of moral theories that have dominated recent Anglo American moral thought: (a) consequentialism, (b) deontologism, and (c) virtue theories. Like all taxonomies, taxonomies of moral theories do violence to the phenomena. However, the advantage of classifying moral theories is that it facilitates inquiries into what particular kinds of moral theories imply about an area of concern. A good taxonomy enables one to learn what moralists of a category are likely to believe about a topic. A particular consequentialist might hold an opinion at variance with the common run of consequentialist opinion, but it still serves inquiry well to ask what consequentialists think, even if answering the question seldom tells one what all consequentialists think.

Consequentialism

Consequentialism means that the rightness or wrongness of an action depends solely, whether directly or indirectly, on its consequences. Most readers are familiar with one variant of consequentialism, namely, utilitarianism, which in its classical form required persons to do whatever maximized expected total utility. Applied to the question of What should a psychologist's policy be in regard to expert testimony? consequentialism favors a psychologist's refusing to testify as an expert, except when he or she has scientific expertise to contribute. If either he or she does not know the relevant science or there is no relevant science, he or she should not testify, even if such a testimony is admissible under current law as opinion testimony.

The argument for this position is straightforward on consequentialist grounds. For example, a mistaken verdict is a bad outcome on consequentialist grounds. *Ceteris paribus*, then, is something that consequentialists will seek to avoid. The purpose of expert testimony is to enable the fact finders to improve their decision making by having available the expert information that the fact finders would otherwise lack, making it less likely that they will reach a mistaken verdict. Although if they rely on the opinion of somebody who is not an expert, especially when there is somebody available who is an expert, they reduce the likelihood of reaching a correct verdict. Testifying in that instance increases the likelihood of a bad outcome, which is something a consequentialist should not do.

Furthermore, if a psychologist offers an expert opinion when there is no science to back it up, he or she is again failing to meet his or her consequentialist duty of working to secure the best expected outcome. Psychologists are in court by virtue of having relevant expertise. An expert without expertise reduces the likelihood of reaching a good outcome and thus should not testify. Pure opinion testimony without scientific proof is not an expertise, in the sense that it will help the trier of fact reach a better verdict. It may make the trier more confident in his or her decision, but it does not increase the accuracy of that decision.

This argument for the moral impermissibility of psychologists testifying as experts when they lack supporting science may seem to involve a confusion over truth in science and truth in the courts. In law, truth is sought through the adversarial process. Lawyers for each side attempt to make their case and to undermine that of the opposition. Psychologists, however, do not rely on an overtly adversarial procedure. Instead, the establishment of truth is guided by the scientific method. Psychologists rely on procedures designed to minimize the possibility that false hypotheses may be accepted. The requirements of the scrupulous collection of evidence, of elimination of alternative hypotheses, of controlled often double-blind experiments, of peer review, and of replicability are scientific devices for finding out the truth.

Moreover, although the jury is left to its own devices to determine what should be the significance of the evidence for the questions before it, science often has specific conventions about how good the evidence for a hypothesis must be to be embraced as true. For example, psychology journals routinely require a significance level of .05 to reject the null hypothesis. This means that the scientists' data would only occur if the null hypothesis were true, 1 out of 20 times. Juries, by contrast, lack explicit mathematical criteria for accepting or rejecting hypotheses or reaching a verdict.

Given the differences between the methods of seeking truth in law and science, it may seem morally appropriate to let the courts decide whether to omit the opinion testimony of psychologists because courts have their own methods of assuring the quality of testimony. Respecting these methods is the course most likely to produce the good outcomes that consequentialists care about. In addition, the scientific convention of insisting that scientific claims pass an exacting evidentiary standard to count as science has the potential to rob fact finders of valuable information if psychologists refuse to offer opinion testimony that falls below the standard of science. Judges and juries are willing in many circumstances to settle for a lower evidentiary standard than the scientist is (e.g., *Barefoot v. Estelle*, 1983).

There is no denying that much of this objection has substance. Nevertheless, psychologists are being called to court as experts in the science of human behavior. One of the reasons for the marvelous progress of science is that scientists have insisted on an exacting evidentiary standard. This standard distinguishes a science journal from shoddy journalism. If one asks What habits of mind best serve a scientist? it is a scrupulous adherence to scientific standards when he or she is in the role of scientist. When he or she jettisons those standards, he or she has ceased to be a scientist and has ceased to be a bona fide expert.

For instance, the preparedness of a psychologist to offer testimony on whether an uncorroborated true recovered memory or unsubstantiated allegation of molestation obtained in a clinical hour is veridical is a matter that can be appraised by other scientists by generally accepted standards. However, there is no generally accepted standard for the presentation of opinion testimony that falls short of accepted scientific standards, whether the opinion reflects expertise or not. Without reliance on a set of standards to guide one's evaluation, there is no grounds for thinking that a jury can reach a reasonable conclusion about whether the expert's conjecture is a reasonable one or even a probable one. The result is that the trier of fact must rely on irrelevant criteria, such as communicator characteristics (see, e.g., Wursten & Sales, 1992).

Absent an argument that a fact finder is actually, rather than imaginarily, assisted by the reliance on a psychologist's offering opinions that are not part of psychological science, a consequentialist moral theory supports the conclusion that the best outcome is served by psychologists limiting their testimony to what is substantiated by the known science. When we factor in the absence of a public, scientific standard for appropriate expert opinion testimony with the inevitable battle of experts' opinions on matters outside the scope of science, considerations of cost favor the conclusion that for consequentialists, opinion testimony not derived from science is morally inappropriate.

Deontology

Deontologists believe that the rightness or wrongness of an act is not solely a function of its consequences. In its classical formulations, such as Kant's (1785/1964), the stress is on respecting persons, on never treating them solely as a means to achieve an end. If there is something deontologically objectionable to a psychologist's testifying beyond his or her expertise, then moral wrongness does not depend solely on the possible bad consequences that may occur because of the testimony.

A powerful deontological objection to a psychologist's testimony that is not rooted in science derives from deontological requirements relating to veracity. For deontologists, failures of veracity involve using other persons. Consider Lothario (from *The Fair Penitent* by Nicholas Rowe) who lied to obtain sexual access to a woman. Her willingness to have sex with him depended on his lying representation of himself. If the woman had known the truth, she might have made a different choice. Lying manipulates people. Deontologically, it is irrelevant that a lie might have the best consequences. The root wrong of lying is that it prevents persons from acting autonomously, thereby failing to respect them as ends in themselves.

When psychologists testify as expert witnesses, they are assuming the mantle of truth. Their duty of veracity requires that they not give testimony that is likely to create false beliefs about what truths psychology has to impart about the issue at hand. Given that there is at present no known way of enabling laymen to distinguish portions of testimony that are accurate from those that are not, veracity requires psychologists' testimony to reflect that fact. When psychologists offer opinion testimony that is not rooted in science, they are representing opinion as fact when it has failed to meet the scientific standards for ascertaining knowledge. Such opinions may come from an alleged expert but are not someone's expertise. Even if future science vindicated such testimony, the need for vindication shows that the testimony was not at the level required for scientific expertise.

Some readers may object to this argument, asserting that expertise in law is not the same as expertise in science. In law, as already noted, courts look to a putative expert's qualifications, as given by education, licenses, credentials, and the like, to determine whether the person qualifies as an expert. The court is also likely to be concerned over an expert's knowledge of an issue, as might be evidenced by the expert's having been exposed to the phenomena in question, having written about it, or recognition by other experts. Unfortunately, however, this inquiry often becomes one of form rather than substance where opinion testimony is concerned. The focus is usually on credentials and perhaps recognition by peers; the expert's expertise is not judged by standards of science (i.e., its accuracy) but by indirect indexes of expertise and standards of rhetoric (i.e., its persuasiveness).

Within the scientific community, experts achieve recognition by other means. Possession of an advanced degree is at most a tracker or concomitant of expertise; it is not proof of expertise. The expert in a field of psychology is somebody whose knowledge of a topic has been demonstrated. That Francis Crick (e.g., 1995) has no degree in neuropsychology is beside the point for scientists. Instead, his publications in peer-reviewed journals mark him as an expert in the field. Moreover, scientists look to an expert's ability to bring a breadth of understanding to his or her topic and, just as important, the quality of his or her work, as evidenced, for example, by publications in the "best" journals or by membership in prestigious bodies, such as the National Academy of Science, to determine who are the best experts. An esteemed scientist's unpersuasiveness on a witness stand would not undermine his or her credibility in the scientific community, even if it devastated his or her reputation in the legal community. Conversely, overwhelming persuasiveness as an expert witness does not a *nobel laureate* make.

Thus, the argument that the level of expertise required in law is lower than in science is both true and irrelevant. It states only what is legally permissible, not what is morally appropriate, on the part of the psychologist who has been asked to provide expert testimony. Incongruity between the legal and moral determinations of experts does not absolve psychologists of their moral responsibilities. The law's seeming divorce of being an expert from having expertise, at least in the case of opinion testimony, does not morally entitle psychologists to serve as experts when they know or should know that they lack the relevant expertise. In addition, the importance of persuasiveness in a good witness may make some true psychologists–experts ill suited to serve as expert witnesses; conversely, it does not morally entitle nonexperts to testify in ways likely to create false belief in others or beyond their actual competence. Even if the most distinguished looking psychologist could testify in a manner that would persuade the average juror, it would be wrong for him or her to do so until such time as there are scientifically reliable methods for identifying the scientific basis for his or her conclusions. From the deontological perspective, the distinction between legal and scientific experts and expertise either imposes an additional duty on the proffered expert to be scientifically accurate or suggests a need for legal reform.

Virtue Ethics

Virtue ethics, rooted in the writings of Aristotle, had a renaissance with the publication of MacIntrye's (1984) *After Virtue*, although virtue ethics is less amenable to formalization than either consequentialist or deontological ethics. Central to the virtue ethics approach is a tendency to shun questions concerning whether actions are right or wrong, good or bad. Rather, virtue ethics seeks to offer "thick" descriptions of actions and agents (Geach, 1977; Pincoffs, 1986). An action might be cowardly or heroic, sneaky or straightforward. In terms of characterizing agents, virtue ethics encounter difficulty in specifying a list of morally desirable properties, even though courage, temperance, conscientiousness, and honesty are almost always conceded to count as virtues while cowardliness, gluttony, laxity, and mendacity are universally counted as vices.

For psychologists who are potential expert witnesses, their role as psychologists places constraints on virtuous behavior. Certainly, a preparedness to offer testimony as a psychologist who fails to offer accurate facts falls short of the conscientious behavior that is expected by virtue ethics.

Judicious, conscientious psychologists do not allow their opinions to be offered as a substitute for genuine expertise. Such opinions may be perfectly appropriate in therapeutic contexts but should not be offered as facts to influence the jury or the judge. Indeed, the scientific underpinnings of training in psychology should teach one to restrain from one's natural credulity. The role constraints of expert witnessing, with its associated virtues and vices, impose a moral obligation not to offer opinions in place of knowledge. Because psychologists come to court as a result of their presumed scientific knowledge, conscientious psychologists limit their testimony accordingly. For further discussion of the institutional reasons why expert witnessing is not likely to reflect virtuous behavior, see Sales and Simon (1993).

PRINCIPLES AND MORAL THEORIES

As already explained, differences over the grounds for holding moral principles do not prevent there being a consensus on them. The principles of autonomy, beneficence, nonmaleficence, and justice—as accepted by Beauchamp and Childress (1994) and the similar principles set forth in *The Belmont Report* (National Commission for the Protection of Human Subjects, 1978), which also include a principle of fidelity to science—are principles that most people are prepared to recognize, even if they disagree about why these are moral principles worthy of assent.

Such widely recognized moral principles, like the moral theories discussed above, imply that psychologists should limit their expert testimony to opinions supported by psychological science. This does not mean that a psychologist may never state that he or she disagrees with a widely accepted finding, but it does mean that it is immoral to testify, as was done by the two psychiatrists in *Barefoot v. Estelle* (1983), that one knows that a person is going to be dangerous in the future when the scientific literature disagrees with that assessment. At most, the psychiatrists expressing these opinions could have explained why they disagreed with the substantial evidence that supports the conclusion that it is extremely difficult to predict whether a person will perform violent acts in the future and that the majority of predictions of violent acts will be false. In testifying that they could make such predictions, we believe that these psychiatrists failed to observe the principle of nonmaleficence. By ignoring the relevant scientific knowledge, they also appeared to ignore the principle of fidelity to one's profession (and the scientific knowledge base underlying that profession).

The idea that psychologists can give expert testimony on true recovered memories also violates two moral principles. First, testifying that they can identify true recovered memories, absent corroborative evidence of the occurrence of the allegedly remembered events, violates the principle of fidelity to the science. Second, in violating their duty to respect the principle of fidelity to science, the psychologists would also be violating their duty of nonmaleficence because they place the accused in danger of needless harm.

The case for holding that expert testimony that a memory is a true recovered memory of a past event is a violation of the principle of fidelity to the science is straightforward. To date, there is no scientific consensus on the ability of psychologists to use science to distinguish a true recovered memory from a false one. In fact, given what is known about memory, there is every reason to be skeptical of memories elicited in psychotherapy. There is unanimity that memory is not a picture of past events. Instead, memories are constructions of past events. Furthermore, the claim that one can distinguish true recovered memories from false ones is premised on a confused epistemology.

When anybody reports a memory, there is the possibility of error. For clinical psychologists, the conceptual riddle is how to distinguish somebody's seeming to remember an episode from the actually remembering of an episode. All people confront this problem from time to time. You have a "memory" of placing your keys on the TV and not having moved them. When you go to retrieve them, they are not there. You can no longer accurately say that you actually remember placing the keys on the TV and not moving them, but you can still say that you seem to remember doing so.

The phenomenology of actual memories is no different from the phenomenology of seeming to remember memories. In both cases, you can represent the memory to yourself in the same way. Whether you actually remember does not depend on how you represent matters to yourself but on how the representation "fits" what actually happened. Nor does it matter how vividly you remember placing your keys on the TV. You can have, and probably have had, vivid memories of where you laid your keys that proved to be wrong.

When a male client tells his female psychologist during psychotherapy that he remembers being molested as a boy, with or without prodding from the psychologist, she has no way of knowing, from his memory report, whether he is having a true recovered memory or a false one. She may believe that he is remembering falsely, even though she may have every reason to believe he sincerely believes that the episode occurred, or she may believe that he is having a true recovered memory. Whatever she believes, however, has nothing to do with whether he is in fact having a false or true recovered memory. It is unfortunate that clients are not transparent. Clients do not "glow true blue" when having true recovered memories and do not blush at either their intentional or inadvertent duplicities. The belief that it is possible to tell whether a client is having a false or true recovered memory is epistemically no better than the belief that you can tell whether you left your keys on the TV by simply inspecting your memory representation. It rests on a remnant of Cartesianism, namely, that accurate representations carry an "internal" marking, such as being clear and distinct, that distinguishes them from inaccurate representations.

In addition, it is at odds with what is generally conceded. When one seeks to establish, in difficult cases, whether somebody is telling the truth, one turns to such deficient devices as the polygraph because one has reason to believe that these devices are, despite their inadequacies, still superior to a clinician's just listening to the client's report. The matter is even more difficult in the case of assessing whether a client is having a true recovered memory or a false one because the client is likely—as you are with your keys—to believe that his or her memory is accurate; it is probably easier to find the refutation of the memory in the case of the lost keys than of past molestations.

In response to this argument regarding conceptual limitations on the ability of psychologists to distinguish false recovered memories from true recovered memories, some clinicians may be tempted to insist that there is an important disanalogy. The patients with true recovered memories, it may be urged, suffer from disorders, such as dissociative disorders, or symptoms caused by abuse (Bass & Davis, 1988; Briere, 1992; Terr, 1994). So when a client does have a memory of abuse, this behavior is what would be expected, given the disorder or symptoms the client has. The etiology of symptoms and disorders provides corroboration of the memory, making it reasonable to count it as a true recovered memory rather than a false recovered memory.

This reply has at least two problems. First, even if it is true that abuse causes dissociative disorders, it does not follow that the abuse the client is reporting he or she remembers actually occurred. It might be that some other episode of abuse or elements of past abuse, such as who was the perpetrator, are falsely remembered, whereas other elements of the reported memory are true. Consider the case of one of us. He has broken his nose on several occasions. In fact, he has a memory of a boy named "Roy" throwing a ball that broke his nose, but he was told by other witnesses that it was a boy named "Greg." Who actually did what is not settled by simply referring to the memory report. Nothing in memory research makes this implausible. In fact, what we know about memory makes it likely that various elements are not correctly represented or reported. Second, and more important, the etiology of disorders connected with recovered memories is a hypothesis without adequate scientific support. On this topic, Dawes (1994) argued powerfully against the view that false and true recovered memories are reliably detectable or are known to be crucial in the etiology of psychopathology. Given that, testimony by clinicians that say they can distinguish false from true recovered memories appears to go well beyond science. Thus, the critic's reply lacks merit.

We wish to stress that we do not claim that clients never have true recovered memories; they do. Kaszniak, Nussbaum, Berren, and Santiago (1988) described a recovered memory of a same-sex rape. However, Kaszniak et al. did not scrutinize reports of their client to determine that he was having a recovered memory. Instead, they obtained corroboration of the rape's occurrence. Thus, we maintain that circa 1996, there is no known way of distinguishing false from true recovered memories, and scientific testimony should be consistent with that fact.

The arguments just offered in connection with recovered memories apply, as philosophers say, mutatis mutandi and *salva veritate* (without changing the form of the argument) to allegations by children of having been abused or sexually molested. Again, the issue of a fit between allegation and the world is crucial. It verges on a tautology that the most credible allegations of child molestation will be accompanied by corroborating evidence. But the best evidence will be external to what takes place between accusing children and their therapists. Within the limits of a therapy session, a therapist can at best establish such claims as that the child has told a consistent story, elements of the story are beyond the experience of most children, and the child resembles, psychologically, other children who are known to have been abused. At present, it is not possible to establish that an accusation, however sincerely believed, is veridical simply by recourse to "truth-finding" procedures in an assessment session. For example, anatomically detailed dolls are popular with some clinicians far beyond their ability to segregate molested from unmolested children. Wolfner, Faust, and Dawes (1993) and Realmuto, Jensen, and Wescoe (1990) noted the shocking inadequacy of these dolls for identifying genuine molestations (for a good coverage of this work, see Dawes, 1994). To make a long story short, these techniques are remarkable for their inability to detect sexual abuse, even though that has not deterred many clinicians from relying on them. The failure of clinicians to be able to distinguish allegations of abuse from the fact of abuse by only relying on materials obtainable in a session should come as no surprise. In the current state of psychological science, we do not know enough about the sequelae of molestation, the possibilities of mistakenly suggesting abuse however inadvertently, or the base rates of abuse in children who allege it to testify that we, as scientists, know, independently of extrasession evidence, whether a particular child complainant has been molested. We are aware that this may mean that absent corroboration, "monsters" may go free, but that is not justification for doing what we cannot and should not do. Rather it is an argument for more and better police work.

Sadly, we know of no empirically validated clinical indicators for distinguishing veridical from fabricated molestation stories. There have been horrendous, life-destroying fictions. Terr (1994) documented a case in which a child had lyingly accused her therapists of having sexually abused her, evidently as a result of her mother's and subsequent therapists' suggestions. Terr's vindication of the accused did not, we hasten to add, result from relying on evidence internal to her assessment session with the child. Instead, she discovered, for example, that a child's recollection of having been abused with a white vibrator could be accounted for on the basis of the child's mother's own admission of having caught the child masturbating with the mother's vibrator. Psychologists must remember that even in child-molestation cases, the purpose of a trial is not to ensure that the state prevails but to ensure that nobody is convicted without the state making its case beyond a reasonable doubt.

Finally, we wish to stress that we do not claim that either memory or allegations of molestations are normally mistaken. For perfectly good evolutionary reasons, most memories recollected in ordinary circumstances without suggestive prompting are going to be correct. Rather, our skepticism is vigorous when a memory of abuse or allegation of molestation emerges seemingly *ex nihilo* during the course of therapy or assessment. We hope that more research will be undertaken to help establish base rates for the accuracy of recovered memories and allegations of molestation for a wide range of circumstances and of methods that do not suggest abuse to clients. We note that it would be remarkable if memories or allegations that first emerged in therapy were veridical as often as memories or allegations that had existed prior to psychic excavations of a therapist—believer in such memories.

IS APA'S ETHICS CODE CONSISTENT WITH MORAL TEACHINGS?

So far, our analysis suggests that psychologists should restrict their expert testimony to scientific facts. Several moral theories and widely embraced moral principles support restricting a psychologist's testimony to what the science supports at the time of the testimony. Testifying as an expert is not the time to air novel scientific hypotheses or to present one's unproven, and in some cases unprovable, beliefs or clinical conjectures. Enforceable duties on psychologists to so restrict their testimony are not now generally recognized. This state of affairs arises because there is no necessary coincidence, as we have earlier observed, among the requirements, permissions, and proscriptions of morality, ethics, and law. Despite this conclusion, it is arguable that ethics also require a limit on the expert testimony of psychologists that have not been generally recognized heretofore.

For the majority of psychologists in this country, the regulative ethics code is APA's (1992b). All licensed members of APA have a membership derived and legally derived (through both state licensure and tort law) obligation to perform their professional duties in conformance with at least the ethics code's standards.

It is important to realize that the APA ethics code has two ethically relevant parts that impose different kinds of duties on APA-member psychologists. The ethics code has a preamble and six general principles listed as Principles A to F: (A) competence, (B) integrity, (C) professional and scientific responsibility, (D) respect for people's rights and dignity, (E) concern for others' welfare, and (F) social responsibility. The preamble and these six principles are aspirational, namely, that a psychologist's failing to observe them can generate no disciplinary sanctions by APA. However, even though violation of these principles does not sustain disciplinary actions, the principles serve to guide the interpretation of APA's ethical code that is binding for APA members. Failure to observe these standards can result in disciplinary action by APA and, as just noted, can form the factual basis for a legal complaint against the psychologist.

APA's ethics code has eight groups of ethical standards that receive further adumbration: (1) general standards; (2) evaluation, assessment, and interventions; (3) advertising and other public statements; (4) therapy; (5) privacy and confidentiality; (6) teaching, training supervision, research, and publishing; (7) forensic activities; and (8) resolving ethical issues. These groups include 102 standards that spell out, with differing levels of clarity and precision, what a psychologist's compliance with the standards requires.

Although professional codes of ethics, including the APA ethics code, have many conceptual and moral inadequacies (which we do not address in this chapter), such codes serve several highly useful functions. First, they clarify that there is a professional consensus of the ethical standards a professional group's members are required to meet. Second, codes provide public notice of a profession's current ethical standards. Third, codes make it more likely that a profession's members, in determining what their obligations are relative to a particular set of facts, will agree on a range of acceptable and unacceptable behaviors. Finally, codes, by virtue of their being written, make it easier for members to identify deficiencies in the code's formulation.

Given the value of such codes—and the fact that the APA ethics code permits expert testimony, as already noted in the introduction to this chapter—the question becomes whether the code provides clear ethical limits on such testimony that might coincide with our conclusions about the moral limits on such professional work. We conclude that the answer to this question is *yes*.

Simply because the law permits a particular kind of testimony does not mean that psychologists are ethically (morally) right to give it. Thoughtful commentators, such as Grisso (1986), illustrated our point with their position that even though the law might permit psychologists to give an opinion on "ultimate questions," such as whether a defendant was insane or acting under an irresistible impulse, they ought not to do so. The easiest way to understand this claim that psychologists should not offer opinions on ultimate questions in law is to understand it as an insistence that psychologists confine themselves to giving opinion on matters that psychologists are experts on. Ultimate questions in law are not part of the psychological science, even though knowledge of the science may be wondrously clarifying to fact finders in a trial. For example, psychologists can assist the court in understanding the cognitive, affective, and behavioral consequences of having bipolar disorder, but there is no psychological diagnosis of legal insanity. Furthermore, psychologists can share their scientific knowledge of human behavior and psychopathology to assist fact finders in answering for themselves whether a defendant is legally insane.

Because there is no legal requirement that a psychologist must testify that a reported memory is accurate, there is no identifiable conflict between the position we have argued for and the requirements placed on expert witnesses. Even if there were such a conflict, members of APA have an ethical obligation to resolve it in favor of the ethics code. Section 1.02 of the ethics code reads that "if psychologists' ethical responsibilities conflict with law, psychologists make known their commitment to the Ethics Code and take steps to resolve the conflict in a responsible manner" (APA, 1992b, p. 1600). This obligation is reiterated in section 7.06. Furthermore, section 7.01 amplifies this obligation in connection with forensic testimony: "Psychologists who perform forensic functions, such as assessment, interviews, consultations, reports, or expert testimony, must comply with all other provisions of this Ethics Code to the extent that they apply to such activities" (p. 1610).

Our previously stated argument against the possibility of reliably distinguishing true from false recovered memories entails that until special assessment techniques are available, if ever, for identifying veridical memories, no weight should be given to clinical claims that a clinician can "just tell" when a client is or is not being truthful. We also note that the APA Working Group on Investigation of Memories of Childhood Abuse (in press) yielded no consensus on the topic. If anything, the scientific opinion aligned itself against the phenomena. From our perspective, the failure of the task force to reach a consensus supports our point. There is no reason to expect that any expert is an expert at identifying true recovered memories. Our skepticism is also bolstered by the work of Loftus and Ketcham (1994). The onus probandi is on clinicians and scientists who believe in true recovered memories and believe that these memories cause mental disorders to make the case for their hypotheses. Their belief, however sincere, is not sufficient to warrant testifying that a client, for example, has a dissociative identity disorder because of having been abused or that the abuse is known to have occurred because the client has the "right" kind of disorder and has had true recovered memories of the abuse and the molestations that caused it. From the point of view of expert testimony, it would not even matter if a therapist turned out to be unusually good at identifying memories that were subsequently corroborated. Until this clinical "seer" has had his or her method explained and scientifically tested, it is not a part of psychological science; hence, it is morally inappropriate to convey it in court testimony as an expert.

But is there an ethical basis for prohibiting such testimony? Once again, we conclude that the answer is *yes*. Principle A, an aspirational principle requiring competence, places a *prima facie* limitation on opinion testimony by psychologists. Among the obligations imposed by Principle A is a duty to "recognize the boundaries of their particular competencies and the limitations of their expertise" (APA, 1992b, p. 1599). Furthermore, psychologists "provide only those services and use only those techniques for which they are qualified by education, training, or experience" (p. 1599). Given what is known at present, it is appropriate to testify, for example, that there are many reasons to be skeptical about memory reports of long "forgotten" events. Testimony regarding the nature and limitations of memory, including scientifically validated testimony relating to the conditions necessary for accurate memories as well to what is known and not known about the etiology of various psychological problems and disorder, is permissible and well within the competence of many psychologists. However, currently, it does not appear possible for a psychologist to be an expert in spotting true or false recovered memories, knowing that a molestation caused a client to exhibit multiple personalities or specific symptoms, or knowing whether an allegation of molestation by a child is veridical or fantasy. It may be that in the future psychological research will vindicate those who believe these hypotheses, but it is not the case today that a psychologist could give competent expert testimony that a person had a veridical, uncorroborated memory of an etiologically potent episode of abuse. That being the case, it is a violation of Principle A to give such testimony.

Because Principle A is an aspirational principle, rather than an ethical standard, its violation is not grounds for holding that a psychologist has acted unethically. However, the standards themselves place limits on what kind of testimony a psychologist should offer. In particular, section 1.06 of the ethics code reads that "psychologists rely on scientifically and professionally derived knowledge when making scientific or professional judgments or when engaging in scholarly or professional endeavors" (APA, 1992b, p. 1600). Given what is known about putatively true recovered memories and the etiology of mental disorders, section 1.06 could be interpreted to place severe limitations on what psychologists can ethically testify to. To illustrate our contention, consider the clinician offering the testimony that a child was accurately reporting an account of sexual molestation. To be ethical, the clinician's testimony would have to take into account the research on the suggestibility of child witnesses, and the clinician would have to make known the limitations that the research places on her or his confidence in the testimony. In other words, professional opinion can never substitute for scientific fact or lack thereof.

This requirement on scientifically based testimony is further strengthened in the forensic assessment section of the ethics code. Section 7.04(b) states that "whenever necessary to avoid misleading, psychologists acknowledge the limits of their data or conclusions" (APA, 1992b, p. 1610). So even though it is ethically acceptable for a psychologist to testify that some psychologists believe that true recovered memories are to be expected in the treatment of certain mental disorders and that these recovered memories are of events that actually happened and were important in causing these disorders, his or her ethical testimony must include appropriate caveats.

Furthermore, because psychologists offering such testimony are testifying as psychologists, we believe that section 1.06 makes it inappropriate for them to offer their opinion that those hypotheses are correct. We also note that section 1.06 requires that forensic testimony, a "professional endeavor," be rooted not just in a psychologist's "professionally derived knowledge" but in his or her "*scientifically* and professionally derived knowledge" (italics added; APA, 1992b, p. 1600). Hence, it is a violation of 1.06 for psychologists to justify their professional opinion solely on the basis of their professionally derived knowledge from working with, to use one example, clients with multiple personalities who report true or false recovered memories.

CONCLUSION: THE PRACTICAL IMPLICATIONS

Our analysis may be troubling to many clinicians. Indeed, as ardent supporters of clinical psychology and professional practice, we share their concerns. Yet, when we considered three species of moral theory, widely accepted moral principles, and the APA ethics code, we concluded that they all lead to the same conclusion regarding expert testimony by psychologists. Psychologists in the role of expert witnesses should restrict their testimony, despite the admissibility rules for experts, to what the psychological science warrants at the time of the testimony. A court of law is no place for psychologists to retail novel hypotheses or regale fact finders with their personal opinions. The recovered memory controversy and controversies involving molestation allegations have served as two illustrative cases, but our point is general. Psychologists have moral and ethical responsibilities to be circumspect in their testimony.

The courts, however, are not likely to bar opinion testimony. To exclude it could create precedent for excluding all other expert opinion testimony, including that of automobile mechanics and every other expert who cannot invoke the mantle of science or benefit from scientific findings (for a detailed discussion of this issue, see Shuman & Sales, in press).

So what purpose should our observations in this chapter serve? At a minimum, psychologists should seriously reconsider what they have to offer the court before testifying. When scientific research is available, they should offer that research in place of conjecture and opinion. When research is not available to address the question, they should present their testimony hemmed with disclaimers alerting the jury that it is not scientifically based and as yet unproven or unprovable. In fact, given *Daubert*, if a claim is indeed unprovable, there is a case to be made that it is not admissible as scientific testimony. Clearly, attorneys will try to elicit only that testimony that best supports their client's position. Yet, that does not preclude a psychologist's full disclosure of the limits of that testimony if asked on cross-examination. Moreover, psychologists should educate attorneys and triers of fact about their true expertise and limits of psychological knowledge. Such actions would not only fulfill one's moral duties but also improve the quality of expert testimony and the decision making in courts of law. Last, we hope that this chapter stimulates thoughtful discussion and debate about the issues raised herein. For even if others disagree with our analyses or conclusions, the issues we raised about the relationship of morals, ethics, and law, in relation to both expert witnessing and more generally in psychology, have not received the substantial or serious attention that they warrant.

REFERENCES

American Psychological Association. (1992a). *Ethical principles of psychologists and code of conduct.* Washington, DC: Author.

American Psychological Association. (1992b). Ethical principles of psychologists and code of conduct. *American Psychologist, 47,* 1597–1611.

American Psychological Association Working Group on Investigation of Memories of Childhood Abuse. (in press). Final report of the Working Group on Investigation of Memories of Childhood Abuse. *Psychology, Public Policy, and Law.*

Barefoot v. Estelle, 463 U.S. 880 (1983).

Bass, E., & Davis, L. (1988). *Courage to heal.* New York: Harper & Row.

Beauchamp, T. L., & Childress, J. F. (1994). *Principles of biomedical ethics* (4th ed.). New York: Oxford.

Briere, J. (1992). *Child abuse trauma.* Newbury Park, CA: Sage.

Crick, F. (1995). *The astonishing hypothesis: The scientific search for the soul.* New York: Touchstone Books.

Daubert v. Merrell Dow Pharmaceuticals, Inc., 509 U.S., 113 S. Ct. 2786 (1993).

Dawes, R. M. (1994). *House of cards: Psychology and psychotherapy built on myth.* New York: Free Press.

Federal rules of evidence. 28 U.S.C. (Foundation Press 1974).

Frye v. United States, 293 F.1013 (D.C. Cir. 1923).

Geach, P. (1977). *The virtues.* Cambridge, England: Cambridge University Press.

Grisso, T. (1986). *Evaluating competencies: Forensic assessments and instruments.* New York: Plenum.

Kant, I. (1964). *Groundwork of the metaphysics of morals* (H. J. Paton, Trans.). New York: HarperCollins (Original work published 1785)

Kaszniak, A. W., Nussbaum, P. D., Berren, M. R., & Santiago, J. (1988). Amnesia as a consequence of male rape: A case report. *Journal of Abnormal Psychology, 97,* 100–104.

Loftus, E., & Ketcham, K. (1994). *The myth of repressed memories.* New York: St. Martin's Press.

MacIntyre, A. (1984). *After virtue* (2nd ed.). Notre Dame, IN: University of Notre Dame Press.

Mill, J. S. (1960). *Autobiography of John Stuart Mill.* New York: Columbia University Press.

National Commission for the Protection of Human Subjects of Biomedical and Behavioral Research. (1978). *The Belmont report: Ethical guidelines for the protection of human subjects* (DHEW Publication No. OS 78-0012). Washington, DC: U.S. Government Printing Office.

O'Connor, M., Sales, B. D., & Shuman, D. W. (1996). Mental health professional expertise in the courtroom. In B. D. Sales & D. W. Shuman (Eds.), *Law, mental health, and mental disorder* (pp. 40–60). Pacific Grove, CA: Brooks/Cole.

Perrin, G. I., & Sales, B. D. (1994). Forensic standards in the American Psychological Association's new ethics code [Special section]. *Professional Psychology: Research and Practice, 25,* 376–381.

Pincoffs, E. L. (1986). *Quandaries and virtues: Against reductivism in ethics.* Lawrence: University of Kansas Press.

Realmuto, G. M., Jensen, J. B., & Wescoe, S. (1990). Specificity and sensitivity of sexually anatomically correct dolls in substantiating abuse: A pilot study. *Journal of the American Academy of Child and Adolescent Psychiatry, 29,* 743–746.

Sales, B. D., Shuman, D. W., & O'Connor, M. (1994). In a dim light: Admissibility of child sexual abuse memories in court. *Applied Cognitive Psychology, 8,* 399–406.

Sales, B. D., & Simon, L. (1993). Institutional constraints on the ethics of expert testimony. *Ethics and Behavior, 3,* 231–249.

Shuman, D. W., & Sales, B. D. (in press). The admissibility of expert testimony based on clinical judgment and scientific research. *Psychology, Public Policy, and Law.*

Terr, L. (1994). *Unchained memories: True stories of traumatic memories lost and found.* New York: Basic Books.

Wolfner, G., Faust, D., & Dawes, R. M. (1993). The use of anatomically detailed dolls in sexual abuse evaluations: The state of the science. *Applied and Preventive Psychology, 2,* 1–11.

Wursten, A., & Sales, B. (1992). Utilization of psychologists and psychological research in legislative decision making on public interest matters. In D. K. Kagehiro & W. S. Laufer (Eds.), *Handbook of psychology and law* (pp. 119–138). New York: Springer-Verlag.

II

THE ROLE OF EXPERT WITNESS

4

THE TRIALS AND TRIBULATIONS OF A NOVICE EXPERT WITNESS

MAGGIE BRUCK

In this chapter, I present my retrospective memories (aided by transcripts of my courtroom testimony) of my first two experiences as an expert witness in criminal trials. Both cases involve allegations of sexual abuse made by young children against their day-care workers and other adults. In both cases, I appeared as an unpaid expert for the defense.[1] I have written this chapter to warn the novice about the pitfalls of performing this service—ones that I had never been warned about or imagined.

LITTLE RASCALS CASE: *STATE V. ROBERT KELLY*

Bob and Betsy Kelly owned and operated the Little Rascals Day Care Center in Edenton, North Carolina. Betsy was primarily responsible for the day-to-day running of the Little Rascals, whereas Bob, a licensed plumbing contractor and golf pro, helped out as needed. Set in an idyllic hamlet in northeastern North Carolina, by all appearances Little Rascals was the

---

[1] In the second case, a small amount of money was donated to a research account at McGill University to be used for my work on child witnesses.

premier nursery school for middle-class and upper-middle-class parents to send their preschoolers. All of this changed in the winter of 1989.

In January 1989, a parent of one of the children enrolled at Little Rascals alleged that Bob Kelly had sexually abused her son at the day-care center. This allegation was investigated by Brenda Toppin, an officer with the Edenton Police Department and by the county's Department of Social Services. On the basis of their interviews with several children enrolled at Little Rascals, the department concluded that the allegation was valid.

In February 1989, three additional children made allegations. Soon a wave of panic gripped this small town, as parents became more uneasy about whether their own children had also been abused. The local police advised parents to have their children evaluated for abuse, and the police supplied parents with a list of recommended therapists.

Although few children made disclosures when questioned by their parents and police officers about suspected abuse, eventually these children would make allegations after many therapy sessions. Some of these children took up to 10 months of therapeutic intervention before they began to make allegations.

Eventually, 90 children would make allegations involving physical and sexual abuse, and 85% of the children were evaluated and treated by three therapists. Most of the alleged events were claimed to have occurred between September 1988 and December 1988—3–6 months earlier. Although the initial allegations had involved only Bob Kelly, soon they expanded to include dozens of people in the town. Eventually, seven adults were arrested and charged with sexual abuse. These included Betsy Kelly, Dawn Wilson, Robin Byrum, Shelly Stone—all young women who worked at the day-care center—and Scott Privott, the son of a judge, the president of the country club, and the owner of the local video store. (Privott claimed to have never set foot in the Little Rascals Day Care Center.) Darlene Harris, another of the accused, worked at a Head Start center, which was located several miles from Little Rascals.

The charges against these defendants involved rape, sodomy, and fellatio. Children told of having to perform sexual acts on other children, having their pictures taken while performing such acts, and having assorted objects, such as pins and markers, placed into their vaginal or anal openings. There were allegations involving "ritualistic" abuse: Betsy and Bob burned a cat with a candle, they murdered babies. Some children claimed to have been tied up, hung upside down from trees, set on fire, and given drugs that made them feel sick and drowsy. Finally, even more improbable claims were made, such as being thrown overboard into a school of circling sharks.

One of the more surprising aspects of this case, and others like it, was the fact that none of the parents of the Little Rascals children had observed anything that caused them to suspect that their children were being abused or tortured during the period of the alleged abuses; there were no reports of unusual incidents from their children. Nor did the parents detect anything unusual when, without notice, they dropped in early to pick up their children from the day-care center (e.g., to take them to a doctor appointment). It was only after allegations began to grow that parents also began to remember events or behaviors that were consistent with their child was being abused.

I first learned about this case in May 1991 when the PBS program *Frontline* aired Ofra Bikel's (1991) documentary *Innocence Lost*, which describes the fabric of the case. This powerful documentary eventually won an Emmy Award. It created much discussion among both my professional and my nonprofessional peers as to how these children could come to make such allegations and how the parents could come to believe that such terrible things had happened to their children. I was haunted by this piece.

A few weeks later, I received a phone call from Jeff Miller, one of Bob Kelly's attorneys. I was asked to testify about the research on children's suggestibility at Kelly's trial. I was hesitant. I did not consider myself to be a seasoned expert who would be an asset to any trial but particularly for one of this visibility and magnitude. At that point, my colleague, Stephen Ceci, and I had just completed a comprehensive review article on children's suggestibility (Ceci & Bruck, 1993). We had also begun a study of children's memories of a stressful pediatric procedure. But that was the sum total of my experience. Miller assured me that I had the background to provide valuable testimony to the court. After all, most so-called experts were consumers of research rather than producers of it. Reluctantly, I agreed. In part, my decision reflected on my reaction to the *Frontline* documentary. The defendants were not unknown to me; rather, these were three-dimensional characters with ruined lives. I hoped that perhaps my small area of knowledge might help inform the court—whether it be to the detriment or to the benefit of the defendants themselves.

When I agreed, Miller then explained that he would be sending me (and other experts) all of the materials that the defense had. I learned that even as these attorneys were going to trial, they still did not have all the facts of the case. This is because in North Carolina, there is very limited discovery for criminal trials. As such, the defense did not have any reports or copies of interviews with the child witnesses, nor did they know which witnesses would be called by the prosecution. (Similarly, the prosecution did not know which witnesses the defense would call.) The defense tried to use this rule as much as possible to their advantage. Thus, if all went according to plan, the prosecution would not know the identity of the defense's expert witnesses until they took the stand. As seen later, this procedure did have some influence on my own experiences in the courtroom.

Miller and his cocounsel Mike Spivey began sending out materials.

Starting around June, I received weekly packages of documents to review. To begin with, there were therapists' and medical reports. As I read these, a deep despair consumed me. I thought "How could these children have possibly gotten it wrong when it says right here in the therapist's report that the child said that he was abused?" Along these same lines, medical professionals in the field of sexual abuse at the University of North Carolina had conducted physical examinations of the children and had concluded that their symptoms were consistent with those of sexual abuse. Although I knew that my job was not to determine the guilt or innocence of the defendant or to present a one-sided or biased picture of the research to support the defendant's case, nevertheless, I found myself craving at least an element of doubt that the defendant was guilty. Nowhere was that craving sated.

Only later was I to learn how to read these reports. I learned that just because a professional concluded in a report that the child was abused, it did not necessarily mean that the child had reported abuse in the manner contained in the report or that the child had spontaneously reported the abuse. I learned that these reports could reflect situations in which the child was repeatedly questioned and finally assented to abuse in response to an interviewer's leading questions (see Ceci & Bruck, 1995, for some examples). It would be years (and cases) later before I would fully appreciate the host of contextual factors that could affect reported disclosures.

Bob Kelly's trial finally began in August 1991. Twelve children and their parents were among the many witnesses who testified about incidents that allegedly had occurred 3 years earlier. These children's memories appear to have been refreshed by their therapy sessions, meetings with the prosecution, repeated discussions with their parents about the events, and attending "court school" to prepare them for their testimony in court. The parents' memories were refreshed through their diaries and meetings conducted by the district attorney's office.

The prosecution rested right before Christmas 1991. I was scheduled to appear in court on Tuesday, January 16, 1992. Because the defense had limited funds, I was asked if I would arrive before Saturday in order to take advantage of the discount airfares from Montreal to Greenville, North Carolina (where the trial was being held). I agreed.

Before I left for Greenville, my colleagues and friends had many questions; some offered advice. One common question was "Aren't you nervous?" I was not. I had taught courses. I had also given many invited lectures and talks at meetings and had been trained to present evidence clearly and to deal with questions and criticisms of my work. This training and experience seemed perfectly suited to the job that I was asked to do in the courtroom, or so I thought. I was wrong. Also my friend and colleague, Steve Ceci, lectured me on the ethics of being an expert witness. He warned me about some of the traps and conundrums that might await me in a courtroom. He warned me of the evils of being "a hired gun" and that it was important for me to provide a balanced and neutral review of the relevant literature to the court and to allow each side to make what they would of the research. He told me it was important to cooperate with both sides and to try to give the prosecutor nonpartisan replies during the cross-examination. I went armed to my inaugural day in court with the best of intentions.

When I arrived in North Carolina, I met with Miller for several hours. He had read a draft of the *Psychological Bulletin* article that I had coauthored with Steve (Ceci & Bruck, 1993). He had also read much of the other literature in the field. During this meeting, he merely asked me a number of questions that he would ask during the direct examination. These questions were based on the article. To the best of my memory, I do not recall that either of us made suggestions for editing his questions or my answers. I was certainly *not* told how to phrase answers or what studies I should or should not talk about. It seemed easy enough.

I then spent the rest of the day making notes for my courtroom appearance. My major goal was to be as concise as possible, so as to hold the attention of the jury. I wanted to spend most of the time reviewing the most current studies that I thought best characterized the present field of knowledge on children's suggestibility and were most germane to the issues of the case (i.e., Are children suggestible? Could they be led to make claims about central, important events that had never occurred? Are children most prone to suggestion when they have been repeatedly interviewed under a number of suggestive circumstances? What effect does stereotype induction have on children's reports?) In preparing my testimony, I decided not to refer to any of the case material that I had been sent. In part, I did this because I felt that my testimony on the scientific literature would be perceived as more balanced if it was not explicitly tied to the facts at bar. Also, I did not want to be grilled by the prosecution on the facts of the case.

Although I did not include any facts of the case in my testimony, for several reasons I came to learn about the facts of the case over the next 3 days. First, after preparing my testimony on Saturday, I had Sunday and Monday with nothing to do except to look through the materials that were available in the attorney's office. During this time, the attorneys, their assistant, and another expert witness (on the interviewing of children) were working through the materials in the same office. It was difficult not to become involved in their conversations about the evolution of the children's allegations. Also, "free time" was spent having meals with the attorneys and Rachel Miller (Miller's wife, who assisted the defense during the trial). This social part of the day was spent discussing the case and learning about the prosecution's maneuvers and the defendants' ruined lives. The more I heard, the more it sounded like a witch hunt. I also was feeling more and more respect for the defense team. These were state-appointed attorneys who had devoted several years of their lives and given up much of their private practice for this case. The financial burdens as well as the extreme stress were at times overwhelming. I was in awe of their dedication. I was becoming less of an impartial witness by the minute.

On Monday night, I was pulled even further off center. I had dinner with Betsy Kelly (Bob Kelly's wife), herself accused and awaiting trial. Out on bail, she was financially destitute. She spent the weekends visiting her 8-year-old daughter in a town outside of Edenton (one of the conditions of her bail was banishment from Edenton); during the week, she helped the defense team in the courtroom. During the time in the courtroom, she also tried to provide her husband with whatever emotional support was tolerated (the court had decreed that she was not allowed within touching distance of him). Despite these hardships, Betsy was surviving. She was an engaging, bright, and warm woman.

After dinner, the attorneys asked that I rehearse my testimony for the next day. There were no comments about my performance, and everyone seemed confident that it would go well. My only element of concern was having Betsy listen to this. I told her that I was sorry that she had to listen to all this scientific verbiage when she was in such pain. She told me how important it was for her to hear this background to begin to understand what had happened to these children. As might be imagined, not only was I now feeling compassion for the defense attorneys, the defendant, and his family, but I also was now thinking that my role was to comfort defendants and to provide them with some explanations for the children's behaviors.

Tuesday finally arrived. The attorneys had assured me that my testimony would go smoothly and quickly and that I should be on the 6:00 p.m. plane back to Montreal that night. Never plan your life around an attorney's projected schedule of events. As it turned out, I did not take the stand first but had to wait for the prosecution to cross-examine one of the defense's witnesses from the previous week. The witness was Debbie Forrest, who had sent her child to the Little Rascals Day Care Center and had refused to believe that her child had ever been abused.

I watched Mrs. Forrest testify.[2] She was poised and articulate. She appeared confident. Then the bubble burst when the prosecutor unleashed a barrage of seemingly libelous questions.

> Isn't it true that your son was not being cared for at home? That you were known as an unfit mother? That your child looked like he had been dressed by someone who didn't care if he was clean or not? That he was unsupervised and swimming by himself with his cowboy boots

---

[2]In North Carolina, witnesses are permitted into the courtroom prior to giving testimony. In many other jurisdictions, witnesses are not allowed into the courtroom until after they have testified (i.e., "the rule" is imposed to bar witnesses from hearing other witnesses' testimony).

on? That your mother fired you from your job? (*State v. Robert Fulton Kelly, Jr.*, 1991–1992, pp. 5199–15277)

Mrs. Forrest appeared calm and deliberate when she consistently replied, "that is not true. I do not believe that is true, sir. No sir, I have never heard that before" (p. 15277). I was feeling shaky, as I began to wonder for the first time whether I too would be the object of reproach.

I was ready to take the stand after lunch. But first, I was introduced to the defendant, Bob Kelly. He was the first defendant I had ever met— at least in a criminal trial. I wondered how this mild man could be guilty of such egregious crimes. I was growing angrier and more convinced of the defendant's innocence. Especially after hearing the prosecution in the morning, I was incensed over their treatment of witnesses and their way of handling this trial. Whatever aspirations of neutrality I had had 3 days ago were gone.

I took the stand at 2:00 p.m. I was prepared for my testimony—I had a few pages of notes that I carried just for good luck. (These contained reminders of the major areas that I wanted to cover as well as some notes of details of studies, in case I became distracted during my testimony.) I looked at the clock and calculated that I could still be finished by 5:00 p.m. and back to Montreal on the 6:00 p.m. flight. At the very worst, I would catch a flight on Wednesday morning, giving me enough time to get ready for two invited talks that I was scheduled to give at McGill on Thursday.

The direct examination lasted 1 hr, finishing at 3:00 p.m. I felt that I had made the most important points without losing the jury's attention. I had talked about the concepts of suggestibility, and I had reviewed one or two of the most important early studies on the topic of suggestibility (Binet, 1900, and Varendonck, 1911); I had then described elements of interviews that might make them suggestive (e.g., nonverbal factors, repeated questioning, stereotype induction). I had talked about the effects of delay on children's suggestibility. I had reviewed studies that provide data to support these claims. I had discussed studies where the interviewing procedures were similar to those used with the children in this case.

The direct examination ended with a question of opinion and a question of fact. For the first, Miller asked "So Doctor, in your opinion can children learn matters from the adult interviewing process so as to create an event that never actually occurred or one that's not actually in the child's memory?" (*State v. Kelly*, 1991–1992, p. 15329). I replied, "yes, they can" (p. 15329). Finally, I was asked about my fees. I told the court that I was not being paid for my testimony other than compensation for travel and living expenses.

I was now ready for the cross-examination—or so I thought. As it turned out, I was not ready because I had never been warned that the prosecutor (in this case, William Hart) might ask seemingly irrelevant questions or that I might have to provide evidence for the sources of my testimony. This is what happened. In part, looking back, I now suspect that the prosecutor was stalling for time, so that his team could find out about me. Mine was not a known name in the field, and the prosecution had obviously never heard of me. They needed to get on the phone and find out about my academic and forensic background. The next day, I learned that they had called a friend and colleague at the University of North Carolina at Chapel Hill to learn about my background—its strengths and its weaknesses. Unfortunately for the prosecution, this informant was unwilling to provide any negative information.

Because I was not prepared for the next few hours of questions, I became unsettled and anxious. I forgot that I was not the one on trial. The examination began with Hart asking me whether I had brought any of the studies that I had talked about with me today. He asked what materials I had reviewed for my testimony. He wanted to have copies of everything that I had used to prepare my testimony. I did not know how to respond. I could not remember what I had read and whether I had brought it to North Carolina, and if so where it was. Years later, as I wrote this chapter, I realized that I had only used material from the *Psychological Bulletin* article (Ceci & Bruck, 1993), but at that time, I was worried about being underinclusive, perjuring myself, or both; I had images of spending months in jail. Next, I was asked about what materials I had read from the case. Hart questioned me about the names of the child witnesses. I did not remember their names. (In reviewing my testimony, I saw a personal example of how stress affects memory retrieval.)

Before the afternoon break, the prosecutor asked for my notes that I had referred to during my direct testimony (they would copy these notes during the break). Hart was indeed thorough because as he looked through the notes that I had handed to him, he noticed that there were two blank pages of white paper. While I was still under oath, he asked me, "the two white pages there, what are these?" (*State v. Kelly*, 1991–1992, p. 15341). I replied that these were blank pieces of paper. He played to the jury by asking "How did these help you prepare?" (p. 15341). This line of questioning took up another few minutes. As I left for the break, I was asked to search Miller's car (parked in front of the courthouse) for any materials that I might have used to prepare my testimony. I was also asked to search my hotel room and to return in the morning with any additional material that I might have.[3] So much for me catching the 6:00 p.m. flight.

After the break, the questioning continued. It quickly occurred to me that I had become an expert witness on cars rather than on children's

---

[3]It is still not clear what the motivation for this search was. One possibility is that the prosecution hoped that by mistake some experts might turn over the defense's work product and strategies on the case.

suggestibility, as reflected in the following interchange (*State v. Kelly*, 1991–1992).

Q Doctor Bruck, um, when you went—ah, I believe you said you had the briefcase in your car?
A Yes.
Q Did you drive down here from Canada?
A No, I didn't.
Q How did you get here?
A I flew.
Q Okay. And whose car was the briefcase in when you went out to the parking lot?
A Mr. Miller's car.
Q So it wasn't in your car; it was in Mr. Miller's car?
A That's correct.
Q Okay. Now, you and Mr. Spivey went out to the vehicle which is actually a Ford Explorer; is that correct?
A Okay. I don't know what kind of car.
Q Okay.
A It's a black car.
Q Okay.
A It's big.
Q Okay. Sort of a like a big station wagon, right?
A Okay. Yes. (p. 15344)

One piece of Monday morning wisdom: If you are an expert witness, never try to figure out why you are being asked questions. Just answer them to the best of your ability or expertise.

For some reason, Hart now decided that it was time to cross-examine me on my direct testimony. His questions were not what I expected. He started grilling me about the details of some of the studies I referred to; he wanted to know the exact numbers of participants or the exact procedures. I can never remember the number of participants in my own studies, much less in those of other researchers. Because my memory did not save me from these questions, I was getting closer and closer to becoming an uncooperative witness.

But there was a period of calm where he asked questions that were relevant, questions about the *Psychological Bulletin* article (Ceci & Bruck, 1993) in which a century of knowledge on children's suggestibility is synthesized, and questions about the empirical study of children's memories of their visits to their pediatrician. Along the way, I summarized some studies that I did not mention in direct testimony. I explained to the prosecutor that I did not review these studies in my direct testimony because the interviewing techniques were unlike those used with the children in the present case. My reply seemed to infuriate Hart, who berated me for citing a historical study by Varendonck (1911) rather than studies that the prosecutor deemed more relevant to his case. Although the prosecutor tried to accuse me of being biased in my presentation, I was willing to discuss in detail the studies omitted from my direct testimony and to show why I thought these were not relevant to the case at bar.

Hart was quickly becoming my enemy, and I was getting ready to do battle. Even as I read the transcript of my testimony 3 years after the event,[4] I could still hear the stinging sarcasm and drama in his voice. I could still feel my anger that this man was not trying to get at the truth, rather he was trying to cloud it. He treated the science as though it had a personality, embracing it when it suited his purpose but disdaining it otherwise. For example, he wanted to know about other studies that I had not mentioned—about whether children will make false claims about being touched. I described for the first time a study by Ceci, DeSimone, Putnick, and Nightingale (1993), which was in press at the time. This study demonstrates that children could be led to make false claims about being kissed in the bathtub or not being kissed in the bathtub, depending on the interviewer's tone during the questioning. Hart had been instructed; he knew to ask how many participants there were for each study. Somewhere, he had learned that small sample sizes allow one to overlook the importance of the results of a study. When I told him that there were only 2 children in each condition in the Ceci et al. bathtub study, Hart acted triumphant and subsequently referred to that study as the "two-subject study."

At 5:00 p.m. when court was adjourned, I was reminded to go back to my hotel room to search for all the materials that I had reviewed in relation to the case. I spent the rest of the evening hoping for a miracle—one that would prevent me from ever going back into the courtroom again. I thought that Debbie Forrest had had an easy time on cross-examination compared with my treatment. The attorneys did their best by telling me to stay calm and to just answer the questions.

The next day, the cross-examination continued along the same tracks as the day before. I was asked questions that seemed irrelevant. I was asked about my graduate training (from 25 years previously). More surprisingly, I was asked, throughout the day, questions about my coauthor, Ceci. I was asked about his opinions and his work. On several occasions, I was read quotes from his articles (before our collaboration) and asked whether I agreed with these statements. I disagreed with some of them because they were written several years previously and the evidence had changed significantly since he had written some of these conclusions. The prosecutor did not understand this. In fact, it became clear throughout the day that the prosecutor confused *research* with *researchers*. I wonder whether this is a common confusion among nonscientists.

Furthermore, the prosecutor had the mistaken idea that a conclusion

---

[4]This chapter was written in the spring of 1995.

written in a book or a paper was somehow equated with "the truth" and with the "unchangeable" opinion of one researcher. The idea that conclusions need not always be based on results or that the interpretation of results is not an automatic computational process was foreign to the prosecutor and one that I had to explain repeatedly. I tried to explain the difference between results and conclusions and that a scientist does not agree or disagree with results of an experiment (unless, of course, the data are fabricated). One can agree or disagree with the conclusions and the generalizability of the results. The prosecutor did not seem to understand that as knowledge accumulates, ideas change.

As I think about all of this years later, I see what a mistake it is to confuse researchers with research. Although it is easy to do because one comes to represent a "researcher" with a specific point of view, this is a mistake in terms of the profession's applied image. You should try your best in the courtroom not to talk about researchers; rather, you should only talk about studies. These studies should not be associated with names or personalities.

For a good part of the morning, it seemed to me, I was asked questions outside of my area of expertise and of the issues of the case. I was asked about IQ tests. Hart asked me about the developmental stages that children go through. He asked about perception and about the stages of memory development; he asked about the effects of child abuse on different developmental stages. I did not realize that this would be like a doctoral examination—one that I had not studied for. One thing I quickly learned during this line of questions was to make clear the area of expertise for which I was brought into the courtroom. No matter how much an attorney may belittle you, there is no shame in saying that you were not asked to give expert testimony in a specific area in which you feel uncomfortable or unprepared to give expert testimony. This is something the novice expert should write on an index card and read often. It is to be his or her mantra.

I was on the stand for the entire day. Much of the time, the prosecutor repeated his line of questioning. Other times, he read long passages from book chapters and asked me whether I agreed or disagreed. At times, I was asked for my opinion on parts of the testimony given during the trial. I tried as much as possible to stay within my expertise and to only reply when I thought that there was relevant scientific evidence. At times, I overstepped this boundary and replied on the basis of common sense that comes from being a parent. This was clearly a mistake—I was not brought to North Carolina because of my keen common sense or parental abilities. As the day progressed, I became more intransigent about being asked to speculate and offer personal opinion. I only answered questions if I could base my answers on scientific data.

As I reviewed my testimony 3 years later while writing this chapter, it is clear (to me at least) that the prosecutor had had several major goals in his cross-examination. The first, as already mentioned, was to stall for time. The next was to discredit me professionally in the eyes of the jury by trying to show that my presentation of the literature was biased and that I did not know everything about child development. Finally, the prosecutor tried to bore or confuse the jury to the point that they would no longer remember my direct testimony.

With this knowledge, it is important for experts to know that when they go into a courtroom, they should be prepared for what they think are irrelevant questions. Experts should be prepared to become bored and very tired. It also is important to remember that the primary objective is not to decimate your cross-examiner but to try to keep paramount the interest of the court's truth-seeking mission. This may be very difficult, if not impossible.

My cross-examination ended at 4:15 p.m. I felt depleted and panicky. Not only would I have to cancel all my invited talks for the next day, but I would have to spend another day on the stand. The redirect took only 15 min. It was now 4:30 p.m., and it then went back to the prosecutor. This went very smoothly. In fact, he must have also been tired because he asked questions that helped to reinforce many of the points I was trying to make during my testimony. At 4:55 p.m., the prosecutor announced that he had no further questions—great timing! But as I later learned, this was probably perfectly timed. The prosecution wanted to be sure that the defense would not present another witness on Wednesday, for fear that they might have to cross-examine on Thursday. The prosecution assured that they would have Friday when court was adjourned and the weekend to prepare for the next "surprise" witness.

I left the stand exhausted and exhilarated that it was all over. But it was not all over. I had to say goodbye to the defendant, who had stayed behind to thank me for my testimony. I found this a very difficult experience. By now, I was certainly no longer neutral to the defendant's guilt or innocence. I felt that the facts of the case were such that this man had been unjustly charged and imprisoned. I saw how members of a small town had banded together in such a way that people who had initially believed in the defendant's innocence were outcast and, even worse, threatened with being charged of similar crimes. I saw the devotion of the defense attorneys who had worked day and night on this case for the past 2 years, and I saw how firmly they believed in the innocence of their client. These defense attorneys were paid by the state, and because of their devotion to the case, their law practices had virtually ceased to exist, as had a sufficient income to support their families and the expenses of the present trial. It was an emotional good-bye. The next 2 weeks were very difficult. I was disoriented. I was emotionally and physically exhausted.

Bob Kelly's trial lasted 8 months and was the most expensive criminal proceeding in North Carolina's history. It also was a media sensation, with national newspapers, magazines, and electronic media covering it. The media coverage, outside of North Carolina, was decidedly slanted toward the defense. Despite the media outcry against the state's evidence, on April 22, 1992, a jury returned "guilty" verdicts on 99 of 100 charges against Bob Kelly, and he was sentenced to serve 12 consecutive life sentences. He would not be eligible for parole during his lifetime. One year later, Dawn Wilson was convicted of five counts of abusing four children; she was sentenced to life imprisonment. In December 1993, Betsy Kelly, who had already spent 2 years in prison awaiting trial, pleaded no contest. After serving 1 year of a 7-year prison sentence, she was released on parole. In June 1994, Scott Privott pleaded no contest to 37 charges involving 16 children. After having served 3½ years in jail before posting bond in June 1993, Privott was placed on probation for 5 years.

But the story is not over. On May 2, 1995, the appellate court of North Carolina reversed the lower courts' verdicts in the trials of Bob Kelly and Dawn Wilson. In December 1996, the prosecution dropped all charges against Robin Byrum, Shelly Stone, and Darlene Harris. As this chapter goes to press, the prosecution has come forward with new charges against Bob Kelly, who will face a new trial.

When I first read my courtroom testimony several months after the trial, I had widely different feelings. At times, I thought my testimony was brilliant, I was articulate, I made the literature and the problems of the field come alive. At other times, I was horrified. I saw how I unraveled as a result of the persistent and unmotivated (at least to me) questioning of the prosecutor. I worried that I had tried too hard to fight him, that I had become a biased witness. But as I reread the testimony years later (to write this chapter), I saw that I did accurately summarize the literature. I did not make false claims about what the literature showed and what it did not show. Rather, I kept trying to talk about how the literature showed ways children may be interviewed that could produce unreliable, inconsistent, fabricated reports. But I was also angered by how the prosecution tried to impeach my scientific credibility. I did go into the courtroom with good intentions: to inform the court—the defense, the prosecution, and the jury—about the literature on children's suggestibility. I tried to provide the best informed answers to both the defense's and prosecution's questions. I did not try to present a biased picture of the literature. At times, however, it seemed that these good intentions were quickly eroded by fear, confusion, fatigue, and boredom.

I wrote a first draft of this first part of the chapter in May 1993. At that point, I concluded by asking myself the question Would I ever repeat this experience? I wondered if my testimony had any long-term impact in the courtroom. Surely, the defense attorneys could have shown the jurors how the children's stories emerged, and the jurors could have seen for themselves how the prosecution's case was built. Did the defense really need experts to tell jurors that children can be influenced through repetitive interviewing? Was the emotion so strong in this and other cases that it overrode reason, leaving researchers to come into the courtroom and say the obvious?

THE MARTENSVILLE TRIALS

In June 1992, I read in the Montreal newspaper that the police in Martensville, a small town just north of Saskatoon, Saskatchewan, Canada, had charged 9 adults with the sexual abuse of several small children. The allegations involved children being sodomized, beaten, thrown into cages, and threatened with guns, knives, and ropes. There were rumors that these activities were organized by members of a satanic cult. The suspects included Linda Sterling, who ran a day-care center; her husband Ron Sterling, who was the deputy director of the Saskatoon Correctional Center; Travis Sterling, their son; and their 20-year-old daughter. In addition, five police officers, one of whom was not from Martensville, were charged.

The investigation began when a mother reported that her 2-year-old child had swelling and redness around her genital area; the young child who had had episodes of diarrhea throughout the day was cared for by the Sterlings. The case was assigned to a new member of the local police force, Claudia Bryden, herself a victim of childhood sexual abuse. Bryden soon learned that another complaint about sexual abuse, involving the Sterling's son, had been brought to the police's attention 3 years earlier; but this complaint did not result in any charges. Given Ron Sterling's links with many of the police officers in the town, Bryden became suspicious of a cover-up. Shortly after the parents of the 2-year-old had lodged their complaint, Bryden began contacting all the parents of the other children who were cared for by the Sterlings. Bryden gave the parents some general information about ritual sexual abuse and told the parents of her own sexual abuse. When the parents began interrogating their children, the children initially claimed that nothing had happened. Bryden and another member of the police force, Rod Moor, conducted intense and repeated interviews with the children, some of whom were questioned 60 times. Gradually, as was the case with the Little Rascals children, allegations of abuse began to emerge; some of these were quite bizarre. One child claimed that he had seen people being killed by one of the accused, acid had been poured on someone's face, and he had been forced to eat feces. Two children claimed that an axe handle and vibrator had been inserted into their anus. However, there was no medical evidence for these or other allegations. Nor did the children complain to their parents at the time. This case seemed like the Canadian counterpart of the Little Rascals case.

The first of the defendants, the Sterling's young daughter, was tried in March 1993. She was convicted and sentenced to 2 years in prison. The defense did not call any expert witnesses to testify about the reliability of young children's testimony. In June of that same year, one of the police officers was tried. He was cleared and judged innocent when the child complainants were unable to identify him in the courtroom. In the fall of 1993, Ron, Linda, and Travis Sterling were tried in a Saskatoon courtroom. I was asked by Hugh Harradance, the lawyer representing Linda Sterling, to appear as an expert witness.

I agreed to do so on two related conditions. First, I asked Harradance to send me a brief outline of the facts of the case as well as some material on the interviewing procedures used with the children, so that I could be sure that the suggestibility of young children was a key issue in this case. Second, I told Harradance that I would come to court, but I did not want to be informed of any other facts or legal proceedings in this case. I did not want to know about the defendants—their past or present. I merely would come into court and review the scientific literature, much as my coauthor and I have done in our writings (e.g., Ceci & Bruck, 1993, 1995) and in our talks to scientific and professional audiences. In making this demand, I hoped to remove myself emotionally from the case at bar, so that I would be as unbiased and as neutral a witness as possible. Harradance agreed to my terms. Thus, from the beginning, this experience was very different from the Little Rascals case.

There was also another difference. Unlike in North Carolina, in the Province of Saskatchewan, there is "discovery" in criminal trials. The prosecution knew that I would be an expert witness. One of the prosecutors had telephoned me to discuss my testimony and had requested certain scientific articles, which I then faxed to her office.

Harradance faithfully followed my request by not telling me anything about the case or the trial. Since mailing me the initial documents in June, he only sent me the trial testimony of one of the prosecution's experts as well as a book that had been read to the child witnesses to help them recall their alleged abusive experiences. Furthermore, when I arrived in Saskatoon on the day before the trial, he was careful not to discuss the case with me and to ensure that other people involved in the defense did not discuss the case with me. As it turned out, I only learned the details of the case after the jury returned its decision.

Although Harradance talked to me about my testimony, he offered no advice on what I should say and what I should not say. His only advice, as I recall, was to remember to address the Canadian judge as "My Lord," not "Your Honor."

I took the stand on a Monday afternoon. As was the case in North Carolina, the direct examination went smoothly. The cross-examination (which lasted approximately 3 hr), although less grueling than that endured in the North Carolina courtroom, was still stressful. I read the transcript of my testimony for the first time as I wrote this section of my chapter in April 1995. There were certain elements of the cross-examination that I found distressing, even 15 months after the fact.

The first element was the prosecution's attempt to attack my credibility as an expert witness. The court had been told that I was not personally remunerated for my appearance in the courtroom and that I had not studied the facts or the testimony of the case to avoid putting a "spin" on my review to make it fit the facts at bar. To counteract the effect of my actions, the prosecutor questioned me two times about one incident in an attempt to show the jury that I was not an unbiased scientist. The following is part of that testimony (*The Queen v. Ronald Sterling, Linda Sterling, and Travis Sterling*, 1994).

> Prosecutor: Doctor, did you appear on the show *20/20* in the fall of 1993?
> A: Yes, I did.
> Prosecutor: Okay. And the segment that you were on was regarding child sexual abuse and the interviewing of children. Is that correct?
> A: Yes.
> Prosecutor: And you made the following answer to the following question, "You think there are dozens of people in jail now who are totally innocent," and your answer was "Yes, I do." Is that correct?
> A: That's correct.
> Prosecutor: And Doctor in order to come to that conclusion were you present for the trial of these people and listened to the evidence and come to a different conclusion than the jury? (p. 100)

I did not justify my statement to the prosecutor, other than to tell him that it was taken out of context of a larger conversation. I also explained that this was not a statement that was made in my scientific writings or presentations; it was merely my personal opinion. I have been chided by some of my colleagues for having made this statement in a public forum; however, logically, the statement should be correct, given the numbers of adults who have been imprisoned for crimes of sexual abuse of children and the percentage of defendants found guilty for crimes they did not commit. On the basis of this reasoning, one would expect that there would be dozens of innocent people in jail for child abuse, just as there are dozens of innocent people in jail for any other frequently committed crime. Nevertheless, it was a lesson about how careful one must be to lead a "clean life" if one wants to testify as an expert in a courtroom.

As was the case in *State v. Kelly* (1991–1992), the prosecutor also tried to discredit me as a witness by asking me questions about fields that were not my area of expertise (e.g., the effects of child abuse on different developmental stages of children, the developmental stages of children in terms of memory). This time, however, I had no difficulty simply stating that I was not an expert in these areas. I simply came to court to talk about my area of expertise—the suggestibility of children.

But the most frustrating parts of the cross-examination were when the prosecutor attempted to ask about and attack the science of psychology itself. It is one thing not to understand the scientific process, but when this is compounded by a desire to attack what you do not understand, the expert is left with the task of "trying to nail Jello to the wall." Expert witnesses, I imagine, learn that attorneys do not use appropriate scientific terminology or concepts and that they have to explain such terminology to them. This is difficult to accept, given the many experiences I have had talking to attorneys and judges in a public forum. In these contexts, they seem to easily understand the basic concepts I am trying to get across.

In the present case, the prosecutor had some professional assistance. He had hired a developmental psychologist, employed by a local university, to help with the scientific literature. It appears to me that this assistant's main task was to attempt to tear apart two studies (Ceci, Loftus, Leichtman, & Bruck, 1994; Leichtman & Ceci, 1995) that I had discussed in my direct testimony. Unfortunately, this paid consultant did not give the prosecution very informative feedback. As a result, the prosecutor dwelt on minor points of the studies that were unimportant for the final interpretation—and often he himself misinterpreted the results of the study. One could argue that perhaps this was due to the fact that the studies were not well designed or the articles were not well written. As it turned out, these two articles were published in two highly prestigious, peer-reviewed journals, where each underwent extensive reviews by experts in the field. So the fault was not in the articles or the studies themselves.

But this experience in the courtroom shows how trained experimental psychologists can become paid advocates for one side to view the results in a way that is consistent with the side that is paying them. It is also unfortunate that these trained researchers do not explain to the prosecutor that it is important to look at a wide variety of studies, not just one line in one article or chapter. In fact, this was the most frustrating part of my testimony. Because the prosecutor wanted to go over each line in each article and each result, I tried to explain the importance of looking at the bigger picture, that it was important to review a number of studies and to determine the consistency of results and the parameters or generalizability that could be given to these results. I tried to explain that one study is not sufficient to provide evidence about the reliability of children's reports or the conditions under which such reports are suggestible.

I had wanted to provide the court with the current state of the art in the field of children's suggestibility, but the result was an attempt by the prosecution to feign ignorance of the scientific process, to impeach the credibility of the expert, and to confuse the jury. Again, I became depressed.

Although the tone of the cross-examination was milder than that in the North Carolina courtroom (there was no sarcasm, overt rudeness, or histrionics), the judge was more active and more critical in the Canadian court, as evidenced by his statements (*The Queen v. Linda Sterling*, 1994).

> Now, Mr. Bauer [the prosecutor], I'm sitting here wondering how much importance any of this [referring to the details of my testimony] is to the issues the jury is going to have to decide. (p. 143)

> Well, all right. I'm going to be telling the jury not to waste too much time analysing any studies. . . . Maybe the jury will see it differently. (p. 143)

> You see this is exactly the problem with almost all the expert evidence. These ladies and gentlemen and I don't have to be alerted to the risks and problems that they're going to have in dealing with the testimony of these children, and all the expert evidence in the world is not going to help them out. (p. 156)

> Dr. Bruck, I'm going to have to stop you. I mean the jury is going to assess the testimony and the credibility of the children. They don't have to be told that the reports may or may not be inaccurate. (p. 158)[5]

I have shown this judge's comments to some attorneys, who expressed the opinion that he had overstepped his bounds.

When I finished giving my testimony, I immediately left for Montreal. On the way to the airport, the defense attorney thanked me for coming to court and urged me to do more of this work because he thought I was a very effective witness. I have not testified in a jury trial since that time.

I went back to my life in Montreal with none of the emotional or physical problems that I had experienced in the aftermath of my testimony in Edenton (NC). I had never met the Martensville witnesses (although some of the accused police officers did introduce themselves to me), and as he had promised, Harradance did not tell me of their past, present, or future.

On February 2, 1994, Ron and Linda Sterling were found not guilty on all counts. Travis Sterling was convicted on eight sex-related counts and later sentenced to 5 years in prison. He was released pending appeal. On February 10, 1994, the Crown stayed all charges against the remaining four police officers and announced that it would not appeal the Sterlings' acquittal. In May 1995, the conviction of the Sterlings' daughter was reversed by a court of appeals.

---

[5]It is important for the reader to know that the judge's comments were made in response to my statements about the scientific literature. I never made any comments about the case at bar or about the child witnesses in that case.

CONCLUSION

I have painted a very dreary picture of what goes on in North American courtrooms. I ask myself why would anyone willingly subject themselves, their profession, and their science to such abuse? I often wonder whether my testimony really helped the triers of fact determine the truth or it just became another weapon for the attorneys to use to win their case, regardless of the innocence or guilt of the accused. Perhaps if I had accepted personal remuneration for my court appearances, I would feel differently; in such a case, I could reason that I was only doing my job.

The novice expert witness should be warned that no matter how good one's initial intentions to be neutral and to inform the court in the fairest manner possible, one side will use whatever techniques they have available to discredit your person, your integrity, and your science and to confuse the jury.

Having warned the novice of some of the pitfalls of testifying in court, it is equally important to emphasize the necessity of having knowledgeable experts accurately present the science in the courtroom. It would be unfortunate for any scientist whose area of expertise is relevant to the case at hand to retreat to his or her laboratory because of the unpleasantries of the courtroom. With some warning and preparation, one can learn to deal with the negative situations described above in a professional and impersonal manner. In this era of pseudoscience and antiscience, scientists have an obligation to educate and provide the court with the most current review of their field as is relevant to the case at hand.

REFERENCES

Bikel, O. (1991, May 7). Innocence lost. *Frontline* (Show No. 918). Public Broadcasting System.

Binet, A. (1900). *La suggestibilité* [Suggestibility]. Paris, France: Schleicher Frères.

Ceci, S. J., & Bruck, M. (1993). Suggestibility of the child witness: A historical review and synthesis. *Psychological Bulletin, 113,* 403–439.

Ceci, S. J., & Bruck, M. (1995). *Jeopardy in the courtroom: A scientific analysis of children's testimony.* Washington, DC: American Psychological Association.

Ceci, S. J., DeSimone, M., Putnick, M., & Nightingale, N. (1993). Age differences in suggestibility. In D. Cicchetti (Ed.), *Child witnesses, child abuse, and public policy* (pp. 117–183). Norwood, NJ: Ablex.

Ceci, S. J., Loftus, E. F., Leichtman, M., & Bruck, M. (1994). The role of source misattributions in the creation of false beliefs among preschoolers. *International Journal of Clinical and Experimental Hypnosis, 62,* 304–320.

Leichtman, M. D., & Ceci, S. J. (1995). The effects of stereotypes and suggestions on preschoolers' reports. *Developmental Psychology, 31,* 568–578.

The Queen v. Ronald Sterling, Linda Sterling, and Travis Sterling, Jud. Centre of Saskatoon, Sask., *Q.B.J.* No. 74 (1994).

State v. Robert Fulton Kelly, Jr., Superior Criminal Court, Pitt County, NC, #91-CRS-4250–4363 (1991–1992).

Varendonck, J. (1911). Les témoignages d'enfants dans un procès retentissant [The testimony of children in a resounding interview]. *Archives de Psychologie, 11,* 129–171.

5

THE EXPERT WITNESS IN CHILD SEXUAL ABUSE CASES: A CLINICIAN'S VIEW

RICHARD J. LAWLOR

Over the past decade, the question "What can an expert tell the court" seems in many respects to have been answered with "just about anything." Although states vary significantly in the extent to which they allow experts to give opinion testimony in child sexual abuse cases—and particularly how much the court will allow an expert to comment regarding the reliability of statements made by children—the following is clear from both a review of the recent psychological literature (Ceci, 1994; Ceci & Bruck, 1993a, 1993b) and my own review of numerous depositions and transcripts of courtroom testimony, provided by attorneys: A significant portion of what passes for expert testimony in child sexual abuse cases is poorly grounded in the psychological research literature, reflects a lack of the knowledge of this constantly expanding literature, and often demonstrates a significant role confusion on the part of many experts who testify in court. Even psychologists, who presumably have both a research and clinical underpinning to their testimony, seem to be prey to the same difficulties as most other expert witnesses in these cases. Of even more concern is the fact that much of the investigation done in cases of child sexual abuse appears to be done by the least trained professionals and paraprofessionals, without adequate knowledge, skills, experience, training, and sometimes even motivation to apply the knowledge and skills that they have been taught. Even though some child interviewers seem to be intuitively good and able to adapt to the constantly evolving research knowledge, this positive situation does not seem to reflect what occurs in the majority of cases.

As defense lawyers have increasingly become aware of the body of literature that does exist and have been successful in recruiting experts to testify regarding that literature, legitimate concerns have been raised about a backlash against children who allege sexual abuse. The potential for discounting children's testimony, after a decade of gains in this area for the admissibility of children's testimony, seems to be a warranted concern at present.

A number of issues need to be considered by expert witnesses, so that testimony given in court is defensible both on scientific and clinical grounds; to make their testimony defensible, experts providing such testimony need to develop an adequate understanding of the knowledge base that exists and to use that knowledge effectively in their clinical involvement with children. It is also important that the experts recognize the limitations of the current state of knowledge and remain open to the constantly increasing information available in this area. Whether the expert is a therapist, a forensic evaluator, or a researcher, it is imperative that when acting as an expert witness, he or she is aware of a number of overlapping areas of concern. These areas include confusing the role of therapist and evaluator, testifying in ambiguous ways through connotation rather than denotation, generally keeping abreast of the developing research in this area, and being aware of personal biases about a number of issues.

In addition, failure to consider such issues as mental set, confirmatory biases, personal biases, possible impact of iatrogenic effects from abuse investigation, and inappropriate use of props (e.g., drawings and anatomically detailed dolls) can lead to inappropriate expert testimony. Experts need significant background information in these areas to give scientifically and clinically well-grounded testimony to the court. These areas need to be considered in some detail as a basis for concluding what experts can tell a court legitimately.

AREAS OF CONCERN

The Therapist–Evaluator Dilemma

One concern that emerges in the evaluation of potentially sexually abused children is the use of child therapists in the simultaneous roles of evaluator and therapist. The roles of therapist and evaluator are distinctly different, and professionals assuming each of these roles go into them with different sets of assumptions. It is indefensible to mix the two roles, and it is mandatory that clinicians working in this area understand the reasons for this caveat.

The basic assumption of the forensic evaluator has to be one of absolute impartiality. This impartiality has to be maintained in a highly volatile atmosphere of distressed children, anxious parents, and law enforcement officials who may already have decided that they know what has occurred. A competent forensic evaluator needs to maintain a neutral stance, a stance of objectivity, and to engage in as thorough and complete a forensic evaluation as is possible under the circumstances of the particular case. Particularly during the interview of a young child, this approach means that the forensic evaluator has to have a grasp of the developmental literature, which alerts the evaluator to the capacities of children of various ages; a knowledge of the suggestibility and lying behavior literatures, which warn of the many pitfalls to be avoided in these cases; and a thorough grounding in research methodology, which allows the evaluator to read the literature with some degree of sophistication. This latter point is particularly important, in that not all studies or articles that exist in this area are of equal weight or validity (Ceci & Bruck, 1993b; Ekman, 1985; Ekman & Sullivan, 1991).

A competent forensic evaluator is aware of the research literature that shows that under favorable circumstances and in a neutral setting, children, even as young as 3 years of age, are capable of providing valid and useful information to a court. However, these children are also capable of distortions in either their memory or recounting of events based on potential cognitive and social factors that could invalidate the information they provide (Ceci & Bruck, 1993b).

A common scenario seen in many of these cases is for a child to give an adult some type of incomplete statement that raises suspicions that something of an abusive nature may have occurred and for that adult to engage in some degree of questioning with the child. Ultimately, the child is brought to the appropriate legal personnel, and further interviewing takes place. Reviews of hundreds of tapes of these types of interviews suggest that some are done well and many are done quite poorly. The reviews also suggest that the information obtained ranges from appearing to be quite valid to highly questionable.

In some instances, the initial questioners or investigators are unable to obtain information from the child, but suspicions remain that something has happened. A common approach is to then suggest that the child see a therapist. The child then sees the therapist over a period of weeks or months, and in many instances, the child gradually begins to reveal information about incidents of abuse that have occurred. The therapist, during this period, reports the emerging findings to the appropriate legal authorities and continues with the therapy of the child. In most areas of the country, some therapists become known as quite helpful in this regard, and they are frequently able to find information that is useful in the prosecution of sexual abuse cases. Depending on the hearsay exception rules of the particular state, these therapists often testify in subsequent legal proceedings about what the child has said and about the consistency of the child's behaviors or reactions with those of children who have truly been abused.

However, there is a significant problem with mixing the roles of therapist and forensic evaluator. The most significant difficulty stems from the assumption or mental set (Leeper, 1935) the therapist has when entering into the relationship with the child. The child has typically been sent to the therapist because he or she is suspected by others of having been abused. The therapist enters into the relationship with this suspicion and often engages in a variety of therapeutic techniques that may have some validity in therapy but are dangerous when used forensically to elicit information. For example, repetitive interviewing or even repetitive direct questioning of a young child about possible events has been shown to have potential for distorting the child's recollections (Ceci & Bruck, 1993b). In addition to this, however, reviews of numerous therapy notes, and in some instances transcripts of recorded sessions, suggest that the interviews themselves are often conducted in a way that indicates that certain other basic psychological principles are being ignored.

One thing that has been known for many years from the experimental research literature is that there is a possible effect on the results of research from what is known as experimenter bias (Christensen, 1980; Orne, 1962; Rosenthal, 1967). It is important to remember that this area of research shows that when experimenters told graduate students running experiments what results might be expected, a small but reliable bias to confirm the experimenters' expectations of the results typically emerged.

This area of research dealing with demand characteristics of the experimental setting has significant implications for the generalizability of such experiments' results because cues other than the independent variable may actually produce the dependent variable. In a therapy situation, an analogous type of bias is often operating, and the therapist frequently has an assumption about what the child may eventually reveal. This assumption may be based on suspicions conveyed by parents, legal authorities, social workers, or others who have had prior incomplete contacts with the children. But the danger of this initial information is that in the context of the therapy setting, it often produces demand characteristics quite similar to those in the experimental setting when experimenters have expectancies about the results to be obtained. One way this is often seen in the therapy setting is through the phenomenon known as confirmatory bias from the decision-making literature (Kahneman & Tversky, 1972, 1973; Tversky, 1972; Tversky & Kahneman, 1971, 1973).

Confirmatory bias is often seen concretely in transcripts of therapy sessions or even in detailed notes of therapy sessions when the therapist, in interviewing the child, clearly tends to focus on verbalizations produced by the child that move in the direction of confirming the expected revelation of abuse and when the therapist engages in a variety of behaviors that are clearly extinction behaviors by ignoring verbalizations of the child that are either irrelevant or tend to disconfirm the therapist's underlying hypothesis. An example of this kind of situation is a transcript of a recording by a therapist. The child described how her father, during the course of a visit, took her to the bedroom, laid her on the bed, took her panties down, and then allegedly fondled her. During the course of the conversation, the child seemed to be engaging in what was probably fantasy as she talked about her father suddenly running out of the room, going to the street to get a stick, and coming back and inserting the stick in her vagina. Aware that there were absolutely no physical findings of any kind of penetration, the therapist tended to distract the child from these statements, ignore the statements, and gradually produced through the mechanisms of extinction and shaping (Ten Eyck, 1982) a coherent narrative that was consistent with fondling and no physical injury. In other words, therapy sessions not infrequently reflect mechanisms of reinforcement of verbalizations that confirm the therapist's hypothesis and ignore nonreinforcement (extinction) statements that may disconfirm the hypothesis. This combination, based on the confirmatory biases of the therapist, frequently shapes the child's statements to gradually conform to the therapist's expectations. This pattern seems to occur because the therapist assumes that the child has been sent because something bad has happened, and the therapist does not engage in the requisite hypothesis-testing procedures of a trained forensic evaluator.

Advocacy

One reason therapists inadvertently act in this way is because they enter into the relationship with the child as an advocate. Being an advocate for a child is a role that therapists are quite comfortable with, which is appropriate within the context of therapy but clearly violates the principle of impartiality demanded of a forensic evaluator. In mixing the roles of forensic evaluator and therapist, the therapist makes the assumption that the child needs an advocate on the basis of suspicion that the child has been abused. Unfortunately, however, this frequently leads to the types of interviews with the child that violate the caveats that emerge from the research literature.

Anatomically Detailed Dolls

A frequent technique used both in forensic evaluations and in therapy is the introduction of anatomically detailed dolls into either the investigative or therapy setting as an aid in eliciting verbalizations from the child. Although the early research (Boat & Everson, 1988) seemed to suggest that these props could be of some utility in the investigations of these cases, more recent research (Ceci, 1994; Wolfner & Faust, 1993) suggests that particularly with children under age 5, anatomically detailed dolls have no incremental validity, add nothing of value to the investigatory situation, and may actually distort significantly children's recollections about events involving their own bodies. The American Psychological Association (1991) issued a position statement suggesting that highly trained individuals might be able to continue to use the dolls in forensic settings, but the most recent research clearly raises questions about even this cautious endorsement of a limited appropriate use for these tools, particularly with the very young child.

Connotation Versus Denotation in Testimony

One area of frequent testimony by therapists is that a child's degree of upset or psychological disturbance is "consistent with" or perhaps even "indicative of" child sexual abuse. This labeling of any nonspecific finding, such as particular symptoms as indicative of sexual abuse, is wrong. Similarly, the use of the term *consistent with* is an attempt to do through connotation what cannot be done through denotation. It is a statement designed to leave an impression that is clearly not warranted by the underlying facts. The impression is that sexual abuse is in some way confirmed by the behavioral or emotional disturbances displayed by a child. This type of testimony ignores two basic but critically important principles from systems theory that are relevant to diagnostic procedures. These principles are equifinality and equicausality (Baker, 1969), which are reminders that a human is appropriately seen as an open system and conforms to the rules of open systems. According to the principle of *equifinality*, an open system can reach the same end point (e.g., set of symptoms) by a variety of different paths from different starting points. *Equicausality* refers to the situation when the same cause or starting point can produce a wide range of end points. These principles warn of the danger in concluding that a particular cause (abuse) has produced a specific set of symptoms. Children who have been sexually abused can exhibit widely varying emotional reactions and behaviors, including showing no overt emotional disturbance. Thus, utilization of consistent with analyses in a courtroom is erroneous based both on theoretical and research grounds.

Iatrogenesis

Sometimes expert witnesses, whether therapists, researchers, or forensic evaluators, draw conclusions in their testimony regarding the presence or absence of abuse on the basis of the existence of symptoms of disturbance in a child. Is this a legitimate thing for an expert to do?

When therapy notes are reviewed at the request of courts or attorneys dealing with cases of child sexual abuse, one unfortunate but relatively frequent pattern emerges. This pattern is of a child displaying few or no symptoms of emotional disturbance prior to the revelation of possible sexual abuse or to the elicitation of an ambiguous statement indicating possible abuse. Often the child is then referred to therapy, as both a precaution and elicitation for further information. When one looks at the progress notes of such therapy, it is often clear the child is not displaying any symptoms of emotional disturbance in the early stages, but several weeks to several months later, the child clearly displays signs of various emotional disturbances, most frequently anxiety. The question becomes "Where did this anxiety come from?" Can one legitimately use behavioral symptoms that emerge in the course of therapy itself as corroborative evidence for the existence of sexual abuse? Both Goodman et al. (1992) and Jones (1991) have discussed the phenomenon of iatrogenic harms. Goodman et al. noted that the anticipation of testifying in criminal court cases could have detrimental emotional effects on child sexual assault victims. They specifically found that the short-term effects are often negative although the long-term effect is generally one of improvement. They acknowledged that the legal system could play a role in either exacerbating or lessening a child's vulnerabilities to disturbance, and their research shows that there are age differences in the extent to which children are affected. Goodman et al. also found certain buffering effects that can be produced by factors such as support within the family. It seems that single instances of testifying are significantly less likely to produce untoward effects than multiple instances of testifying. There is also a suggestion that when the child's testimony is the only evidence against the defendant and there is a lack of corroborative evidence, there is a greater likelihood of an increase in symptomatology. It is interesting to note that she did not find that the legal outcome of the case predicted improvement or decline in the child's functioning.

Jones (1991) discussed several components or sources of iatrogenic harm, including overzealous professional intervention, repeated interviews or use of multiple interviewers, the use of disclosure work by therapists, repeated physical examinations, possible declining living standards of the child and family after disclosure, and "unnecessary" restrictions on access to or visitation with the child when the child is placed outside the home. These studies suggest that therapists often overreach in court with testimony about the extent to which children's behaviors or symptoms are consistent with child sexual abuse. Clearly, the research suggests that in some instances, the disturbances used to support the allegation of abuse may actually have been produced within the context of the therapy or investigative situation itself. Thus, such statements should never be taken at face value without a thorough exploration of the context within which such symptoms developed. Clearly, if the symptoms developed subsequent to the initial suspicions of abuse and after the child entered therapy, serious questions may exist about their corroborative value.

Maggie Bruck (as quoted in Ceci, 1994) introduced an analogy to the therapy situation that might produce iatrogenic effects. She suggested a hypothetical situation in which there existed a drug known to be effective for the treatment of cancer in a certain percentage of people with cancer. This drug, however, was also known to create cancer in some people who were actually cancer free. If one did not know which individuals had cancer, should the drug be administered to everyone? Clearly, the answer to this question would be *no*. Yet, referring children to therapy, which research shows is not always a benign process, is in many ways a similar situation because many of the children are not known in fact to have been abused. Yet, because the therapy situation is potentially highly suggestive as a result of and often uses memory-eliciting or memory-enhancing techniques, such as probing interviews, fantasy play, repetitive discussions, and so forth, it can actually produce children who think they have been sexually abused. This iatrogenic effect can result in children who become for all intents and purposes indistinguishable from truly abused children. The research literature also suggests that at least during some of the time under this type of circumstance, children are unable to recognize the difference between events that actually occurred and events about which they have had increasingly specific discussions with their therapist but in fact never occurred in reality. This situation results from the phenomenon of source monitoring difficulty or source misattribution, which is discussed in the developmental literature (Ceci & Bruck, 1993b).

One is then faced with the potential that the very technique used to investigate the existence of possible sexual abuse may in fact in some instances produce cognitive distortions, particularly in young children, that cause the child to believe and behave as if he or she were actually abused. This danger is enhanced if techniques such as stereotype induction, fantasy induction, teaching the child techniques of self-empowerment, hypnotic age regression, and symbolic interpretation of the child's play are used extensively. Therapists who engage in these kinds of techniques when using therapy as a forensic investigative technique, for which it was never intended, are engaging in what Gardner (1991) has sarcastically referred to as the role of "validator," which is a potentially harmful role.

Lying

A forensic evaluator needs to always keep in mind that in addition to revealing factual information, a child either may be presenting material that has been distorted through some extraneous influences or may in fact actually be lying. The clinical literature is replete with suggestions that young children are incapable of lying, at least in any sophisticated way; yet the research literature (Ekman, 1985, 1987) does not confirm this view. This impression is also at variance with what most parents of preschoolers know. One of the most extreme examples of deliberate lying behaviors I have seen was a presentation by a 5-year-old girl who had accused her mother of sexually molesting her. The child's story essentially consisted of an allegation that the mother, naked herself, had leaped into the room, pulled the girl's panties down, and inserted her finger into the girl's vagina. In spite of the improbability of such a scenario, the child's statements were taken at face value by the child-protective authorities. The child was removed from the mother's home and placed with the father. She was then referred for further evaluation at the request of the mother's attorney.

Spontaneously, after entering the evaluator's office, the girl announced that on the previous day during the course of a visit, her mother had told her daughter to tell the psychologist that it was not her mother who had molested her but was in fact her stepmother. This kind of detail is often used by evaluators as an index of the truthfulness of a child's statements, and it is generally felt by therapists that young children such as this one are incapable of this kind of elaboration unless it is true. Knowing, however, that all contact with the mother was supervised at this point, the evaluator was able to immediately contact the supervisor to confirm that no such event had occurred and that the observer had been present with the mother and child throughout the whole visit.

The child further alleged that a maternal aunt had become angry with her while she was at a clinic and had accused her of lying about her mother. This statement was also disconfirmed by clerical staff who had observed the aunt and child the whole time they were together and had documented only delightful, interactive play between the two.

When the child was then confronted with the knowledge of the falsity of her statements in each of these instances, the child said "I forgot she was there" (the observer) and "I didn't know anybody else was watching" (the clerical staff). When later asked to tell what actually happened with regard to the allegations against her mother, the child said "tell me what you know and I'll know what to say."

Subsequently, it turned out that this child had been questioned for more than 2 years during visits with her father about possible bad things that her mother had done to her, had been exposed to many of the traditional good touch–bad touch teaching materials including a videotape from the local library, and had for a long period of time had a close relationship with her father and actually wanted to live with him.

This particular case is a good example of the fact that children's motivations to lie closely mirror the same motivations found in adults; the ideas about the content of allegations they make can be gleaned from repetitive prior conversations. Without the ability of the forensic evaluator to appropriately confront the contradictory statements or information, forensic evaluations will often be unproductive. Therapists are rarely willing to be confrontational in this manner because confrontation is likely to destroy the therapeutic alliance the therapist is trying to build. The therapist is also unlikely to seek out the kind of information that would even allow for appropriate confrontation about contradictions in the child's statements.

This example essentially demonstrates the need to constantly test alternative hypotheses in the course of interviewing as a forensic evaluator—something that is almost never done in the course of therapy. This kind of approach, which follows up all statements of the child, not just ones convergent with the hypothesis of abuse, and checks out information from extraneous sources, is consistent with the maxims to avoid premature closure, avoid confirmatory bias, and deal effectively with the effects of prior mental sets when evaluating a child in a forensic context.

These concerns clearly suggest again that the roles of therapist and forensic evaluator should not be mixed. The roles have different purposes, and the therapy situation itself is inherently suggestive and may produce the exact harm, at least from the perspective of the child's cognitive reality, that everyone involved is trying to avoid. Children should not be referred to therapy for investigative purposes. If a child suspected of being abused displays emotional disturbance or behavioral symptoms, referral to therapy is appropriate. If the child does not display emotional disturbance, however, as is the case with many children, referral to therapy is inappropriate.

The issue arises as to what should be done with the child who displays emotional disturbance prior to any clear-cut statements revealing abuse. This seems to be an area that needs further discussion in the profession. Ceci (1994) has suggested that perhaps supportive therapy and the avoidance of any techniques that the research literature warns may be suggestive might be an appropriate approach. This approach, however, would certainly require that therapists have a complete understanding of what their role is as well as an awareness of the potential for distortion of children's memories in the therapy context. This suggestion, absent of any other research evidence to support other positions, seems preferable to the extremist positions of those who would suggest avoiding all therapy referrals until the legal proceedings are over and those who defend the use of any techniques in therapy prior to the conclusion of the legal proceedings.

Personal Biases and the Developmental Literature

Often the initial impetus for an investigation of a child comes from statements that the child made with regard to bathing behaviors, sleeping behaviors, or statements about genital touching. Again, unless one is aware of the research literature and can use that literature as a roadmap during the course of investigations or evaluations, the mental health expert is likely to react on the basis of personal prejudices, biases, or assumptions.

Research on familial bathing patterns (Rosenfeld, Siegal, & Bailey, 1987) indicates that child–parent bathing is relatively common up to about age 8 or 9, the frequency of such common bathing declines with age, and there is a positive correlation between bathing together and genital touching. This literature clearly indicates that one cannot automatically conclude that parent–child bathing is an indication of molestation without evidence that something more in fact has occurred. The behavior itself is common enough that molestation is probably not even appropriately suspected without evidence of other kinds of questionable behavior.

Similarly, the frequency of incidental genital touching of a parent by a child is also not, alone, evidence supportive of molestation. The research literature (Rosenfeld, Bailey, Siegal, & Bailey, 1986) suggests that such activity is not uncommon even up to age 10 and an automatic assumption of sexual abuse is unwarranted. If there are other indications of questionable behavior or if the touching is not incidental but seems to be the primary focus, then a full investigation is warranted to either rule in or rule out abuse. This approach corresponds to the legal notion that a crime consists of both an act (*actus reus*) and an intention on the part of the actor (*mens rea*).

Finally, children sleeping in the parental bed is also a common behavior, and at times, it does occur in reaction to some type of sleep problem or perhaps in reaction to parental awareness of the parent's own emotional withdrawal from the child (Lozoff, Wolf, & Davis, 1985). Such sleeping patterns seem relatively common and are frequently associated with separation anxiety. Most frequently, this sleeping pattern is transient if the child and parents are doing well in other aspects of their lives. Again, standing alone, there is no implication of sexual abuse in the example of children sleeping in the parental bed, yet such behaviors often trigger intensive investigations, repetitive questionings, and even referrals to therapy.

Personal biases are sometimes activated in both therapy and forensic evaluations by countertransference issues (Freedman, Rosenberg, Gettman-Felzien, & Van Scoyk, 1993) when the evaluator or therapist is faced with topics such as sleeping, bathing, genital touching, and children's drawings. Many male psychologists reported having experienced some degree of physical or sexual abuse in the past. Such personal experiences would seem to indicate a need for careful training to develop competence to work in the area of sexual or physical abuse. This acknowledgement of a need to recognize one's own potential needs and anxieties in this area seems to be a legitimate caveat.

Children's Drawings

Much is often made by evaluators of children's drawings during the course of evaluative sessions. Some of these drawings are produced spontaneously; some are done at the behest of the examiner. Some are done in neutral settings, whereas others are done in settings in which demand characteristics are coercive or leading. Sometimes the drawings are interpreted symbolically—for which there is no research support, but it is important to know what the incidence of genitalia in children's drawings is. Hibbard, Roghmann, and Hoekelman (1987) compared the drawings of children who were alleged sexual abuse victims with those of children in a control group where there was little likelihood that the children had been molested. Their findings suggest that approximately 10% of children in the allegedly sexually abused group (5 of 52) produced genitalia in their drawings. Only 2% of children in the control group (1 of 52) produced genitalia. It is clear that the numbers are extremely low in each case; thus, there is not much predictive value from genitalia in drawings of young children. Furthermore, it is not at all clear that the context within which the genitalia were produced in the group of children alleged to have been sexually abused was not suggestive as a result of the same demand characteristics found in the play and interactions of children interviewed with anatomically detailed dolls after a pediatric examination, which then resulted in statements that erroneously indicated they had been subjected to genital examinations (Ceci, 1994).

APPROPRIATE TECHNIQUES

Although it is beyond the scope of this chapter to present in detail all of the issues with regard to the suggestibility literature, the developmental literature, the social psychology literature, the cognitive and learning literatures—which are necessary for a full understanding—or the principles of forensic evaluation, some of the basic principles that should be adhered to and seem to be generally recognized can be presented. Dozens of articles in the literature present appropriate techniques for dealing with sexual abuse allegations (e.g., Cooke & Cooke, 1991). Many of these articles actually present suggestions that may be at variance with the research literature (e.g., the suggestion of a need for repetitive sessions), and others present contradictory recommendations within the same article. The basic principles that can be presented, however, are relatively straightforward and seem to conform to both commonsense notions and ideas based on the general body of psychological research literature, which cuts across numerous subfields. The first and foremost of the recommendations is that to be an effective forensic evaluator, one must be involved with the case as early as possible. In many instances, this is a difficult principle to adhere to strictly because there have been many informal interviews by parents or other adults, which are rarely documented, long before the child has been brought for a formal investigation. The possible effects of these former interviews are always questionable, and the extent to which details of this former questioning of the child can be elicited is an important consideration in any forensic evaluation. An assessment of the possible motivations of those who have talked to the child previously should be an important consideration.

Often before the trained forensic evaluator can interview the child, the child has been interviewed by untrained or poorly trained child-protective workers or therapists, who may not really understand the delicate issues involved in these kinds of interviews and interrogations. Thus, even if the forensic evaluator is relatively early in the time frame, he or she may still be faced with the fact of prior repetitive questioning of the child.

In addition to being involved as early as possible, the forensic interviewer needs to be aware of such basic principles as obtaining as much background information as is possible about the child, the circumstances of the first revelations or quasirevelations, to whom the child has talked, the child's behaviors and emotional development prior to the current investigation, and the possibility of previous incidents or suspicions. After this information is gathered, the interviewer needs to begin with as relaxed an atmosphere as possible and one in which the child is encouraged to give a free-recall presentation of whatever information he or she may have. Only after the child has presented, even with encouragement, as much free recall as he or she can should the interviewer begin to ask direct questions based on the information provided in the free-recall situation. At no point should the investigator introduce data or information that has not been presented by the child.

If the child mentions particular individuals, it is extremely important that the evaluator remains neutral and does not indulge in the induction of stereotypes about the individuals with negative comments about those persons or comments that reinforce the child's sense of self-empowerment with regard to those individuals.

It needs to be borne in mind, however, that even leading, suggestive, and highly coercive interviews may at times bring out the truth but may also destroy the credibility of the evidence that has been brought out. One of the most outstanding tapes I reviewed was an almost 1-hr-long interview of a 4-year-old boy in his home by relatives who suspected his father of sexually molesting the boy. This interview consisted of repetitive demands for the child to "tell the truth," "tell us what he did to you," "you can tell us, we know he did something," and "tell us and this will be over, you won't have to do this again." Fifteen minutes into the tape, the child was in hysterics, choking, sobbing, and repetitively denying that his father had done anything. Finally, after almost 1 hr of this kind of coercive interviewing, with the child in hysterics throughout much of the interview, the child finally admitted that his father had molested him and told what his father had done.

When the tape inadvertently fell into the hands of the prosecutor because the family members conducting the interview thought it would be "helpful," the prosecutor was bound to reveal the existence of the tape. A review of the tape clearly showed it to be an extreme example of all of the various techniques designed to suggest information, coerce information, and bribe a child for presenting certain kinds of information. Thus, the credibility of the child's statements was clearly undermined. The interesting thing about this particular case, however, was that the father had molested his child, and there was other evidence that could be used. Eventually, the father confessed and entered into a plea bargain with the state. This example illustrates the fact that not every coercive and leading interview produces inaccurate information. However, such interviews, to the extent that they can be documented to have been suggestive, leading, or coercive, are likely to be called into question, and the evidence produced is likely to be found incredible or even suppressed. This fact is another illustration of why those doing forensic evaluations and interviews need to be cognizant of the factors that research identifies as important in such interviews.

WHAT SHOULD THE EXPERT TELL THE COURT?

The ideas previously presented suggest that an expert can legitimately tell the court in the area of child sexual abuse information that is elicited using the research findings as a road map; this clearly needs to be information that is not based on personal bias, individual assumptions, or nonobjective role behaviors of the mental health professional. The amount of information that can be provided by therapists, if presented objectively, is likely to be limited in nature. If the therapist is familiar with the research in this area, it may be possible for him or her to present information regarding the appropriateness or inappropriateness of various interviewing techniques, the utility of certain interviewing props such as anatomically detailed dolls, the developmental capacities of a particular child, and a comparison of those capacities with other children of the child's age. Generally, given the inability of mental health professionals to accurately detect lying behavior or actual cases of abuse (Ekman & O'Sullivan, 1991; Horner, Guyer, & Kalter, 1993), it would not be appropriate to even approach the issue of the child's credibility from a strictly clinical perspective.

Forensic evaluators also need to be, even more so than therapists, fully aware of the expanding research literature and should be able to discuss the reasons for particular interviewing approaches, the limitations of the information obtained, and the range of objective, research-based, validated procedures that exist.

Both therapists and evaluators should be aware generally of the appropriate guidelines for diagnostic procedures, noting that appropriate diagnostic considerations generally require a consideration of as many possibilities initially as are compatible with the symptoms or complaints in the preliminary presentation: the most common diagnoses, a logical approach to testing the alternative hypotheses, the use of branching and screening techniques, and cost–benefit calculations with regard to the increasing numbers of diagnostic techniques used. Finally, both therapists and forensic evaluators need to consider disconfirmatory as well as confirmatory evidence and to seek and evaluate data that tend to both rule in and rule out the various hypotheses (Elstein, Shalman, & Sprapka, 1978).

An area of concern regarding what can legitimately be presented in courts is that courts sometimes refer to even relatively sophisticated mental health professionals' questions that are likely to be impossible to resolve. A classic example involves the situation when a child had been subjected to repeated interviews over many weeks, months, or perhaps even 1 year or more. During the course of these interviews, the child gave contradictory statements. Finally, exasperated, the court referred the child to an evaluator who had both the knowledge base and the clinical skills required to conduct an appropriate and sophisticated evaluation. Unfortunately, the likelihood of obtaining objective information from another series of interviews at this point was almost nonexistent. The child's memory for the original event at this point may have been actually overwritten by the demand characteristics of the previous interview situations. Or the child may in fact have taken on the views of a particular individual or group of individual authority figures with whom he or she had been in contact over this time period. Most often, in this scenario, the only legitimate response is that it is impossible to ever know at such a late date what actually occurred.

Under ideal circumstances when appropriate documentation and hopefully recording of the initial interviews are available, it may be possible to either affirm or criticize the techniques used and suggest on the basis of this type of information that the initial responses show signs of having been produced in a nonsuggestive, nonleading atmosphere. Other than this kind of information, however, evaluators who are brought in late to a case are unlikely to be able to present definitive information to a court.

Evaluation of allegations of sexual abuse is an extremely complex and difficult area. Clinicians presented with the same data have typically produced widely varying assessments of the likelihood of abuse and widely varying recommendations (Ceci, 1994; Horner et al., 1993). These data suggest that even the most sophisticated clinicians tend to pay attention to and weight various kinds of information presented by and about children inaccurately.

The most valid statements about the status of children in sexual abuse cases are likely to be produced on the basis of statements made by children that are spontaneous, primarily of a free-recall nature, and generally well documented during the early stages of the investigation. Statements are often produced as a result of repetitive interviews; interviews conducted in suggestive, leading, or coercive situations; or interviews conducted using inappropriate props. Thus, the ability to draw accurate conclusions is likely to be minimal. Therefore, what a clinician can contribute to the court in the investigation of sexual abuse, more so than in most areas of expert testimony, is highly dependent on the use of the research from several areas of psychology, the possession and use of excellent clinical training and skills, and a willingness to enter this arena with an absolute commitment to neutrality, impartiality, and objectivity.

CONCLUSION

When all is said and done and the above cautions are taken seriously, it is apparent that the average clinician, and particularly the average therapist, has little, if anything, to contribute reliably in a courtroom where issues of child abuse and child sexual abuse are being considered. It appears that relatively few therapists of any discipline have the requisite training and background to be involved in the courtroom proceedings. Therapists may have the background to deal with sexually abused children but generally do not have the background to assess whether that abuse had occurred in the first place. This is clearly the role of the forensic evaluator. The background information the forensic evaluator brings to this situation allows the evaluator to draw more reliable conclusions than can a general clinician who does not have the requisite background and training. It becomes apparent that in many situations, these types of courtroom trials will pit trained evaluators against relatively untrained clinicians and therapists. At those times, it will be necessary for the forensic evaluator to explain the differences in the functioning of the two types of clinicians, therapists and evaluators, and to clarify clearly the limits of expertise as well as what the expertise can provide in these situations.

REFERENCES

American Psychological Association. (1991, February 8). *Statement on the inclusion of anatomically detailed dolls in forensic evaluations* (as adopted by the APA Council of Representatives). Washington, DC: American Psychological Association. (Available from Governance Affairs)

Baker, F. (1969). Review of general systems concepts and their relevance for medical care. *Systematics, 7*(3), 209–229.

Boat, B., & Everson, M. (1988). The use of anatomical dolls among professionals in sexual abuse evaluations. *Child Abuse & Neglect, 12,* 171–186.

Ceci, S. J. (1994). Cognitive and social factors in children's testimony. In B. Sales & G. VandenBos (Eds.), *Psychology in litigation and legislation* (Master Lectures series, pp. 13–54). Washington, DC: American Psychological Association.

Ceci, S. J., & Bruck, M. (1993a). The child witness: Translating research into policy. *Society for Research in Child Development Social Policy Report, 7*(3), 1–30.

Ceci, S. J., & Bruck, M. (1993b). Suggestibility of the child witness: A historical review and synthesis. *Psychological Bulletin, 113,* 403–439.

Christensen, L. B. (1980). *Experimental methodology* (2nd ed.). Boston: Allyn & Bacon.

Cooke, G., & Cooke, M. (1991). Dealing with sexual abuse allegations in the context of custody evaluations. *American Journal of Forensic Psychology, 9*(3), 55–66.

Ekman, P. (1985). *Telling lies: Clues to the deceit in the marketplace, politics and marriage.* New York: Norton.

Ekman, P. (1987). *Why kids lie.* New York: Scribner.

Ekman, P., & O'Sullivan, M. (1991). Who can catch a liar. *American Psychologist, 46,* 913–920.

Elstein, A. S., Shalman, L. S., & Sprapka, S. A. (1978). *Medical problem solving.* Cambridge, MA: Harvard University Press.

Freedman, M. R., Rosenberg, S. J., Gettman-Felzien, D., & Van Scoyk, S. (1993). Evaluator countertransference in child custody evaluations. *American Journal of Forensic Psychology, 17,* 61–73.

Gardner, R. (1991). *True and false accusations of child sex abuse.* Cresskill, NJ: Creative Therapeutics.

Goodman, G. S., Taub, E. P., Jones, D. P. H., England, P., Port, L. K., Rudy, L., & Prado, L. (1992). Testifying in criminal court: Emotional effects on child sexual assault victims. *Monographs of the Society for Research in Child Development, 57*(5, Serial No. 229).

Hibbard, R. A., Roghmann, K., & Hoekelman, R. A. (1987). Genitalia in children's drawings: An association with sexual abuse. *Pediatrics, 79,* 129–137.

Horner, T. M., Guyer, M. J., & Kalter, N. M. (1993). Clinical expertise and the assessment of child sexual abuse. *Journal of the American Academy of Child and Adolescent Psychiatry, 32*, 925–933.

Jones, D. P. H. (1991). Professional and clinical challenges to protection of children. *Child Abuse & Neglect, 15*(Suppl. 1), 57–66.

Kahneman, D., & Tversky, A. (1972). Subjective probability: A judgment of representatives. *Cognitive Psychology, 3*, 430–454.

Kahneman, D., & Tversky, A. (1973). On the psychology of prediction. *Psychological Review, 80*, 237–250.

Leeper, R. W. (1935). A study of a neglected portion of the field of learning: The development of sensory organization. *Journal of Genetic Psychology, 46*, 41–75.

Lozoff, B., Wolf, A. W., & Davis, N. S. (1985). Sleep problems seen in pediatric practice. *Pediatrics, 75*, 477–483.

Orne, M. T. (1962). On the social psychology of the psychological experiment: With particular reference to demand characteristics and their implications. *American Psychologist, 17*, 776–783.

Rosenfeld, A. A., Bailey, R., Siegal, B., & Bailey, G. (1986). Determining incestuous contact between parent and child: Frequency of children touching parents' genitals in a nonclinical population. *Journal of the American Academy of Child Psychiatry, 25*, 481–484.

Rosenfeld, A. A., Siegal, B., & Bailey, R. (1987). Familial bathing patterns: Implications for cases of alleged molestation and for pediatric practice. *Pediatrics, 79*, 224–229.

Rosenthal, R. (1967). Covert communications in the psychological experiment. *Psychological Bulletin, 67*, 356–367.

Ten Eyck, R. L. (1982). *Verbal conditioning: An overview.* Unpublished manuscript, Indiana University Medical Center and Larue Carter Hospital, Indianapolis.

Tversky, A. (1972). Elimination by aspects: A theory of chance. *Psychological Review, 79*, 281–299.

Tversky, A., & Kahneman, D. C. (1971). Belief in the law of small numbers. *Psychological Bulletin, 76*, 105–110.

Tversky, A., & Kahneman, D. C. (1973). Availability: A heuristic for judging frequency and probability. *Cognitive Psychology, 5*, 207–232.

Wolfner, G., & Faust, D. (1993). The use of anatomically detailed dolls in sexual abuse allegations: The state of the science. *Applied and Preventive Psychology, 2*, 1–11.

6

PSYCHOLOGICAL AND ETHICAL CONSIDERATIONS IN THE PREPARATION OF THE MENTAL HEALTH PROFESSIONAL AS EXPERT WITNESS

KYLE D. PRUETT AND ALBERT J. SOLNIT

Serving the judicial process well while upholding ethical and competency standards of mental health practice is a daunting, often enervating task. The most experienced clinician thinks twice before crossing from consulting room to courtroom, where clinical expertise can seem as much a liability as an asset. The very competence toward which one strives over a lifetime of practice and research propels many professionals to try to influence the judicial process in its struggle with resolving conflict, especially when such conflict affects the lives of children.

Yet most practitioners discover quickly that competence in practice does not automatically translate to feeling competent on the witness stand. Lessons about the rigors of testimony and the adversarial process as a whole are hard won and not always successfully integrated into increasing efficiency as an expert witness. Serving as an expert witness offers opportunities to help inform officers of the court (and bench) to improve the opportunities for children caught in competing systems of care or control over their lives. Ultimately, it is a process that works best when the expert is, as Provence (a pediatrician and developmentalist) described (in Goldstein, Solnit, & Freud, 1986), "unafraid to recognize the difference between the caring expert and the usurper of parental authority; and to incorporate the view that good professional practice requires soft-heartedness as well as hard-headedness" (p. XII).

To be of use in the adversarial domain, even seasoned clinicians must adapt their skills and their language to that of courtroom culture. This chapter is devoted to a discussion of these adaptations and how one is prepared to serve as a competent expert witness in court, particularly in matters of child maltreatment and placement. To serve this role, we have spent several decades in collaboration with legal professionals, designing and facilitating training experiences for hundreds of physicians, psychologists, and other health professionals. The principles that serve as the underlying foundation of our practice have been translated into our training approaches as well. We (a) make the important distinction between professionally informed opinion and personally held value preference, (b) resist the frequent temptation to exceed one's authority or competence on a given question, (c) eschew the morass of serving dual agency as both evaluator and therapist, and (d) respect the limited boundaries inherent in serving as a caring informed expert and not as the decider or trier of fact. In the sections that follow, we focus on what we have found most and least useful in this process.

DIFFERENCES BETWEEN LEGAL EXPECTATION AND THE CLINICAL VIEW

The courtroom is a forum for the resolution of disputes over rights and property. It is not a domain for clinical intervention or the display of erudition or clinical virtuosity. Sales and Shuman (1993) have articulated one of the inherent conflicts between the goals of the attorney and the goals of the expert.

> Attorneys need partisan experts to persuade the trier of fact (judge or jury), which weighs in favor of the selection of the most articulate, understandable, predictable, and persuasive expert, rather than the best scientist. Even when there are good scientists who fit the bill, attorneys have a strong incentive to choose the person whose presentation and interpretation of the data is most supportive to the attorney's case. (p. 225)

Implicit in training to serve as an expert witness is adherence to the principle that the expert must be an expert *practitioner* before becoming an expert *witness*. Consequently, clinical (or research) competence is the first obligation, with the clinician or evaluator striving to focus only on knowledge without being unduly influenced by an attorney's specific needs in any given case. Unfortunately, the temptation is always to stretch the science to fit the problem.

In this chapter we focus on preparing mental health experts, both experienced and those still in training, as expert witnesses, not as witnesses of fact. Expert witnesses testify for specific reasons on certain matters before the court and are generally not otherwise considered to have standing in a case. Practitioners serving as witnesses of fact may be subpoenaed in a trial because of certain information they have either acquired or generated in the course of routine clinical practice. They are not specifically asked to address larger medical or scientific matters before the court in a particular case. Whereas witnesses giving expert and fact testimony must have many similar skills, we distinguish them here because witnesses giving fact testimony implicitly have standing in a particular case and consequently need to have counsel themselves. Both types of witnesses are required to be fundamentally psychologically and medically competent and ethical.

QUALITIES OF GOOD FORENSIC TRAINING

To articulate the content of the professional preparation of the expert witness, we begin with certain assumptions about the characteristics of good training: (a) the availability of experienced, senior mentorship, the value of which cannot be overemphasized, and seeing it done is believing that it can and should be done (technical performance matters deeply if testimony is to be persuasive); (b) the opportunity to read legal cases and testimony, to critique transcripts with experienced attorneys and clinicians, to attend trials; and (c) to have moot court experience as expert witness. These training experiences should form the curriculum of any professional training course of instruction.

Most useful of all is sustained contact with experienced teachers or mentors who supervise ongoing work. Supervision is the process by which two people join in a collaborative effort to maintain competence and elevate such competence through increasing the knowledge base and accumulating experience in a reflective, collaborative, systematic, and regularly scheduled context. The reflective stance inherent in good supervision refers to teaching and learning perspectives through emphasizing the ability to understand and explain the reasons for how work is done in a particular context. Collaboration is founded on a model of shared authority and power, wherein the supervisor or mentor respects the student's knowledge of the clinical contact, and the student, in turn, values the pooling of expertise. Supervision can be effective only when it is conducted on a regular basis, despite the pressures of time for direct service and report writing. Nothing protects competence more efficiently.[1] In our training program, we require that every case assigned be supervised by a senior clinician with courtroom experience. Collection of data and report writing, and sometimes even testimony, are directly supervised. Furthermore, the supervisors meet regularly for group discussion and feedback on supervision, often leading to curricular changes in the next training round.

CHARACTERISTICS OF GOOD FORENSIC EXAMINERS

Objective Opinions

Professional, not personal, opinions are the end point of the supervisory process. The expert witness should be able to identify opinions that are personal to minimize the chance that they cloud or distort testimony in matters on which he or she can testify with reasonable medical certainty. As Haas (1993) summarized in a discussion of the competence and quality of forensic performance, "judging by the sort of complaints that reach ethics committees and licensing boards, more professional attention needs to be addressed to the issues of competence and quality in psychological courtroom work" (p. 251). Specific professional opinion is the final product of professional skill in harvesting and summarizing relevant information in an expert manner.

Controlling Empathy

Empathic skills are an essential tool in the mental health professional's competence. Yet when he or she is asked to evaluate certain parties in a case, those empathic skills must be constrained in a manner unusual for clinical practice but essential for fair, ethical, evaluative interaction. Because this is counterintuitive to most less experienced trainees at first glance, we include empathy control as an essential element in curricular preparation. Shuman (1993) summarized current standards on the use of empathy in forensic examinations.

> It is unfair for the forensic examiner to reflect the defendant's cognitive or affective experiences in a manner that erroneously implies a therapeutic alliance or a comfort level that would lead the defendant to slip into a therapeutic mind-set. Psychiatrists and psychologists are trained to enhance therapeutic relationships by employing certain joining techniques with their patients. These techniques go beyond the

---

[1]For a thorough discussion of the supervision and mentorship process, see Fenichel (1992).

inherently human awareness of receptive empathy, and are entirely inappropriate in a court-ordered examination. (p. 298)

Staying Within Professional Boundaries

Therapeutic relationship building, though an efficient pathway to important psychological data, is not a viable forensic technique. The very skills that allow clinicians to approach adults and children, and their capacity to talk intimately about their strengths and weaknesses, successes and failures, must be applied in an atypical manner. Once again, apprenticeship or supervised experience with a forensic practitioner is especially critical in this matter because of real

> questions about the transferability of the clinician's data gathering and interpretative skills from one setting to another. ... Clinical examinations in the child placement process are undertaken for the purpose of responding to questions formulated not by the expert but by court, agency, or counsel about matters they consider relevant to decisions at invocation, adjudication, or disposition. Such examinations are carried out ... in an atmosphere of nonconfidentiality and under court-determined deadlines. (Goldstein, Solnit, & Freud, 1979, p. 230)

A further distinction analogous to the nonconfidentiality of the clinical interview is that the interview occurs in a circumstance that is not necessarily voluntary for any of the parties who are participating. The best interests of the patients or clients involved are at best served indirectly, and the clinician generally has been asked to provide a specific service by a court or by an advocate for a specific purpose for which he or she is usually paid.

What Can the Responsible Expert Discuss?

If this, then, is a confusion to be eschewed, toward what clarity must trainees strive in preparing themselves to collect information that usefully can be brought to bear on the legal matters at hand? Furthermore, are the professional boundaries between involved disciplines clear enough for expert opinion to be separated from less rarified thought? We find this warning useful:

> All professionals may be fact finders, but not all facts are for them to find. While all may be opinion givers, not all opinions are for them to give. "Am I qualified to find this fact or to give this opinion?" is a question all professional participants should ask themselves or be pressed to confront. (Goldstein et al., 1986, p. 21)

Whether the expert is to interview parties with standing in a particular case, or merely review or present scientific data in testimony, the following itinerary is a useful guide. Our expertise is of greater use to the court as a whole when appointed by the court, rather than when hired by one adversary to face another.

Initial Contact

The pathway from initial contact to investigation typically proceeds in four stages.

1. The expert must make clear to the attorney or court that his or her time and expertise are being contracted for, not an anticipated, favorable opinion. One is paid for time and expertise; professional opinions are not for sale.
2. The expert must clarify that the objectivity essential to high standards of practice will be maintained. Consequently, one must insist that all available relevant data be supplied, whether or not it is helpful to a particular attorney's client. Such objective inquiry is frequently challenged when the clinician evaluator requests to see *all* of the important people affecting a child's life in a particular case, regardless of whether they may be favorable to a particular attorney's position.
3. The court or its officers must define the area of inquiry sufficiently so that it fits within one's area of expertise. If such a fit exists, only then it is appropriate to discuss the cost and form of the evaluation and the timetable for its completion.
4. Important documents must be exchanged in an orderly, coherent, and ethically sound fashion even before the interviews have begun.

Having described a beginning guideline for the trainee's access to data, we review the differing uses for which attorneys and physicians may want to put this ethically obtained data, bearing in mind Holden's (1989) caution.

> In the majority of legal cases, attorneys do not care about the discovery of scientific truth (or arguably, any other type of truth or justice). Instead, they are concerned only with winning the case for their client. This means that they may maximize the data in testimony that support their case and minimize those data and facts that conflict with their theory of the facts. (p. 1658)

The bottom line: All would-be expert witnesses should be aware that "lawyers seemingly want articulate but partisan experts with integrity" (Champagne, James, & Rubin, 1991, p. 387).

Ellis (1984) has presented a thoughtful review of the myriad reasons that courts choose to request expert witness involvement, particularly in cases involving child maltreatment or child placement. She gave special emphasis to the problems that arise when the "important dialogue concerning what the judge expects and what the expert can offer does not occur" (p. 599). She documented the common struggles between courts and expert witnesses with regard to the degree of scientific certainty. When the expert comes into court "and testifies about children in general, rather than a particular child, the expert may not serve this judge's emotional need for certainty adequately, and conflict arises" (p. 611). She concluded, quite rightly in our experience, that "courts are not equipped to be forums for ascertaining scientific precision. Instead, judges must accept that the best they can do is to follow the least arbitrary and least intrusive means of making use of expertise" (p. 630).

When the court does decide to make use of expert testimony, she argued that it seems best to assume that "experts should be required to have both academic and clinical training. . . . Credentials per se, however, should not govern. . . . The expert should at a minimum have completed the full curriculum for a chosen program" (p. 621). She proposed that a standard be written to ensure that the expert is qualified

> not by profession alone but by special knowledge of children's emotional lives. . . . The important capacity to put oneself in the place of a child, to use the ability to identify with the emotional life of the very young, cannot be learned through study alone. (p. 622)

Knowing how to be of use to the court even when one's knowledge does not fully address the court's concerns is another curricular topic. Staying within established professional boundaries when the expert is not able to advise the court regarding specific long-term predictors about child placement, Goldstein et al. (1986) still felt it would be

> corrosive and damaging to the children if the court were to postpone a final decision in the false hope that further investigation would produce what only hindsight might ultimately reveal. When the psychological reasons for making a choice between two available alternatives are substantially in balance, the one remaining critical factor for the long-term benefit of the children is that the choice be made quickly and unconditionally and that the uncertainty and doubt about to whom they belong should be removed. (p. 44)

Because we address testimony regarding children, including their placement and maltreatment, dilemmas particular to evaluating sexual abuse in general, and the exploitation of physical intimacy in caregiving circumstances, we review certain additional theoretical constructs. These constructs are principles on which clinical practice rests regarding opinion and judgment about adequate protective nurturant care. They go far beyond the adversarial curiosity about whether a given traumatic event may have occurred. These are especially helpful guidelines because, in the vast majority of sexual abuse cases, it is usually impossible to know or corroborate what a child has experienced without direct, preserved medical evidence or corroboration. Because the fundamental need of all children is for consistent, continuous caretaking relationships, testimony about specific abuse must be articulated in terms of (a) the overriding significance of human relationships to the well-being and development of the child, (b) the inextricable intertwining of environment and endowment, (c) the maturational forces that shape a child's life over time, (d) the measurable differences between the way children perceive their world and their drive to be competent in it and the way caretaking and other adults perceive that same world, and (e) the profound (and important) differences between a child's and adult's sense of time.

The Report

The cardinal difference between typical clinical investigation and the forensic evaluation is that the latter must expressly address relevant legal issues, regardless of their importance or even relevance to the overall well-being of a child. Bank and Poythress (1982) have posited a useful review of court testimony and forensic report preparation by mental health professionals and the differing forms required by the questions framed by the legal questions. Training should emphasize interacting with the smallest number of people critical to the question at hand. One cannot assume that any given attorney, no matter how competent legally, socially, or personally, understands clinical material or even the intricate processes of forensic examination. The clinician is trying to answer certain questions about a child's life and development and develop recommendations that might profoundly affect the course of that life. Consequently, one should not be surprised if consultation is terminated prior to the request for a written report, especially if the weight of such a report is not expected to be favorable to an attorney's case.[2]

Information in the report should include (a) the nature and dates of clinical contacts, followed by the nature of the data collected and the sources of information summarized in the report; (b) the circumstances of the referral and the focus of the legal questions at hand; (c) a brief recounting of relevant information whenever possible (complex histories of previous evaluations, clinical intervention, or trauma may require clarification and summarization); (d) a compilation of any assessment instruments or observations used to summarize the clinical findings; (e) when necessary and possible, a clear description of overall developmental and

---

[2] This is one of the chief reasons that experts should discuss fees prior to submitting an opinion: to protect their objectivity throughout the course of the evaluation (Melton, Petrilla, & Poythress, 1987).

psychological functioning; and (f) a clear statement of the relevance of the clinical material to the placement issues being decided.

Testifying

It is crucial that a supervisor prepare the less experienced expert for his or her role in the evidentiary and adversarial process. He or she is merely an element, not an advocate. Blau (1984) stated that "anything the expert can do to avoid thinking in terms of 'our side,' 'our case,' 'winning' or 'beating them' will be helpful in maintaining perspective and appropriate behavior as an appropriate witness" (p. 226). Mental health professionals work for the child's best interests, regardless of who hires them.

In preparing strategies for testifying, it is worth reviewing briefly the special dilemmas faced by an expert witness when one has also been a responsible treating clinician.

> With only the rarest exceptions, one should not serve as an expert in the interest of the court concerning a child whom one is treating. The probability that the therapeutic alliance will be distorted or destroyed is too great a risk to take. When it is clear that testimony will be required either as expert witness or as a treating clinician, consult with the child's attorney who will be questioning you about the nature, extent, vulnerability, and scope of the cross-examination of testimony. The rehearsal of specific questions and answers, however, is relatively useless, because the stilted quality of rehearsed answers impresses no one and usually erodes credibility. (Pruett, 1993, pp. 7–12)

Usually it is an inherently impossible task to serve the primary interests of both the court and the child simultaneously, when the latter, not the former, was the reason for clinical involvement in the first place. In summary,

> our clinical experience suggests that professional persons generally cannot effectively perform dual roles. Potentially conflicting loyalties tend to prevent either assignment from being faithfully discharged. Therefore, we believe that the operative presumption for legislature, agency, and court ought to be against the assignment of dual professional roles. The presumption for professional participants ought to be against accepting or assuming such roles. (Goldstein et al., 1986, p. 80)

Expert witness testimony is usually called at the end of the evidentiary portion of the trial. Once sworn in, the expert faces the *voir dire*, the beginning examination of a witness to ascertain competence and qualifications. This is a guided interrogation designed to clarify for the judge usually the chronological history of the witness's training, education, and justification for expertise in the matters before the court.

Court cases begin with direct examination, followed by cross-examination, redirect, and recross. The attorney who contracted for the expertise begins by leading the witness through the findings in the "direct" in such a way as to be generally supportive of the client's position. A jargon-free understanding of the complexities of the clinical material rendered in an authoritative and articulate manner usually shortens time on the witness stand. It is most appropriate to address one's remarks to the fact finder (judge or jury, if present). Opposing counsel makes objections, which are either allowed or overruled by the judge.

Cross-examination is a unique aspect of testifying in court. Skillful attorneys use cross-examination to pressure the witness or to convert the witness into a weapon directed at the adversary. As part of the turn-taking rhythm of trial dialogue, redirect is next. No new material can be introduced. Only strengthening or clarifying comments of either substantive or peripheral challenges can be used. Recross is the opposing counsel's last crack at the witness. Fear of this process has contaminated many forensic forays by inexperienced clinicians. Proper training can help one make proper judgments about defending one's hard-won opinion.

> Professional persons who participate in the child placement process must strike a balance between too general and too specific a definition of disciplines. They must encourage the existence of borders and, despite the absence of firm guidelines, must differentiate between situations when they can and when they cannot go beyond these borders. (Goldstein et al., 1986, p. 78)

Common pitfalls in testimony that should be reviewed by the supervisor and supervisee include giving lengthy treatises, using jargon, appearing to be professionally arrogant, and overadvocating a particular opinion.

Before reviewing special expert witness training issues surrounding child sexual abuse, it is useful to review competence issues. In a discussion of competence and quality in forensic performance, Haas (1993) has identified certain common pitfalls of competence to which all are frequently prey because of the seductive power of the courtroom and the subtle gratifications of being on stage as the expert (p. 259). He cited (a) not understanding the judicial system and the requirement that evidence support conclusions; (b) professional arrogance, such as relying completely on one's memory and ignoring documentation; (c) advocating, rather than testifying; (d) not attending to changes in the knowledge base; (e) cynicism, impairment, or simply being "burned out"; and (f) greed in the expansion of substantiating work to flesh out a billing cycle. This litany of challenges to forensic competence serves as a useful checklist for the trainees and their supervisors to ensure their work is coherent and comprehensive.

We would add two final measures of competence derived from our training and clinical experience—acknowledging the limits of knowledge and the awareness of strongly held value preferences. Because the clinical child expert is constrained by the auspices under which an evaluation is conducted and by the limits of child development and behavior knowledge, he or she should realize that saying "I don't know" or "I can't answer that question" can be an indication of expertise and especially of how limited we are in making long-term predictions. The evaluative method is inherently constraining and seductive because the lack of confidentiality and the inability of the expert to provide treatment or assistance does not encourage a realistic alliance with the involved child or adults that would enable them to remember or focus on relevant experiences and feelings. At the same time, despite the ethically correct warning to child and parent that the interviews and play sessions are not confidential—that is, a formal report will be made to the judge and other officers of the court—the practiced skill of clinical child experts in interviewing adults and playing with children often leads adults and children to reveal attitudes and information to the expert witnesses that may not be in their manifest interests. Presumably, the clinical child expert witness is guided by the best interests of the child about which disputing adults or agencies are in conflict.

Clinical child experts generally agree that their value preferences are those that support the autonomy and integrity of the family. When the family ceases to function adequately in meeting the community's standards of care and safety for the child, then it is the child's best interests that become paramount. Clinical child experts also can agree that they are at risk of unwittingly, moralistically misjudging the way parents or agencies provide care for children by applying their own lifestyle preferences as the standard. Such awareness can minimize or mitigate the "freight" that each clinical child expert carries from his or her own background and training.

FRUSTRATING THE COURT'S DESIRE FOR EXACT KNOWLEDGE

Special concern needs to be taken in preparing the mental health professional to be of use in sexual abuse cases because of the nature of the abuse and the complexity in investigating it psychologically. As Holder (1985) emphasized, "in some ways, the most difficult type of child abuse to diagnosis or investigate is sexual abuse. If it is serious or aggressive enough, it is not only child abuse, it is also rape (statutory at least)" (p. 223). This implies that it may be tried in ordinary criminal court, and evidence must be preserved in such a way as to be admissible at trial.

Another reason sexual abuse is complex for the courts is that even developmentally appropriate objects of intense interest or desire in children are often unpredictable. This quote from *Before the Best Interests of the Child* (Goldstein et al., 1979) clarifies the unwelcome limitations necessitated by our knowledge of child development.

> Children are not always unwilling partners in sexual activities initiated
> by the parent. On the contrary, parental sexual advances are met only

too frequently by a child's willingness to cooperate. Initial shock and surprise do not preclude pleasurable, erotic excitement from the fulfillment of secret fantasies. Parents are, after all, typically the best loved people in a child's life, toward whom he turns for affection. Indeed, children regularly develop fantasies to become the partner of the parent of the opposite sex and replace the marital partner. Normal as these fantasies are, the child's mental health and emotional development depend on their not being realized. Parents must not allow a child's emotional ties to them to go beyond the limits of affection. (p. 63)

This is a reminder of how important it is to remain humble in such work.

Having articulated the limitations with regard to what can and cannot be understood regarding a child's responsibility in reporting, we need to guard against attributing negatively to our investigational schemata. As stated above, even for those trained as child experts, without medical corroboration, it may be impossible ever to know what a child has experienced physically and sexually. The expert assesses and describes the child's developmental status and the quality of her or his relationship to important adults, as well as the adult's capacity to protect and adequately nurture the child's growth. It is also recommended that "anatomically correct" dolls be used only by child experts. At present, no reliable data suggest that playing with such dolls can be interpreted as an accurate historical rendering of an experience a child has had. All children, whether abused or not, have fantasies about their own and their parents' sexuality. These can be misunderstood or assessed incorrectly by individuals not trained to understand children and their play (Solnit, Nordhus, & Lord, 1992).

CONCLUSION

In concluding this discussion of professional competence and training issues, we remind the reader of the overriding significance of a senior clinician's mentorship and perspective. When paired with the opportunity to review legal cases and testimony on a regular basis, competence stabilizes and improves over time, allowing more compelling and effective forensic collaboration.

Finally, consider this word about the seductions of collegiality in forensic consultation. The loneliness of the work for the mental health clinician may tempt him or her to seek out or use the attorney as friend or coworker in the process, to be part of a "team," and this can be risky or detrimental to the case. The clinician often is interested primarily, if not solely, in the child and may be the best informed advocate for the child in the adversarial setting.

REFERENCES

Bank, S. C., & Poythress, N. G. (1982). The elements of persuasion in expert testimony. *Journal of Psychiatry and Law, 10,* 173–204.

Blau, T. (1984). *The psychologist as expert witness.* New York: Wiley.

Champagne, A., James, R., & Rubin, S. (1991). An empirical examination of the use of the expert witnesses in American courts. *Jurismetrics, 31,* 375–392.

Ellis, J. W. (1984). Evaluating the expert: Judicial expectations of expert opinion evidence in child placement adjudications. *Cardozo Law Review, 5,* 587–634.

Fenichel, E. (Ed.). (1992). *Learning through supervision and mentorship: A sourcebook.* Washington, DC: Zero to Three/National Center for Clinical Infant Programs.

Goldstein, J., Solnit, A., & Freud, A. (1979). *Before the best interests of the child.* New York: Free Press.

Goldstein, J., Solnit, A., & Freud, A. (1986). *In the best interests of the child.* New York: Free Press.

Haas, L. J. (1993). Competence and quality in the performance of forensic psychologists. *Ethics and Behavior, 3,* 251–266.

Holden, C. (1989). Science in court. *Science, 243,* 1658–1659.

Holder, A. R. (1985). *Legal issues in pediatrics and adolescent medicine* (2nd ed.). New Haven, CT: Yale University Press.

Melton, G., Petrilla, J., & Poythress, N. G. (1987). Consultation, report writing and expert testimony. In *Psychological evaluations for the court* (pp. 347–371). New York: Guilford Press.

Pruett, K. D. (1993). Bearing witness for babies. *Zero to Three, 13,* 7–12.

Sales, B. D., & Shuman, D. W. (1993). Reclaiming the integrity of science in expert witnessing. *Ethics and Behavior, 3–4,* 223–229.

Shuman, D. W. (1993). The use of empathy in forensic examinations [Special issue]. *Ethics and Behavior, 3,* 289–302.

Solnit, A. J., Nordhus, B. F., & Lord, R. (1992). *When home is no haven: Child placement issues.* New Haven, CT: Yale University Press.

7

THE EXPERT AS EDUCATOR

JOSEPH S. MILLER AND RONALD J. ALLEN

When other means fail, people resort to the trial as a method for resolving conflicts about legal rights and the underlying facts that determine them.[1] For example, a child custody dispute may require that contested facts relevant to a parent's custodial fitness be settled, or the dispute may be limited to determining what arrangement will be in the child's best interest in light of certain undisputed facts. Similarly, a criminal defendant may deny any involvement in a crime or may concede his or her involvement but argue that the act was justified, as with the defense of self-defense. The trial embraces all such disputes because it is, at its core, simply a collection of procedures developed to focus a pair of disputants on the legally critical portions of their disagreement and to allow them to provide the fact finder with as much information about the disputed facts as is practicable.[2]

---

[1]We use *trial* in its broadest sense, referring to methods of adjudication ranging from an administrative hearing at a state agency to a "full dress" trial in federal district court. The key elements unifying these procedures are (a) an independent and neutral adjudicator (b) who presides over an adversarial presentation of the relevant evidence and (c) settles the parties' legal rights and liabilities (d) according to the facts found in light of that evidence.

[2]Whereas a judge can and sometimes must serve as the fact finder, a jury typically plays this role, whether the case is a civil or criminal one. For the sake of simplicity, however, we use the generic term *fact finder* throughout this chapter.

Among the collection of procedural tools grouped under the label *the trial* is the body of law known as the rules of evidence, the dominant goal of which is to increase the chances that the facts found at trial are true. These rules govern, among other things, the *admissibility* of the evidence that the parties offer (i.e., whether the fact finder can properly consider a given piece of information in reaching his or her judgment). The judge who presides at a trial implements the rules of evidence by making admissibility decisions, usually at the request of the party who opposes the reception of a given item into evidence. These admissibility decisions help to direct the fact finder's deliberative process toward a factually accurate outcome because the decisions filter the proffered information through the sieve of a relevance-driven rule of admissibility. This rule states that (a) irrelevant evidence is not admissible and (b) all relevant evidence is admissible unless otherwise excluded by some specific rule, such as the rule against hearsay (*Federal Rules of Evidence*, 1994, Rule 402).[3] The legal conception of *relevant evidence*, evidence having any tendency to make the existence of a legally material fact more or less likely (Rule 401), provides the primary foundation for the rules.

After the parties have introduced the relevant evidence they deem important, the fact finder brings his or her own knowledge and experience to bear by deliberating to his or her best judgment as to what, for purposes of the law, "really happened." The structure of this process—the presentation of relevant evidence, culminating in reasoned deliberation to judgment—has developed according to a generally accepted view of the most reliable way to implement the dominant goal of increasing the chances that the facts found at trial are true. Lacking an unimpeachable source of correct answers to questions of historical fact (i.e., a yardstick against which to measure independently the relative accuracy of the trial method), our society has continued to refine the trial along the dimension that we can control and assess, namely, its integrity as a process. In other words, reasoned deliberation about the relevant evidence is the best available means to achieve the goal of accurate fact finding.

The expert witness serves an important function in trials that focus on matters amenable to specialized or atypical training or experience. Specifically, an expert can enhance the likelihood of an accurate outcome by putting at the fact finder's disposal the ability to "draw inferences from the facts which [he or she] would not be competent to draw" (McCormick, 1954, p. 28) without such assistance. Indeed, under the rules of evidence, an expert witness is simply a person "who ha[s] some specialized or unusual

---

[3]Throughout this chapter, we refer, when appropriate, to the *Federal Rules of Evidence* that embody a particular approach or illustrate a particular point in the discussion. Although binding only in the federal courts, the *Federal Rules of Evidence* have served as a model for the states since their adoption in 1975 (Allen & Kuhns, 1989, p. xvii). Indeed, many states' rules of evidence are now virtually indistinguishable from their federal counterparts.

training, experience, or ability that permits [him or her] to piece together or to interpret data in a manner that would not be readily apparent to the average layperson fact finder" (Allen & Kuhns, 1989, p. 734; see also *Federal Rules of Evidence* Rule 702). And as the questions that people litigate become ever more complex, the legal system's need to tap such extralegal expertise continues to grow. The legal professional, although an expert in law, cannot avoid the hundreds of fields of specialized knowledge that the contemporary trial calls into play without undermining the trial's viability as a method for resolving disputes. Nor can the legal professional navigate these fields of knowledge without the help of those who study and work in them on a daily basis. An increased resort to the assistance of expert witnesses is essentially unavoidable.

Despite the increasing prevalence of expert testimony in most varieties of civil and criminal litigation, a number of controversies continue to focus one's attention on its uses and abuses. The existence of the volume, of which this chapter is a part, says as much. As we demonstrate in the next section, these controversies persist because expert testimony cannot help but straddle a fault line concealed in the traditional model of the trial as a process of reasoned deliberation. In summary, concerns about rising costs, to both the parties and the system, push the legal system toward the practice of deferring to an expert's largely unexplained opinions—a practice fundamentally at odds with the notion that the fact finder should determine the outcome by reasoned deliberation. The decline in accuracy that may result from increased deference to expert opinions cannot easily be assessed, which is in itself cause for concern.

To help both forensic experts and the lawyers who work with them better understand the role the expert witness should play—namely that of an educator—we set that role in context, describing in the first part of this chapter some basic principles that shape the rules of evidence. These principles illustrate both the potential benefits of and the severe limitations on the usefulness of expert testimony. In the second part, we review some uses and abuses of expert testimony in the context of child sexual abuse prosecutions, underscoring the importance of the expert's educative function in a system that emphasizes reasoned deliberation. In the third part, we conclude with some specific suggestions for experts, from psychology or any other field, who hope to serve as witnesses in a manner that benefits both the legal system and their chosen profession.

TRIAL PRINCIPLES AND THE EXPERT'S ROLE

Consider the conventional jury trial, civil or criminal. Potential jurors are drawn from the community in which the court sits. Knowledge of the event at issue in the trial does not, as some might suspect, disqualify a person from serving on the jury; only knowledge that would qualify one as a lay witness in the case necessarily disqualifies one from jury service because a juror cannot testify as a witness in a case he or she helps to decide [*Federal Rules of Evidence* Rule 606(a)]. Instead, prospective jurors remain eligible if they are willing to set aside any specific knowledge they may have of the event at issue (e.g., from news broadcasts or other media outlets) and to decide the case on the basis of their reasonable judgments about the information provided by the parties. The critical feature to note about the jury is that it samples the common knowledge, experiences, and judgment of the community in which the court sits. In other words, the legal system, far from constituting the jury according to some "blank slate" model, relies on jurors to adjudicate a given dispute according to their vast collective resources of conventional knowledge and common modes of reasoning, to give flesh to the bones of evidence by reference to their own experiences.[4]

The general rules of evidence, as we have indicated, regulate the sorts of information that the parties can present to the fact finder at trial and, to a degree, the manner in which they can present it. These rules are enormously complex and require a large investment of time and energy to master. All the same, this maze of rules has developed according to a few core principles, the two most important of which are (a) authenticity, according to which all evidence must be shown to be what it purports to be,[5] and (b) completeness, according to which the introduction of a part of a piece of evidence entitles one's opponent to introduce as much of its remainder as is needed to give an accurate picture of the whole. These two principles help to anchor the presentation of evidence in the U.S. legal system's chosen method of fact finding, reasoned decision making. After reviewing these principles and some of the rules that illustrate them, we explore the expert's proper role at trial in greater detail.

Authenticity

The principle of authenticity animates a number of evidentiary rules; all of which are variations on a basic requirement that constrains the presentation of evidence from all three of the conventional domains—real (i.e., tangible items that played a role in the litigated event, such as a bloody glove found at the crime scene), demonstrative (i.e., tangible items that help the fact finder understand the litigated issue, such as a chart or

---

[4] In this important sense, any fact finder—whether jury, judge, or administrative adjudicator— is largely self-informing. The important differences among them are largely limited to the comparative breadth and depth of the information they bring to their respective tasks.
[5] The process of authenticating a piece of proffered evidence is typically referred to as "laying the foundation" (Allen & Kuhns, 1989, p. 170) for the evidence. We use the term *authenticity* rather than *foundation* because it better captures the broad scope of the principle.

map), and testimonial (i.e., witness statements). For example, if the prosecution in a drug trafficking trial wishes to introduce a sample of an illegal substance alleged to have been seized at the crime scene, the prosecution must introduce evidence sufficient to support the finding that the sample is, indeed, of an illegal substance seized at the crime scene [*Federal Rules of Evidence* Rule 901(a)]. Similarly, if a party wishes to use a photograph to prove the truth of something shown therein, such as an X-ray film offered to prove the location and severity of a bone fracture, he or she must introduce evidence sufficient to support the finding that the photograph is the original or account for the original's absence (Rule 1002). Finally, if a party wishes to introduce the testimony of a witness, he or she must introduce evidence sufficient to support the finding that the witness has first-hand knowledge of the matter about which he or she will testify (Rule 602). Of course, the evidence supporting the finding that one's testimony comes from first-hand knowledge may simply be part of the testimony itself (e.g., Q: "Were you there at the time?" A: "Yes." Q: "What did you see?" etc.). In all three instances, the basic requirement is the same: The proponent of the evidence must demonstrate that it is what it purports to be.

The principle of authenticity also animates the rhetoric of 19th- and early 20th-century cases to the effect that a lay witness could testify only about factual observations and could not offer opinions (McCormick, 1954, p. 19). Although expert witnesses are conventionally thought to be exempt from this restriction, the origin and current status of the rule merit some detailed analysis. The so-called rule against opinion testimony—formulated at a time when the word *opinion* primarily denoted speculation or conjecture—was a natural corollary to the principle of authenticity as expressed in the testimonial domain (i.e., the firsthand knowledge requirement; McCormick, 1954, pp. 19, 21–22). According to his review of 18th century cases, Wigmore (1978) concluded that

> the disparagement of "opinion" always had reference to the testimony of a person who had no "facts" of his observation to speak from, and the skilled witness [i.e., the expert] was the person who had to be received by way of exception to that notion. Thus, when an ordinary or lay witness took the stand, equipped with a personal acquaintance with the affair and therefore competent in his sources of knowledge, the circumstances that incidentally he drew inferences from his observed data and expressed conclusions from them did not present itself as in any way improper. It would not occur to any judge that this witness was doing a wrong thing. In short, it was only "opinion" as a mere guess or a belief without observation which he would reject; "opinion" as an inference or conclusion from personally observed data he did not think of disparaging. (p. 5)

During the early 19th century, however, this relatively narrow expression of the authenticity principle grew by "careless usage" (McCormick, 1954, pp. 21–22) to the broader rule against any testimony in the form of an opinion, where opinion denotes an inference, as distinct from the report of a sensory observation (see also Wigmore, 1978, p. 8).

Both judges and commentators have since come to recognize that the purported distinction between fact and opinion is, at best, evanescent. One need not ponder the question long to realize that every witness statement expresses a belief, correct or incorrect, about the existence of some state of affairs; this, of course, is the very essence of an opinion or inference. As a result of the legal system's recognition that the fact–opinion distinction is analytically untenable, the rule against opinion testimony has returned to its original scope. Under the contemporary rules of evidence, a lay witness can offer inferences that "are (a) rationally based on the perception of the witness and (b) helpful to a clear understanding of the witness' testimony or the determination of a fact in issue" (*Federal Rules of Evidence*, 1994, Rule 701). In other words, inferences are admissible when they derive from firsthand knowledge (i.e., when they are authentic and helpful to the fact finder).

One might well ask why the rule against opinion testimony should have survived in any form at all, given the apparent flaw in the distinction on which it is based. The answer, we think, lies in its continuing contribution to the legal system's goal of finding facts by a process of reasoned deliberation. As McCormick (1954) has described it, the rule that formerly excluded opinion testimony has now been reconstituted as a rule of preference regarding the form of testimony: "The more concrete description is preferred, to the more abstract" (p. 23). The legal system would, for example, prefer that a witness offer the testimony "He was driving on the left-hand side of the road" rather than the statement "He was driving carelessly." This preference is rooted in the conclusion that the latter form of the testimony provides less concrete information about the observed event, thereby frustrating reasoned deliberation by limiting the extent to which the fact finder can make independent judgments about what happened.

Rather than limit fact finders in this way, the legal system links the goal of permitting deliberations according to reasons to the principle of authenticity. This is done by pushing a witness to restrict his or her testimony to thinly varnished reports of firsthand observations, leaving out so far as is practicable the inferences that he or she believes the observations warrant (Allen & Miller, 1993, p. 1132; Ladd, 1952, pp. 415–417). In this way, the witness provides the fact finder with the external data that he or she needs to determine for him- or herself, according to reasoned judgment, whether those data warrant a particular conclusion. These independent determinations are precisely what the legal system wants fact finders to make. If witnesses were, by contrast, to testify to little more than their conclusions—rather than revealing the data that support them—the fact finder's only real choice would be to rely (or not rely) on a witness's conclusions according to a sort of global credibility judgment. Although one has no independent means for assessing whether facts found according to such a credibility-driven, deferential approach would be more or less accurate on the whole than those found by resorting to a system of reasoned deliberation, it is certain that such a deferential fact-finding process would be far less rational.

As we noted above, according to the conventional view of the rules of evidence, expert testimony is an exception to the rule against opinions that regulates the form of lay witness testimony. In other words, experts are permitted to offer their opinions regarding disputed issues about which they have no firsthand knowledge (*Federal Rules of Evidence* Rule 702), without first testifying as to the underlying facts or data on which these opinions are based (Rule 705). This conventional view and the tensions that it creates sit at the center of many of the ongoing controversies concerning the proper role of expert testimony (Allen & Miller, 1993). Before turning to our analysis of this situation, however, we discuss the second core evidentiary principle, completeness.

Completeness

According to the principle of completeness, the introduction of a part of a piece of evidence entitles one's opponent to introduce as much of its remainder as is needed to give the fact finder an accurate sense of the whole. This principle and the rules and practices that embody it spring from the recognition that accuracy is promoted by evaluating pieces of evidence in light of the available contextualizing information. For example, if a witness refreshes his or her memory of an event while testifying about it by referring to a written document, the opposing party is entitled to inspect the document and to ask the witness questions about it (*Federal Rules of Evidence* Rule 612). Similarly, if a party attempts to undermine the credibility of a witness by introducing extrinsic evidence of his or her prior inconsistent statements regarding the same subject matter, that witness is entitled to an opportunity either to explain the apparently inconsistent statement or to expressly deny having made it [Rule 613(b)]. The completeness principle also extends to permit the introduction of otherwise inadmissible evidence when a party must offer it to combat the opponent's introduction of, or attempt to introduce, inadmissible evidence—a rule known as the doctrine of curative admissibility (Allen & Kuhns, 1989, pp. 289–290).

The most powerful exemplar of the principle of completeness, however, is the practice of vigorous cross-examination, the questioning of a witness who has been called by one's opponent in the litigation. As McCormick (1954) has observed,

> the common law judges and lawyers for two centuries have regarded
> the opportunity for cross-examination as an essential safeguard of the

accuracy and completeness of testimony, and they have insisted that cross-examination is a right and not a mere privilege. (p. 40)

The legal system's estimation of the importance of cross-examination is perhaps most evident in the practices of administrative, as compared with judicial, tribunals. It is now well-settled law in the United States that administrative agency tribunals are not required to follow the rules of evidence that prevail in the courtroom absent an express statutory requirement that the agency do so (Schwartz, 1991, pp. 371–372). An administrative judge may thus admit and consider *any* evidence that (a) possesses probative value and (b) is commonly accepted by prudent people in the conduct of their personal affairs (p. 373). Courts have held, however, that administrative tribunals may not so relax their evidentiary rules as to conduct proceedings that disregard the fundamental elements of due process of law, as these are constitutionally protected aspects of an orderly determination of one's legal rights and liabilities (p. 375). Chief among these fundamental elements of due process is the opportunity to cross-examine the opponent's witnesses (*Goldberg v. Kelly*, 1970; *Greene v. McElroy*, 1959; Schwartz, 1991, p. 383). Thus, in much the same way that authenticity helps to promote accuracy by shaping the role of opinion testimony in the fact-finding process, completeness as embodied by cross-examination links the legal conceptions of fairness (i.e., due process) and accuracy.

Precisely what functions does cross-examination serve? The process of cross-examination promotes completeness, and thus accuracy and fairness, by allowing the opposing counsel to develop additional testimony regarding the physical, cognitive, and affective conditions under which the witness observed the events about which he or she has testified. This additional information helps the fact finder to assess more intelligently the strength and reliability of the testimony. The cross-examiner can also test the consistency between current and prior statements by the witness regarding the subject matter of the testimony, thereby developing additional evidence bearing on the witness's basic credibility. These functions of cross-examination become especially important in settings where the conventional view of expert testimony prevails and thus experts are permitted to offer testimony in the form of unexplained opinions without a previously developed factual basis. In such a situation, only by engaging in rigorous and detailed cross-examination will the party opposing the expert witness be able to uncover the bases for the opinion and thereby provide the fact finder with the sort of information that is needed to assess the persuasiveness of the expert's opinion on an independent basis.

The Educative Function of Expert Testimony

Anglo American courts have called on experts for direct assistance since at least the middle of the 14th century, at which time experts aided the courts by offering opinions on a given matter within their expertise without having experienced any of the relevant underlying events in controversy on a firsthand basis (Wigmore, 1978, p. 3). By the latter part of the 18th century, however, parties themselves began to proffer the opinions of experts to the fact finder along with the rest of their evidence. The tension between receiving opinions from experts and rejecting them from lay witnesses soon became clear (p. 4). As Learned Hand (1901) noted at the opening of this century, "no one will deny that the law should in some way effectively use expert knowledge wherever it will aid in settling disputes. The only question is as to how it can do so best" (p. 40). The tension created by the use of expert testimony continues down to the present day and only becomes more pronounced as the use of expert testimony becomes more common.

As we noted in our discussion of the principle of authenticity, a fundamental premise of the way fact finding is structured in the legal system, at least with respect to all things other than expert testimony, is that the parties must introduce evidence sufficient to allow the fact finder to reach a reasoned judgment about the facts at issue. Witnesses are pushed to report, so far as is practicable, firsthand observations, and all trial participants share enough common background knowledge and experience to communicate with one another effectively about most human affairs. Aided in his or her task by liberal rules of cross-examination, the fact finder mediates among the conflicting versions of the facts at issue by deliberating to judgment.

But what if a witness's testimony emerges from or can only be understood by reference to a set of experiences that the fact finder lacks? Or what if the connection between what the witness says and the full import of what he or she means is so arcane that the chances are virtually zero that the fact finder will understand what the spoken words are meant to convey? Whenever such a distance between common experience and the knowledge necessary for accurate adjudication existed, the common law system of trials perceived two choices that could be made: Either the necessary background information could be provided through additional testimony or the fact finder could defer to the judgments of others. The former option has virtually always been chosen. For example, if a witness does not speak English, a translator is provided; a statement's translation is itself subject to dispute until all the parties are satisfied that the meaning of the witness's statement has been communicated. Likewise, when the routine practices or conventions of a trade or business help to determine a fact at issue, the parties adduce evidence on the topic, so that the fact finder is put in a position to judge what the routine practices or conventions are. The dominant conception of the trial has, in short, been that the parties must tie the trial evidence to the background knowledge and experience of the typical community members who constitute the jury, so that these individuals are in a position to understand what the witnesses are saying and thus to decide the case by means of rational deliberation.

Rather obviously, expert testimony does not fit easily into the common law model of the ideal trial. Experts are usually experts by virtue of years of specialized training, and there may thus be formidable costs, both to the public that subsidizes the justice system and to the parties in suit, associated with educating the fact finder to the point where he or she can follow the reasoning of a given expert in the same way that he or she can follow the reasoning of a lay witness. Enormous pressures arise to defer to the expertise of experts as a means of keeping trials to a manageable length and expense but at the alternative cost of endorsing a method of decision making at odds with the essence of the common law mode of trial—the pursuit of factual accuracy through rational deliberation. The fact finder who is not put in a position to understand the reasoning of a witness can only accept or reject the witness's conclusions on global credibility grounds. But such a fact finder cannot rationally decide which of two or more competing experts to believe without having enough knowledge about the relevant fields to understand the experts' reasoning (Hand, 1901, pp. 54–55). The choice of which expert to credit is not made because the jury understands the reasoning and sees either its cogency or its flaws; it is made for some other reason.

However, expert testimony can be treated just like any other testimony—to be relevant, it must be understandable to the jury (Ladd, 1952, pp. 428–430). To make an expert's testimony understandable requires that the jury be educated about the subject of the expert's testimony. According to this model of the expert's role, the expert explains the general principles relevant to the case, the data relied on in reaching any conclusions, why those data were relied on, and the reasoning used to get from the data to the conclusion(s). All of these elements can be contested to the extent desired by the opposing party. The jury then sorts them out.

Thus, the choice is between deference and education, and it is a complicated one.[6] It is not clear which of the two approaches advances accuracy, although only testimony that seeks to educate the jury can advance rationality. Of course, if the only experts who testified at trials were disinterested in the outcome, truly dedicated to the truth, and sufficiently aware of the limitations of the knowledge generated by their fields of expertise, society might choose to advance accuracy, with no lament for the

---

[6]Deference and education are not analytically distinct methods. They are, instead, distant points on a spectrum. For example, jurors will virtually never see truly "raw" data at trial. Likewise, deference occurs to some extent whenever a jury decides that a witness has testified truthfully. Still, the extent of deference or of education is an important variable. This is particularly obvious when one considers a case involving not only the reporting of sensory experiences (e.g., "the light was red.") but also the drawing of inferences (e.g., "in light of these epidemiological studies, I am of the opinion that Bendectin does not cause birth defects").

loss of rationality. But expert witnesses become advocates often enough to make deference fertile ground for a thicket of abuses in which both rationality and accuracy are lost. Our view of the expert's proper role, focused on the educative function that all evidence should serve, thus offers a benefit far beyond theoretical consistency. As the following examples of expert testimony in cases affecting children show, the legal system enhances the rationality of the fact-finding process and thereby reduces the chances that advocacy will successfully masquerade as expert opinion by insisting that experts educate fact finders rather than provide them with unexplained opinions.

CHILD SEXUAL ABUSE ACCOMMODATION SYNDROME EVIDENCE

Criminal prosecutions for child sexual abuse are perhaps the quintessential example of the difficulties generated at the border of law and psychology, offering dread aplenty for the fact finder that must determine what really happened. Three unavoidable qualities of such prosecutions make the burden especially heavy. First, like other prosecutions that proceed to trial, they must be resolved on a body of evidence that was insufficient to force a plea bargain or alternatively a decision not to prosecute. Accordingly, neither a guilty verdict nor an acquittal would be manifestly irrational. Second, the consequences of a wrongful verdict, so unmistakably dire, magnify the uncertainties endemic to all methods of trying past facts. A wrongful acquittal leaves behind a child twice abused, first by an abuser and next by a trial that failed to redeem his or her courage in coming forward. A wrongful conviction snares an innocent defendant in a net of blame for one of the most odious of crimes. Finally, at the very time the fact finder most craves confidence in the rightness of his or her decision, clashing fragments of the conventional understanding of human affairs undermine the confidence the fact finder can have in any decision, thereby rendering all possible solutions less satisfying: "How could this little boy invent lies about such things? Yes, they must have happened" or "But how could his teacher, whom he trusted, have committed such monstrous acts? No, they cannot have happened."

One cannot be surprised that with the stakes of error so high and the traction of conventional explanations of human affairs so low, the parties to a child sexual abuse prosecution typically present the fact finder with expert testimony to move him or her toward the desired decision (Newman, 1994, p. 182). Such testimony ranges from expert medical testimony regarding the physical manifestations of abuse (or lack thereof) or the child's medical history to expert behavioral science testimony regarding the psychological manifestations of abuse. Although the former sort of testimony is, in the main, quite noncontroversial, the latter sort remains the subject of vigorous dispute in the courts and among commentators.

State v. Michaels (1993), the notorious prosecution for the alleged sexual abuse of children at the Wee Care Day Nursery in Maplewood, New Jersey, presented the state's intermediate appellate court with a dramatic example of the abuse of the opportunity to introduce expert testimony. The specific expert testimony at issue was purportedly based on a variation of the child sexual abuse accommodation syndrome (CSAAS; as documented by Summit, 1983).

In 1988, the prosecution proffered at the trial the testimony of Eileen Treacy, an expert in child psychology and the treatment of sexually abused children. Her testimony, admitted over the defense's objections, consisted of both background information and child-specific statements. She discussed, as a general matter, "the memory capability of young children, their developing sense of good and bad, their ability to distinguish reality from fantasy, and their sexual development patterns" (State v. Michaels, 1993, p. 498). Then, on the basis of her analysis of the pretrial interviews and trial testimony of each child as well as the behaviors attributed to the children by their relatives, Treacy testified that with respect to all the children involved but one, their testimony and conduct "were consistent with child sexual abuse" (p. 499). According to the court, "she defined consistent with as having a 'high degree of correlation,' 'over point six [.6]' in numerical terms of probability" (p. 501). At the close of the trial, the jury convicted Margaret Michaels of 115 counts of sexually abusing 19 children and of endangering the welfare of a 20th child, after which she was sentenced to a prison term of 47 years.

A three-judge appeals court panel overturned Michaels's conviction in 1993, 5 years into her sentence, on the basis of among other things the illicit manner in which Treacy's expert testimony had been used. The appellate court concluded that Treacy's "testimony constituted nothing less than substantive evidence of defendant's guilt, albeit Treacy's opinion thereof" (State v. Michaels, 1993, p. 501). Applying the New Jersey Supreme Court's decision in State v. J.Q. (1993), announced less than 3 months earlier, the court held that the admission and use of Treacy's testimony as substantive evidence of Michaels's guilt were enough, by themselves, to require that her convictions be overturned (State v. Michaels, 1993, p. 502).

In State v. J.Q. (1993), the New Jersey Supreme Court reversed a conviction of child sexual abuse on the ground that expert testimony purportedly based on CSAAS had been admitted and used to prove that sexual abuse had, in fact, occurred. After a careful discussion of Summit's (1983) work on CSAAS, the court held that an expert witness could "describe traits found in victims of such abuse to aid jurors in evaluating specific defenses" (State v. J.Q., 1993, p. 1197) but could not offer the opinion that abuse had, in fact, occurred. As the court observed, Summit's research had been conducted with a population of known victims of sexual abuse and tried to present "a common denominator of the most frequently observed victim behaviors" (Summit, 1983, p. 180). In other words, the syndrome does not diagnose or detect abuse on the basis of a set of observations but instead explains children's responses and behaviors in light of the abuse that is known to have occurred. The trial court erred in *State v. J.Q.* (1993), according to the New Jersey Supreme Court, because

> the CSAAS evidence was not presented to the jury in accordance with its scientific theory, *i.e.*, the evidence was not offered to explain the conflicting behavioral traits in this case either of accommodation or delayed disclosure. Rather, the evidence was presented to the jury as though it were to prove directly and substantially that sexual abuse had occurred. (p. 1207)

Only when offered to rebut an attempt to impeach the victim's testimony (e.g., "she recanted once already, so she ought not be to believed," "he would have spoken up sooner if such terrible things had actually happened") does CSAAS evidence remain anchored to the theory and data sample according to which it was developed.

Ironically, in recognition of the potential for abuse latent within expert testimony, Summit (1992) has himself recently made all this quite clear:

> The words *identification, detection, diagnosis, symptom, disorder, illness* and *pathology*, which might imply a diagnostic focus, do not appear in the paper, nor is there a promise of verifying the alleged abuse with such words as *test, validate, evaluate, confirm,* or *prove.* . . . The CSAAS is meaningless in court discussion unless there has been a disputed disclosure, and in that instance the ultimate issue of truth is the sole responsibility of the trier of fact. The CSAAS acknowledges that there is no clinical method available to distinguish "valid" claims from those that should be treated as fantasy or deception, and it gives no guidelines for discrimination. . . . The CSAAS is used appropriately in court testimony not to prove a child was molested but to rebut the myths which prejudice endorsement of delayed or inconsistent disclosure. (pp. 158, 160)

Similarly in *State v. Michaels* (1993), the prosecution's expert conceded that the theory on which she had based her testimony was "not designed for diagnostic purposes, but rather was to be used to create . . . a framework for understanding what a sexually abused child experiences" (p. 498).

The appellate court in *State v. Michaels* (1993) cast its discussion of the errors that had occurred with respect to Treacy's testimony in terms that parallel those developed by the New Jersey Supreme Court in *State v. J.Q.* (1993). According to the panel,

> child-abuse expert evidence is admissible only for the purpose of rehabilitation—explaining traits often found in children who had been abused. When such testimony is used, the expert would be expected to testify that that *specific* behavior of the victim, while appearing to be inconsistent, *may* in fact be consistent with sexual abuse. The expert should not be asked to give an opinion about whether a particular child was abused. Therefore, care should be taken to avoid giving the jury an impression that the expert believes based on CSAAS . . . [that] a particular child has been abused. (*State v. Michaels*, 1993, p. 499)

Because Treacy's testimony far surpassed a simple effort to explain apparently inconsistent behaviors among the alleged victims and "no amount of cross-examination could have undone the harm caused by [her] purported validations" (*Stave v. Michaels*, 1993, pp. 501–502), Michaels's conviction was necessarily invalid. The New Jersey Supreme Court denied the prosecution's petition for certification of this part of the intermediate appellate court's decision, leaving that court's opinion as the last word on this particular issue in the case (*State v. Michaels*, 1994, p. 1374).

Treacy's testimony and its relationship to Summit's (1983) findings powerfully illustrate the vulnerability that results from the law's need to tap extralegal expertise as well as the potential for abuse in a system that encourages deference to experts. We know, on reflection, that Treacy's testimony went beyond any position that Summit's findings would explicitly justify or support. Yet, if Treacy is the expert to whom we wish the fact finder to defer, we have no obvious reason to keep her inferences and opinions regarding the likelihood that abuse occurred from being admitted into evidence. Indeed, only when we assess Treacy's testimony by reference to the expert's role as an educator does the problem become clear: The trial judge ought not to have allowed Treacy's testimony because it had no rigorous scientific basis that was articulated to the fact finder (i.e., it had not been shown to be authentic). Her assertion that the testimony and conduct of the children bore a .60 correlation to child sexual abuse can easily mislead through its apparent conflation of innocent correlation with the genuine predictive power of a causal model, bolstering the causal implication of her statement that the children's testimony and conduct "were consistent with child sexual abuse" (*State v. Michaels*, 1993, p. 499).

As Newman (1994) wryly indicated,

> a claim that [the complainant child's] behavior is "consistent with" the sex abuse syndrome does not reveal causes for the behavior other than sex abuse that may exist. The symptom of headache is consistent with being hit over the head with a blunt instrument, but [blows by] blunt instruments do not cause most people's headaches. (p. 196)

Legal actors must be attuned to the use of such potentially misleading language and the unauthenticated assertions that may slip in under its cover.

Treacy's testimony regarding a .60 correlation also lacks, so far as we are aware, a basis in any controlled studies. She could just as easily have testified to a correlation of .99 or .01, with no more or less violence to the truth, precisely because the testimony was based on no hard data whatsoever. As Newman (1994) explains, "experts [on CSAAS] offering to provide the causation probabilities associated with the different causative possibilities are attempting to resolve the ultimate issue for the court and are going beyond what their science can support" (p. 196). Again, her testimony could not be authenticated in the manner the law requires. Insisting that Treacy thoroughly explain the basis of her statements, on the view that an expert is to be an educator, would probably have exposed the deficiencies in her testimony and should have resulted in its exclusion at Michaels's trial.

The decisions in *State v. Michaels* (1993) and *State v. J.Q.* (1993) regarding the proper uses of CSAAS evidence are quite consistent with an education-centered approach to the use of expert testimony. In both cases, the courts reversed a conviction obtained, at least in part, on evidence that was purportedly based on CSAAS but actually ranged well beyond the domain of assertions that CSAAS could support—statements grounded on the false premise that the syndrome had been developed to serve and actually functioned well as a diagnostic tool. By cutting their testimony loose from any theory that could link their conclusions to the data about which they testified, the experts made it impossible for a jury to do anything but defer to their opinions regarding the fact of abuse. By allowing the experts to do so, the trial courts in these two cases failed to act as gatekeepers against the influence of nonrational factors of decision. The appellate courts, by contrast, circumscribed the proper use of CSAAS testimony by insisting that the expert witness remain tethered to the data of the case by the theory on which he or she purported to rely (i.e., by asking what improved understanding of an impeached behavior of a specific child complainant [recanting etc.] could be achieved by resorting to the evidence about CSAAS). The experts could proceed only so far as a valid scientific connection to the pertinent inquiry could take them.

In these two decisions, the New Jersey courts have followed both the reasoning and the outcome of a large number of state court decisions on this issue. For example, in *State v. Myers* (1984), an early case in dealing with CSAAS issues, the Minnesota Supreme Court affirmed Myers's conviction on charges of criminal sexual conduct, obtained in part on the basis of the prosecution's expert testimony on CSAAS. According to the court,

> the nature ... of the sexual abuse of children places lay jurors at a
> disadvantage. Incest is prohibited in all or almost all cultures, and the

common experience of the jury may represent a less than adequate foundation for assessing the credibility of a young child who complains of sexual abuse. If the victim of a burglary failed to report the crime promptly, a jury would have good reason to doubt that person's credibility. A young child subjected to sexual abuse, however, may for some time be either unaware or uncertain of the criminality of the abuser's conduct. As Dr. Bell testified, uncertainty becomes confusion when an abuser who fulfills a caring–parenting role in the child's life tells the child that what seems wrong to the child is, in fact, all right. Because of the child's confusion, shame, guilt, and fear, disclosure of the abuse is often long delayed. When the child does complain of sexual abuse, the mother's reaction frequently is disbelief, and she fails to report the allegations to the authorities. By explaining the emotional antecedents of the victim's conduct and the peculiar impact of the crime on other members of the family, an expert can assist the jury in evaluating the credibility of the complainant. (*State v. Myers*, 1984, p. 610)

The state supreme courts are in great agreement on this point: Admit CSAAS expert testimony solely for the purpose of rehabilitating the credibility of a child complainant witness.[7] In all these instances, the courts have demonstrated the proper concern for guaranteeing that an expert assist, rather than supplant, the fact finder by helping him or her to understand the information the parties have presented.

SOME SUGGESTIONS FOR THE EXPERT WITNESS

Expert witnesses are, like lawyers, hired hands by definition. The parties' lawyers, not their witnesses, control the development and presentation of their respective cases. For this reason, the most important aspect of dealing with specialized evidence—namely, the lawyer's solid working grasp of the general principles to which necessary expert testimony relates—remains out of the expert witness's control. Nevertheless, a professional who has been retained by a lawyer to serve as a potential expert witness can offer valuable assistance and exert important kinds of leverage at a variety of points in the process, thereby crafting the most beneficial contribution to the legal system possible while acting consistently within his or her particular professional ethical duties. To help bring about more satisfying interactions of legal and extralegal expertise, we offer a small number of suggestions to the would-be expert witness.

First, think of educating as the primary activity—educating your client (i.e., the lawyer who has retained you), the fact finder, and yourself

---

[7]See, for example, *State v. Lindsey* (1986), *Wheat v. State* (1987), *State v. Hester* (1988), *State v. Myers* (1986), *State v. Foret* (1993), *State v. Black* (1986), *Duckett v. State* (1990), and *State v. Catsam* (1987).

about the best way to serve an educative function. Of course, lawyers like other professionals develop areas of specialty, so you may not need to educate your client all that much about the particular substantive area at issue in a case; substantive review might be limited to the latest developments in the field. Your lawyer–client will always need, however, to learn some matters that only you can teach. The potential benefits and limitations of your testimony may turn, to a degree, on your theoretical orientation and professional choices and commitments. Are you, for example, a Freudian analyst or a behavior modification therapist? Because such considerations are probably more important for, say, social workers than structural engineers, personal judgment is called for; one should probably err on the side of being overinformative. Equally important, provide your lawyer–client with a realistic assessment of the investment of time, energy, and money that will be necessary to make your services productive. This sort of upfront communication about the features that distinguish you from other potential experts, and that a lawyer may not know enough to ask about, will help to prevent conflicts down the road.

Second, having educated your lawyer–client on the preliminaries, cooperate with him or her to create a plan for the presentation of your testimony on direct examination that will effectively link it to the experience and knowledge base of the average fact finder at as many points as possible. This is, admittedly, a tall order, but both the legal system and your profession are better served by interactions that promote rational decision making. In addition, an education-focused presentation style is almost always better trial strategy because the fact finder will usually be more persuaded by knowledge that they have internalized, through connections to preexisting concepts.

Third, help your client to cross-examine the opponent's expert witnesses—yes, there will almost always be at least one—as effectively and productively as possible. The emphasis here should be on exposing the ways in which the opposing expert's opinions cannot be grounded in reliable data or methodologies (i.e., by using the leverage provided by the principle of completeness to probe the authenticity of the opposing expert's testimony). Because the lawyer you are working for may be far less equipped than you are to spot the nuances of the opposing expert's departures from solid scientific ground, this function is critically important.

On a related point, you should also prepare yourself, with your lawyer–client's help, for your inevitable cross-examination at the hands of the opposing counsel. If the opposing counsel has made good use of his or her expert witness(es), the focus of the cross-examination will be on exposing the ways in which your opinions cannot be grounded in reliable data or methodologies. The opposing counsel may also pursue one or more other standard line of questioning used with expert witnesses, such as the fees you received for testifying, your prior or continuing employment as an expert witness, your credentials, the adequacy of your clinical examination (if such was undertaken), and your knowledge of the learned treatises in your field of expertise. Whatever approach the opposing side opts for, rehearsal of the cross-examination process will help both to reduce the stress of the experience and to identify the weak links in your direct examination presentation.

Finally, know your own limits. For example, resist the natural temptation to broaden your testimony into the fringes of your expertise and beyond in an effort to be helpful. The only way to provide help that also preserves the rationality of the fact-finding process is to limit your testimony to matters you can thoroughly ground. Similarly, know at the outset, to the maximum degree possible, the matters to which you cannot or will not testify. If a lawyer discourages your efforts to make an educative contribution with your testimony, strongly consider walking away.

REFERENCES

Allen, R. J., & Kuhns, R. B. (1989). *An analytical approach to evidence: Text, problems, and cases.* Boston: Little, Brown.

Allen, R. J., & Miller, J. S. (1993). The common law theory of experts: Deference or education? *Northwestern University Law Review, 87,* 1131–1147.

Duckett v. State, 797 S.W.2d 906 (Tex. Crim. App. 1990) (in banc).

Federal rules of evidence, 28 U.S.C. (1994).

Goldberg v. Kelly, 397 U.S. 254 (1970).

Greene v. McElroy, 360 U.S. 474 (1959).

Hand, L. (1901). Historical and practical considerations regarding expert testimony. *Harvard Law Review, 15,* 40–58.

Ladd, M. (1952). Expert testimony. *Vanderbilt Law Review, 5,* 414–431.

McCormick, C. T. (1954). *Handbook of the law of evidence.* St. Paul, MN: West.

Newman, S. A. (1994). Assessing the quality of expert testimony in cases involving children. *Journal of Psychiatry & Law, 22,* 181–234.

Schwartz, B. (1991). *Administrative law* (3rd ed.). Boston: Little, Brown.

State v. Black, 537 A.2d 1154 (Me. 1986).

State v. Catsam, 534 A.2d 184 (Vt. 1987).

State v. Foret, 628 So.2d 116 (La. 1993).

State v. Hester, 760 P.2d 27 (Id. 1988).

State v. J. Q., 617 A.2d 1196 (N.J. 1993).

State v. Lindsey, 720 P.2d 73 (Ariz. 1986).

State v. Michaels, 625 A.2d 489 (N.J. Superior Ct. App. Div. 1993).

State v. Michaels, 642 A.2d 1372 (N.J. 1994).

State v. Myers, 359 N.W.2d 604 (Minn. 1984).

State v. Myers, 382 N.W.2d 91 (Iowa 1986).

Summit, R. (1983). The child sexual abuse accommodation syndrome. *Child Abuse & Neglect, 7,* 177–192.

Summit, R. (1992). Abuse of the child sexual abuse accommodation syndrome. *Journal of Child Sexual Abuse, 1,* 153–161.

Wheat v. State, 527 A.2d 269 (Del. 1987).

Wigmore, J. H. (1978). *Evidence in trials at common law* (Vol. 7, Chadbourn rev.). Boston: Little, Brown.

III

EVIDENCE IN TESTIMONY

8

HOW VALID ARE CHILD SEXUAL ABUSE VALIDATIONS?

CELIA B. FISHER AND KATHERINE A. WHITING

In 1984, Ben Bussey was found guilty of child sexual abuse following eyewitness testimony to the alleged offense. At trial, a psychiatrist testifying for the prosecution explained to the Kentucky court that the alleged child victim exhibited symptoms of the child sexual abuse accommodation syndrome (CSAAS; Summit, 1983). The Supreme Court of Kentucky reversed the conviction on the grounds that the lower court had erred by allowing the expert testimony into evidence because CSAAS was not a medically accepted scientific concept (*Bussey, Jr. v. Commonwealth*, 1985). This case marked the first in a series of child sexual abuse convictions overturned by the Supreme Court of Kentucky on the basis of the failure of CSAAS expert testimony to meet the legal–scientific standards of *People v. Kelley* (1976) and *Frye v. United States* (1923; see also Stewart & Young, 1992).[1]

---

[1]The cases of *Kelley* and *Frye* represent findings that expert opinion based on a scientific technique is inadmissible unless the technique is "generally accepted" as reliable in the relevant scientific community. This criteria does not necessarily apply for expert testimony that does not claim to be an application of scientific techniques (Elias, 1992). In a more recent case, the U.S. Supreme Court ruled that the Frye test, and by definition the "general acceptance" criteria, is superseded by adoption of the *Federal Rules of Evidence* (*Daubert v. Merrell Dow Pharmaceuticals, Inc.*, 1993). According to the opinion of the court, delivered by

A 3-year-old boy told his maternal grandmother, mother, and maternal aunt that during court-ordered visits with his divorced father "Daddy pulled my petey" (for a detailed description of this case, see Brooks & Milchman, 1991). The mother contacted the state social work agency, and the validity of the boy's allegations was subsequently evaluated by a number of mental health professionals, including a social worker, a psychologist, and a psychiatrist. The professionals used a variety of assessment techniques, including individual and conjoint sessions with the boy and other family members, play therapy, and anatomically detailed drawings. One professional was unable to reach any conclusions regarding the alleged abuse. A second found the child to be a victim of oral–genital contact and masturbation. A third found the child to be a victim of another's delusion and recommended that the child be protected from the mother's belief that he had been sexually abused. A fourth testified that the father could not have victimized his son because he did not have the profile of a pedophile. The judge ruled that whereas custody should remain with the mother, the father could continue to have unsupervised visits. The case continued to be litigated in family court over a period of several years, as the child continued to allege that he was being abused by his father.

In 1988, Kelly Michaels was accused of sexually abusing 20 New Jersey nursery schoolchildren under her care. A psychological expert, hired by the prosecution, testified that the behaviors of the alleged victims were consistent with child sexual abuse. A substantial portion of the expert's testimony was based on child interviews and parental responses to a 32-item checklist describing the children's behaviors. Among the psychological evidence presented as supporting the charge of sexual abuse was the presence of at least four of the five phases of the child sexual abuse syndrome (CSAS; Sgroi, 1982) and the relative absence of confounding variables (other than abuse), which could have produced the CSAS symptomatology. Michaels was convicted of 115 counts of sexual offenses and imprisoned. Five years later, the conviction was successfully appealed. The New Jersey Court of Appeals ruled that the data on which the expert psychological testimony was based were unreliable, invalid, and probative of sexual abuse and could not be used as evidence of guilt (*State v. Margaret Kelly Michaels*, 1993/1994).

These cases illustrate the professional and ethical challenges facing psychologists when they draw on currently available theory and assessment techniques to validate allegations of child sexual abuse for forensic pur-

---

Justice Blackmun, "under the Rules the trial judge must ensure that any and all scientific testimony or evidence admitted is not only relevant, but reliable" (*Daubert*, 1993, p. 9). Blackmun defined the term *scientific* to imply a grounding in the methods and procedures of science and the term *knowledge* to connote more than subjective belief or unsupported speculation.

poses. In recent years, psychologists have been called on to assist the courts in drawing conclusions about the probability that an alleged child victim has been sexually abused. This has necessitated a shift in focus from clinical interviews primarily designed to provide a foundation for appropriate treatment plans, to investigatory interviews designed to substantiate whether a child has been abused (Sink, 1988; White & Edelstein, 1991). In contrast to interviews conducted to determine appropriate therapeutic procedures for identified victims of abuse, data collected for judicial evidentiary purposes must rigorously avoid interview bias (e.g., a priori assumptions that the abuse occurred) and contamination of the child's recollections (Fisher, 1995; Haugaard & Reppucci, 1988; White & Edelstein, 1991). This is often difficult because in many situations a complaint has already been filed and the child has been questioned by one or several other investigators prior to seeing the psychologist (McGovern, 1991).

Most interview protocols and assessment instruments currently available for evaluating child sexual abuse do not meet basic standards for test construction and evaluation as required by the *Standards for Educational and Psychological Testing* (1985). For example, commonly used interview formats and behavioral checklists, intended to document the presence or absence of abuse, have not been subjected to tests of validity designed to demonstrate the degree to which the assessments elicit appropriate, meaningful, and useful data in determining whether abuse has occurred. Similarly, there is a paucity of reliability tests indicating the degree to which the data derived from sexual abuse assessment strategies are free from errors of measurement, including interviewer bias and stability of individual characteristics under consideration (Conte, 1992; Conte, Sorenson, Fogarty, & Rosa, 1991; Fisher, 1995; White & Edelstein, 1991).

According to the American Psychological Association's (APA; 1992) Ethical Principles of Psychologists and Code of Conduct, "psychologists' forensic assessments, recommendations, and reports are based on information and techniques (including personal interviews of the individual, when appropriate) sufficient to provide appropriate substantiation for their findings" [Standard 7.02(a), p. 1610]. It is the premise of this chapter that many psychologists who engage in forensically relevant child sexual abuse assessments are at risk of violating this standard because of the current lack of psychometrically valid and reliable instruments and techniques used to determine if child sexual abuse occurred. The primary focus of this chapter is to contribute to the ongoing efforts of mental health and legal practitioners to meet forensic and ethical demands for valid sexual abuse assessment by providing an overview and critique of instruments and techniques currently applied to the validation of child sexual abuse. We begin with the problem of accepting a singular definition of child sexual abuse.

DEFINING CHILD SEXUAL ABUSE

One reason for the lack of techniques and instrumentation directly applicable to child sexual abuse assessment is the multifaceted nature of sexual abuse (Ammerman, Cassisi, & Hersen, 1986; Clarke & Hornick, 1988; O'Donohue & Elliott, 1991). First, the definition of sexual abuse includes a broad range of behaviors, including exhibitionism, kissing, fondling, digital penetration, intercourse, oral or anal sex, and insertion of objects into the sex organs. Second, these acts can be perpetrated across a broad range of intrafamilial and extrafamilial relationships, including family members (fathers, mothers, siblings, aunts, uncles, cousins), familiar adults (e.g., mother's boyfriend, clergy, neighbor, teacher), and strangers. Third, across these different abusive behaviors and relationships, there is considerable variability in the duration (e.g., months, years) and frequency (e.g., once, weekly) that a child may be victimized.

Under the best of circumstances, such variability in the behavioral, relational, and temporal aspects of child sexual abuse would make it difficult to apply a single assessment standard to the evaluation of alleged victims. The problem is further compounded by the fact that the psychological and behavioral sequelae of abuse are also influenced by the victim's gender and level of cognitive and social development, the reaction of family members to knowledge of the abuse, and the culture or society view of sexual victimization (National Research Council, 1993; Zuravin, 1991). Moreover, children's reactions to sexual abuse are heterogeneous (O'Donohue & Elliott, 1991; Robin, 1991). Whereas some reactions may occur more frequently than others, sexually abused children exhibit a wide spectrum of behavioral and emotional reactions, including asymptomatic reactions (Kendall-Tackett, Williams, & Finkelhor, 1993).

In many cases, sexually abused children are observed to be less symptomatic than or indistinguishable from nonabused clinical child populations and nonreferred populations (Friedrich, Beilke, & Urquiza, 1988a, 1988b; Friedrich et al., 1992; Kendall-Tackett et al., 1993; White, Halpin, Strom, & Santilli, 1988). Consequently, no single constellation of psychological symptoms or behavioral indicators can be applied to validate that child sexual abuse has occurred. Unfortunately, many of the validation techniques currently in use are based on the erroneous single standard assumption. In the sections that follow, we identify and report on the empirical validity of assessment techniques frequently used by psychologists who engage in child sexual abuse validations.

THEORETICAL MODELS APPLIED TO THE VALIDATION OF CHILD SEXUAL ABUSE

Several well-known theoretical models have been used by psychologists who testify in courts to support the use of specific behaviors as evidence that a child has been sexually abused. Prominent among these are the CSAS (Sgroi, 1982), the CSAAS (Summit, 1983), posttraumatic stress disorder (PTSD; Walker, 1990), and the traumagenic dynamics model (Finkelhor & Browne, 1985). These symptom-based models have been traditionally developed from observations of practitioners working therapeutically with children who have experienced documented or suspected child abuse. Although they provide clinically rich material for identifying and treating behavioral and emotional sequelae of abuse, such observations have not been subjected to the more rigorous tests of objectivity required to apply them as a means of assessing whether sexual abuse actually occurred (Fisher, 1995).

Unfortunately, some mental health professionals serving the courts as sexual abuse validators have incorporated these symptoms into behavioral checklists designed to substantiate the presence of clusters of behavioral indicators of child sexual abuse. These checklists are often idiosyncratic to specific groups of sexual abuse validators (Benedek & Schetky, 1987; Fisher, 1995; Robin, 1991) and have not been constructed according to current standards of psychological testing (e.g., *Standards*, 1985). For example, in a *PsycLIT* computer search on articles and chapters published between 1984 and 1994, we found no reports of empirical studies testing the validity of checklists based on these theoretical models. Thus, the application of these theoretical models in the form of either direct interview or parental checklists for the purposes of providing forensic evidence that a child has been sexually abused may violate APA ethical standards designed to foster the construction and use of psychometrically valid and reliable assessment techniques [APA, 1992, Standards 2.03, 2.04(a), and 7.02; Fisher, 1995].

THE CHILD SEXUAL ABUSE SYNDROME AND THE CHILD SEXUAL ABUSE ACCOMMODATION SYNDROME

The seminal works of Sgroi (1982) and Summit (1983) on behaviors associated with child sexual abuse provide practical approaches to the heartrending and complex challenges of working therapeutically with sexually abused children. The CSAS conceptualizes child sexual abuse as a situation in which an adult with authority and power coerces a child who is lacking in emotional, maturational, and cognitive development into sexual compliance. The syndrome consists of 20 behavioral indicators of child sexual abuse, which arise in response to a spectrum of sexually abusive behaviors (e.g., exhibitionism, penile penetration) and "predictable" patterns of sexual encounters between adults and children (an engagement phase, sexual interaction phase, secrecy phase, disclosure phase, and suppression phase).

The original CSAAS was composed of five categories: (1) secrecy;

(2) helplessness; (3) entrapment and accommodation; (4) delayed, conflicted, and unconvincing disclosures; and (5) retraction (Summit, 1983). The syndrome was intended to highlight the tendency of the adult world to ignore evidence of child sexual abuse and the accommodating efforts of the child not to complain (Summit, 1983, 1992).

In developing their theories, both practitioners drew on their extensive clinical experiences with children to relay their observations regarding the behavioral and psychological sequelae of sexual abuse to "individuals clamoring for expert advice" (Sgroi, 1982, p. 6). Both wrote sensitively about the fact that a tendency for many child victims not to initially disclose abuse or to recant once a disclosure was made tended to discredit the reliability of their testimony in court (Sgroi, 1982; Summit, 1983, 1992). Neither practitioner claimed that their observations and recommendations should be taken as the final word on the investigation or validation of child sexual abuse, and both cautioned that there are no definitive answers.

The practitioner who seeks to be in compliance with current APA ethical requirements for the construction and use of assessment techniques (e.g., Standards 2.02 Competence and Appropriate Use of Assessment and Interventions and 2.03 Test Construction; APA, 1992) should be aware that neither Sgroi (1982) nor Summit (1983, 1992) provided scientific evidence for the validity or reliability of child abuse assessment protocols based on their syndromes. Unfortunately, a small cadre of practitioners testifying in child abuse cases have applied the CSAS and CSAAS models to the construction of idiosyncratic, psychometrically unsound behavioral checklists to identify clusters of behaviors said to demonstrate that child sexual abuse has occurred (Fisher, 1995). These practitioners have exploited such clinical concepts as "ammunition for battles in court" in collusion with false claims advanced by prosecutors and attempts by defense to "strip" the concepts of "any worth or relevance" (Summit, 1992, p. 153).

Approximately 10 years after his seminal writings and in response to what he saw as the "abuse" of the CSAAS by prosecution and defense experts, Summit (1992) more clearly outlined his views on the forensic limitations and values of syndrome evidence. In this article, he strongly asserted that CSAAS does not address an illness or disorder; that it is a clinical opinion, not a scientific instrument; and that "the cause-and-effect relationship among the factors themselves and with the possible problem is generally obscure" (Summit, 1992, p. 157). He also warned that using "syndrome evidence" for diagnostic testimony does not meet the criteria for scientific reliability required by *Kelley–Frye*. According to Summit (1992), "the CSAAS is used appropriately in court testimony, not to prove a child was molested but to rebut the myths which prejudice endorsement of delayed or inconsistent disclosure" (p. 160).

Summit's (1992) more recent description of the role of CSAAS testimony in court is consistent with findings in several recent legal cases (e.g., New Jersey's *State v. Michaels*, 1993/1994; and Indiana's *Stewart v. State*, 1988; see also Reichard, 1992). The decisions in these cases allowed CSAS or CSAAS expert testimony to be admitted to inform the fact finders that inconsistent accounts and recantations of allegations are not necessarily indicative of deceit in children. The courts also ruled that such testimony must be limited to a discussion of victims as a class, not extended to the evaluation of a particular child witness.

Posttraumatic Stress Disorder

The flawed tendency to apply syndrome evidence to prove child sexual abuse extends to the use of PTSD symptoms as diagnostic criteria for the validation of sexual abuse. According to the *Diagnostic and Statistical Manual of Mental Disorders* (4th ed. [DSM-IV]; American Psychiatric Association, 1994), a diagnosis of PTSD represents a group of behavioral indicators designed to help clinicians better understand the dynamics of an adult's or child's response to an uncommon traumatic event. Diagnostic criteria for PTSD include (a) a direct or indirect exposure to a traumatic event, (b) persistent reexperiencing of the event, (c) persistent avoidance of stimuli associated with the trauma; (d) persistent symptoms of arousal not present before the trauma, (e) symptom duration of more than 1 month, and (f) clinically significant stress or impairment (American Psychiatric Association, 1994).

Certain patterns of PTSD symptoms have been viewed as consistent with a child's reaction to sexual abuse: (a) reexperiencing of the stressful event through repetitive play, frightening dreams, or a reenactment (i.e., inappropriate sexual behaviors); (b) an avoidance of any object or person who is related to the trauma, including concentration difficulties, an unwillingness to discuss the abuse, or both; and (c) an increase in arousal, including difficulty falling asleep, anger, aggression, distractibility, or a combination of the above (McLeer, Deblinger, Atkins, Foa, & Ralphe, 1988; Walker, 1990). According to McLeer et al., a diagnosis of sexual-abuse-related PTSD must meet the following criteria: The child needs to demonstrate at least one symptom in the reexperiencing of the stressful event category, three or more symptoms in the avoidant behavior category, and at least two symptoms in the autonomic hyperarousal category.

The validity evidence for the relationship between these symptoms and child sexual abuse is at best weak. For example, McLeer et al. (1988) found that in a sample of 31 clinic-referred sexually abused children, only 48% met these criteria. Along similar lines, Kiser et al. (1988) found that a little more than half (55%) of a group of children who had been physically abused, sexually abused, or both exhibited PTSD symptoms whereas others exhibited anxiety, depression, externalizing behaviors, and behavioral problems. Moreover, in a recent study, no significant group differences emerged when a PTSD symptom checklist was used to compare sexually abused psychiatric patients with physically abused and nonabused patients (Deblinger, McLeer, Atkins, Ralphe, & Foa, 1989).

The absence of a consistent pattern of PTSD disorders in sexually abused children underscores the ethical and forensic problems associated with using it as a diagnostic category to substantiate that a child has been sexually abused. It should be noted, however, that whereas the PTSD model lacks validity for substantiating whether sexual abuse has occurred, it has been used as a basis for psychometrically valid instruments designed to assess the impact and therapeutic implications of known cases of sexual abuse (V. V. Wolfe & Gentile, 1992; V. V. Wolfe, Gentile, Michienzi, & Wolfe, 1991).

Psychologists applying the PTSD diagnosis as validation of child sexual abuse fail to recognize the tautological nature of this position (Fisher, 1995). According to *DSM-IV* (American Psychiatric Association, 1994), the essential feature of PTSD is "the development of characteristic symptoms *following exposure*, to an extreme traumatic stress" (italics added, p. 424). Thus, the validity of the PTSD diagnosis depends on first establishing that the child has been a victim of an uncommon trauma. Accordingly, to meet ethical and forensic demands for scientifically based evidence of child sexual abuse, a PTSD diagnosis cannot be established in the absence of independent documentation that sexual abuse has occurred.

In some cases, PTSD-like behaviors may be a consequence of the stressful nature of repeated interrogations by investigators, parents, therapists, or some combination of these people who attempted to substantiate whether sexual abuse had occurred (Fisher, 1995; Gardner, 1994). For example, in some instances, overenthusiastic social workers, police investigators, or psychologists may attempt to elicit from a child information regarding suspected abuse by describing lurid accusations made by others about the accused (see Bruck, Ceci, & Rosenthal, 1995). According to *DSM-IV*, learning about serious harm experienced by family or close friends may also trigger PTSD symptoms. Gardner suggested that court-appointed evaluators of child sexual abuse should attend to the temporal framework of PTSD symptoms, thereby distinguishing between abuse-related PTSD symptoms due to a sexual abuse trauma (usually present, to varying degrees, during and immediately following the discontinuation of the abuse) and investigatory-related PTSD that does not appear until after the disclosure and interrogation. Other investigatory-related PTSD-like symptoms, such as repetitive play in a therapist's office, may be a product of the repetitive nature of the therapy sessions rather than a pathological acting out of a traumatic event (Fisher, 1995).

In addition to the practical limitations of applying the PTSD model to the validation of child sexual abuse discussed above, Finkelhor (1987) has raised some conceptual limitations. First, the PTSD theoretical model emphasizes symptoms that are not typically found in sexual abuse research. For example, PTSD diagnoses tend to focus on imagery, nightmares, and a lack of affect and social relations, whereas sexual abuse researchers have observed fear, sexual problems, low self-esteem, emotional upset, and self-blame (Conte & Schuerman, 1987; Finkelhor, 1987). Second, the PTSD model offers a list of symptoms but does not explain how these symptoms are developed or what their source is (Finkelhor, 1987). The PTSD model provides little guidance concerning what a psychologist should expect to see, for example, from a child who has been abused over a period of years by his or her father in contrast to a child that was victimized once by a neighbor. Third, the PTSD diagnosis was developed from observations of individuals who had a sudden and dangerous experience, whereas much sexual victimization occurs through "manipulation of the child's affections and misrepresentation of social standards" (Kendall-Tackett et al., 1993, p. 174). Finkelhor has attempted to address some of these issues by proposing a conceptualization of the impact of sexual abuse on children's cognitive and emotional orientations.

The Traumagenic Dynamics Model

The traumagenic dynamics model was developed to help clinicians and researchers conceptualize how sexual abuse can affect a child's cognitive and affective capacities (Finkelhor & Browne, 1985). Whereas some mental health practitioners conducting forensic evaluations have drawn on this model to provide "syndrome evidence" of abuse, throughout his writings Finkelhor (1987) has made clear his position that the impact of sexual abuse trauma is too complex to enable a singular diagnosis that could meet forensic demands.

The traumagenic dynamics model consists of four trauma-causing factors that can distort a child's self-concept, worldview, and emotional orientation. The first, traumatic sexualization, represents how a child's sexual behaviors, feelings, and attitudes are shaped in developmentally inappropriate ways. Behaviors that may be associated with this trauma are sexual preoccupation, sex play, excessive masturbation, and exploitation of younger children. The second, betrayal, emphasizes hostility, anger, and distrust as potential reactions to the child's realization that someone they were vitally dependent on caused them harm. The third trauma, powerlessness, focuses on the dynamic consequences of having one's will continuously contravened and can be behaviorally manifested through fear and anxiety, impaired coping skills, or the need for control or dominance. The fourth trauma, stigmatization, is characterized by self-destructive behaviors reflecting the child's sense of negative self-worth (Finkelhor, 1987; Finkelhor & Browne, 1985).

Finkelhor and his colleagues (Finkelhor, 1987; Finkelhor & Browne, 1985; Kendall-Tackett et al., 1993) have repeatedly emphasized the absence of any specific syndrome or single traumatizing process in children who have been sexually abused. In a recent review of 45 empirical studies, Kendall-Tackett et al. noted the variability of symptoms across age, gender, relationship to the perpetrator, duration, and type of molestation. The review also indicates that whereas general PTSD symptoms, fears, behavior problems, low self-esteem, and sexualized behaviors were most frequently associated with sexual victimization no one symptom characterized a majority of sexually abused children. The authors concluded that the diversity of symptoms, the possibility of multiple symptom patterns, and the absence of symptoms in approximately one third of victimized children indicate that practitioners cannot rely on the presence or absence of symptom patterns to validate sexual abuse.

TRAUMATIC SEXUALIZATION

As described by Finkelhor and Browne (1985), sexual victimization can result in developmentally inappropriate and dysfunctional sexual feelings, attitudes, and behaviors. This process of traumatic sexualization can result in confusion about sexual self-concepts, unusual emotional responses to sexual activities, or age-inappropriate sexual behaviors. Within the framework of the traumagenic dynamic model, the extent and quality of traumatic sexualization vary as a consequence of the child's understanding of the sexual implications of the abusive activities, the sexual values transmitted by the abuser, and the seductive versus forceful nature of the abuse. Drawing on this theoretical model, some mental health professionals who engage in child sexual abuse validation have used checklists of sexual behaviors, anatomically detailed drawing, and sexualized doll play as evidence of victimization. However, as with other forms of symptom evidence, at present there is no empirical evidence that such behaviors can serve as evidence that a child has been sexually abused.

Sexualized Behavior

Sexualized behaviors most often observed to be related to child sexual abuse include putting objects into the anus or vagina, excessive or public masturbation, seductive behavior, initiation of intercourse or sexual stimulation with adults or peers, and age-inappropriate sexual knowledge

(Beitchman, Zucker, Hood, daCosta, & Ackman, 1991; Deblinger et al., 1987; Friedrich et al., 1992; Gale, Thompson, Moran, & Sack, 1988; Goldston, Turnquist, & Knutson, 1989; Kendall-Tackett et al., 1993; Kolko, Moser, & Weldy, 1988). The most extensive research on normative and clinical patterns of child sexual behavior has been conducted by Friedrich and his colleagues at the Mayo Clinic (Friedrich et al., 1988a, 1988b; Friedrich, Grambsch, Broughton, Kuiper, & Beilke, 1991; Friedrich et al., 1992). Across a range of well-controlled studies, Friedrich and his colleagues have demonstrated that sexually abused children exhibit more sexual behavior problems than either nonabused clinical samples or nonreferred children.

To measure more comprehensively and objectively children's sexual behavior, Friedrich and his colleagues developed the Child Sexual Behavior Inventory (CSBI; Friedrich et al., 1991, 1992), a 35-item parent-report measure designed to assess the frequency of specific behaviors during the past 6 months. Sexual behaviors assessed on the CSBI include items related to self-stimulation, sexual aggression, gender-role behavior, and personal boundary violations (Friedrich et al., 1991, 1992). In a recent study, a comparison of CSBI responses of 276 children ages 2 to 12 with a confirmed history of sexual abuse and 880 same-age children screened for the absence of such history demonstrated a significantly greater frequency in the abused sample for 27 out of the 35 items (Friedrich et al., 1992). Among the 8 nondiscriminating behaviors were cross-gender-related behaviors, kissing nonfamily members, undressing in front of others, and scratching or exposing one's crotch. Among the most discriminating items were those behaviors related to the initiation of sexual activities with individuals or objects. Among the least discriminating behaviors were an interest in the opposite sex and touching or stimulating one's sex parts in the home.

The CSBI has been found to be reliable with respect to both interitem and test–retest measures. Support for the validity of the instrument as a method of discriminating between groups of sexually abused and nonabused children is evidenced by significant differences among most items, higher scores for the sexually abused sample on the CSBI total score, and the relationship of scores to specific features of sexual abuse, including severity, force, and number of perpetrators (Friedrich et al., 1992). Whereas the CSBI has reasonable sensitivity for distinguishing among groups of sexually abused and nonabused children, Friedrich et al. questioned the utility of the instrument as proof that a specific child has been abused and recommended that it not be relied on in isolation as the primary indicator of sexual abuse. White et al. (1988) has recommended similar restraint with respect to using specific items to diagnose sexual abuse.

We share Friedrich and his colleagues' (1991, 1992) caution in supporting the utility of the CSBI for decisions regarding individual cases.

First, each differentiating behavior on the CSBI was exhibited by at least one nonabused child and never more than 42% of the abused sample. Second, the instrument is not as sensitive in discriminating between abused and nonabused samples of girls 7–12 years of age (Friedrich et al., 1992)— a pattern also reported for 2- to 6-year-old girls by White et al. (1988). This should be a point of some concern because girls are more likely than boys to be the victims of child sexual abuse (Finkelhor, Hotaling, Lewis, & Smith, 1990). Third, nonabusive circumstances, such as the level of family nudity, opportunities for the child to witness intercourse, and television-watching practices, were found to be related to the CSBI total score in the normative sample. Fourth, whereas both Friedrich et al. (1991, 1992) and White et al. (1988) have found total sexualized behaviors to be more frequent in abused than nonabused children, patterns of specific behaviors vary across the different studies, suggesting caution in relying on isolated sexualized behaviors as a substantiation of abuse. Fifth, Friedrich et al.'s (1992) own work and the research of others (D. A. Wolfe & Mosek, 1983) suggest that family variables, such as life stress and socioeconomic status, are associated with the expression of sexual behavior in children. In this regard, the generalizability of recent findings to individuals is further constrained by the fact that normative and clinical samples typically vary on these family dimensions. Behavioral and demographic differences between abusive and nonabusive families make definitive conclusions regarding the impact of sexual abuse as distinct from other dysfunctional family dynamics difficult to assess and risk a greater frequency of false-positive sexual abuse validations in distressed and economically struggling families.

Genitalia in Children's Drawings

A logical extension of the traumatic sexualization model is that sexually abused children will indicate their precocious knowledge of adult genitalia in their drawings (Miller & Veltkamp, 1989; Sturner & Rothbaum, 1980). Other researchers have theorized that artistic expression serves to elicit ventilation of internalized conflict stemming from the trauma of sexual abuse, thereby facilitating its identification and recognition by both the child and practitioner (Burgess, McCausland, & Wolbert, 1981; Sgroi, 1982). Some child abuse validators have thus looked to the presence of sexually relevant detail in children's human figure drawings as a means of identifying trauma in children who may be too young to verbally communicate their experiences. In a recent survey of mental health professionals conducting sexual abuse investigations, Conte et al. (1991) found that almost two thirds (66%) use anatomically correct drawings as tools for assessing whether a child has been sexually abused. However, legal experts question the adequacy of human figure drawing as a means of corroborating victimization or of providing information on the child's understanding of what actually happened during an abusive incident (Riordan & Verdel, 1991).

One reason for this skepticism regarding the use of sexual detail as an indicator of child sexual abuse is that the presentation of genitalia in children's spontaneous drawings is rare in both abused and nonabused children (Di Leo, 1973; Hibbard, Roghmann, & Hoekelman, 1987; Koppitz, 1968). It is perhaps for this reason that the consideration of genitalia is not mentioned as a rating category for the Goodenough Draw-a-Man Test, the most widely used standardized figure-drawing test (Brill, 1935; Goodenough, 1926). One of the few empirical tests of the association between genitalia in children's drawings and sexual abuse was conducted by Hibbard et al. Using a standardized format, the investigators obtained male and female drawings from fifty-seven 3- to 7-year-olds referred to child-protective services as alleged sexual abuse victims (36 of whom had allegations supported by physical evidence, a witness, or a confession) and 55 nonabused children. The drawings were examined for the inclusion of eyes, vulva–vagina, penis, and anus. Whereas sexual abuse victims were approximately five times more likely to draw genitalia, only 10% (5 out of 57) actually drew sexual features. Hibbard et al. concluded that whereas the presence of sexual detail in young children's human figure drawings may be suggestive of child abuse, the absence of such detail does not rule out the possibility that the child has been victimized.

A second reason for the skepticism regarding the use of children's human figure drawings as corroboration of child sexual abuse is that it is difficult to clarify whether what one observes represents genitalia without questioning the child. In investigatory interviews, such questioning may influence the nature of the child's verbal response, subsequent drawings, or both, thus contaminating the forensic value of the assessment. Additionally, other contextual factors (e.g., the birth of a sibling, family nudity, bathing with siblings) may influence the extent to which sexual details appear in nonabused children's drawings. At present, the absence of standardized techniques, appropriate norms, reliable ratings, and criterion-related validity for assessing the meaning of sexual details in children's drawings does not support the use of this technique for validation interviews or admissibility as evidence in legal proceedings.

Anatomically Detailed Dolls

Perhaps the most popular and yet most controversial of the diagnostic tools focusing on traumatic sexualization is the use of anatomically detailed dolls. Although there is as of yet no standardization of design, the dolls usually have oral and anal orifices, with the mature male dolls having a penis, scrotum, and pubic hair and the mature female dolls having a vagina, breasts, and pubic hair. Originally developed in 1978 to help children illustrate sexually abusive acts that they might find difficult to verbally communicate, the dolls were rapidly adopted as an assessment tool by practitioners who engage in the assessment of child sexual abuse (Friedemann & Morgan, 1985). A recent survey of mental health professionals who engage in child abuse validation indicates that the vast majority (92%) used anatomically detailed dolls in child abuse evaluations (Conte et al., 1991). The rapid, widespread use of the dolls evokes popular concern over the appropriateness of presenting explicitly sexual material to children, professional concern over their potentially coercive and suggestive nature, and judicial concern regarding their ability as assessment tools for the validation of child sexual abuse to meet the scientific standards required by *Kelley–Frye* (*In re Amber B. and Teela B.*, 1987; *In re Christine C. and Michael C.*, 1987).

Whereas empirical studies indicate that sexually abused children are more sexual or more sexually aggressive in their play with both anatomically detailed and nondetailed dolls (August & Forman, 1989; Friedrich et al., 1992; Jampole & Weber, 1987; White, Strom, Santilli, & Halpin, 1986), the generalizability of such findings to individual diagnosis has been questioned. One reason is that although the frequency of sex play was lower for children with no history of sexual abuse, a percentage of nonreferred children did manipulate the doll's genitals and demonstrate behaviors indicative of sexual intercourse (Dawson, Vaughan, & Wagner, 1991; Glaser & Collins, 1989). A related reason is the lack of professional consensus regarding the classification of specific forms of doll play behavior as an indicator of sexual abuse (Boat & Everson, 1988). For example, Herbert, Grams, and Goranson (1987) found that approximately half the doll play behavior of 3- to 5-year-old nonabused children was categorized as probable sexual abuse when raters were asked to evaluate the children as if an actual sexual abuse allegation had been made. Additional concerns arise from research demonstrating that asking children specific questions about sexual and aggressive behaviors increases the manifestation of these behaviors in doll play (McIver, Wakefield, & Underwager, 1989). Because such leading questions are unfortunately common in child sexual abuse validations (Bruck et al., 1995), the use of anatomically detailed dolls as part of a child sexual abuse investigation runs the risk of creating a situation of entrapment (Sivan, Schor, Koeppl, & Noble, 1988; Skinner & Berry, 1993).

In recent years, there have been several excellent reviews illustrating problems with the standardization of training, administration, and scoring procedures for presenting anatomically detailed dolls to children as well as the absence of a psychometrically sound basis for considering anatomical doll play as a valid test of child sexual abuse (e.g., Boat & Everson, 1988, 1993; Cohn, 1991; Kendall-Tackett & Watson, 1992; Kenyon-Jump, Burnette, & Robertson, 1991; Sivan et al., 1988; Skinner & Berry, 1993;

White, 1988; White & Quinn, 1988; Yates & Terr, 1988a, 1988b). The reader is advised to refer to these chapters and articles for an extensive review of the advantages and disadvantages of using anatomically detailed dolls for the purposes of treatment and forensic application.

Factors underlying the importance of considering the psychometric properties of anatomical dolls for child sexual abuse validation have been identified by several writers (Boat & Everson, 1993; Skinner & Berry, 1993). First among these factors is the popularity of the dolls in child sexual abuse validations. Recent surveys indicate that doll usage is widespread, ranging between 68% to 92% among professionals recognized as having expertise in investigating or assessing allegations of sexual abuse (Boat & Everson, 1988; Conte et al., 1991; Kendall-Tackett & Watson, 1992). A second factor pertains to issues raised regarding whether anatomically detailed doll use for sexual abuse validation is in compliance with professional guidelines for test construction and use as outlined in the *Standards for Educational and Psychological Testing* (1985). Ethical issues associated with the lack of psychometric evidence for the validity and reliability of doll use became a primary concern following the assertion of APA's Committee on Psychological Testing and Assessment that anatomical dolls are "a psychological test and are subject to the standards when used to assess individuals and make inferences about their behavior" (Landers, 1988, p. 25). A related factor concerns the admissibility of anatomically detailed doll-based assessments as evidence meeting the standards of the scientific community as required by *Kelley–Frye* and *Daubert v. Merrell Dow Pharmaceuticals, Inc.* (1993). A fourth issue regards the relationship of certain demographic variables, such as race, socioeconomic level, and family variables (e.g., the pregnancy of a female relative or birth of a sibling), to sexualized doll play in normative samples (Dawson et al., 1991; Kenyon-Jump et al., 1991). For example, in a recent study, Everson and Boat (1990) found that 4- to 5-year-old nonreferred, presumably nonabused African American lower socioeconomic status boys were significantly more likely to demonstrate sexually explicit doll play than other normative samples. This finding raises the ethical concern that false-positive substantiations of sexual abuse based on anatomical doll play may be more frequent for children from poor minority families (Standard 2.04, APA, 1992; Fisher, 1995; Fisher, Hatashita-Wong, & Isman, in press).

This brief overview of the now extensive research on the use of anatomically detailed dolls indicates that at present, there is no evidence that their use constitutes a valid assessment of whether an individual child has been sexually abused. APA (1991) has taken a somewhat equivocal stance toward this issue. Whereas recognizing that there are no uniform standards for conducting interviews, no standardization of doll design, and no normative data, as of 1991 APA's position is that "doll-centered assessment of children when used as part of a psychological evaluation and interpreted by experienced and competent examiners, may be the best available practical solution" for the investigation of child sexual abuse. APA may want to reconsider the ethicality of using anatomically detailed dolls as a diagnostic test of child sexual abuse in forensic settings, in light of the greater specificity with which assessment responsibilities are addressed in the organization's Ethical Principles of Psychologists and Code of Conduct (Standard 7.02a; APA, 1992) and APA Division 41's (Forensic Psychology) Specialty Guidelines for Forensic Psychologists (Section VI-A; Committee on Ethical Guidelines for Forensic Psychologists, 1991). Both documents emphasize the psychologist's responsibility to select forensically relevant evaluation procedures that can provide substantiation of findings consistent with professional and scientific standards. We concur with the conclusion drawn by Skinner and Berry (1993) that given the current lack of supporting evidence for the psychometric validity of anatomically detailed dolls as a means of substantiating child sexual abuse, psychologists using these dolls as a diagnostic instrument risk operating in an ethically indefensible manner.

INTERVIEWING CHILDREN ABOUT SEXUAL ABUSE

The absence of psychometrically sound assessment instruments for validating child sexual abuse has led a number of professionals to develop semistructured interview formats designed to increase the accuracy of a clinician's analysis of the presenting problems by reducing factors that contribute to investigator bias, coercion, misinterpretation, and suggestion (e.g., Robin, 1991; Sink, 1988; Walker, 1990; White & Edelstein, 1991; White & Quinn, 1988; Yuille, Hunter, Joffe, & Zaparniuk, 1993). These protocols share a sensitivity to several interfering and facilitative factors influencing the accuracy of children's responses to investigatory interviews. First, the formats seek to maximize a child's recall of abusive events through investigator familiarity with age-appropriate retrieval strategies and developmental differences in the ability to provide details. Second, many of the newer protocols are designed to minimize trauma and the potential for interfering with the child's ability to benefit from subsequent treatment (e.g., allowing the child some sense of control during the interview, letting the child know that help is available).

A third characteristic of these interview protocols is an emphasis on the integrity of the investigation to meet judicial evidentiary standards. One means of accomplishing this is by keeping careful records, including an audiotape or videotape of the interview. An additional integrity safeguard is to avoid taking an advocate position by assuming an impartial stance. Such efforts are facilitated when a validator is able to interview all involved parties, including the child, the alleged offender, and accusing adults (Bresee, Stearns, Bess, & Packer, 1986; Walker, 1990; White & Edelstein, 1991). Some examiners, like Gardner (1994), strongly encourage court orders requiring all three parties to be involved in the examination. Unfortunately, obtaining interviews of all parties involved in the allegation is not the norm. In their survey of child abuse validation experts, Conte et al. (1991) found that only 43% of respondents periodically interviewed alleged abusers.

Most protocols also attempt to prevent contamination of a child's report of abusive incidents by avoiding repeated interviews and leading questions and moving from general, open-ended inquiries to more specific questions. The use of open-ended questions as a means of avoiding contamination through leading questions can, however, weaken the probative value of the interview. That is, this semistructured format leads to a lack of standardization in interview procedures across different children and for the same child across multiple interviews. This lack of standardization, in turn, compromises the ability to provide the court with psychometrically sound comparative judgments regarding responses typifying abused versus nonabused children as well as estimates of the reliability of a particular child's statements elicited during different interview sessions.

Miller and Veltkamp (1989) have attempted to apply a uniform interview format using the Fable Assessment of Child Trauma (FACT). In having a child respond to a series of fables, the FACT allows the investigator to elicit spontaneous information about the child's fears, family relationships, and other abuse-relevant dimensions in a nonthreatening, standardized context. The FACT format also enables the investigator to evaluate the child's level of comprehension and cognitive processing and how these may have affected the child's reaction to an abusive event and the child's ability to communicate these reactions. Although the FACT offers a novel approach to reducing the stress associated with more common validation interviews, its limitations include the unsubstantiated assumption that the fables elicit psychological reactions to actual trauma, the absence of a developmental framework for evaluating children of different ages, and a lack of a standardized scoring system.

Gardner (1994) has attempted to redress this latter problem by setting up detailed guidelines for assigning "true" and "false" scores to 62 items designed to distinguish true from false allegations of child abuse. These items address a range of affects and behaviors assumed to be consistent with a child's response to sexual victimization, including the extent of details and consistency with which the child describes the abusive events, the presence of trauma-specific behaviors and attitudes, indications of psychopathology, and creative outlets for working through the trauma. According to Gardner, the more true scores a child receives, the more likely it is that he or she has been abused. Gardner's protocol illustrates two critical flaws characterizing all of the recently developed interview formats. First, the interview items are typically derived from clinical observations and a review of the extant literature, but these items have not been subjected to empirical tests to establish their reliability and validity for identifying whether a child has been abused. Second, the protocols do not provide explicit criteria for objectively rating the data or concluding that a child's interview responses support or contradict the abuse allegation.

The development of the statement validity analysis (SVA) as a tool for assessing the credibility of children's allegations of sexual abuse is an attempt to overcome the limitations of current interview procedures by providing a reliable and valid criterion-based method for evaluating children's narratives (Raskin & Esplin, 1991; Raskin & Yuille, 1989; Steller & Kohnken, 1989; Yuille, 1988). The SVA comprises three interrelated components: (a) interview guidelines, designed to elicit an unstructured narrative of the abuse allegations; (b) criteria-based content analysis (CBCA), an analysis of material elicited by the interview guidelines designed to establish whether transcribed statements meet 18 criteria for whether the described event actually occurred; and (c) a validity checklist, which takes into account the specific investigatory context, including the psychological characteristics of the child witness and the adequacy of the interview.

The CBCA is the core feature of the SVA and has thus far been the only component subjected to empirical tests. The 19 CBCA criteria were derived from the Undeutsch hypothesis (Steller, 1989) that statements reflecting actual experiences contain different characteristics than statements reflecting imagined experiences. Several studies applying the CBCA to children's real and imagined narratives (Steller, 1989; Steller, Wellershaus, & Wolf, 1988; Yuille, 1988) and transcripts from confirmed and doubtful cases of child sexual abuse (Esplin, Boychuk, & Raskin, 1988) demonstrate high interrater reliabilities and support the use of the method as a tool for discriminating true statements from false statements. However, Anson, Golding, and Gully (1993) found only moderate to low interrater correlations for the CBCA criteria when chance-corrected reliabilities were applied. Moreover, in a recent study, Lamb et al. (1997) found that although the CBCA was helpful in distinguishing between plausible and implausible accounts, many of the criteria were present in the implausible statements as well. At present, empirical examination of the other two SVA components has yet to be completed (Horowitz, 1991), and the external validity of existing field studies has been questioned (Wells & Loftus, 1991). Accordingly, questions remain regarding the psychometric reliability, validity, and practical use of this technique for corroboration of sexual abuse allegations. See Ruby and Brigham (1997) for a comprehensive critique of the CBCA.

CONCLUDING COMMENTS

Until recently, psychologists interviewed sexually abused children for the purpose of obtaining a clinical assessment, a diagnosis, and a treatment plan that would help the child overcome the trauma of abuse and resume a path of adaptive development. Within the past decade, this role has shifted; psychologists find themselves interviewing alleged victims of child abuse for the purpose of assisting the courts in determining the truthfulness of the child's allegations. In response to this new forensic demand to validate child sexual abuse, psychologists have presented data based on symptom checklists, observations of sexualized behaviors, and semistructured interview protocols as scientifically based evidence that can corroborate or contradict an accusation of sexual abuse. However, in the absence of empirically based psychometric foundations for these assessment strategies, expert testimony may not be meeting current ethical or judicial standards.

At present, psychological evaluations cannot establish whether an alleged child victim has been abused. Indeed, the current use of the term *validation* to describe child abuse assessments introduces false expectations that psychologists are capable of determining whether a child has been abused (Fisher, 1995; Sullivan, 1989). Child sexual abuse is not a psychological disorder. Child sexual abuse encompasses a heterogeneous group of behaviors perpetrated on children by abusers. A diagnostic assessment of a child's psychological well-being should not be confused with the evidence of an abuser's behavior. Expert witnesses providing such evaluations render opinions beyond their professional expertise and potentially usurp the role of judge and jury to determine whether child sexual abuse allegations are true or false (Fisher, 1995; Melton, 1990; Melton & Limber, 1989).

The adversarial nature of the U.S. legal system is increasingly dividing mental health professionals serving as expert witnesses into two different camps. Those adhering to a "child-protective" position (Milchman, 1992) tend to approach child abuse investigations with an a priori belief that abuse has occurred (Bruck et al., 1995; Fisher, 1995; Jones & McGraw, 1987) and a tendency to deny the possibility of false accusations, memory distortions, and suggestibility (Milchman, 1992). Those adhering to a "defense-protective" position (Milchman, 1992) tend to see adult defendants as victims of false accusations, inaccurate memories, and coercive and leading child interview techniques. The overzealous forensic use of clinically relevant, but diagnostically unsubstantiated, techniques for assessing symptoms of child sexual abuse and the corresponding attempts to discount all psychological data as irrelevant to judicial decisions are threatening the perceived credibility of psychologists as expert witnesses and violating the welfare and rights of both victimized children and innocent defendants.

Psychologists have an important role to play in the legal proceedings when professional expertise is needed to assist the triers of facts in evaluating the credibility of child sexual abuse allegations. Conclusions drawn from clinical observations and psychometrically sound assessment tools regarding an alleged child victim's cognitive and affective status, his or her behaviors across a variety of contexts and interpersonal relationships, and the presence or absence of developmental psychopathology are critical facts needed to help judges and juries test rival hypotheses concerning a sexual abuse defendant's guilt or innocence. However, psychologists providing expert testimony in child sexual abuse cases risk usurping the role of the triers of fact and violating ethical guidelines when they confuse clinical opinion for scientific fact and the role of fact finder with the role of child advocate.

REFERENCES

American Psychiatric Association. (1994). *Diagnostic and statistical manual of mental disorders* (4th ed.). Washington, DC: Author.

American Psychological Association. (1991, February 8). *Statement on the use of anatomically detailed dolls in forensic evaluations* (as adopted by the APA Council of Representatives). Washington DC: Author. (Available from Governance Affairs)

American Psychological Association. (1992). Ethical principles of psychologists and code of conduct. *American Psychologist, 47,* 1597–1611.

Ammerman, R. T., Cassisi, J. E., & Hersen, M. (1986). Consequences of physical abuse and neglect in children. *Clinical Psychological Review, 6,* 291–310.

Anson, D. A., Golding, S. L., & Gully, K. J. (1993). Child sexual abuse allegations: Reliability of criteria-based content analysis. *Law and Human Behavior, 17,* 331–341.

August, R. L., & Forman, B. D. (1989). A comparison of sexually and nonsexually abused children's behavioral responses to anatomically correct dolls. *Child Psychiatry and Human Development, 20,* 39–47.

Beitchman, J. H., Zucker, K. J., Hood, J. E., daCosta, G. A., & Akman, D. (1991). A review of the short term effects of child sexual abuse. *Child Abuse & Neglect, 15,* 537–556.

Benedek, E., & Schetky, D. (1987). Problems in validating allegations of sexual abuse. Part 1: Factors affecting perception and recall of events. *Journal of the American Academy of Child and Adolescent Psychiatry, 26,* 916–921.

Boat, B. W., & Everson, M. D. (1988). Use of anatomical dolls among professionals in sexual abuse evaluations. *Child Abuse & Neglect, 12,* 171–179.

Boat, B. W., & Everson, M. D. (1993). The use of anatomical dolls in sexual abuse evaluations: Current research and practice. In G. S. Goodman & B. L. Bottoms (Eds.), *Child victims, child witnesses: Understanding and improving testimony* (pp. 47–70). New York: Guilford Press.

Bresee, P., Stearns, G. B., Bess, B. H., & Packer, L. S. (1986). Allegations of child sexual abuse in child custody disputes: A therapeutic assessment model. *American Journal of Orthopsychiatry, 56,* 560–569.

Brill, M. (1935). The reliability of the Goodenough Draw-a-Man Test and the validity and reliability of an abbreviated scoring method. *Journal of Educational Psychology, 26,* 701–708.

Brooks, C. M., & Milchman, M. (1991). Child sexual abuse allegations during custody litigation: Conflicts between mental health expert witnesses and the law. *Behavioral Sciences and the Law, 9,* 21–32.

Bruck, M., Ceci, S., & Rosenthal, R. (1995). Amicus brief in *Michaels v. State of New Jersey. Psychology, Public Policy, and Law, 1,* 242–322.

Burgess, A. W., McCausland, M. P., & Wolbert, W. A. (1981). Children's drawings as indicators of sexual trauma. *Perspectives in Psychiatric Care, 19,* 50–58.

Bussey, Jr. v. Commonwealth, Appellee Supreme Court, September 6, 697 S.W.2d 139 (Ky. 1985).

Clarke, M. E., & Hornick, J. P. (1988). The child sexual abuse victim: Assessment and treatment issues and solutions [Special issue]. *Contemporary Family Therapy—An International Journal, 10*(4), 235–242.

Cohn, D. S. (1991). Anatomical doll play of preschoolers referred for sexual abuse and those not referred. *Child Abuse & Neglect, 15,* 567–573.

Committee on Ethical Guidelines for Forensic Psychologists. (1991). Specialty guidelines for forensic psychologists. *Law & Human Behavior, 15,* 655–665.

Conte, J. R. (1992). Has this child been sexually abused? Dilemmas for the mental health professional who seeks the answer. *Criminal Justice and Behavior, 19,* 54–73.

Conte, J. R., & Schuerman, J. (1987). The effects of child abuse on children: A multidimensional view. *Journal of Interpersonal Violence, 2,* 380–390.

Conte, J. R., Sorenson, E., Fogarty, L., & Rosa, J. D. (1991). Evaluating children's reports of sexual abuse: Results from a survey of professionals. *American Journal of Orthopsychiatry, 61,* 428–437.

Daubert v. Merrell Dow Pharmaceuticals, Inc., 509 U.S., 113 S. Ct. 2786 (1993).

Dawson, B., Vaughan, A. R., & Wagner, W. G. (1991). Normal responses to sexually anatomically detailed dolls. *Journal of Family Violence, 7,* 135–152.

Deblinger, E., McLeer, S., Atkins, M., Ralphe, D., & Foa, E. (1989). Post-traumatic stress in sexually abused, physically abused, and non-abused children. *Child Abuse & Neglect, 13,* 403–408.

Di Leo, J. (1973). *Children's drawings as diagnostic aids.* New York: Brunner/Mazel.

Elias, H. M. (1992). Commentary: "Abuse of the child sexual abuse accommodation syndrome." *Journal of Child Sexual Abuse, 1,* 169–171.

Esplin, P. W., Boychuk, T., & Raskin, D. C. (1988, June). *A field validity study of criteria-based content analysis for children's statements in sexual abuse cases.* Paper presented at the North Atlantic Treaty Organization Advanced Study Institute on Credibility Assessment, Maratea, Italy.

Everson, M. D., & Boat, B. W. (1990). Sexualized doll play among young children: Implications for the use of anatomical dolls in sexual abuse evaluations. *Journal of the American Academy of Child and Adolescent Psychiatry, 28,* 736–742.

Finkelhor, D. (1987). The trauma of child sexual abuse: Two models. *Journal of Interpersonal Violence, 2,* 348–366.

Finkelhor, D., & Browne, A. (1985). The traumatic impact of child sexual abuse: A conceptualization. *American Journal of Orthopsychiatry, 55,* 530–541.

Finkelhor, D., Hotaling, G., Lewis, I. A., & Smith, C. (1990). Sexual abuse in a national study of adult men and women: Prevalence, characteristics, and risk factors. *Child Abuse & Neglect, 14,* 19–28.

Fisher, C. B. (1995). The American Psychological Association's ethics code and the validation of sexual abuse in day-care settings. *Psychology, Public Policy, and Law, 1,* 461–468.

Fisher, C. B., Hatashita-Wong, M., & Isman, L. (in press). Ethical and legal issues in clinical child psychology. In W. K. Silverman & T. H. Ollendick (Eds.), *Developmental issues in the clinical treatment of children and adolescents.* Boston: Allyn & Bacon.

Friedemann, V., & Morgan, M. K. (1985). *Interviewing sexual abuse victims using anatomical dolls: The professional's guidebook.* Eugene, OR: Shamrock Press.

Friedrich, W. N., Beilke, R. L., & Urquiza, A. J. (1988a). Behavior problems in young sexually abused boys: A comparison study. *Journal of Interpersonal Violence, 3,* 21–28.

Friedrich, W. N., Beilke, R. L., & Urquiza, A. J. (1988b). Children from sexually abused families: A behavioral comparison. *Journal of Interpersonal Violence, 2,* 391–402.

Friedrich, W. N., Grambsch, P., Broughton, D., Kuiper, J., & Beilke, R. L. (1991). Normative sexual behavior in children. *Pediatrics, 88,* 456–464.

Friedrich, W. N., Grambsch, P., Damon, L., Hewitt, S. K., Koverola, C., Lang, R. A., Wolfe, V., & Broughton, D. (1992). The Child Sexual Behavior Inventory: Normative and clinical comparisons. *Psychological Assessment, 4,* 303–311.

Frye v. United States, 54 App. 46, 47, 293 F. 1013 (D.C. Cir. 1923).

Gale, J., Thompson, R. J., Moran, T., & Sack, W. H. (1988). Presenting problems of sexually abused girls receiving psychiatric services. *Journal of Abnormal Psychology, 98,* 314–317.

Gardner, R. A. (1994). *Protocols for the sex-abuse evaluation.* Cresskill, NJ: Creative Therapeutics.

Glaser, D., & Collins, C. (1989). The response of young, non-sexually abused children to anatomically correct dolls. *Journal of Child Psychology and Psychiatry, 30,* 547–560.

Goldston, D., Turnquist, D., & Knutson, J. (1989). Sexual abuse in young children: Its clinical presentation and characteristic patterns. *Child Abuse & Neglect, 12,* 163–170.

Goodenough, F. L. (1926). *Measurement of intelligence by drawing*. New York: Harcourt, Brace, & World.

Haugaard, J., & Reppucci, N. D. (1988). *The sexual abuse of children*. San Francisco: Jossey-Bass.

Herbert, C. P., Grams, G. D., & Goranson, S. E. (1987). *The use of anatomically detailed dolls in an investigative interview: A preliminary study of "non-abused" children*. Unpublished manuscript, University of British Columbia, Department of Family Practice, Vancouver, British Columbia, Canada.

Hibbard, R. A., Roghmann, K., & Hoekelman, R. A. (1987). Genitalia in children's drawings: An association with sexual abuse. *Pediatrics, 19*, 129–136.

Horowitz, S. W. (1991). Empirical support for statement validity assessment. *Behavioral Assessment, 13*, 293–313.

In re Amber B. and Teela B., 191 Cal. App. 3d 682 (1987).

In re Christine C. and Michael C., 191 Cal. App. 3d 676 (1987).

Jampole, L., & Weber, M. K. (1987). An assessment of the behavior of sexually abused and non-sexually abused children with anatomically correct dolls. *Child Abuse & Neglect, 11*, 187–192.

Jones, D., & McGraw, J. (1987). Reliable and fictitious accounts of sexual abuse to children. *Journal of Interpersonal Violence, 2*, 27–45.

Kendall-Tackett, K. A., & Watson, M. W. (1992). Use of anatomical dolls by Boston-area professionals. *Child Abuse & Neglect, 16*, 423–428.

Kendall-Tackett, K. A., Williams, L. M., & Finkelhor, D. (1993). Impact of sexual abuse on children: A review and synthesis of recent empirical studies. *Psychological Bulletin, 113*, 164–180.

Kenyon-Jump, R., Burnette, M. M., & Robertson, M. (1991). Comparison of behaviors of suspected sexually abused and nonsexually abused preschool children using anatomical dolls. *Journal of Psychopathology and Behavior Assessment, 13*, 225–240.

Kiser, L. J., Ackerman, B. J., Brown, E., Edwards, N. B., McColgan, E., Pugh, R., & Pruitt, D. B. (1988). Post-traumatic stress disorder in young children: A reaction to purported sexual abuse. *Journal of the American Academy of Child and Adolescent Psychiatry, 27*, 645–649.

Kolko, D. J., Moser, T. M., & Weldy, S. R. (1988). Behavioral/emotional indicators of sexual abuse in child psychiatric inpatients: A controlled comparison with physical abuse. *Child Abuse & Neglect, 12*, 529–541.

Koppitz, E. M. (1968). *Psychological evaluation of children's human figure drawings*. New York: Grune & Stratton.

Lamb, M. E., Sternberg, K. N. J., Esplin, P. W., Hershkowitz, I., Orbach, Y., & Hovav, M. (1997). Criterion based content analysis: A field validation study. *Child Abuse & Neglect, 21*, 255–264.

Landers, S. (1988). Use of "detailed dolls" questioned. *The APA Monitor, 19*, 24–25.

McGovern, K. B. (1991). Was there really child sexual abuse or is there another explanation? *Child & Youth Services, 15*, 115–127.

McIver, W., Wakefield, H., & Underwager, R. (1989). Behavior of abused and non-abused children in interviews with anatomically correct dolls. *Issues in Child Abuse Accusations, 1*, 39–48.

McLeer, S., Deblinger, E., Atkins, M., Foa, E., & Ralphe, D. (1988). Post-traumatic stress disorder in sexually abused children. *Journal of the American Academy of Child and Adolescent Psychiatry, 27*, 650–654.

Melton, G. B. (1990). Ethical dilemmas in playing by the rules: Applied developmental research and the law. In C. B. Fisher & W. W. Tryon (Eds.), *Ethics in applied developmental psychology: Emerging issues in an emerging field* (pp. 145–162). Norwood, NJ: Ablex.

Melton, G. B., & Limber, S. (1989). Psychologists' involvement in cases of child maltreatment: Limits of role and expertise. *American Psychologist, 44*, 1225–1233.

Milchman, M. S. (1992, Spring). Professional controversies in child sexual abuse assessment. *Journal of Psychiatry and Law*, 49–83.

Miller, T. W., & Veltkamp, L. J. (1989). Assessment of child sexual abuse: Clinical use of fables. *Child Psychiatry and Human Development, 20*, 123–132.

National Research Council. (1993). *Understanding child abuse and neglect*. Washington, DC: National Academy Press.

O'Donohue, W., & Elliott, A. N. (1991). A model for the clinical assessment of the sexually abused child. *Behavioral Assessment, 13*, 325–339.

People v. Kelley, 17 Cal.3d 27 (1976).

Raskin, D. C., & Esplin, P. W. (1991). Assessment of children's statements of sexual abuse. In J. Doris (Ed.), *The suggestibility of children's memory: Implications for eyewitness testimony* (pp. 172–176). Washington, DC: American Psychological Association.

Raskin, D. C., & Yuille, J. C. (1989). Problems in evaluating interviews of children in sexual abuse cases. In S. J. Ceci, M. P. Toglia, & D. F. Ross (Eds.), *New perspectives on the child witness* (pp. 184–207). New York: Springer.

Reichard, R. D. (1992). Is the grass greener on the other side of the river? The child sexual abuse accommodation syndrome in Indiana's courts. *Journal of Child Sexual Abuse, 1*, 143–146.

Riordan, R. J., & Verdel, A. C. (1991). Evidence of sexual abuse in children's art products. *The School Counselor, 39*, 116–121.

Robin, M. (1991). Beyond validation interviews: An assessment approach to evaluating sexual abuse allegations. *Child and Youth Services, 17*, 93–113.

Ruby, C. L., & Brigham, J. C. (1997). The usefulness of the criteria-based content analysis technique in distinguishing between truthful and fabricated allegations. *Psychology, Public Policy, and Law, 3*, 705–737.

Sgroi, S. M. (1982). *Handbook of clinical intervention in child sexual abuse*. Lexington, MA: Lexington Books.

Sink, F. (1988). A hierarchical model for evaluation of child sexual abuse. *American Journal of Orthopsychiatry, 58,* 129–135.

Sivan, A. B., Schor, D. P., Koeppl, G. K., & Noble, L. D. (1988). Interaction of normal children with anatomical dolls. *Child Abuse & Neglect, 12,* 295–304.

Skinner, L. J., & Berry, K. K. (1993). Anatomically detailed dolls and the evaluation of child sexual abuse allegations: Psychometric considerations. *Law and Human Behavior, 17,* 399–421.

Standards for educational and psychological testing. (1985). Washington, DC: American Psychological Association.

State v. Margaret Kelly Michaels, 625 A.2d 489 (N.J. Superior Court 1993), *aff'd,* 642 A.2d 1372 (1994).

Steller, M. (1989). Recent developments in statement analysis. In J. C. Yuille (Ed.), *Credibility assessment* (pp. 135–154). London: Kluwer.

Steller, M., & Kohnken, G. (1989). Criteria-based statement analysis. In D. C. Raskin (Ed.), *Psychological methods in criminal investigation and evidence* (pp. 217–245). New York: Springer.

Steller, M., Wellershaus, P., & Wolf, T. (1988, June). *Empirical validation of criterion-based content analysis.* Paper presented at the North Atlantic Treaty Organization Advanced Study Institute on Credibility Assessment, Maratea, Italy.

Stewart v. State, 521 N.E.2d 675, 677 (Ind. 1988).

Stewart, W. F., & Young, R. (1992). The rehabilitation of the child sexual abuse accommodation syndrome in trial courts in Kentucky. *Journal of Child Sexual Abuse, 1,* 133–141.

Sturner, R., & Rothbaum, F. (1980). The effects of stress on children's human figure drawings. *Journal of Clinical Psychology, 36,* 324–331.

Sullivan, M. J. (1989, May 4). *Eliminating chaotic practices in child sex abuse evaluations.* Paper presented at a meeting of the Brooklyn Bar Association, Brooklyn, NY.

Summit, R. C. (1983). The child sexual abuse accommodation syndrome. *Child Abuse & Neglect, 7,* 177–193.

Summit, R. C. (1992). Abuse of the child sexual abuse accommodation syndrome. *Journal of Child Sexual Abuse, 1,* 153–163.

Walker, L. E. (1990). Psychological assessment of sexually abused children for legal evaluation and expert witness testimony. *Professional Psychology: Research and Practice, 21,* 344–353.

Wells, G., & Loftus, E. (1991). Commentary: Is this child fabricating? Reactions to a new assessment technique. In J. Doris (Ed.), *The suggestibility of children's recollections* (pp. 168–171). Washington, DC: American Psychological Association.

White, S. (1988). Should investigatory use of anatomical dolls be defined by the courts? *Journal of Interpersonal Violence, 3,* 471–475.

White, S., & Edelstein, B. (1991). Behavioral assessment and investigatory interviewing. *Behavioral Assessment, 13,* 245–264.

White, S., Halpin, B. M., Strom, G. A., & Santilli, G. (1988). Behavioral comparisons of young sexually abused, neglected, and nonreferred children. *Journal of Clinical Child Psychiatry, 17,* 53–61.

White, S., & Quinn, K. M. (1988). Investigatory independence in child sexual abuse evaluations: Conceptual considerations. *Bulletin of the American Academy of Psychiatry and Law, 16,* 269–273.

White, S., Strom, G., Santilli, G., & Halpin, B. (1986). Interviewing young children with anatomically correct dolls. *Child Abuse & Neglect, 10,* 519–529.

Wolfe, D. A., & Mosek, M. D. (1983). Behavioral comparisons of children from abusive and distressed families. *Journal of Consulting and Clinical Psychology, 51,* 702–708.

Wolfe, V. V., & Gentile, C. (1992). Psychological assessment of sexually abused children. In W. O'Donohue & J. H. Geer (Eds.), *The sexual abuse of children: Clinical issues* (Vol. 2, pp. 143–187). New York: Erlbaum.

Wolfe, V. V., Gentile, C., Michienzi, T., Sas, L., & Wolfe, D. A. (1991). The Children's Impact of Traumatic Events Scale: A measure of post-sexual-abuse PTSD symptoms. *Behavioral Assessment, 13,* 359–383.

Yates, A., & Terr, L. (1988a). Anatomically correct dolls: Should they be used as a basis for expert testimony? *Journal of the American Academy of Child and Adolescent Psychiatry, 27,* 254–257.

Yates, A., & Terr, L. (1988b). Issue continued: Anatomically correct dolls: Should they be used as a basis for expert testimony? *Journal of the American Academy of Child and Adolescent Psychiatry, 27,* 387–388.

Yuille, J. C. (1988). The systematic assessment of children's testimony. *Canadian Psychology, 19*(3), 247–261.

Yuille, J. C., Hunter, R., Joffe, R., & Zaparniuk, J. (1993). Interviewing children in sexual abuse cases. In G. S. Goodman & B. L. Bottoms (Eds.), *Child victims, child witnesses: Understanding and improving testimony* (pp. 95–116). New York: Guilford Press.

Zuravin, S. J. (1991). Research definitions of child physical abuse and neglect: Current problems. In R. Starr & D. Wolfe (Eds.), *The effects of child abuse and neglect: Issues and research* (pp. 100–128). New York: Guilford Press.

9

EXPERT SCIENTIFIC TESTIMONY ON CHILD WITNESSES IN THE AGE OF *DAUBERT*

MARGARET BULL KOVERA AND EUGENE BORGIDA

In June 1993, the U.S. Supreme Court decided the case of *Daubert v. Merrell Dow Pharmaceuticals, Inc.* (1993). According to any number of legal commentators (e.g., Ayala & Black, 1993; Faigman, Porter, & Saks, 1994; Hutchinson & Ashby, 1994; Klein, 1994; Miller, Rein, & Bailey, 1994; Monahan & Walker, 1994; Walker & Monahan, 1996), the *Daubert* decision has changed the standard for the admission of scientific evidence in federal courts. Although it is still too early to determine how many state courts will follow the federal lead, at least 35 states modeled their evidentiary rules after the *Federal Rules of Evidence* (1975) and therefore can be expected to adopt some version of *Daubert* when ruling on the admission of expert scientific testimony in a variety of cases, including child sexual abuse cases. In *Daubert*, the U.S. Supreme Court basically changed the rules relating to

The research reported in this chapter was supported in part by Grant 90-CA-1273 from a subcontract from the National Council of Jewish Women's Center for the Child and the National Center on Child Abuse and Neglect and by a University of Minnesota Graduate School Grant-in-Aid of Research. We wish to thank Brian L. Cutler and Bradley D. McAuliff for their helpful suggestions on a draft.

185

the admissibility of expert testimony, holding that the Frye test of "general acceptance" (*Frye v. United States*, 1923) had been superseded by the *Federal Rules of Evidence*. The new test, as presented in *Daubert*, requires a focus on Rule 702 (*Federal Rules of Evidence*, 1975), which states that

> if scientific, technical, or other specialized knowledge will assist the trier of fact to understand the evidence or to determine a fact in issue, a witness qualified as an expert by knowledge, skill, experience, training, or education, may testify thereto in the form of an opinion or otherwise. (p. 14)

Under the U.S. Supreme Court's decision in *Daubert*, district courts are supposed to perform a "gatekeeping role" with respect to expert witness evidence. The trial judge in particular must ensure "that an expert's testimony both rests on a reliable foundation and is relevant to the task at hand" (p. 2799). The court in *Daubert* offered a formula for the admission of scientific expert testimony: admissibility = reliability + relevance. Reliability is established if expert testimony involves "scientific knowledge"; the term *scientific* implies a grounding in the methods and procedures of scientific inquiry, and knowledge must be based on more than subjective belief or unsupported speculation. Relevance is established if such testimony "will assist the trier of fact to understand the evidence or determine a fact in issue"; this requires a fit between scientific knowledge and a disputed issue. Thus, the focus of the inquiry under *Daubert* is clearly on the underlying scientific assumptions, methods, data, and interpretations of the expert's testimony and less on professional qualifications or general acceptance.

In addition, *Daubert* addressed a nonexclusive list of factors ("secondary indicia") to consider in determining reliability and relevance. The key factor is whether the expert's theory or technique was developed under the scientific method of hypothesis testing. Important, but nondispositive, considerations include whether the theory or technique has been subjected to peer review and publication; what are its known or potential rates of error; whether, under *Federal Rules of Evidence* Rule 403, the probative value of such testimony is outweighed by the danger of "unfair prejudice, confusion of the issues, or misleading the jury"; and whether the theory or technique is "generally accepted" among peers (i.e., the Frye test).[1]

Thus, under *Daubert*, Rule 702 governs the admissibility of expert testimony in federal courts. It should be noted that "helpfulness" to the jury is at the heart of Rule 702 and is interpreted rather broadly. Rule 702 confines the court's review to the relevance and reliability of expert testi-

---

[1]The court noted in *Daubert* that Rule 403's balancing of the probative against the prejudicial value of evidence has a special role in cases involving expert witnesses. Because expert evidence is often more influential (and potentially misleading) than other evidence, Rule 403 gives the trial judge more power over experts than over lay witnesses.

mony, leaving issues of weight and credibility to the jury. In fact, to the contention that overturning *Frye* would leave "befuddled juries . . . confounded by absurd and irrational pseudoscientific assertions," the court wrote,

> in this respect respondent seems to us to be overly pessimistic about the capabilities of the jury, and of the adversary system generally. Vigorous cross-examination, presentation of contrary evidence, and careful instruction on the burden of proof are the traditional and appropriate means of attacking shaky but inadmissible evidence. (*Daubert*, 1993, p. 2798)

Under *Daubert*, in other words, doubts about whether the expert testimony helps the jury should be resolved in favor of admissibility on the assumption that traditional "safeguards" like cross-examination, opposing experts, or judicial instruction on the burden of proof (individually or in combination) are effective. It is in this sense that *Daubert* has been interpreted by various legal commentators as having "lowered" the standard for admissibility of expert evidence. By abolishing the rule that an expert's method of analysis must first obtain (as in the Frye test) "general acceptance" in the scientific community (*United States v. Dorsey*, 1995), admission of expert testimony is probably made more likely.[2]

The admissibility of expert psychological testimony in child sexual abuse trials now must be scrutinized in light of the *Daubert* decision. To this end, we briefly review the psychological literature that is relevant to the disposition of child sexual abuse cases, highlighting the varying reliability of the relevant psychological evidence. Recall that the *Daubert* decision also requires that admissible scientific evidence be more probative than prejudicial. One method of determining whether expert testimony is prejudicial is to conduct jury simulations that include expert testimony and to assess whether the expert testimony unduly or inappropriately influences juror decisions. Thus, we review jury simulation studies that examined the impact of expert testimony on juror decisions in child sexual abuse cases. Finally, relying on previous studies from the subdisciplines of social, cognitive, and legal psychology, we evaluate the likelihood that the judicial safeguards mentioned in *Daubert* would prove effective remedies for unreliable scientific evidence that might be admitted in court.

---

[2]Many courts and commentators have viewed the Frye test of scientific evidence critically. For example, the Frye test is generally viewed as the most conservative test because of its emphasis on the "general acceptance" of disputed science. However, there has been little agreement as to when a particular scientific finding has passed the threshold test into general scientific acceptance. Moreover, as scientific knowledge has exploded and crossed disciplinary boundaries, courts have had difficulty identifying the pertinent scientific field in which to measure general acceptance.

As the frequency with which attorneys introduced expert psychological testimony about child witnesses at trial increased (Myers et al., 1989), psychologists and legal scholars began to examine the scientific and legal status of expert testimony about child witnesses (e.g., Levy, 1989; Sagatun, 1991). In particular, scholars have discussed the admissibility of different types of testimony that could be offered by an expert psychological witness in the context of a child sexual abuse trial (e.g., Askowitz & Graham, 1994; McCord, 1986; Myers, 1993; Myers et al., 1989; Roe, 1985; Serrato, 1988). Most commonly, these discussions have dealt with expert testimony on children's mnemonic capabilities, behavioral symptoms of child sexual abuse, and child witness credibility. These different types of expert testimony vary in their scientific status within the field of psychology; consequently, courts have had varied responses to this novel scientific evidence.

Although scholars have devoted much attention to whether social science evidence should be admissible in child sexual abuse cases, researchers have conducted few studies that examine the impact that this evidence would have on juror decisions if it were admitted in court. However, from our perspective, it is essential to conduct jury simulation studies that investigate the possible effects of expert psychological testimony on jury decision making in child abuse cases. These studies can directly address the issue of whether the prejudicial influence of this expert testimony outweighs its probative value, a critical issue when determining admissibility of expert testimony or any other form of evidence (*Federal Rule of Evidence* Rule 403).

For the remainder of this section, we discuss those areas of psychological inquiry that have been introduced as expert testimony in child sexual abuse trial simulations: children's mnemonic capabilities, behavioral evidence of child sexual abuse—including but not limited to child sexual abuse accommodation syndrome (CSAAS; Summit, 1983) and children's manipulation of anatomically detailed dolls—and child witness credibility. In addition to discussing the state of our knowledge in these areas, we describe the empirical research that investigates the impact of this information on jurors' decisions.

Expert Testimony on Children's Mnemonic Capabilities

Research and Case Law on Children's Memory

Although reviewers of the literature have differed in the optimism with which they have evaluated children's mnemonic capabilities (e.g., Bruck & Ceci, 1995; Ceci & Bruck, 1993; Myers, 1995; Myers et al., 1989), they have agreed on a subset of findings. For example, young children (i.e., preschoolers) generally recall less information than do older children, although the proportion of accurate statements in the free-recall reports does not vary with age (e.g., Goodman, Hirschman, Hepps, & Rudy, 1991). Preschool children also are more susceptible to incorporating misleading information into their reported memories for events than are older children and adults (Rudy & Goodman, 1991). Moreover, young children (i.e., younger than 6) have difficulty remembering the source of their memories (i.e., whether the source of a memory was a real event or an imagined one; Foley, Johnson, & Raye, 1983). Thus, although research has reliably demonstrated that older children perform similarly to adults, it has also demonstrated that very young children provide less accurate testimony than do older children or adults.

Scholars who have an optimistic view of child witnesses' capabilities argue that the prosecution should offer expert testimony on children's memory to rehabilitate a child's credibility after the defense has attacked the child's testimony by claiming that children lack the cognitive capacity to remember and to testify accurately to events surrounding the abuse (Myers et al., 1989). Other authors have provided the court with reviews of the child witness literature on the defense's behalf (as was the case in *State v. Michaels*, 1994), arguing that children are often less competent witnesses than are adults, in part because of age differences in suggestibility (Bruck & Ceci, 1995; Ceci & Bruck, 1993). Although currently the case law addressing the admissibility of this type of expert testimony is meager, expert evidence on child witness memory probably would be admissible under *Daubert*. Clearly, children's capabilities to remember forensically relevant events are relevant when determining whether a child's allegations of sexual abuse are credible. Moreover, the psychological research on this topic is reliable; it is grounded in scientific methods, has been subjected to peer review, and is generally accepted by the relevant scientific community (as evidence of its general acceptance, 45 psychologists cosigned the amicus brief on children's memory submitted in *State v. Michaels*, 1994). Indeed, one appellate court has judged research on children's suggestibility to be both relevant and reliable (*United States v. Rouse*, 1996). To date, however, little direct evidence addresses whether this type of expert evidence is more probative than it is prejudicial.

Effects of Testimony About Children's Mnemonic Capabilities

Expert testimony on the factors that influence adult eyewitnesses' memories sensitizes jurors to the impact of various witnessing conditions on eyewitness accuracy (see, e.g., Blonstein & Geiselman, 1990; Cutler, Dexter, & Penrod, 1989; Cutler, Penrod, & Dexter, 1989; Fox & Walters, 1986). However, little research has examined the effects of expert testimony about child witnesses' mnemonic capabilities on jury decision making. Although some factors (e.g., exposure to misleading postevent information) negatively impact the memories of both children and adults (for a review, see Ceci & Bruck, 1993), other issues such as reality monitoring (e.g., Foley & Johnson, 1985; Foley et al., 1983; Lindsay, Johnson, & Kwon, 1991) and the role of cognitive development in memory (e.g., Farrar & Goodman, 1990; Goodman & Reed, 1986; List, 1986) are specifically relevant to child witnesses. It is possible that expert testimony that highlights the inadequacies in children's cognitive processes may not affect juror judgments because of jurors' unflagging beliefs in children's credibility. For example, if jurors strongly believe that young children do not lie about child sexual abuse, this belief may overpower any impact of expert testimony about children's suggestibility. Therefore, it is important that researchers empirically investigate whether expert testimony on children's memory has any impact on juror judgments.

To date, only one investigation of this kind has been conducted. Crowley, O'Callaghan, and Ball (1994) showed a videotaped simulation of a child sexual abuse trial to college students and jury-eligible community members; the alleged victim was either 6, 9, or 12 years old. In this simulation, a court-appointed expert who was questioned by the judge and cross-examined by the defense attorney provided information about age differences in memory accuracy, suggestibility, and reality monitoring (i.e., differentiation of reality from fantasy). The gist of the expert's testimony on all of these topics was that children under the age of 6 may have poorer recall for events and people, may be more susceptible to suggestive questions, and may have trouble differentiating fantasy from reality. The expert also argued that the mnemonic capabilities of children over the age of 6 do not differ significantly from the capabilities of adults. In addition to this testimony about cognitive development, the expert provided limited testimony about children's behavioral responses to abuse; that is, the expert argued that delayed disclosure is a typical reaction to abuse and provided some possible reasons why a child would delay disclosure (e.g., fear of retaliation, guilt, or self-blame). Crowley et al. (1994) found that the presentation of this expert testimony affected jurors' perceptions of a child's memory; specifically, jurors who heard expert testimony believed the child victim—irrespective of the child's age—was less likely to be susceptible to suggestion. It is important to note that the age of the alleged victim did not interact with the presence of expert testimony. In addition, the presentation of expert testimony did not influence juror verdicts.

Unfortunately, the method used by Crowley et al. (1994) has several limitations. These authors confounded the presentation of behavioral evidence about child sexual abuse and the presentation of expert testimony on cognitive development. Therefore, it is unknown whether expert testimony on age differences in memory has a unique impact on juror decisions. Moreover, because the authors did not present jurors with a child victim who was under the age of 6—the age at which children begin to remember as accurately as adults, according to their expert—the authors could not demonstrate whether expert testimony sensitized jurors to age differences in memory. To do so, the authors would have to present jurors with a very young victim (under 6 years old) and an older victim (i.e., over 6 years old) and examine whether the presence of expert testimony caused jurors to differentiate between the mnemonic capabilities of these two victims. Further research must be conducted to determine whether expert testimony on children's mnemonic capabilities sensitizes jurors to the effects of age on eyewitness memory. Thus, the research to date does not conclusively establish whether expert testimony on child memory is more probative than prejudicial.

Expert Testimony on Behavioral Responses to Child Sexual Abuse

Research and Case Law on General Behavioral Evidence

Researchers have examined a number of potential correlates of sexual victimization, including posttraumatic stress disorder, behavioral problems, sexualized behaviors, aggression, and mental illness. A recent review of the literature comparing sexually abused and nonabused children found that abused children generally exhibited more symptoms than nonabused children (Kendall-Tackett, Williams, & Finkelhor, 1993), but the authors of that review concluded that no one symptom was exhibited by a majority of abused children. Moreover, no clear-cut pattern of behavioral symptoms was correlated with abuse. Indeed, fully a third of abused children exhibited no symptoms at all. Similarly, Berliner and Conte (1993) concluded that there is no evidence that behavioral symptoms can be used to discriminate between abused and nonabused children. These authors argued further that some of the behavioral symptoms that have been investigated as potential indicators of abuse (e.g., reluctance to discuss the allegations) are equally plausible indicators of nonabuse.

Prior to the *Daubert* decision, expert evidence on behavioral reactions to child sexual abuse was often judged inadmissible as substantive evidence of abuse (for a review of the pre-*Daubert* case law, see Myers et al., 1989). That is, courts often ruled that it was impermissible for an expert to offer evidence that the child witness exhibited behaviors that were typical of child sexual abuse victims to substantiate the child's allegations of abuse. Courts were more likely to accept this kind of expert testimony if it was offered to rehabilitate the child's credibility (i.e., to explain inconsistent responses on the part of the alleged victim).

It is not yet clear whether any court's decisions about the admissibility of behavioral reactions testimony will change in light of *Daubert*. However, we believe that the research conducted on behavioral correlates of sexual victimization would survive a *Daubert* hearing. For example, this research has included the proper comparison groups (e.g., nonabused samples) and has been subjected to peer review. Moreover, this scientific evidence is clearly probative. The fact that a child exhibits some of the symptoms associated with sexual abuse, although not dispositive, increases the likelihood that the child is an abuse victim.[3] Moreover, jury simulation studies are beginning to demonstrate that testimony on behavioral reactions to sexual abuse is not prejudicial to the defendant.

Effects of Testimony About Behavioral Responses to Sexual Abuse

Jurors who are not exposed to expert testimony may expect a truthful child victim to behave in a very circumscribed manner (e.g., in a confident and consistent manner, like any other truthful witness) and thus may judge a child to be less credible when his or her testimony violates these expectations (Leippe & Romanczyk, 1989). An expert's testimony on behavioral reactions to sexual abuse may provide jurors with new information about counterintuitive behaviors that are typical of a sexually abused child (e.g., delays in reporting) or address certain misconceptions that jurors may have about child sexual abuse (McCord, 1986; Myers et al., 1989; Roe, 1985; Serrato, 1988). In addition, an expert may explain that a child victim's hesitation when describing his or her abuse could stem from a child's lack of sexual knowledge or from fear of an abuser rather than from the child's deception or subterfuge. This testimony may cause jurors to judge a nervous, hesitant child witness more leniently.

Expert testimony may increase the credibility of the child witness by linking the content and presentation of the child's testimony to the "unusual behaviors" and reactions that children in general have to sexual abuse (McCord, 1986; Serrato, 1988). Because expert testimony may broaden jurors' understanding of abuse and victims' reactions to abuse, jurors exposed to expert testimony should be better able to link the counterintuitive reactions of a particular child witness (e.g., a delay in reporting the abuse) with an understandable—and believable—sexual abuse scenario. For example, jurors—relying on their preconceived beliefs and expectations—may infer that a child who nervously fidgets while testifying is lying, because they believe that nervousness and fidgeting are behavioral indicants of deception (e.g., Zuckerman, DePaulo, & Rosenthal, 1981). However, if jurors have heard an expert testify that sexually abused children often appear nervous and uncertain when describing their experience, they may be more likely to believe a child who nervously fidgets on the stand because his or her behavior is congruent with the typical behavior of abuse victims. Indeed, a child who is confident and poised during testimony may be

---

[3]It should be noted that the probability that a particular child has been abused is also dependent on the base rate of abuse in a population of children.

judged a liar by jurors who have heard expert evidence suggesting that this is atypical behavior for an abuse victim.

A few researchers have investigated the impact of behavioral reactions testimony on juror decisions in child sexual abuse cases. These studies have addressed several empirical questions. Is behavioral reactions testimony more influential when the child victim–witness is a particular age (Gabora, Spanos, & Joab, 1993; Kovera & Borgida, 1992)? Does the way in which the testimony is presented (e.g., standard testimony vs. testimony that concretely links the case facts to the psychological research) attenuate its influence on juror decisions (Gabora et al., 1993; Kovera & Borgida, 1992; Kovera, Gresham, Borgida, Gray, & Regan, 1997)? Does behavioral reactions testimony bolster the credibility of the child, or does it sensitize jurors to the typical behavioral reactions of child sexual abuse victims (Kovera, Gresham, et al., 1997)?

To investigate whether behavioral reactions testimony may have a greater impact on juror decisions when the child victim–witness is a particular age, Gabora et al. (1993) conducted a jury simulation study in which they manipulated the age of the child witness (13 vs. 17 years old) and the presence of expert testimony on behavioral reactions to child sexual abuse. In the expert testimony conditions, the expert was described as a clinician who specialized in child sexual abuse cases. In the general expert testimony conditions, the expert talked about the psychological research on children's behavioral reactions to abuse; specifically, she described common reactions to child sexual abuse and explained some seemingly unusual victim behaviors such as delayed disclosure. In the specific expert testimony conditions, the expert described the same psychological research as she did in her general testimony, but she also linked the research to the case at hand. This specific expert testimony also included a description of the expert's interview with the child, and the expert offered an opinion that the child had been abused. Expert testimony of either form did not significantly affect juror verdicts, either independently or in interaction with child witness age.

It is not altogether surprising that Gabora et al. (1993) found no impact of behavioral reactions expert testimony on verdicts in their jury simulation study. Although the researchers varied both witness age and the presence of expert testimony in a single trial scenario, the ages of the children in this simulation present problems for assessing whether expert testimony sensitizes jurors to a sexual abuse victim's behavioral reactions. The witnesses in Gabora et al. were 13 and 17 years old. Because people believe that children under the age of 12 are unlikely to have detailed sexual knowledge (Isquith, Levine, & Scheiner, 1993; Scheiner, 1988), the Gabora et al. study does not provide information about the impact of behavioral reactions testimony on jurors' perceptions of children who presumably are able to fabricate allegations of abuse because of their sexual knowledge (e.g., children who are 13 or older) and on their perceptions of children who presumably would be unable to fabricate (e.g., children who are 12 or younger). If one expects that expert testimony enhances child witnesses' credibility by explaining that their counterintuitive behavioral reactions to abuse are not necessarily indications of fabrication, it is crucial to compare jurors' perceptions of child witnesses who vary in their perceived ability to fabricate abuse allegations (e.g., children who are younger and older than 12).

Kovera and Borgida (1992) conducted a study that addressed these issues. In this study, participants watched a 3.5-hr videotape simulation of a child sexual abuse trial. The child witness was played by either an 8-year-old or a 14-year-old actress. In addition, the authors varied the type of expert psychological testimony they presented to their participants; jurors heard either standard expert testimony on behavioral reactions, standard expert testimony that was concretized with a hypothetical example, or no expert testimony. In the standard expert testimony, the expert described the typical set of victim reactions to child sexual abuse, including behaviors such as nightmares and delayed reporting of the allegation (i.e., standard behavioral responses testimony). The expert also explained that children often do not have the knowledge to communicate effectively about their abusive experiences; therefore, they sometimes appear confused when discussing the abusive episodes. In the concrete expert testimony, after the expert presented the standard summary of the psychological research on typical behavioral responses to sexual abuse, the prosecuting attorney described a hypothetical abuse scenario that closely paralleled the case fact pattern. The expert was then asked to discuss whether the child in this hypothetical scenario behaved in a manner consistent with the psychological research on behavioral reactions to sexual abuse.

Kovera and Borgida (1992) found that in the absence of any expert testimony, jurors were more likely to convict the defendant when the child witness was 14 than when the child was 8. Moreover, jurors who did not view expert testimony were more likely to find the evidence to be consistent with the alleged victim's story when the child was 14 than when the child was 8. The child witness's age did not influence any juror judgments when jurors were presented with expert psychological testimony of either type (i.e., standard or concrete); that is, expert testimony eliminated any effects of child witness age on juror judgments.

Several studies have demonstrated that jurors perceive adolescent victims of sexual abuse to be less credible than child victims (e.g., Bottoms & Goodman, 1994; Duggan et al., 1989); unexpectedly, Kovera and Borgida (1992) did not replicate these findings in their no expert control condition. Indeed, the findings from their study suggest the opposite: Jurors find teenage victims to be more credible than child victims. Although Kovera and Borgida hypothesized that behavioral reactions expert testimony would increase the credibility of the older child because the testimony would explain her counterintuitive reactions may not be indicative of fabrication, this testimony decreased conviction rates when the alleged victim was an adolescent. Perhaps the portion of the expert's testimony in which she explained that young children do not have the requisite sexual knowledge for fabrication was responsible for this effect. If the expert's testimony made the issue of sexual knowledge more salient to the jurors, then this information may have increased the accessibility of jurors' age-related beliefs about fabrication (e.g., Isquith et al., 1993; Scheiner, 1988). In fact, internal analyses revealed that juror beliefs about children's abilities to fabricate allegations of sexual abuse mediated the interactive effects of witness age and expert testimony on juror judgments.

These studies of the influence of expert testimony about the typical behavioral reactions of child sexual abuse victims on juror decision making do not address a critical question raised by the *Daubert* decision: Does expert testimony educate the jury (i.e., sensitize the jury to factors that increase the probability that a child has been abused), or does such testimony prejudicially influence the jury (i.e., bolster the credibility of a witness, irrespective of whether the trial evidence is congruent with the expert's testimony)? More succinctly, is expert testimony on behavioral reactions to child sexual abuse more probative than prejudicial? Kovera, Gresham, et al. (1997) addressed this question by investigating the impact of expert testimony on juror decision making in cases in which the child witness seemed either prepared or unprepared for her testimony.

Survey data suggest that the preparation of a child witness for a courtroom experience is one prosecutorial strategy for increasing witness credibility (Kovera, Gresham, et al., 1997). This pretrial preparation may increase the likelihood that the child witness remains composed and provides consistent responses while testifying (Saywitz & Snyder, 1993). Children who have been prepared for the courtroom experience and, consequently, have become more comfortable in the courtroom might appear more confident, composed, and credible. Not only might they demonstrate poise on the witness stand, but they also might provide more coherent testimony relatively free from hesitancies and nonfluencies.

Although preparation is designed to protect the child from stress attendant to testifying in court, prosecutors believe that preparation also strengthens their case. Another prosecutorial strategy for enhancing child witness credibility is the presentation of behavioral reactions expert testimony. However, it is possible that the combined use of these two strategies may backfire on prosecutors. When presenting evidence about behavioral reactions to sexual abuse, experts may testify that young children do not have knowledge that allows them to understand sexual behavior; therefore, these children often appear confused and uncertain when describing their abuse. Thus, a prepared child who appears calm and composed on the stand is exhibiting behavior that directly contradicts the behavioral responses evidence presented by the expert. If expert testimony sensitizes jurors to an abuse victim's typical behavioral responses, then a prepared child should be judged less credible than an unprepared child, a somewhat counterintuitive finding. If, however, expert testimony bolsters an alleged victim's testimony, then jurors should judge a child witness to be more credible in the presence of expert testimony than in its absence, irrespective of the child's preparation. A direct test of these sensitization and bolstering hypotheses can be conducted if expert testimony and child witness preparation are manipulated within a single study.

To examine these hypotheses, Kovera, Gresham, et al. (1997) showed participants a simulated trial in which the actress portraying the child witness acted either prepared (e.g., the child made eye contact, sat still, and responded confidently) or unprepared (e.g., the child looked down, fidgeted, and responded hesitantly) for her testimony. The trial contained no expert testimony, standard expert testimony on sexual abuse victim's typical behavioral responses, or testimony in which an expert explicitly linked the psychological research on victim's behavioral responses with the trial evidence by means of a hypothetical scenario (concrete expert testimony).[4] In both expert testimony conditions, the expert explained that the combination of a child's fear, guilt, and lack of sexual knowledge often results in a child appearing confused and hesitant when describing sexual abuse. Therefore, the unprepared child's behavior was congruent with the expert's description of typical victim behavior, whereas the prepared child's behavior was incongruent with the expert's description.

Kovera, Gresham, et al. (1997) found that jurors who heard behavioral responses expert testimony in the form of a hypothetical example were more likely to make pro-prosecution judgments when a child witness's behavior was congruent with the expert's testimony (i.e., unprepared) than when her behavior was incongruent with that testimony (i.e., prepared). Specifically, those jurors who viewed concrete expert testimony judged the defendant to be less credible and were more likely to convict the defendant when the child witness was unprepared than when the child witness was prepared. Conversely, jurors who heard standard testimony about victim's behavioral responses were more likely to make pro-prosecution judgments when the child's behavior was incongruent with the expert's testimony (e.g., prepared) than when it was congruent (e.g., unprepared). Specifically, jurors who heard standard expert testimony about victim's behavioral re-

---

[4]Attorneys may use a hypothetical scenario to help them demonstrate how the psychological research relates to the case at hand. In the hypothetical scenario, the prosecuting attorney described a hypothetical situation that closely paralleled the evidence presented by the prosecution and then asked the expert psychologist to explain what the research would lead her to conclude in this hypothetical case (i.e., whether the evidentiary pattern suggested that the child had been abused). The expert then explained how she would use the research to evaluate the facts presented in the case.

sponses rated the defendant less favorably and were more likely to convict when the child was unprepared than when the child was prepared. This interaction suggests that concrete expert testimony sensitizes jurors to behavioral correlates of sexual victimization; standard testimony does not serve this sensitization function. Moreover, independent of child witness preparation, standard testimony increased the child's credibility and conviction rates; however, concrete testimony did not produce such an increase. Thus, standard testimony appears to bolster a child's testimony, whereas concrete testimony does not.

These findings suggest that the explicit link between the psychological research on typical victim behavior and the specific behavior of a particular alleged victim that is provided exclusively in the concrete expert testimony is essential if the expert testimony is to educate the jury as intended (see also Brekke & Borgida, 1988). The concrete link provided in the hypothetical testimony enables jurors not only to use the information provided by the expert but also to use the information when it is appropriate to do so (i.e., where juror misconceptions about human behavior shape their perceptions of witness credibility). In contrast, standard expert testimony that does not bridge the gap between the psychological research and the case evidence appears to bolster the credibility of the child, a legally impermissible outcome. Thus, when evaluating the admissibility of expert testimony it is important to consider not only the reliability of the scientific evidence to be proffered but also the form that this expert testimony takes.

Child Sexual Abuse Accommodation Syndrome Evidence

Pre-*Daubert* rulings have also addressed the admissibility of specific subtypes of expert testimony on children's behavioral reactions to sexual victimization. One such subtype was based on Summit's (1983) description of CSAAS. From his clinical observations of sexually abused children, Summit gleaned five characteristics typically seen in abuse victims: secrecy, helplessness, entrapment and accommodation, delayed and inconsistent disclosure, and recantation. Experts who testify about this syndrome generally use CSAAS as a framework to explain children's seemingly unusual reactions to child sexual abuse (e.g., delays in reporting, recantation of the allegations). Advocates of this syndromal approach argue that child sexual abuse victims engage in prototypical behaviors such as delayed reporting of the abuse, showing fear of men, having nightmares with assaultive content, and recanting their allegations; if a child exhibits these prototypical behaviors, then some experts argue that a psychologist may infer that abuse has occurred.

However, Summit never intended CSAAS to be used as a diagnostic tool; rather, Summit originally described this syndrome to provide therapists with a common framework for discussing sexual abuse. Moreover, the reliability of CSAAS as a diagnostic tool has been questioned (e.g., Myers et al., 1989) because of the lack of empirical evidence supporting the syndrome's ability to discriminate between abused and nonabused children (see Levy, 1989; Melton & Limber, 1989). Thus, when CSAAS is proffered as substantive evidence, it is unlikely to meet the *Daubert* standards for reliability. Although CSAAS does not diagnose sexual abuse, Summit (1992) has argued that research on the syndrome provides evidence that children who have been abused may delay disclosure or retract their allegations. It is possible, therefore, that CSAAS may be admissible for rehabilitative purposes under *Daubert* (Mason, 1995). Indeed, replying on an analysis of the *Federal Rules of Evidence*, appellate courts in New Jersey and Indiana recently have held that CSAAS testimony was improperly admitted as substantive evidence but that it was admissible to rehabilitate the credibility of a child witness (*State v. Michaels*, 1993; *Stewart v. State*, 1995).

Only one empirical study examines whether CSAAS evidence prejudicially influences juror decisions. Specifically, Kovera, Levy, Borgida, and Penrod (1994) examined the impact of CSAAS expert testimony on juror decision making in a child molestation case. They showed jury-eligible participants a 2.5-hr videotaped trial that consisted of edited footage from an actual California criminal trial. Some participants were shown expert testimony about CSAAS. In her testimony, the psychologist explained CSAAS and related the social science research on children's typical emotional and behavioral reactions to sexual abuse. Furthermore, the expert described several common fears of child sexual abuse victims, including fears of men and of being alone. The expert also informed the jurors about prototypical behavioral indicators of abuse, such as nightmares with assaultive content, delays in reporting, and sexual knowledge inconsistent with the child's age. The expert then stated that the child appeared to fit the description of a child with CSAAS. Participants who heard this CSAAS testimony were more likely to convict the defendant than were jurors who heard no expert testimony.

Anatomically Detailed Dolls Evidence

Critics have also debated the merits of another type of expert testimony based on children's behavioral responses: expert testimony reporting on clinical interviews with children during which anatomically detailed (AD) dolls are used as an investigative or therapeutic tool (Koocher et al., 1995; Sagatun, 1991). Some therapists and investigators have used AD dolls to aid children when they describe their experiences of abuse (Everson & Boat, 1994). AD dolls may be a particularly helpful tool when the alleged victim is a very young child who may not have an adequate vocabulary to describe sexual behavior; the dolls may provide the child with an anatomical model for learning the names of body parts or may serve as props to assist the child in describing their experience (Koocher et al., 1995). However, some experts who use this technique assume that because young children usually do not have detailed sexual knowledge, only sexually abused children have the necessary knowledge to demonstrate sexual acts with the AD dolls.

The current empirical database does not support this assumption. Research investigating how nonreferred—and thus presumably nonabused—children interact with AD dolls found that these nonreferred children often examine and touch sexual body parts, although they rarely demonstrate sexual activity such as oral–genital contact or sexual intercourse (for a review, see Koocher et al., 1995). Although some empirical research comparing the play of abused and nonreferred children has supported the assumption that abused children are more likely to engage in sexualized behavior with AD dolls than are nonabused children (e.g., August & Forman, 1989; Jampole & Weber, 1987; White, Strom, Santilli, & Halpin, 1986), other studies have not found differences between these groups (e.g., Cohn, 1991; Kenyon-Jump, Burnette, & Robertson, 1991). Unfortunately, some of this research suffers from methodological constraints, such as the lack of information regarding the reliability of behavioral coding, small sample sizes, and lack of experimenter unawareness of group (e.g., abused vs. nonabused) membership (for methodological criticisms, see Koocher et al., 1995; Levy, 1989; Maan, 1991; Sagatun, 1991).

Prior to *Daubert*, some courts have excluded AD dolls testimony (e.g., *In re Amber*, 1987; *In re Jennifer*, 1988), whereas other courts admitted this testimony (*D. A. H. v. G. A. H.*, 1985; *In re Christine C.*, 1987; *In re J. K.*, 1987; *In re Rinesmith*, 1985). Recently, however, eminent scholars in the child sexual abuse domain have produced two influential reviews of the AD doll literature (Bruck & Ceci, 1995; Koocher et al., 1995) in which they conclude that there is scant empirical evidence to support the discriminative validity of AD doll interviews. Therefore, it is unlikely that expert testimony that relies on AD dolls to diagnose sexual abuse will pass muster using *Daubert*'s admissibility criteria.

In their investigation of the impact of AD testimony on juror decisions, Kovera et al. (1994) presented some jury-eligible participants with expert evidence on AD dolls. In the AD dolls testimony, the expert described the therapy session in which the alleged victim first disclosed her allegations of sexual abuse. On hearing the child's allegations, the expert provided the child with AD dolls to aid the child in relating her experience. The expert described the dolls to the jury and explained that children who have been abused are more likely to demonstrate sexual activity with the dolls than are children who have not been abused. The expert further stated that the child's display of the abusive behavior using the dolls was an accurate reenactment of the child's memory of the incident. Participants who heard this AD dolls expert testimony were more likely to convict the defendant than were jurors who did not hear expert testimony. Given the questionable validity of the AD doll testimony provided in this trial, there is some evidence that AD doll evidence may be more prejudicial than probative.

Expert Testimony on Child Witness Credibility

Research and Case Law on Witness Credibility Evidence

In expert testimony on child witness credibility, an expert directly vouches for the alleged victim's credibility as a witness. The assumption underlying the introduction of credibility testimony is that clinicians' vast experience in dealing with child sexual abuse victims provides a better foundation for making judgments of credibility than does the foundation provided by the common experience of the jury. However, professional clinicians may be no more accurate than laypeople in their judgments of witness credibility or detection of malingering (Faust & Ziskin, 1988). Moreover, such testimony may usurp the function of the jury.

Rarely has expert psychological testimony on credibility evidence been admitted as substantive evidence of a child's credibility. For example, although the Hawaii Supreme Court admitted expert testimony on a child witness's credibility in *State v. Kim* (1982), the court later overturned this ruling in *State v. Batangan* (1990). In *Batangan*, the court ruled that witness credibility evidence should be inadmissible because an expert's conclusions about a child's truthfulness and credibility do not assist the jury and are prejudicial to the defendant. Similarly, other courts have judged credibility testimony to be inadmissible (e.g., *People v. Bledsoe*, 1984; *People v. Roscoe*, 1985; *State v. Erickson*, 1990; *State v. Holloway*, 1986; *State v. Mueller*, 1983; *State v. Myers*, 1984). Given a lack of empirical evidence supporting the reliability of credibility evidence (see Faust & Ziskin, 1988; Myers et al., 1989), it is unlikely that this type of testimony would meet *Daubert*'s criteria for admissibility.

Effects of Witness Credibility Evidence on Juror Judgments

Only a single empirical investigation of witness credibility testimony's impact on juror decisions has been conducted. Kovera et al. (1994) also examined the impact of witness credibility testimony on juror judgments. In one version of their trial simulation, the expert described the frequency of her therapy sessions with the alleged victim and the relationship she had formed with her client. The expert further detailed the extent of her experience working with victims of sexual abuse. After the psychologist related her client's disclosure of the events surrounding the alleged abusive incident, the prosecuting attorney asked the expert whether her vast experience in working with child sexual abuse victims allowed her to form an opinion about the credibility of the alleged victim. The expert responded that she had formed the opinion that the alleged victim was telling the truth about her victimization. Jurors who heard this witness credibility testimony were more likely to convict the defendant than were jurors who heard no expert testimony. Given the unreliability of witness credibility evidence and the findings from Kovera et al., it is likely that witness credibility evidence is more prejudicial than it is probative. This study, therefore, provides additional support for those who argue against the admissibility of witness credibility evidence (e.g., Faust & Ziskin, 1988; Myers et al., 1989).

Direct Comparisons of Expert Evidence Type

The *Daubert* decision highlights the importance of *Federal Rule* 403 (i.e., the tension between prejudicial impact and probative value) when evaluating the admissibility of expert testimony. Perhaps some types of expert testimony are more prejudicial (or more probative) than others. This determination of the relative impact of expert testimony on juror judgments requires the direct comparison of expert evidence type within a single study. Kovera et al. (1994) conducted such a study in which they compared the influence of the more controversial forms of sexual abuse expert testimony (i.e., CSAAS, AD dolls, and witness credibility) on juror decisions. Examining these three types of testimony also allowed the authors to examine the validity of competing categorization schemes for predicting the relative influence of expert testimony.

Imwinkelreid (1981) proposed one such categorization scheme. He argued that juror perceptions of how "scientific" the evidence is will mediate the impact of expert testimony on jurors' decisions. In addition, Imwinkelreid divided expert evidence into three broad categories: (a) techniques that provide quantitative results (e.g., the gas chromatograph or "breathalyzer"), (b) techniques that result in nonquantitative visual displays (e.g., the polygraph or "lie detector"), and (c) techniques that rely on an expert's intuition or judgment (e.g., a psychiatrist's assessment of insanity). According to Imwinkelreid, testimony based on expert judgment is least likely to impress the jury. Furthermore, he has suggested that jurors perceive techniques that produce visual displays as more scientific than techniques that are based on expert judgment. In the same vein, perhaps jurors may view diagnostic AD dolls testimony—which relies on a visual behavioral display—as more scientific than witness credibility or CSAAS testimony, both of which are based on more subjective clinical judgments by the expert.

Social cognitive research on decision making suggests a competing categorization scheme. Researchers in this tradition have investigated the extent to which individuals use group probability data or base-rate information when making decisions (e.g., Bar-Hillel, 1980; Taylor & Thompson, 1982). Perhaps the probabilistic content of expert testimony—rather than perceived differences in scientific status—drives differences in jurors' perceptions of expert testimony. Probabilistic testimony (i.e., scientific generalizations based on groups of respondents) may have a relatively weak impact on juror judgments because it is less concrete, vivid, and salient to the decision maker than is the anecdotal evidence provided in case studies (Saks & Kidd, 1981). In keeping with this hypothesis, Brekke and Borgida (1988) demonstrated that probabilistic expert evidence (e.g., syndromal evidence) influences juror judgments only under extremely constrained circumstances (e.g., when the testimony is presented before any other testimony and the research is linked to the case at hand through a hypothetical example). Perhaps jurors may be less likely to use expert evidence based on probabilistic data (i.e., CSAAS testimony) than they are to use expert evidence based on more vivid case history data (i.e., witness credibility or AD doll testimony).

Only Kovera et al. (1994) have compared the influence of probabilistic evidence with the influence of testimony based on an expert's assessment of a particular individual. Specifically, they examined whether the perceived scientific status or the probabilistic qualities of the expert evidence accounted for differences in the impact of different types of child sexual abuse expert testimony. To this end, Kovera et al. (1994) presented participants with a videotaped child sexual abuse trial simulation in which they varied the type of expert testimony proffered; participants heard either CSAAS, witness credibility, AD doll, or no expert testimony (see previous sections for descriptions of the expert testimony used in the simulation). Participants then made a variety of judgments about the trial and the trial participants. Participants' ratings of the expert and her testimony were less positive when the expert presented CSAAS evidence (i.e., probabilistic information) than when she presented credibility or AD doll evidence (i.e., case history information). Most important, participants actually recalled less of the evidence presented by the CSAAS expert. However, expert evidence type did not influence conviction rates, although it is possible that the high conviction rates in all expert testimony conditions ($M = 83\%$) prevented detection of any differential influence of expert evidence type.

Although it did not detect differences in conviction rates, the Kovera et al. (1994) study suggests that expert testimony involving AD dolls and witness credibility does seem to influence decision making in a direction that is favorable to the child witness (i.e., a pro-prosecution shift in judgments) by influencing participants' perceptions of the expert and expert testimony. These findings suggest that witness credibility and AD doll testimony may be more prejudicial than CSAAS testimony. Yet because

Kovera et al. did not vary the consistency between the expert testimony and the other trial evidence, this study provides no information about whether any of these types of expert testimony (i.e., CSAAS, witness credibility, or AD doll testimony) sensitizes jurors to the factors associated with child sexual abuse. Thus, the Kovera et al. study provides no information about the probative value of these three types of testimony. Until empirical evidence demonstrates that these forms of testimony have some probative value, it may be prudent to limit their admissibility in court because of their possible prejudicial nature.

PSYCHOLOGICAL RESEARCH ON THE EFFECTIVENESS OF *DAUBERT'S* SAFEGUARDS

Some scholars have argued that the *Daubert* decision opens the floodgates, increasing the likelihood that unreliable scientific evidence finds its way into the courtroom (e.g., Simard & Young, 1994; Tamarelli, 1994). They argue that judges arc ill prepared to serve as gatekeepers; judges do not have the requisite training to evaluate accurately the reliability of novel scientific evidence (e.g., Black, Ayala, & Saffran-Brinks, 1994; Tamarelli, 1994). Furthermore, they opine that jurors are unlikely to make distinctions between reliable and unreliable expert evidence because they lack scientific training (e.g., Black et al., 1994; Sanders, 1994; Simard & Young, 1994). Yet the U.S. Supreme Court does not share these reservations. Indeed, in the *Daubert* decision, the U.S. Supreme Court argued that traditional legal safeguards like judicial instruction on the burden of proof, forceful cross-examination, and the presentation of inconsistent evidence provide sufficient means to educate the jury about scientific reliability.

We argue that the *Daubert* decision is not well informed by psychological science. Empirical research has demonstrated that other legal safeguards presumed to be effective may not be (e.g., Stinson, Devenport, Cutler, & Kravitz, 1996). Moreover, psychological evidence already on the shelf suggests that *Daubert's* safeguards do not provide effective means for discrediting any unreliable expert evidence that may be admitted at trial. Indirect evidence for the ineffectiveness of the *Daubert* safeguards comes from the legal psychology research on judicial instructions and from the social psychological literature on belief perseverance and methodological reasoning. Moreover, direct evidence on the ineffectiveness of the cross-examination and opposing experts safeguards is beginning to mount. In the remainder of this section, we review both the indirect and direct evidence that bears on the effectiveness of the safeguards mentioned in *Daubert*.

Indirect Evidence

Judicial Instructions

It is unlikely that judicial instructions on the burden of proof help jurors to evaluate the reliability of novel scientific evidence. Simply put, jurors do not comprehend judge's pattern instructions. Indeed, in their classic investigation of juror comprehension of judicial instructions, Elwork, Sales, and Alfini (1977) found that jurors who heard judicial instructions understood the law no better than jurors who did not hear instructions.

Moreover, empirical research has demonstrated that in particular, jurors do not understand judicial instructions on the burden of proof. Strawn and Buchanan (1976) found that approximately half of their sample understood judicial instructions about the burden of proof (i.e., that the prosecution must prove their case beyond a reasonable doubt). Similarly, Reifman, Gusick, and Ellsworth (1992) found that although jurors who had heard instructions had a better understanding of procedural law (e.g., the appropriateness of considering consequences of the verdict, burden of proof) than did jurors who were not instructed, absolute levels of juror comprehension were low. That is, less than one *third* of the jurors who served on criminal juries knew that the prosecution had the burden of proving their case beyond a reasonable doubt. This body of research suggests that the judicial instruction safeguard mentioned in *Daubert* is ineffective.

Belief Perseverance

Social psychological research on belief perseverance demonstrates that once people have formed an opinion, they are unlikely to be swayed by contradictory evidence. For example, Ross and Anderson (1982) have noted that people often produce naive theories about causal relationships with minimal information. Ross and Anderson also argued that once people are told that there is a relationship between two variables (e.g., a child who engages in sexualized play with AD dolls is a child who has been sexually abused), individuals generate their own logical explanations for the relationship. Moreover, belief perseverance research suggests that people might maintain beliefs they generate during the expert's direct testimony despite the opposing attorney's subsequent efforts to discredit the basis for these beliefs through either cross-examination or the presentation of contradictory evidence (Jelalian & Miller, 1984). For example, jurors' beliefs about the reliability of the expert's scientific evidence may persevere despite the presence of *Daubert*'s safeguards because the jurors may have generated a causal explanation that the opposing attorney did not undermine, discredit, or even address.

In addition, social psychological research on belief perseverance supports the hypothesis that *Daubert's* safeguards may be effective in guarding against the undue influence of some types of expert evidence but not of others. Anderson (1983) demonstrated that concrete data (i.e., vivid case history data) lead to stronger belief perseverance than do abstract data (i.e., statistical summaries). That is, it is easier to undermine beliefs that were generated from abstract, probabilistic data than from more vivid, anecdotal data. Therefore, even a strong cross-examination of an expert witness or an opposing expert may be ineffective in reducing belief perseverance, if the expert's testimony relies on vivid, anecdotal evidence (e.g., AD doll evidence; witness credibility evidence). However, this body of research also suggests that a strong cross-examination might be sufficient to discredit jurors' beliefs associated with an expert's presentation of probabilistic evidence (e.g., child witness memory evidence, CSAAS evidence). Thus, it is conceivable that *Daubert's* safeguards, ironically, may be effective in discrediting some rather reliable evidence that is based on group probability data (e.g., expert testimony on child witness memory) but ineffective in discrediting relatively unreliable evidence that is based on case history data (e.g., witness credibility evidence).

Methodological Reasoning

Despite the U.S. Supreme Court's optimistic evaluation of jurors' capabilities, recent research on laypersons' methodological and statistical reasoning skills suggests that jurors may be unable to accurately assess scientific reliability without additional training (e.g., Nisbett, 1993). For example, Tversky and Kahneman (1974) showed that participants do not recognize that results from small samples are more likely to be fallacious than are results from larger samples. Other researchers also have demonstrated that participants have difficulty applying the law of large numbers to everyday events such as social behavior (Jepson, Krantz, & Nisbett, 1983; Nisbett, Fong, Lehman, & Cheng, 1987). Therefore, it is reasonable to expect that although jurors may use simple heuristics (e.g., a published study is better than an unpublished study) to evaluate the reliability of scientific evidence, jurors may be insensitive to variability in methodological quality (e.g., the representativeness of a sample and sample size).

Yet some studies have revealed that formal training in methodological reasoning can improve individuals' reasoning about everyday life events. For example, Lehman, Lempert, and Nisbett (1988) demonstrated that graduate students in disciplines emphasizing methodological reasoning (e.g., psychology) were more likely to apply these reasoning skills to everyday problems than were graduate students in other disciplines (e.g., law). In addition, Fong, Krantz, and Nisbett (1986) found that people given brief training in methodological and statistical reasoning provided more statistically sophisticated answers to a series of real-world problems. If jurors are insensitive to factors that influence scientific reliability, perhaps they can be trained through cross-examination and opposing experts to be sensitive to these factors when evaluating expert evidence. However, in their studies of statistical training on reasoning ability, Nisbett and his colleagues used training techniques that required trainees to practice the new skills that they had learned; it seems unlikely that either cross-examination or opposing experts could provide comparable statistical training. Jury simulation studies that manipulate the strength of cross-examination or the presence of opposing experts can shed some light on the court's assumption that these safeguards are sufficient to highlight inadequacies in the reliability of expert evidence.

Direct Evidence

Cross-Examination

As the *Daubert* decision notes, cross-examination is one method of highlighting the inadequacies of any scientific research entered into evidence (Saks & Kidd, 1981). Of course, an effective cross-examination is predicated on the knowledge of the attorney; if the attorney is unaware of the factors associated with scientific reliability, it is impossible for him or her to mount an effective cross-examination that undermines unreliable scientific evidence. Recall that Lehman et al. (1988) demonstrated that individuals who have studied the law have poor methodological reasoning skills in comparison to individuals who completed graduate work in psychology. Therefore, it is possible that attorneys may not have the requisite knowledge to illuminate methodological problems with an expert's novel scientific evidence.

If attorneys do not possess the knowledge required to attack the scientific foundation of an expert's testimony, it is also possible that they would recognize this deficit in their knowledge and hire scientists or consultants to assist them in preparing their cross-examinations of experts. Thus, it is also important to determine whether cross-examination is an effective method of undermining unreliable testimony. Is cross-examination worthy of the faith scholars have in this safeguard against "junk" science inappropriately influencing jury verdicts? Berman, Narby, and Cutler (1995) found that a cross-examination that highlighted inconsistencies in an eyewitness's testimony effectively discredited the witness's identification. Expert witnesses, however, are different from eyewitnesses in that experts have specialized knowledge and training. Moreover, anecdotal evidence supports cross-examination's effectiveness in undermining an expert witness's testimony, but little directly relevant empirical evidence supports these claims.

To our knowledge, only one study has investigated whether a more rigorous cross-examination of an expert's testimony on child sexual abuse is more effective in discrediting that testimony. In their investigation of expert testimony's influence on juror judgments, Kovera et al. (1994) varied the strength of the defense attorney's cross-examination of the expert witness in their research design. That is, three types of expert testimony on child sexual abuse (i.e., CSAAS, AD doll, and witness credibility) were subjected to strong or weak cross-examination. In the weak cross-examination conditions, the defense attorney asked the expert a few questions on a very narrow aspect of her testimony. The defense attorney attacked the expert and her testimony on several grounds and did so in a much more hostile, adversarial style in the strong cross-examination conditions than he did in the weak cross-examination conditions.

Although mock jurors reported that the strong cross-examination of the expert was indeed stronger than the weak cross-examination, the manipulation of the cross-examination strength did not influence participants' verdicts, their perceptions of the expert, or their perceptions of the scientific status of the psychological research presented by the expert. Moreover, recent research on expert evidence in sexual harassment trials suggests that cross-examination does not sensitize jurors to issues of construct validity or ecological validity (Kovera, McAuliff, & Hebert, 1997). These findings suggest that once jurors form beliefs about the reliability of expert evidence, these beliefs are relatively resistant to change. So although a number of commentators have suggested that attorneys should use a stunning cross-examination to discredit unreliable scientific evidence (Melton & Limber, 1989; Saks & Kidd, 1981; Tamarelli, 1994), the Kovera et al. (1994, 1997) data suggest that cross-examination may not be an effective means of discrediting expert evidence, calling into question the effectiveness of *Daubert's* cross-examination safeguard.

Opposing Experts

Cross-examination is but one legal safeguard that can be used to discredit unreliable scientific evidence. In their research on belief perseverance, Ross and Anderson (1982) demonstrated that individuals' beliefs may be changed either by attacking the information on which the beliefs are based or by presenting individuals with new data that contradict their beliefs. Cross-examination of an expert witness is akin to attacking the credibility of the information that provides the basis for jurors' beliefs. Yet attacking the expert in cross-examination does not appear to be an effective means of discrediting participants' initial beliefs about the scientific status of the expert's evidence (Kovera et al., 1994). However, in the *Daubert* opinion, the U.S. Supreme Court also argued that the presentation of new and contradictory information by an opposing expert may be an effective way of discrediting the testimony of an expert witness who presents unreliable scientific evidence.

The empirical evidence from an as of yet unpublished study suggests that the U.S. Supreme Court may have been overly optimistic in its assessment of opposing experts as a viable safeguard against unreliable expert evidence. In their investigation of juror evaluations of the reliability of eyewitness identifications, Cutler and Penrod (1995) varied the favorability of the witnessing and identification conditions in addition to the expert testimony that was proffered at trial (i.e., no expert, a defense expert who describes the psychological research on eyewitness memory, the defense expert plus a refuting prosecution expert). Although the defense expert alone increased participants' sensitivity to the witnessing and identification conditions, Cutler and Penrod found that the addition of an opposing expert led to juror insensitivity to these conditions as well as juror skepticism about the eyewitness identification. Generalizing these findings to situations in which jurors are asked to evaluate the reliability of scientific evidence, one might expect that an opposing expert would make jurors skeptical of *all* scientific evidence, not just *unreliable* scientific evidence. Clearly, this outcome was not the U.S. Supreme Court's intent by suggesting opposing expert's data as a safeguard for unreliable evidence. Thus, these data suggest that an opposing expert may not be an effective means of educating jurors about scientific reliability and question the effectiveness of the third, and final, *Daubert* safeguard.

CONCLUSIONS

The recent U.S. Supreme Court decision in *Daubert* (1993) requires a reevaluation of the reliability of scientific evidence that is likely to be offered in child sexual abuse trials. Our review of the literature suggests that although some types of evidence are likely to meet the *Daubert* criteria for admissibility (i.e., evidence on child witness memory and on behavioral reactions to sexual victimization), other types of evidence that could be offered as evidence in sexual abuse trials suffer from questionable reliability and may, in fact, be prejudicial to the defendant (i.e., CSAAS, witness credibility, and AD doll evidence). When the U.S. Supreme Court overturned the Frye rule, however, it was clearly advocating the more liberal admissibility standards of the *Federal Rules of Evidence*. Given this change in admissibility standards, some unreliable evidence on child sexual abuse may be heard by juries.

If unreliable psychological evidence does reach juries, are the *Daubert* safeguards sufficient to educate juries about scientific reliability and to help them make informed decisions about scientific evidence? Judicial instructions do not educate jurors about the burden of proof (Reifman et al., 1992; Strawn & Buchanan, 1976). In at least one study, cross-examination was ineffective in discrediting unreliable scientific evidence on CSAAS, witness credibility, and AD dolls (Kovera et al., 1994). Furthermore, there is preliminary evidence that the presentation of contradictory evidence through an opposing expert increases skepticism of a witness's testimony but not sensitivity to the factors that would render that testimony unreliable (Cutler & Penrod, 1995). Taken together, the evidence suggests that the legal safeguards mentioned in the *Daubert* decision may well be ineffective at educating jurors about the factors that indicate scientific reliability (e.g., replication, falsifiable hypotheses, appropriate control groups). Therefore, more attention should be paid to the gatekeeping role that judges will play in their assessments of scientific status.

Yet there is some evidence that legal training does not prepare judges for this gatekeeping role (Lehman et al., 1988). Some commentators have argued that judges must acquire knowledge about scientific reliability to perform their gatekeeping function competently (Black et al., 1994), perhaps by attending seminars devoted to educating them about science and scientific reliability (Tamarelli, 1994). Fortunately, case books designed to educate judges (and attorneys) about scientific evidence are surfacing (e.g., Faigman, Kaye, Saks, & Sanders, 1997; see also Walker & Monahan, 1996). Only time will reveal whether these efforts are effective in preparing judges to evaluate the likely avalanche of novel scientific evidence— reliable and unreliable—that will confront them on the bench.

REFERENCES

Anderson, C. A. (1983). Abstract and concrete data in the perseverance of social theories: When weak data lead to unshakable beliefs. *Journal of Experimental Social Psychology, 19,* 93–108.

Askowitz, L. R., & Graham, M. H. (1994). The reliability of expert psychological testimony in child sexual abuse prosecutions. *Cardozo Law Review, 15,* 2027–2101.

August, R. L., & Forman, B. D. (1989). A comparison of sexually abused and nonsexually abused children's behavioral responses to anatomically correct dolls. *Child Psychiatry and Human Development, 20,* 39–47.

Ayala, F. J., & Black, B. (1993). Science and the courts. *American Scientist, 81,* 230–239.

Bar-Hillel, M. (1980). The base rate fallacy in probability judgments. *Acta Psychologica, 44,* 211–233.

Berliner, L., & Conte, J. R. (1993). Sexual abuse evaluations: Conceptual and empirical obstacles. *Child Abuse & Neglect, 17,* 111–125.

Berman, G. L., Narby, D. J., & Cutler, B. L. (1995). Effects of inconsistent eyewitness statements on mock-jurors' evaluations of the eyewitness, perceptions of defendant culpability and verdicts. *Law and Human Behavior, 19,* 79–88.

Black, B., Ayala, F. J., & Saffran-Brinks, C. (1994). Science and the law in the wake of *Daubert:* A new search for scientific knowledge. *Texas Law Review, 72,* 715–802.

Blonstein, R., & Geiselman, R. W. (1990). Effects of witnessing conditions and expert witness testimony on credibility of an eyewitness. *American Journal of Forensic Psychology, 8,* 11–19.

Bottoms, B. L., & Goodman, G. S. (1994). Perceptions of children's credibility in sexual assault cases. *Journal of Applied Social Psychology, 24,* 702–732.

Brekke, N., & Borgida, E. (1988). Expert psychological testimony in rape trials: A social–cognitive analysis. *Journal of Personality and Social Psychology, 55,* 372–386.

Bruck, M., & Ceci, S. J. (1995). Amicus brief for the case of *State of New Jersey v. Michaels* presented by committee of concerned social scientists. *Psychology, Public Policy, and Law, 1,* 272–322.

Ceci, S. J., & Bruck, M. (1993). Suggestibility of the child witness: A historical review and synthesis. *Psychological Bulletin, 113,* 403–439.

Cohn, D. S. (1991). Anatomical doll play of preschoolers referred for sexual abuse and those not referred. *Child Abuse & Neglect, 15,* 455–466.

Crowley, M. J., O'Callaghan, M. G., & Ball, P. G. (1994). The juridical impact of psychological expert testimony in a simulated child sexual abuse trial. *Law and Human Behavior, 18,* 89–105.

Cutler, B. L., Dexter, H. R., & Penrod, S. D. (1989). Expert testimony and jury decision making: An empirical analysis. *Behavioral Sciences and the Law, 7,* 215–225.

Cutler, B. L., & Penrod, S. D. (1995). *Mistaken identification: The eyewitness, psychology, and the law.* New York: Cambridge University Press.

Cutler, B. L., Penrod, S. D., & Dexter, H. R. (1989). The eyewitness, the expert psychologist, and the jury. *Law and Human Behavior, 13,* 311–322.

D.A.H. v. G.A.H., 371 N.W.2d 1 (Minn. App. 1985).

Daubert v. Merrell Dow Pharmaceuticals, Inc., 509 U.S., 113 S. Ct. 2786 (1993).

Duggan, L. M., III, Aubrey, M., Doherty, E., Isquith, P., Levine, M., & Scheiner, J. (1989). The credibility of children as witnesses in a simulated child sex abuse trial. In S. Ceci, D. Ross, & M. Toglia (Eds.), *Perspectives on children's testimony* (pp. 71–99). New York: Springer-Verlag.

Elwork, A., Sales, B. D., & Alfini, J. J. (1977). Juridic decisions: In ignorance of the law or in light of it? *Law and Human Behavior, 1,* 163–189.

Everson, M. D., & Boat, B. W. (1994). Putting the anatomical doll controversy in perspective: An examination of the major doll uses and criticisms of the dolls in child sexual abuse evaluations. *Child Abuse & Neglect, 18,* 113–129.

Faigman, D. L., Kaye, D., Saks, M. J., & Sanders, J. (1997). *Modern scientific evidence: The law and science of expert testimony.* St. Paul, MN: West.

Faigman, D. L., Porter, E., & Saks, M. J. (1994). Check your crystal ball at the courthouse door, please: Exploring the past, understanding the present, and worrying about the future of scientific evidence. *Cardozo Law Review, 15,* 1799–1835.

Farrar, J., & Goodman, G. S. (1990). Developmental differences in the relation between scripts and episodic memory: Do they exist? In R. Fivush & J. Hudson (Eds.), *Knowing and remembering in young children* (pp. 30–64). New York: Cambridge University Press.

Faust, D., & Ziskin, J. (1988, July 1). The expert witness in psychology and psychiatry. *Science, 241,* 31–35.

Federal rules of evidence, 28 U.S.C. (West 1975).

Foley, M. A., & Johnson, M. K. (1985). Confusions between memories for performed and imagined actions. *Child Development, 56,* 1145–1155.

Foley, M. A., Johnson, M. K., & Raye, C. L. (1983). Age-related confusion between memories for thoughts and memories for speech. *Child Development, 54,* 51–60.

Fong, G. T., Krantz, D. H., & Nisbett, R. E. (1986). The effects of statistical training on thinking about everyday problems. *Cognitive Psychology, 18,* 253–292.

Fox, S. G., & Walters, H. A. (1986). The impact of general vs. specific expert testimony and eyewitness confidence upon mock juror judgment. *Law and Human Behavior, 10,* 215–228.

Frye v. United States, 293 F. 1013 (D.C. Cir. 1923).

Gabora, N. J., Spanos, N. P., & Joab, A. (1993). The effects of complainant age and expert psychological testimony in a simulated child sexual abuse trial. *Law and Human Behavior, 17,* 103–119.

Goodman, G. S., Hirschman, J. E., Hepps, D., & Rudy, L. (1991). Children's memory for stressful events. *Merrill Palmer Quarterly, 37,* 109–157.

Goodman, G. S., & Reed, R. S. (1986). Age differences in eyewitness testimony. *Law and Human Behavior, 10,* 317–332.

Hutchinson, C. T., & Ashby, D. S. (1994). *Daubert v. Merrell Dow Pharmaceuticals, Inc.:* Redefining the bases for admissibility of expert scientfic testimony. *Cardozo Law Review, 15,* 1875–1927.

Imwinkelreid, E. J. (1981). A new era in the evolution of scientific evidence—A primer on evaluating the weight of scientific evidence. *William and Mary Law Review, 23,* 261–290.

In re Amber B., 191 Cal. App. 3d 682, 236 Cal. Rptr. 623 (1st Dist. 1987).

In re Christine C., 191 Cal. App. 3d 676, 236 Cal. Rptr. 630 (1987).

In re Jennifer, 517 N.E.2d 187 (Mass. Ct. App. 1988).

In re J. K., 49 Wash. App. 670, 745 P.2d 1304 (1987).

In re Rinesmith, 376 N.W.2d 139 (Mich. Ct. App. 1985).

Isquith, P. K., Levine, M., & Scheiner, J. (1993). Blaming the child: Attribution of responsibility to victims of child sexual abuse. In G. S. Goodman & B. L. Bottoms (Eds.), *Child victims, child witnesses: Understanding and improving testimony* (pp. 203–228). New York: Guilford Press.

Jampole, L., & Weber, M. K. (1987). An assessment of the behavior of sexually abused and nonsexually abused children with anatomically correct dolls. *Child Abuse & Neglect, 11,* 187–192.

Jelalian, E., & Miller, A. G. (1984). The perseverance of beliefs: Conceptual perspectives and research developments. *Journal of Social and Clinical Psychology, 2,* 25–56.

Jepson, C., Krantz, D. H., & Nisbett, R. E. (1983). Inductive reasoning: Competence or skill? *Behavioral and Brain Sciences, 6,* 494–501.

Kendall-Tackett, K. A., Williams, L. M., & Finkelhor, D. (1993). Impact of sexual abuse on children: A review and synthesis of recent empirical studies. *Psychological Bulletin, 113,* 164–180.

Kenyon-Jump, R., Burnette, M. M., & Robertson, M. (1991). Comparison of behaviors of suspected sexually abused and nonsexually abused preschool children using anatomical dolls. *Journal of Psychopathology and Behavioral Assessment, 13,* 225–240.

Klein, M. F. (1994). After *Daubert:* Going forward with lessons from the past. *Cardozo Law Review, 15,* 2219–2235.

Koocher, G. P., Goodman, G. S., White, C. S., Friedrich, W. N., Sivan, A. B., & Reynolds, C. R. (1995). Psychological science and the use of anatomically detailed dolls in child sexual-abuse assessments. *Psychological Bulletin, 118,* 199–222.

Kovera, M. B., & Borgida, E. (1992, August). *Children on the witness stand: A persuasion analysis of jurors' perceptions.* Paper presented at the 100th Annual Convention of the American Psychological Association, Washington, DC.

Kovera, M. B., Gresham, A. W., Borgida, E., Gray, E., & Regan, P. C. (1997). Does expert testimony inform or influence jury decision-making? A social cognitive analysis. *Journal of Applied Psychology, 82,* 178–191.

Kovera, M. B., Levy, R. J., Borgida, E., & Penrod, S. D. (1994). Expert testimony in child sexual abuse cases: Effects of expert evidence type and cross-examination. *Law and Human Behavior, 18,* 653–674.

Kovera, M. B., McAuliff, B. D., & Hebert, K. S. (1997, August). *Juror evaluations of expert evidence validity.* Paper presented at the 105th Annual Convention of the American Psychological Association, Chicago, IL.

Lehman, D. R., Lempert, R. O., & Nisbett, R. E. (1988). The effects of graduate training on reasoning: Formal discipline and thinking about everyday life events. *American Psychologist, 43,* 431–443.

Leippe, M. R., & Romanczyk, A. (1989). Reactions to child (versus adult) eyewitnesses: The influence of jurors' preconceptions and witness behavior. *Law and Human Behavior, 13,* 103–132.

Levy, R. J. (1989). Using "scientific" testimony to prove child sexual abuse. *Family Law Quarterly, 23,* 383–409.

Lindsay, D. S., Johnson, M. K., & Kwon, P. (1991). Developmental changes in memory source monitoring. *Journal of Experimental Child Psychology, 52,* 297–318.

List, J. A. (1986). Age and schematic differences in the reliability of eyewitness testimony. *Developmental Psychology, 22,* 50–57.

Maan, C. (1991). Assessment of sexually abused children with anatomically detailed dolls: A critical review. *Behavioral Sciences and the Law, 9,* 43–51.

Mason, M. A. (1995). The child sex abuse syndrome: The other major issue in *State of New Jersey v. Margaret Kelly Michaels. Psychology, Public Policy, and Law, 1,* 399–410.

McCord, D. (1986). Expert psychological testimony about child complainants in sexual abuse prosecutions: A foray into the admissibility of novel psychological evidence. *Journal of Criminal Law and Criminology, 77,* 1–68.

Melton, G. B., & Limber, S. (1989). Psychologist's involvement in cases of child maltreatment: Limits of role and expertise. *American Psychologist, 44,* 1225–1233.

Miller, P. S., Rein, B. W., & Bailey, E. O. (1994). *Daubert* and the need for judicial scientific literacy. *Judicature, 77,* 254–260.

Monahan, J., & Walker, L. (1994). Judicial use of social science research after *Daubert. Shepard's Expert and Scientific Evidence Quarterly, 2*(2), 327–342.

Myers, J. E. B. (1993). Expert testimony regarding child sexual abuse. *Child Abuse & Neglect, 17,* 175–185.

Myers, J. E. B. (1995). New era of skepticism regarding children's credibility. *Psychology, Public Policy, and Law, 1,* 387–398.

Myers, J. E. B., Bays, J., Becker, J., Berliner, L., Corwin, D. L., & Saywitz, K. J. (1989). Expert testimony in child sexual abuse litigation. *Nebraska Law Review, 68,* 1–145.

Nisbett, R. E. (1993). *Rules for reasoning.* Hillsdale, NJ: Erlbaum.

Nisbett, R. E., Fong, G. T., Lehman, D. R., & Cheng, P. W. (1987). Teaching reasoning. *Science, 238,* 625–631.

People v. Bledsoe, 36 Cal. 3d 236, 203 Cal. Rptr. 450, 681 P.2d 291 (1984).

People v. Roscoe, 168 Cal. App. 3d 1093, 215 Cal. Rptr. 45 (5th Dist. 1985).

Reifman, A., Gusick, S. M., & Ellsworth, P. C. (1992). Real jurors' understanding of the law in real cases. *Law and Human Behavior, 16,* 539–554.

Roe, R. (1985). Expert testimony in child sexual abuse cases. *University of Miami Law Review, 40,* 97–113.

Ross, L., & Anderson, C. A. (1982). Shortcomings in the attribution process: On the origins and maintenance of erroneous social assessments. In D. Kahneman, P. Slovic, & A. Tversky (Eds.), *Judgment under uncertainty: Heuristics and biases* (pp. 129–152). Cambridge, England: Cambridge University Press.

Rudy, L., & Goodman, G. S. (1991). Effects of participation on children's reports: Implications for children's testimony. *Developmental Psychology, 27,* 527–538.

Sagatun, I. J. (1991). Expert witnesses in child abuse cases. *Behavioral Sciences and the Law, 9,* 201–215.

Saks, M. J., & Kidd, R. F. (1981). Human information processing and adjudication: Trial by heuristics. *Law & Society Review, 15,* 123–160.

Sanders, J. (1994). Scientific validity, admissibility, and mass torts after *Daubert. Minnesota Law Review, 78,* 1387–1441.

Saywitz, K. J., & Snyder, L. (1993). Improving children's testimony with preparation. In G. S. Goodman, & B. L. Bottoms (Eds.), *Child victims, child witnesses: Understanding and improving testimony* (pp. 117–146). New York: Guilford Press.

Scheiner, J. (1988, April). The use of the minimalist vignette as a method for assessing the generalizability of videotape trial simulation results. In M. Levine (Chair), *Simulated jury research on the child as a witness.* Symposium conducted at the meeting of the Eastern Psychological Association, Buffalo, NY.

Serrato, V. (1988). Expert testimony in child sexual abuse prosecutions: A spectrum of uses. *Boston University Law Review, 68,* 155–192.

Simard, L. S., & Young, W. G. (1994). *Daubert's* gatekeeper: The role of the district judge in admitting expert testimony. *Tulane Law Review, 68,* 1457–1475.

State v. Batangan, 71 Haw. 552, 799 P.2d 48 (1990).

State v. Erickson, 454 N.W.2d 624 (Minn. App. 1990).

State v. Holloway, 82 N.C. App. 586, 347 S.E.2d 72 (1986).

State v. Kim, 64 Haw. 598, 645 P.2d 1330 (1982).

State v. Michaels, 625 A.2d 489 (N.J. Superior Court 1993).

State v. Michaels, 642 A.2d 1372 (N.J. 1994).

State v. Mueller, 344 N.W.2d 262 (Iowa Ct. App. 1983).

State v. Myers, 359 N.W.2d 604 (Minn. 1984).

Stewart v. State, 652 N.E.2d 490 (Ind. 1995).

Stinson, V., Devenport, J. L., Cutler, B. L., & Kravitz, D. A. (1996). How effective is the presence-of-counsel safeguard? Attorney perceptions of suggestiveness, fairness, and correctability of biased lineup procedures. *Journal of Applied Psychology, 81,* 64–75.

Strawn, D. J., & Buchanan, R. W. (1976). Jury confusion: A threat to justice. *Judicature, 59,* 478–483.

Summit, R. C. (1983). The child sexual abuse accommodation syndrome. *Child Abuse & Neglect, 7,* 177–193.

Summit, R. C. (1992). Abuse of the child sexual abuse accommodation syndrome. *Child Abuse & Neglect, 16,* 153–163.

Tamarelli, A. W., Jr. (1994). *Daubert v. Merrell Dow Pharmaceuticals:* Pushing the limits of scientific reliability—The questionable wisdom of abandoning the peer review standard for admitting expert testimony. *Vanderbilt Law Review, 47,* 1175–1203.

Taylor, S. E., & Thompson, S. C. (1982). Stalking the elusive "vividness" effect. *Psychological Review, 89*, 155–181.

Tversky, A., & Kahneman, D. (1974). Judgment under uncertainty: Heuristics and biases. *Science, 185*, 1124–1131.

United States v. Dorsey, 45 F.3d 809, 813 4th Cir., *cert. denied*, 115 S. Ct. 2631 (1995).

United States v. Rouse, 100 F.3d 360 (8th Cir. 1996).

Walker, L., & Monahan, J. (1996). *Daubert* and the *Reference manual*: An essay on the future of science and law. *Virginia Law Review, 82*, 837–857.

White, S., Strom, G. A., Santilli, G., & Halpin, B. M. (1986). Interviewing young sexual abuse victims with anatomically correct dolls. *Child Abuse & Neglect, 10*, 519–529.

Zuckerman, M., DePaulo, B. M., & Rosenthal, R. (1981). Verbal and nonverbal communication of deception. In L. Berkowitz (Ed.), *Advances in experimental social psychology* (Vol. 14, pp. 1–59). San Diego, CA: Academic Press.

10

EXPERT TESTIMONY REGARDING THE CHARACTERISTICS OF SEXUALLY ABUSED CHILDREN: A CONTROVERSY ON BOTH SIDES OF THE BENCH

MARY ANN MASON

In a widely publicized 1986 New Jersey child sexual abuse case, Margaret Kelly Michaels was convicted on 155 counts of sexual offenses involving 20 children who were students in the Wee Care Nursery School. Psychologist Eileen Treacy was a central prosecution witness. She testified to a pattern of behavior, which she called *child sexual abuse syndrome*, and further offered 32 child behavioral indicators of such abuse. On the basis of her analysis of the pretrial interviews of the children and other information, she gave her opinion on whether the testimony and conduct of the children were consistent with child sexual abuse. She determined that for all but 1 child, the testimony and conduct were consistent.

In 1993, the New Jersey Superior Court Appellate Division reversed this conviction on the basis of the improper introduction of expert testimony regarding child sexual abuse syndromes (*State v. Margaret Kelly Michaels*, 1993/1994). The court claimed that evidence presented regarding the scientific reliability of such testimony was insufficient. The court stated, "unquestionably, this erroneously admitted evidence was capable of producing an unjust result and thus requires the reversal of defendant's convictions" (p. 492).

Prosecutors are faced with a frustrating problem in child sexual abuse cases. Often they must prove a case with no corroborative evidence, no witnesses, and a victim who is reluctant or unable to testify against the defendant. Sometimes that victim is less than 5 years old. Even when the victim does testify, the nature of the testimony may be halting and inconsistent and may completely contradict pretrial testimony. In addition, the child may recant or deny that he or she ever made the allegations. Similar problems of proof occur in civil actions relating to custody, dependency, or tort actions.

However, the stakes are often unusually high for the defendant. The possible outcome for the suspected abuser may be prison in a criminal action or a parent's loss of access to his or her child in a civil action, as well as a lifelong social stigma as a child molester.

To help overcome their evidentiary problems, prosecutors and juvenile and family courts rely increasingly on expert witness testimony. In addition to medical witnesses who testify to the physical symptoms of abuse if there are any, mental health professionals, clinical psychologists, psychiatrists, and social workers are regularly called on as witnesses.

These mental health experts usually offer two kinds of testimony. First, they may testify, on the basis of their experience and training, that they consider a particular child to fit the profile of a sexually abused child. To prepare for this testimony, the expert interviews the child extensively—often with the help of an anatomically correct doll—notes symptoms and behavior patterns, and formulates a diagnosis. This evaluation is sometimes derived over the course of several sessions of therapy. The parents and others who have observed the child may be questioned as well. The expert may claim that the child fits the particular characteristics of a specific syndrome associated with sexually abused children or that the child fits a looser description of characteristics often found in sexually abused children. Usually the expert does not reach this conclusion directly but recites the characteristics of an abused child and then describes most of the same characteristics that he or she has observed with this particular child witness.

The second kind of expert testimony addresses only the general characteristics of a sexually abused child but not the behavior of a particular child. With this kind of testimony, the expert, almost always a clinician, may or may not have evaluated the child and addresses general clinical patterns observed in sexually abused children by himself or herself and by others. Here also the testimony may be presented as a specific syndrome or more loosely described as general behavioral characteristics of a sexually abused child.[1]

---

[1]There is another body of cases in which expert testimony is challenged as hearsay testimony. These cases are not included in this study because this testimony is technically lay, not expert, witness testimony and the witnesses challenged include mothers, teachers, and other nonexperts.

Behavioral syndrome testimony in child sexual abuse cases has provoked serious controversy in the courts, with contradictory appellate court decisions on its admissibility within the same jurisdiction. There is also a serious split regarding the conditions under which such testimony is allowed, with some courts allowing this kind of expert testimony, not as direct testimony, but only to rehabilitate the reputation of a child witness who has been accused of being untruthful.[2]

Although testimony regarding the characteristics of sexually abused children is relatively recent (within the last 13 years), a fairly large body of appellate court judges have ruled on its admissibility. In all of these cases, the expert testimony was allowed at the trial court level, and the appellate court was asked to reverse the decisions against the defendant on the grounds that the expert testimony was wrongfully admitted. From these opinions, it is possible to discern definite patterns of expert testimony and of appellate court response. Although this does not tell the whole story because it only includes those cases that are on appeal, it does provide a representative sample of appellate court judges' responses and reasoning and probably fairly represents the nature of the expert testimony and the identity of the experts they must deal with on appeals.

From the other side of the bench, the mental health community that provides the experts is also divided about testimony regarding behavioral characteristics of sexually abused children. The division falls mainly between the clinicians who treat the patients and the research scientists who study the problem. The scientists have now had many years to test the validity of this syndrome testimony, and the clinicians have had the same number of years to work with many sexually abused children. Their disagreement has, for the most part, grown stronger, focusing now on the appropriate role for syndrome testimony, if any, and the ethics of testifying in court on such matters (Berliner & Conte, 1993; Kendall-Tackett, Williams, & Finkelhor, 1993; MacFarlane, 1992; Summit, 1992).

The state of the controversy on both sides of the bench is addressed in this article, in the belief that the divisions can best be lessened by the widest possible understanding between the two worlds.

THE EXPERTS AND THEIR TESTIMONY

My study of the appellate court decisions between 1980 and 1990 (122 cases identified) reveals several facts regarding the identity of the

---

[2]New Jersey presumably allows syndrome testimony for rehabilitative purposes. The court in the Michaels case discussed this distinction in the law but observed that expert witness Treacy's testimony was not restricted to rehabilitating the witness.

TABLE 1
Expert Witnesses by Profession in a Study of
Appellate Court Decisions (1980–1990)

Profession	n	%
Social worker	54	34
Clinical psychologist	49	31
Counselor–therapist	19	12
Psychiatrist	12	8
Physician	12	8
Other	14	9
Total	160	

Note. There was more than one expert in many cases. The Other category includes professors, police investigators, and school principals.

expert witnesses and the nature of their testimony (Mason, 1991).[3] Nearly all the experts have a clinical orientation, with social workers (licensed clinical social workers or American certified social workers) composing the largest group (34%), followed closely by clinical psychologists (31%), and trailed by counselor–therapists (12%), psychiatrists (8%), and physicians (8%). All other groups are sparsely represented (see Table 1).

Almost all of the experts in these cases are hands-on clinicians rather than behavioral scientists. The great majority are therapists, with a significant number serving as the therapist for that particular child witness. Eighty-seven percent interviewed the child, whereas a large group among those who interviewed the child, 45.9%, treated the child as well. Twenty-three experts specified that they used anatomical dolls in their interview (Mason, 1991).

In qualification discussions, many mentioned having attended workshops but not conducting independent research (with the exception of Roland Summit, who is identified in three cases). Nonetheless, none of the courts excluded their testimony of the basis of lack of qualifications. The criterion for acceptance most often used by the courts was experience in working with sexually abused children (Mason, 1991).

CHARACTERISTICS OF SEXUALLY ABUSED CHILDREN

Seventy-three of these appellate decisions specify indicators of sexual abuse offered by the experts in their trial court testimony. The three largest groupings of indicators deal with truthfulness, sexual behavior, and emo-

---

[3]To accomplish this analysis, I conducted and cross-checked a key word search of both the WESTLAW and LEXIS complete state and federal databases from the years 1980 to 1990. The sample of 122 cases selected by this search was coded to describe the grounds for appeal, the identity of the experts, the nature of expert testimony described, the judges' decisions, and the judges' reasons.

tional upset. The largest cluster, cited by experts 54 times, involves recantation, denial, or reluctance to report that the event occurred. As seen later, this emphasis is in part a function of the rules under which the testimony was admitted. Delayed reporting, retraction–recantation, and conflicting and inconsistent accounts are all frequently presented by the experts as characteristics of sexually abused children (see Table 2).

The anomaly of this central core of descriptors, however, is that by their very denials, children strengthen the expert's belief in their abuse and the jury is given the same message. Furthermore, 15 experts testified that sexually abused children do not lie about their abuse, and 6 stated that consistency in accounting is characteristic of sexually abused children. According to which experts are testifying, then, straightforward truth telling is a characteristic of a sexually abused child, but so are delay, denial, and recantation.

There are other contradictions as well. The second largest category of descriptors deals with the child's sexual behavior. Even though 14 experts cited inappropriate knowledge of sex and sexual preoccupation as characteristics of a sexually abused child, some others (6) believe naïveté and aversion to sexual matters are marks of abuse. In two of the cases, fear of men was recited as a trait of a sexually abused child, whereas 2 experts testified that a desire to protect or to continue to see the abuser was consistent with abuse. In yet another contradiction, pseudomaturity was cited by 2 experts as evidence of sexual abuse, whereas 1 expert cited emotional immaturity (Mason, 1991).

In the third cluster, many experts described emotional or acting out behavior as consistent with sexual abuse, which may be considered typical of many children at some point. These general characteristics include depression and anxiety (15), anger (5), regressive or withdrawn behavior (12), sleep or eating disorders including nightmares and bed wetting (24), and behavioral problems such as running away, problems at school, and other forms of acting out behavior (17; Mason, 1991).

This examination of characteristics offered by expert witnesses in this sample indicates, at the least, an imprecise behavioral profile with a number of critical contradictions. Part of the reason that these characteristics are so contradictory and diverse may be that the expert is tailoring the list to suit a particular child. For example, in *State v. Myers* (1984), the court allowed testimony that the child was abused because she showed symptoms such as fear, confusion, a poor mother–daughter relationship, fear of men, nightmares with assaultive conduct, and sexual knowledge beyond her years. However, the expert in *Ward v. State* (1988) testified that a child could show signs of abuse by sexual behavior, passiveness or aggressiveness, changes in eating habits, underachievement, sleep disturbances, or depression.

TABLE 2
Description of Sexually Abused Children Offered in Testimony

Truthfulness	Sexual behavior	Emotional behavior	Acting out behavior	Other
Delay, denial, inconsistency	Overly sexual	Nightmares, sleep	Problems at school (7)	Play with dolls indicates
Delayed reporting (21)	Knowledge of sex	disorders (13)	Aggression (3)	abuse (12)
Retraction, recantation	inappropriate for	Helplessness (10)	Relationship problems (2)	Secrecy (8)
(19)	age (8)	Fear (10)	Running away (2)	Accommodation (8)
Conflicting and unconvinc-	Sexual preoccupation	Depression (8)	Pseudomaturity (2)	Drawings by child indicate
ing disclosure or incon-	(6)	Bed wetting (7)	Agitation (1)	abuse (3)
sistent accounts (14)	*Aversion to sex*	Anxiety (7)		Inappropriate trust level (2)
Fabrication (1)	Negative attitude	Withdrawal (6)		Minimization of events (2)
Truthful, consistent	toward sex (3)	Regression (6)		Report to nonfamily mem-
Child does not lie, or false	Naive in sexual	Guilt (5)		ber (1)
accounts are rare (15)	matters (1)	Anger (5)		Remember abuse when
Consistency in account (a	Fear of men (2)	Eating disorders or lack		asleep (1)
child is unable to main-		of appetite (4)		Ambivalence (1)
tain a consistent lie		Embarrassment (2)		Poor self-image (1)
over time; 6)		Confusion (2)		Restriction of activity (1)
Child can tell reality from		Suicidal (1)		Sense of betrayal (1)
fantasy (3)		Sense of loss (1)		
		Emotional behavior (1)		
		Dissociative behavior (1)		
		Trauma (1)		

Note. ns are in parentheses. *N* = 122.

TABLE 3
How Experts Labeled Descriptions

Syndrome	n
Child sexual abuse accommodation syndrome	10
Posttraumatic stress disorder	4
Child sexual abuse syndrome	3
Intrafamilial child sexual abuse syndrome	3
Child abuse accommodation syndrome	2
Post-child-molest traumatic stress disorder	1
Child molest syndrome	1
No syndrome named	49
Total	73

LABELS GIVEN TO SYNDROME TESTIMONY

What the experts in these cases called the indicators generally varied widely (see Table 3). In many of the earlier cases, experts labeled the characteristics as the child sexual abuse accommodation syndrome (CSAAS), or some variation of that term, and they often mentioned Ronald Summit—the psychiatrist who is generally credited with formulating this syndrome to describe interfamilial sexual abuse (Summit, 1983). The five characteristics that Summit noted, which are still frequently mentioned even when not identified as CSAAS, are secrecy, helplessness, accommodation, fear of disclosure, and retraction. In later cases, CSAAS or its variations were less frequently noted, and most experts described their testimony generally as a report of characteristics of sexually abused children but did not mention the syndrome per se. This may well be a response to the refusal of some courts to admit the CSAAS on the grounds that it lacks scientific reliability, as evidenced by its exclusion from the *Diagnostic and Statistical Manual of Mental Disorders* (3rd ed., rev. [DSM-III-R]; American Psychiatric Association, 1987). A few of the more recent cases have moved away entirely from sexual abuse classifications and instead refer to posttraumatic stress disorder (PTSD), which is included in the *DSM-III-R* (*Matter of E. M.*, 1987; *State v. Catsam*, 1987; *State v. Reser*, 1989; *Townsend v. State*, 1987). This testimony emphasizes the reluctance of children to report the event immediately or at all.

JUDICIAL RESPONSE TO EXPERT TESTIMONY

Two legal rules regarding the admissibility of expert testimony must be considered by judges. The first is the well-established general rule that the issue of credibility is the sole province of the jury. As one court said, "it is hornbook law [law school textbook] that the credibility of a witness and the weight to be given his testimony rests exclusively with the jury or trier of fact" (*United States v. Rosenberg*, 1952, p. 320). This would be the case, for instance, with the introduction of the results of a polygraph or of an expert who actually claimed that he or she could tell if a witness were lying.

The second rule is that the judge must consider whether the expert testimony is reliable. In making this judgment, appellate courts are guided by the *Federal Rules of Evidence* (1991) or their state's version of them. According to Rule 702, "if scientific, technical, or other specialized knowledge will assist the trier of fact to understand the evidence or to determine a fact in issue, a witness qualified as an expert by knowledge, skill, experience, training, or education, may testify thereto in the form of an opinion or otherwise" (p. 1020). This rule is balanced by Rules 401 and 403, which insist respectively that the evidence must be relevant and that it must not create a substantial likelihood of undue prejudice by confusing the issues or misleading the jury.

In addition to these broad rules, some jurisdictions, including the federal courts, follow the more stringent Frye test (*Frye v. United States*, 1923), which permits expert testimony only when the trial court has found that the scientific principle or discovery underlying the testimony is "sufficiently established to have gained general acceptance in the particular field in which it belongs" (p. 1020).

This rule was recently challenged as too narrow. The U.S. Supreme Court, in a case popularly referred to as the "junk science" case (*Daubert v. Merrell Dow Pharmaceuticals, Inc.*, 1993) involving expert witness testimony in a product liability dispute, loosened the rule somewhat. Instead of insisting on general acceptance in a particular scientific field, the court dictated that the trial judge must make a judgment on whether an expert's testimony is to be admitted based on whether the testimony's underlying reasoning or methodology is scientifically valid. The judge must consider several facts in deciding this and is not limited to one. These factors include

> "whether the theory or technique in question can be (and has been) tested, whether it has been subjected to peer review and publication, its known or potential error rate, and the existence and maintenance of standards controlling its operation, and whether it has attracted widespread acceptance within a relevant scientific community" (*Daubert*, 1993, p. 2792).

In the appellate cases, which were decided between 1980 and 1990 (before the *Daubert* decision), fairly clear patterns of acceptance and rejection can be identified (Mason, 1991). In the 122 cases examined, there is an overall trend in favor of the trial court's admission of expert testimony: 67 appellate courts approved admission, 44 disallowed testimony, and 11 approved admission in part and disallowed in part (see Table 4).

TABLE 4
Response to Challenges of Expert Testimony

Response	Admission		Nonadmission		Total
	n	%	n	%	n
Particular child shows signs of abuse (syndrome and general)	54	63.5	31	36.5	85
General characteristics (not particular to one child)	21	60.0	14	40.0	35
Syndrome testimony (not particular to one child)	3	33.3	6	66.7	9
Testimony based on observations with anatomical dolls	2	22.3	7	77.7	9
Children do not lie about abuse	3	25.0	9	75.0	12
Characteristics of defendant–abuser	1	7.1	13	92.9	14
Total	84		80		164

Note. Cases may have more than one basis for admission–nonadmission. Totals are more than 100% of total cases.

The majority of appellate courts that allow the expert's testimony generally state that it is within the trial court's discretion or that the testimony is helpful. They allow it even when it is applied to a particular child rather than presented as a general phenomenon. The Supreme Court of Hawaii —the first court to allow this testimony—explained that the expert's opinion regarding the complainant's credibility logically followed from his testimony about the behavior of sexually abused children. Therefore, the testimony respecting the credibility of the complainant "cannot be considered to be substantially more prejudicial than the testimony which led to the conclusion" (*State v. Kim*, 1982, p. 1335).

By far the most important reason given for disallowing the trial court's use of expert testimony (see Table 5) is that it is an inappropriate support

TABLE 5
Reasons for Exclusion of Expert Testimony

Reasons	n
Inappropriate support of child's credibility	27
Inappropriately defines characteristics of defendant	13
Not helpful–irrelevant	10
Claim that "children do not lie" usurps jury function	9
Anatomical dolls not scientifically accepted	7
Syndrome not accepted in scientific community	3
Syndrome testimony not allowed to prove abuse occurred	3
Top prejudicial	1

Note. Some courts offer more than one reason for exclusion.

of the child's credibility. In a similar vein, experts who said directly that children do not lie about sexual abuse were disallowed in 9 cases.

Only about 13 of these appellate courts rejected the admission of expert testimony on the grounds that the testimony was not established in the scientific community. These rejections focus on syndrome testimony and on the use of anatomically correct dolls. These appellate courts are less likely to accept testimony about the behavior of sexually abused children with CSAAS, or some version of it, than about a more flexible list of descriptors with no title. Some courts challenge the scientific reliability of the syndrome on the basis that it is not recognized as a diagnostic category by the American Psychiatric Association or the American Psychological Association. As the California court observed In re Sara M (1987),

> the Third District concluded the evidence adduced at the jurisdictional hearing failed to meet the Kelly–Frye Standard. The psychologist testified the syndrome is neither included in the *Diagnostic and Statistical Manual of Mental Disorders* (DSM-III-R) of the American Psychiatric Association nor recognized by the American Psychological Association or other professional organizations. The psychologists described the syndrome as being in the beginning stages of development and acceptance. (p. 560)

Yet some courts do not seem troubled by this lack of acceptance in the relevant scientific community and readily accept syndrome testimony (*People v. Gray*, 1986; *People v. Luna*, 1988).

Although the American Psychiatric Association's diagnostic system does not recognize the CSAAS or any other diagnostic profile of the sexually abused child, the *DSM-III-R* does recognize PTSD. At least one court made this distinction in allowing testimony labeled PTSD about a child's reluctance to admit that sexual abuse had occurred (*People v. Gray*, 1986).

When directly challenged on this issue of testimony that is based on observations with anatomical dolls, most of these appellate courts refuse to accept testimony that a child's play with anatomical dolls reveals evidence of sexual abuse. This technique—widely used by therapists to aid in assessing whether the child has been sexually abused—is sometimes challenged under the Frye rule as a new scientific principle not "sufficiently established to have gained general acceptance in the particular field in which it belongs" (*Frye*, 1923, p. 1022; also see Levy, 1989). The court in *In re Amber B.* (1987) reversed a dependency adjudication on the basis of doll-assisted testimony, arguing that "the purpose [of the California version] of the Frye rule is to prevent fact-finders from being misled by the 'aura of infallibility' that may surround unproven scientific methods" (p. 685; see also Levy, 1989).

THE REBUTTAL PHENOMENON

A close look at the patterns of acceptance or rejection of the admissibility of this kind of expert testimony reveals an extremely significant pattern. The overall pattern of acceptance of expert witness testimony is greatly skewed toward rebuttal rather than direct (see Table 6). Although on direct testimony appellate courts are more likely to disapprove rather than approve of expert witness testimony, they are enthusiastic about admitting expert testimony to rehabilitate the credibility of the witness who has been attacked by the defense. Twenty-seven courts admitted expert testimony on rebuttal, whereas only 7 rejected it. Courts that reject affirmative testimony sometimes express in *dicta* that they would have allowed it for the purpose of rehabilitating the child witness. There has been a movement in this direction among legal scholars as well (see, e.g., Myers et al., 1989).

Even though there is an element of fair play in allowing expert testimony when the child's credibility has been attacked, there are two significant problems with how most appellate courts handle the rebuttal exception. First, courts allow expert witness testimony on recantation, which associates a child's behavior with a syndrome used to diagnose sexual abuse. Second, opportunity for rebuttal becomes an open window through which all kinds of testimony not allowed on direct testimony are thrown.

The typical rebuttal situation occurs when the defense points out that the child delayed, sometimes for months or even years, the telling about the alleged incident of abuse or that the child recanted regarding the original accusation of abuse. For example, in *State v. Middleton* (1983), a 14-year-old girl reported that her father had raped her. Within 1 week, she made consistent reports to her mother's friend, a children's services worker, a doctor, the police, and the grand jury. Six weeks later, she recanted in front of her mother, her father's attorney, and another witness.

When evidence of the child's change of story was brought forth at trial, the expert was then allowed to explain this supposedly incomprehensible behavior by testifying that a characteristic of a sexually abused child is frequent denial following an allegation of sexual abuse, presumably out of fear of the abuser. The Middleton court stated on appeal that

TABLE 6
Pattern of Admission of Testimony

Testimony type	Admit n	Exclude n
Direct	57	73
Rebuttal	27	7

Note. $\chi^2(1, N = 164) = 13.64$, $p < .001$.

if a complaining witness in a burglary trial, after making the initial report, denied several times before testifying at trial that the crime had happened, the jury would have good reason to doubt seriously her credibility at any time. However, in this instance we are concerned with a child who states she has been the victim of sexual abuse by a member of her family. The experts testified that in this situation the young victim often feels guilty about testifying against someone she loves and wonders if she is doing the right thing.... Explaining this bizarre behavior by identifying its emotional antecedents could help the jury better assess the witness's credibility. (*State v. Middleton*, 1983, p. 1222)

Although it may seem fair to allow the expert to counter charges by the defense that recantation indicates lying, the anomaly is that recantation is presented as a characteristic of a sexually abused child, thereby persuading the jury not only that this kind of delay for a child is explainable (as it might be by other theories of children's testimony) but also that it is a characteristic of a sexually abused child. This provides a form of "linkage," which it could be argued is highly prejudicial.

Perhaps even more problematic is that the expert's testimony is often not limited to the fact of recantation. In *Alison v. State* (1986/1987), the child witness was not accused of recantation but of fact complicity with her mother in creating the story. The court then allowed the experts to bring in a very wide range of syndrome testimony, which contained no reliability data, that only touched on complicity and did not mention recantation.

In *People v. Gray* (1986), the 9-year-old child was initially reluctant to disclose the alleged acts of lewd behavior perpetrated by her stepfather and was inconsistent initially in her account by naming a stranger, not her stepfather. The expert witness was permitted to testify that

there are certain behavioral traits seen in molestation victims, *i.e.*, delayed reporting, inconsistent disclosure, accommodation in the sense of outward affection toward an adult a child also fears, and increased likelihood of immediately reporting a stranger than a family member. (p. 216)

In this case, the allegation was brought by the girl's father in the course of a child support battle, whereas the girl's mother reported that the girl had a very good relationship with her stepfather and had shown no signs of emotional distress.

Overall, the rebuttal exception skews the nature of the expert testimony in the courts toward recantation, inconsistency, and delay, as indicated in the previous discussion of the indicators mentioned in the experts' testimony. These indicators become the password by which a wide range of expert testimony is permitted into the courtroom.

PROFESSIONAL CONCERNS ABOUT EXPERT TESTIMONY REGARDING THE CHARACTERISTICS OF SEXUALLY ABUSED CHILDREN

Most appellate courts, then, are concerned with the form in which the expert testimony is presented, that is, not represented as a specific syndrome or offered on rebuttal rather than affirmatively; but they are reluctant to look beyond the form to critically examine the content of the testimony or the standing of this diagnostic tool within its professional community. In addition, appellate courts are generally unconcerned about scientific training and are willing to accept the testimony of expert witnesses as long as they have had significant clinical experience. They do not question the relationship of the expert with the child.

I now cross over to the other side of the bench and examine the standing of syndrome testimony within the relevant community of mental health professionals and scientists. In this community, the divisions and contradictions are nearly as severe as they are in the courts. The major division may be described as that between the research scientists and the clinicians. Generally speaking, clinicians are most likely to treat sexually abused children and most likely to serve as expert witnesses. These clinicians are generally more confident about the reliability of behavioral indicators of abuse. On the other side, research scientists are more likely to test the reliability of syndrome testimony in controlled scientific studies, and they are generally more critical of testimony regarding behavioral indicators of sexual abuse. There is a second issue, usually raised outside the clinical community, about the self-regulating standards that the profession sets, or does not set, with regard to this type of expert testimony. Of particular concern is the relationship of the expert to the child witness (Garbarino, Stott, & the Faculty of the Erikson Institute, 1989).

There is now over a decade of research and publication focusing on the symptomology of sexually abused children. In general, it is fair to say that the research community has grown wary regarding the existence of distinct behavioral characteristics. In two recent studies, prominent researchers (Berliner & Conte, 1993; Kendall-Tackett et al., 1993) evaluated the large number of studies that have investigated the existence of behavioral characteristics. Both groups are critical of the presence of clear indicators of sexual abuse. Kendall-Tackett et al. reviewed 45 of these studies. Their finding is that although sexually abused children demonstrated more symptoms than nonsexually abused children, these symptoms covered a wide range and fell into no clearly discerned pattern. In addition, about one third showed no symptoms at all. In assessing their findings, the authors stated that

> the range of symptoms, the lack of a single predominant symptom pattern, and the absence of symptoms in so many victims clearly sug-

gest that diagnosis is complex. Because the effects of abuse can manifest themselves in too many ways, symptoms cannot be easily used, without further evidence, to confirm the presence of sexual abuse. Yet the absence of symptoms certainly cannot be used to rule out sexual abuse. There are too many sexually abused children who are apparently asymptomatic. This finding is especially important for those conducting forensic evaluations. (p. 175)

The second review article by researchers Berliner and Conte (1993) reaches similar conclusions. The authors stated that

> fundamentally, all the indicator-based assessment strategies suffer the same essential problems. For most criteria there is little or no evidence that the variables actually discriminate between abused and nonabused children. For many of the criteria offered as evidence that abuse did or did not take place, it is just as plausible that an alternative hypothesis is true. For example, several commentators argue that a relevant criterion for a true case of sexual abuse is if the child is very hesitant to talk about the abuse. This is because of an assumption that a sexually abused child will feel ashamed and will have been threatened or bribed not to tell. However, it is just as possible that a child who has told several other adults about the abuse and been supported in that telling or a child who is too young to know what the sexual abuse represents, or a child with high self-esteem or a high level of assertiveness may show no hesitancy in describing the abuse. (pp. 114–115)

Many clinicians would not agree with the general criticism of the lack of a definable pattern or the difficulty in interpreting symptoms, such as a fear of disclosure. They feel that they have been dealt with unfairly by criticism from within their community and from the courts. Kee MacFarlane (1992), a noted clinician and director of the Children's Institute International, commented that

> in sexual abuse cases, the defense will always try to avoid the unpopular appearance of attacking the character of a child. The target becomes whatever else is in the arsenal of the prosecution: the witnesses, the experts, the materials, the research, the literature. It has been particularly difficult for many clinicians to watch the language and tools of the therapeutic process become ammunition for prosecutors and a bull's eye for the defense. (p. 166)

Roland Summit, the original creator of the concept of CSAAS in 1983, has recently lamented the fate of this syndrome in the courts.

> The polarization which inflames every issue of sexual abuse has been kindled further here by the exploitation of a clinical concept as ammunition for battles in court. The excess heat has been generated by false claims advanced by prosecutors as well as a primary effort by defense interests to strip the paper of any worth or relevance. (Summit, 1992, p. 153)

Although Summit (1992) believes his concept has been wrongly applied as a sexual abuse test, he claimed that it still has validity to explain delayed disclosure or inconsistent testimony: "The CSAAS is used appropriately in court testimony not to prove a child was molested but to rebut the myths which prejudice endorsement of delayed or inconsistent disclosure" (p. 160).

Another issue of concern to some mental health professionals, although apparently not to most courts, is the relationship between the child and the expert. In the study described earlier, almost all of the experts interviewed the child. The great majority examined the child sufficiently to claim that this particular child exhibited characteristics of a sexually abused child. A large group (45.9%) among those who interviewed the child treated the child as well. The great majority of these experts are therapists, not research scientists or criminal investigators (Mason, 1991).

Garbarino et al. (1989) have criticized the use of therapists to investigate a child's credibility, claiming that a therapeutic approach is conducive to eliciting a response and to dealing with the subjective reality of the child, but not to determining credibility. At least one court has held this position as well. In *People v. Leon* (1989), the court rejected the testimony of expert witness Roland Summit regarding the CSAAS argument:

> On the one hand is the need to care and treat an abused child and the need as a treatment device to accept as true his (or her) report, whether truthful or not; and on the other hand the preservation of the constitutional right to presumption of innocence in a criminal case. (p. 939)

The neutrality of the expert is a concern for the professional community as well. The American Psychological Association's (1981) Ethical Principles of Psychologists warns psychologists to "avoid relationships that may limit their objectivity or create a conflict of interest" (p. 633). Although not noted by any appellate court in this study, the fact that many of these experts had acted as therapists for the child they were testifying about could be seen as a breach of professional neutrality. According to the aforementioned study, only 13.3% had no contact with the child at al (Mason, 1991).

CONCLUSION

Expert testimony in cases involving sexual abused children is particularly powerful because there is often no other evidence aside from the testimony of the child. The foregoing examination of appellate court decisions reveals that there is a great deal of conflict among courts about the admission of expert testimony regarding the behavioral characteristics of sexually abused children. Nonetheless, the majority of courts are willing to admit this type of testimony, particularly on rebuttal, even when it is applied to a particular child. In contrast to the *State v. Michaels* (1993/1994) case noted in the introduction to this chapter, few courts question the content of the scientific basis of the testimony. Those appellate courts that do reject the testimony do not offer clear guidelines but the general evidentiary rule that this testimony goes to the issue of the child's credibility, which can only be determined by the trier of the facts.

The expert testimony revealed in the appellate opinions includes a very wide range of descriptors, which are often contradictory in nature and many of which could be symptoms of any disturbed child. Because of the nature of the rebuttal, inclusion of the experts' testimony in these cases dwells most often on recantation and inconsistent stories as an indicator of abuse. This puts the jury in the odd situation of being told that a child who tells the truth in a straightforward manner has been abused, but if a child denies abuse or tells conflicting stories, this gives even more weight to the fact of abuse.

There is a growing trend in courts to disallow syndrome testimony in direct examination but to allow it on rebuttal to rehabilitate the witness who has been accused of delay, inconsistent accounts, or recantation (*State v. Michaels*, 1993/1994). However, these characteristics are not more scientifically reliable on rebuttal than they are on direct, and the opportunity for rebuttal becomes an open window through which a wide range of testimony not allowed on direct can enter.

This chapter described the existence of a wide gulf between the scientific and the judiciary communities regarding the content of behavioral syndrome testimony. Although these appellate courts are reluctant to look beyond the form to critically examine the content, the scientific community is very critical of the scientific validity of the content, particularly outside the context of therapy (Berliner & Conte, 1993; Kendall-Tackett et al., 1993). The many studies that have been performed on the indicators of sexual abuse fail to reveal any consistent pattern of behavior that can be identified in the majority of sexually abused children. Moreover, many of the symptoms that do occur in some children can be found in children who are not sexually abused. The clinical community is likely to divide with the scientific community on this issue and claim that there are clear behavioral indicators, although the clinical community maintains no consensus on what these might be, even on the issue of delay or recantation. For instance, in a recent national survey of 212 professionals who evaluate children who may have been abused, the respondents ranked "Child's report of abuse is consistent over time" at 68.5 on the importance index, whereas "Child's disclosure contains retractions or is conflicted" was ranked at 36.8 (Berliner & Conte, 1993).

Finally, even though appellate courts generally accept the credentials of an expert and rarely question his or her relationship with the child, at least some members of the clinical community—and some critics outside of it—question the neutrality of the expert who not only interviews the child but in many cases provides therapy as well.

This chapter suggested three critical issues that need clarification in this very unsettled area of the law. First, a consensus regarding the behavioral characteristics of sexually abused children, if any, that is accepted by the appropriate scientific community should be clearly conveyed to the judiciary. Whereas the U.S. Supreme Court decision on *Daubert* (1993) makes it clear that judges must rule on the scientific reliability of expert testimony, it is difficult for judges to make that decision without appropriate guidance from the scientific community. Second, a clear rationale and strict standards for the admission of rebuttal testimony must be established. Third, guidelines for the acceptance of expert witnesses that consider the qualification of the experts and the potential conflict of therapist and neutral evaluator should be developed.

These issues could best be resolved in a collaborative effort between the three communities: the scientific, the clinical, and the judicial. In this area, as in others, there appears to be a lack of communication among the three communities. Cooperative study and jointly developed standards would be useful to promote judicial uniformity and, therefore, fairness. The scope of this collaboration could spread far beyond the issue of behavioral characteristics of sexually abused children and include other troublesome areas of expert testimony by mental health professionals as well, such as testimony in battered women syndrome or repressed memory cases.

REFERENCES

Alison V. State, 346 S.E.2d 389 (Ga. 1986), *revsd*, 353 S.E.2d 805 (Ga. 1987).

American Psychiatric Association. (1987). *Diagnostic and statistical manual of mental disorders* (3rd ed., rev.). Washington, DC: Author.

American Psychological Association. (1981). Ethical principles of psychologists. (1981). *American Psychologist, 36*, 633–638.

Berliner, L., & Conte, J. (1993). Sexual abuse evaluations: Conceptual and empirical obstacles. *Child Abuse & Neglect, 17*, 111–125.

Daubert v. Merrell Dow Pharmaceuticals, Inc., 509 U.S., 113 S. Ct. 2786 (1993).

Federal rules of evidence, 28 U.S.C. (West 1991).

Frye v. United States, 293 F. 1013 (D.C. Cir. 1923).

Garbarino, J., Stott, F., & the Faculty of the Erikson Institute. (1989). *What children can tell us*. San Francisco: Jossey-Bass.

In re Amber B., 191 Cal. App. 3d 682 (1987).

In re Sara M., 194 Cal. App. 3d 585 (1987).

Kendall-Tackett, K., Williams, L., & Finkelhor, D. (1993). Impact of sexual abuse on children: A review and synthesis of recent empirical studies. *Psychological Bulletin, 13,* 164–180.

Levy, R. (1989). Using "scientific" testimony to prove child sexual abuse. *Family Law Quarterly, 23,* 383.

MacFarlane, K. (1992). Summit's "Abuse of the CSAAS." *Journal of Child Sexual Abuse 1*(4), 165–167.

Mason, M. A. (1991, Fall/Winter). A judicial dilemma: Expert witness testimony in child sex abuse cases. *Journal of Psychiatry and Law,* 185–219.

Matter of E. M., 520 N.Y.S. 2d 327 (Fam. Ct. 1987).

Myers, S., Bays, M., Becker, J., Berliner, L., Corwin, D., & Saywitz, K. (1989). Expert testimony in child sexual abuse litigation. *Nebraska Law Review, 68,* 100.

People v. Gray, 187 Cal. App. 3d 213 (Cal. 1986).

People v. Leon, 214 Cal. App. 3d 925 (1989).

People v. Luna, 204 Cal. App. 3d 726 (1988).

State v. Catsam, 534 A.2d 184 (Vt. 1987).

State v. Kim, 645 P.2d 1330 (Haw. 1982).

State v. Margaret Kelly Michaels, 264 N.J. Superior Court 579, 625 A.2d 489 (1993), *aff'd,* 642 A.2d 1372 (N.J. 1994).

State v. Middleton, 657 P.2d 1215 (Or. 1983).

State v. Myers, 359 N.W.2d 604 (Minn. 1984).

State v. Reser, 767 P.2d 1277 (Kan. 1989).

Summit, R. (1983). The child sexual abuse accommodation syndrome. *Child Abuse & Neglect, 7,* 177–193.

Summit, R. (1992). Abuse of the child sexual abuse accommodation syndrome. *Child Abuse, 1*(4), 153–165.

Townsend v. State, 734 P.2d 705 (Nev. 1987).

United States v. Rosenberg, 23 F.2d 300 (1952).

Ward v. State, 519 S.W.2d 1082 (Fla. App. 1988).

IV

COMMENTARIES: TOWARD A CONSENSUS

11

THE PSYCHOLOGIST AS EXPERT WITNESS: A COMMENT

PETER A. ORNSTEIN AND BETTY N. GORDON

With increasing frequency, psychologists are being called on to provide expert testimony in legal situations involving allegations of child sexual abuse. Some of these experts are clinical psychologists, functioning as forensic evaluators, treating clinicians, or researchers studying sexual abuse and related topics. Others are developmental and cognitive psychologists who focus on relating children's memory and suggestibility to their abilities to provide accurate testimony. As is the case with other professionals who serve as expert witnesses, the involvement of psychologists is based on the assumption that their expertise can facilitate the interpretation of evidence that is presented to the court. Accordingly, psychologists who serve as expert witnesses function as representatives of the discipline who have the serious responsibility of providing triers of fact with the access to what is known about topics such as child development, sexual abuse, memory, and suggestibility. The very interesting set of chapters that is assembled in this volume illustrates just how difficult it is to meet this responsibility. As we see it, difficulties arise because of the nature and extent of the knowledge required for effective testimony and because the demands of the courtroom often do not permit the expert to present this material in a systematic, unbiased manner.

Our reactions to these chapters are based on a set of working assumptions about the testimony of expert witnesses. In this commentary, we spell out these assumptions and discuss the chapters in the context of what we think can reasonably be said in court about sexual abuse and children's memory and suggestibility.

THE IMPORTANCE OF SCIENTIFIC RESEARCH

We approach our analysis from the fundamental perspective that expert testimony by psychologists must be consistent with current scientific research. This viewpoint is espoused in a number of chapters in this volume but is stated most compellingly by Lavin and Sales (this volume, chapter 3), who provide the ethical and moral underpinnings for it. From this perspective, it is essential that clinical psychologists who are questioned about child sexual abuse and its possible sequelae be familiar with the most current information on such topics as the epidemiology of abuse, the factors that may be associated with abuse, and the difficulties of making a diagnosis on the basis of any predefined constellation of presumed symptoms. Moreover, when developmental psychologists are asked to comment on the accuracy of children's reports, their remarks must be based on research on the cognitive aspects of testimony, especially children's abilities to remember and to resist suggestion and their tendencies to lie or distort. It is not necessary that an expert witness be an active researcher (i.e., one who is contributing to the scientific literature), but it is essential for such an individual to read widely and critically and to understand the nature of scientific research.

Thus, we agree with the position taken by Lavin and Sales (this volume, chapter 3) and by other contributors to this volume (e.g., Kovera & Borgida, chapter 9; Pruett & Solnit, chapter 6) that expert testimony must be based on scientific research. But what is "scientific" research? As we use the term, it refers to work that is empirically based and derived from controlled studies that are published in archival peer-reviewed journals. Across a wide range of disciplines, it is generally accepted that some measure of quality control is gained when researchers are required to subject their work to the standards of the field, as reflected in the judgments of their peers who do the reviewing. This emphasis on peer-reviewed journals should not be taken to deny the importance and relevance of work appearing in other outlets (e.g., newsletters, edited volumes), but the expert witness has a professional responsibility to be familiar with original research that meets the standards of the review process. It is important to note, however, that meeting these standards is necessary but not sufficient for a piece of work to be appropriate for citation in expert testimony. Publication in a peer-reviewed journal neither guarantees that laboratory-based research can be applied readily to the specifics of a particular case of abuse nor ensures that a piece of research is without significant flaw. This issue of quality, moreover, may be particularly problematic in the clinical domain when one can find studies that (a) are essentially single-participant anecdotal reports, (b) lack desired (although admittedly sometimes difficult to obtain) control groups, and (c) involve the faulty or unverifiable assignment of participants to groups.

AN EXAMPLE

Let us illustrate these problems by a consideration of the difficulties of accurately assigning participants to abused and nonabused groups. Although many research questions require such a contrast, these comparisons often are seriously flawed because there is no way to determine with absolute certainty whether the individuals studied were or were not actually abused. Thus, for example, participants are necessarily classified as abused or nonabused on the basis of clinical judgments, which themselves may or may not be accurate (Berliner & Conte, 1993). Even studies that rely on confessions or convictions in criminal proceedings as evidence for the validation of abuse are suspect because the legal process itself is not designed for the determination of "absolute truth." In reality, some innocent individuals are convicted, and others who may be guilty are acquitted.

The problem of assignment of participants to groups is illustrated by Fisher and Whiting (this volume, chapter 8) in their discussion of the use of assessment procedures that have not been adequately validated. Consider, for example, the widespread interest in clinical circles that was generated by Summit's (1983) discussion of the child sexual abuse accommodation syndrome. Although it was claimed that there is a systematic pattern to the disclosure of child abuse that involves initial denial, subsequent disclosure, recanting, and finally repeated disclosure, research in support of this presumed sequence (see, e.g., Gonzalez, Waterman, Kelly, McCord, & Oliveri, 1993; Sorensen & Snow, 1991) is problematic because of difficulties with the validation of the abuse (vs. nonabuse) status of the children included in the studies. As far as we can tell, without physical or other corroborative evidence, there is no way to know with absolute certainty whether children who initially deny abuse were or were not abused. The situation is complicated further by conflicting reports in the literature (see, e.g., Bradley & Wood, 1996), leaving us in basic agreement with Ceci and Bruck's (1995) assessment that there is no one pattern of disclosure that accounts for the behavior of all (or even most) children suspected of having been sexually abused.

This state of affairs is most unfortunate because the view of a gradual disclosure process seems to have become part of the "folklore" (Jones,

1996), to such an extent that it has driven the testimony of many experts. Moreover, acceptance of this belief can have a troubling effect on clinical interactions because it encourages the position that when a child denies having been abused, there is nonetheless a high likelihood that he or she was in fact abused. As Fisher and Whiting (this volume, chapter 8) point out, this belief can lead to a clinical approach that involves repeated leading questions and the use of suggestive materials (e.g., books, dolls, props) that are designed to encourage disclosure—a style that would be very problematic with highly suggestive young children. Similarly, Lawlor (this volume, chapter 5) discusses problems that result when children who deny abuse are placed in therapy that is focused on facilitating disclosure, pointing out that one must always consider the possibility that some of these children may not have been abused.

THE EXPERT AS A CRITICAL CONSUMER OF THE LITERATURE

Given the flaws that often occur in published research, it is important for the expert witness to be an active and critical consumer of the literature. As such, the expert must read "defensively" to be on guard for personal opinions of authors that may not be supported by data but that nonetheless may come to be assimilated into the collective belief system of one or more groups of specialists. As an example, it is commonly believed that certain behaviors or symptoms can be taken as indicators of sexual abuse. Indeed, Mason (this volume, chapter 10) discusses the extent to which this perspective is presented by clinicians who testify as experts in abuse cases. Unfortunately, however, an informed analysis of the available data provides little support for this belief (e.g., Berliner & Conte, 1993).

Ideally, to determine if any set of behaviors is associated with abuse, it is necessary to obtain adequate baseline data. As Ornstein, Ceci, and Loftus (1996) pointed out in one section of the report of the American Psychological Association's Working Group on Recollections of Abuse, one needs a set of 2×2 contingency tables in which it is possible to examine the extent to which the presence and absence of certain documented types of abuse are and are not associated with specific well-defined sequelae. Consider, for example, the claim that sexualized behaviors are observed to be common in abused children. This may be the case, but the proposition cannot be evaluated without an understanding of the extent to which nonabused children may also engage in the very same behaviors and of the degree to which some abused children may be asymptomatic. Moreover, even without these contingency tables, it is already clear that (a) many children who have been sexually abused are asymptomatic and (b) some children who have not been abused may evidence many of the symptoms thought to be associated with sexual abuse (Berliner & Conte, 1993; Kendall-Tackett, Williams, & Finklelhor, 1993). Given these findings, we would disagree with Kovera and Borgida's (this volume, chapter 9) claim that "the fact that a child exhibits some of the symptoms associated with sexual abuse ... increases the likelihood that the child is an abuse victim" (p. 192). As we see it, a child who exhibits these symptoms is likely to be experiencing distress that may or may not be related to sexual abuse.

USING DATA CORRECTLY

As critical readers of the literature, expert witnesses have a parallel obligation to use published data in an accurate and precise manner. To illustrate a common misuse of data, let us consider the problems that result when false allegations about sexual abuse are confused with intentional lying. Clearly, not all false allegations involve deliberate lying on the part of the child (see also Yuille, Tymofievich, & Marxsen, 1995). Indeed, a child's statement may be incorrect, but he or she may believe that what is being alleged is true; or parts of what a child says may be true, whereas parts may not be true; or a child may be basically correct in stating what happened, but an incorrect abuser may be named. As it turns out, intentional lying appears to occur in a relatively small subset of cases. Indeed, depending on the age of the child, it is estimated that between 2% and 8% of cases (with higher percentages for older children) involve false reports that are based on intentional lies (Everson & Boat, 1989; Jones & McGraw, 1987).

Although children are not likely to lie deliberately about sexual abuse, a substantial number of child sexual abuse cases—between 23% and 33%—do involve allegations that are not true, with the higher estimates observed in cases involving custody and divorce issues (Jones & McGraw, 1987; Thoennes & Tjaden, 1990). Unfortunately, the extent to which each of the three types of allegations indicated above contributes to the percentage of false reports is not known. It is also unfortunate that the statistics regarding the small percentage of cases involving intentional lying are often cited mistakenly in the clinical literature and in court as reflecting the frequency of all false allegations, thus leading to the erroneous impression that false allegations of any type are rare. As an example of this confusion, consider Coulborn-Faller and Corwin's (1995) claim that "research has provided support for the assertion that children infrequently lie about being sexually abused, *false allegations of sexual abuse by children constituting between 2 and 8% of cases*" (italics added, p. 72). In reality, false allegations constitute a substantial problem for clinical and legal professionals.

INTERPRETIVE CHALLENGES

Although we emphasize the importance of research as a foundation for expert testimony, we readily admit that psychologists will experience many challenges as they attempt to apply the relevant literatures to questions of abuse and children's abilities to serve as witnesses (see Berliner, this volume, chapter 1). As we see it, there are two sets of problems: one involving difficulties of generalization from controlled research in the laboratory to the "real world" and the other reflecting the challenges of doing something close to controlled research outside of the laboratory. As an example of the generalization problem, consider societal and professional interest in what children can remember about abusive incidents in the context of one's inability to examine sexual abuse in an experimental fashion. As such, it is necessary to rely on children's memory for experiences that contain some salient features of abuse (e.g., physical contact, states of undress), and there can be genuine differences of opinion concerning what makes a good analogue event. Consider, as well, that there are always interpretive problems that stem from efforts to apply group data to the specifics of an individual case. And concerning research in the field, interpretive difficulties can often arise from the necessity of working without the controls of the laboratory.

These problems of interpretation clearly increase the challenge of the task assigned to psychologists who serve as expert witnesses. As can be seen, the expert has to operate with a firm understanding of the relevant literatures and a keen sense of research methodology to ensure that the findings can be evaluated critically. Moreover, given both the complexities and the limitations of these literatures, an expert's characterization of current professional thinking is likely to be quite conditionalized. For example, "boundary conditions" may interfere with general statements about the sequelae of abuse or the suggestibility of children, requiring the expert to be prepared to say that "X may hold under certain conditions, but Y may be true in other situations." This is certainly the case when it comes to any claim about young children's cognitive capabilities. Indeed, an emerging literature on context specificity indicates that the contextual conditions prevailing during an assessment or evaluation can have a profound influence on the diagnostic conclusions that are reached about a child's cognitive functioning (Ornstein, 1991; Ornstein, Baker-Ward, & Naus, 1988).

We recognize, of course, that psychologists usually are called by either the prosecution or the defense and that the adversarial system (see Spencer, this volume, chapter 2) does not necessarily welcome presentations that are conditionalized in this manner. We also recognize that there are pressures—sometimes subtle, sometimes severe—put on an expert witness to become a "team player" and thus to identify with the aims of either the prosecution or the defense. Indeed, Bruck (this volume, chapter 4) discusses quite vividly the difficulties confronted by a "novice" expert witness as she tried to maintain a professional neutral posture. These pressures notwithstanding, the neutral, literature-driven type of testimony is required if psychologists are to apply the findings of their discipline in a manner that is professionally responsible. In this way, the psychologist who appears as an expert witness can serve an educational function, leaving the final judgments in any case to the triers of fact. Indeed, there is a real obligation to educate the courts about the complex issues that are involved in any discussion of abuse and testimony. Miller and Allen's (this volume, chapter 7) description of the educational role of expert witnesses is consistent with this orientation.

THE BOUNDARIES OF EXPERTISE

Given our view that expert testimony must be based on a firm understanding of the research literature, we feel strongly that a sophisticated understanding of research methodology must be an entry-level requirement for service as an expert witness. As such, we are distressed by Mason's (this volume, chapter 10) report that most professionals accepted as experts by the courts are qualified primarily on the basis of their attendance at workshops and their work with sexually abused children, not by any demonstration of research competence. In keeping with the Ethical Principles of Psychologists and Code of Conduct of the American Psychological Association, we feel strongly that professionals who serve as expert witnesses have a responsibility to recognize the boundaries of their substantive expertise. For example, other things being equal, we would expect practicing clinicians to be less familiar with the extensive literature on the development of memory than they are with research on trauma, abuse, and neglect. Similarly, cognitive developmentalists may be very familiar with work on suggestibility and the malleability of memory, but they may be less up-to-date in their understanding of the abuse literature. For psychologists to effectively serve the courts, it is essential that we monitor ourselves by indicating frankly the limits of our professional training and experience.

In this regard, the authors of several chapters in this volume (see Lawlor, chapter 5; Mason, chapter 10; and Pruett & Solnit, chapter 6) indicate a critical need for professionals who testify in court to clarify their respective roles in the management of sexual abuse cases. In particular, the roles of the forensic investigator and therapist must be differentiated because the goals and assumptions of each are very different. As Lawlor points out, the goals of therapy are inconsistent with those of obtaining evidence for forensic purposes. Although forensic investigators and treating therapists both should begin their work with active efforts to test alternative hypotheses about the nature and cause(s) of a child's distress, investigators are charged with determining the facts in a case, to the extent to which this is possible. In contrast, therapists have a responsibility for their clients' adjustment, adaptation, and well-being. Moreover, given the intense nature of the relationship between client and therapist, opportunities for confirmatory bias and suggestibility are increased in the treatment context because many therapeutic methods have a great potential to influence children's reports, beliefs, and behaviors. Indeed, such influence is often the major aim of a therapeutic intervention, and clinicians who work to help children deal with their distress should not have to worry about whether the techniques they use foster suggestion. Thus, we feel strongly that the roles of forensic evaluator and therapist should be completely separate and that therapists should not be called on to testify in court about children with whom they are engaged in treatment.

SO WHAT CAN AN EXPERT WITNESS SAY?

Despite the complexities involved in conducting, interpreting, and generalizing research relevant to child sexual abuse, there is consensus among professionals regarding many aspects of this field. Although there are some who raise legitimate questions about the clinical and legal relevance of laboratory studies (see Berliner, this volume, chapter 1), in our view much of what we know about children's memory and suggestibility seems to have a strong empirical foundation (see Kovera & Borgida, this volume, chapter 9) and to be relevant to understanding children's abilities to provide accurate testimony. A consensus view (see Ceci & Bruck, 1995), for example, holds that age differences in children's cognitive functioning can affect the flow of information from initial encoding and storage to subsequent retrieval and reporting. Thus, with increases in age, children are better able to encode information in memory, to establish stable memory representations, to provide spontaneous accounts of what they have experienced, and to retain information over time. Furthermore, consistent with a constructionist account of remembering—with constructive processes being driven by prior knowledge—age-related differences in understanding the events that are being experienced may have profound implications for the later memory of such events (Ornstein, Larus, & Clubb, 1991). At one extreme, a child who does not understand what is happening to him or her may have little basis for subsequently accurately remembering what was experienced.

With increases in age, children are also better able to resist the force of misleading, intervening experiences, including suggestive questioning. A growing body of work indicates that young children (particularly preschoolers) are especially vulnerable to external influences in the form of misleading or suggestive information. Under some conditions, it is even possible to influence young children to report events that have never occurred with such a degree of elaboration and credibility that experts cannot tell whether the events in question did or did not take place (Ceci, Crotteau-Huffman, Smith, & Loftus, 1994; Ceci, Loftus, Leightman, & Bruck, 1994). Admittedly, however, important questions remain concerning the boundary conditions under which children may be resistant to suggestion and the extent to which they may later come to believe statements made initially to conform to the strong pressures of an interviewer.

In the clinical realm, much is known about some aspects of child sexual abuse, whereas a great deal of work remains to be done in other areas. There is a considerable amount of data, for example, related to the epidemiology, sequelae, and risk factors of child sexual abuse (see, e.g., Finkelhor, Hotaling, Lewis, & Smith, 1990). Research clearly indicates that sexual abuse is surprisingly common, although more so among girls than boys, and that perpetrators of abuse are predominately male and are typically known to the child. Furthermore, it has been shown that early sexual abuse is associated frequently (but not always) with significant mental health problems later in life. Also, as indicated above, there is compelling evidence that no one behavioral symptom or set of symptoms can be taken as diagnostic of abuse and that patterns of disclosure cannot be used to identify abused children. However, many important questions remain to be addressed in this relatively young field. In particular, further work is necessary to develop reliable and valid assessment methods, including empirically based guidelines for clinicians charged with the difficult task of interviewing children suspected of having been abused.

CONCLUSIONS

The chapters included in this volume provide an important resource for psychologists who serve as expert witnesses in the courts, in that they establish a framework from which to understand the complexity of this task. An emerging consensus in this book is that of the importance of basing testimony on knowledge that is scientifically validated rather than on personal opinion, even if that opinion is informed by years of clinical experience. In many cases, we believe that psychologists can provide the trier of fact with meaningful and relevant information regarding child sexual abuse and cognitive functioning. However, we caution, as do Lavin and Sales (this volume, chapter 3), that in doing so, we must hold ourselves to a higher standard than that required by the court. Thus, we argue that each expert has a professional obligation to assess carefully the limits of his or her own expertise before agreeing to serve as an expert witness. In this regard, it is important to remember that "saying 'I don't know' or 'I can't answer that question' can be an indication of expertise" (Pruett &

Solnit, this volume, chapter 6, p. 133). In addition to this self-examination of one's areas of competence, we believe that potential witnesses should think deeply about the complex ethical and moral issues that are involved in providing evidence in court. Indeed, because expert psychological testimony has the potential to exert a profound influence on the lives of children and their families, we support the development of training programs that will provide both novice and more seasoned experts with exposure to these issues.

REFERENCES

Berliner, L., & Conte, J. R. (1993). Sexual abuse evaluations: Conceptual and empirical obstacles. *Child Abuse & Neglect, 17*, 111–125.

Bradley, A. R., & Wood, J. M. (1996). How do children tell? The disclosure process in child sexual abuse. *Child Abuse & Neglect, 20*, 881–891.

Ceci, S. J., & Bruck, M. (1995). *Jeopardy in the courtroom: A scientific analysis of children's testimony.* Washington, DC: American Psychological Association.

Ceci, S. J., Crotteau-Huffman, M., Smith, E., & Loftus, E. F. (1994). Repeatedly thinking about non-events. *Consciousness & Cognition, 3*, 388–407.

Ceci, S. J., Loftus, E. W., Leichtman, M., & Bruck, M. (1994). The role of source misattributions in the creation of false beliefs among preschoolers. *International Journal of Clinical and Experimental Hypnosis, 62*, 304–320.

Coulborn-Faller, K., & Corwin, D. L. (1995). Children's interview statements and behaviors: Role in identifying sexually abused children. *Child Abuse & Neglect, 19*, 71–82.

Everson, M. D., & Boat, B. W. (1989). False allegations of sexual abuse by children and adolescents. *Journal of the American Academy of Child and Adolescent Psychiatry, 28*, 230–235.

Finkelhor, D., Hotaling, G., Lewis, I. A., & Smith, C. (1990). Sexual abuse in a national survey of adult men and women: Prevalence, characteristics and risk factors. *Child Abuse & Neglect, 14*, 19–28.

Gonzalez, L. S., Waterman, J., Kelly, R. J., McCord, J., & Oliveri, M. K. (1993). Children's patterns of disclosures and recantations of sexual and ritualistic abuse allegations in psychotherapy. *Child Abuse & Neglect, 17*, 281–289.

Jones, D. P. H. (1996). Editorial: Gradual disclosure by sexual assault victims—A sacred cow? *Child Abuse & Neglect, 20*, 879–880.

Jones, D., & McGraw, J. M. (1987). Reliable and fictitious accounts of sexual abuse in children. *Journal of Interpersonal Violence, 2*, 27–45.

Kendall-Tackett, K., Williams, L., & Finkelhor, D. (1993). Impact of sexual abuse on children: A review and synthesis of recent empirical studies. *Psychological Bulletin, 113*, 164–180.

Ornstein, P. A. (1991). Putting interviewing in context. In J. Doris (Ed.), *The *suggestibility of children's recollections: Implications for eyewitness testimony* (pp. 147–152). Washington, DC: American Psychological Association.

Ornstein, P. A., Baker-Ward, L., & Naus, M. J. (1988). The development of mnemonic skill. In F. E. Weinert & M. Perlmutter (Eds.), *Memory development: Universal changes and individual differences* (pp. 31–50). Hillsdale, NJ: Erlbaum.

Ornstein, P. A., Ceci, S. J., & Loftus, E. F. (1996). Reply to the Alpert, Brown, and Courtois document: The science of memory and the practice of psychotherapy. In J. L. Alpert & P. A. Ornstein (Cochairs), *The Working Group on the Investigation of Memories of Childhood Abuse: Final report* (pp. 106–131). Washington, DC: American Psychological Association.

Ornstein, P. A., Larus, D. M., & Clubb, P. A. (1991). Understanding children's testimony: Implications of research on the development of memory. In R. Vasta (Ed.), *Annals of child development* (Vol. 8, pp. 145–176). London: Jessica Kingsley.

Sorensen, T., & Snow, B. (1991). How children tell: The process of disclosure of child sexual abuse. *Child Welfare, 70,* 3–15.

Summit, R. C. (1983). The child sexual abuse accommodation syndrome. *Child Abuse & Neglect, 7,* 177–193.

Thoennes, N., & Tjaden, P. G. (1990). The extent, nature and validity of sexual abuse allegations in custody/visitation disputes. *Child Abuse & Neglect, 14,* 151–163.

Yuille, J. C., Tymofievich, M., & Marxsen, D. (1995). The nature of allegations of child sexual abuse. In T. Ney (Ed.), *True and false allegations of child sexual abuse* (pp. 21–46). New York: Brunner/Mazel.

12

WHERE RESEARCHERS FEAR TO TREAD: INTERPRETIVE DIFFERENCES AMONG TESTIFYING EXPERTS IN CHILD SEXUAL ABUSE CASES

THOMAS D. LYON AND JONATHAN J. KOEHLER

Debates regarding the admissibility of expert testimony in child sexual abuse cases are often characterized as between clinicians and researchers. Clinicians base their judgment on personal experience and anecdotes, whereas researchers base their judgment on scientific findings. Clinicians are willing to testify that a particular child has been sexually abused, whereas researchers cautiously avoid rendering a judgment about any particular case. Clinicians believe that they can interpret children's statements and behaviors to validate abuse, whereas researchers warn that children's statements and behaviors may be shaped by adults, including clinicians. Clinicians are happy to testify (typically for the prosecution), comfortably adopting the role of advocate for their position. Researchers reluctantly agree to testify (typically for the defense) and are unhappy having done so, finding their neutrality challenged by the inherently adversarial nature of the trial. In short, clinicians rush in where researchers fear to tread.

One might think that debates would cease if clinicians were banished from the courtroom. However, disagreements among researchers are suppressed when they face the common enemy of intuitive, unscientific judgment. Once that enemy is removed, differences within the ranks are highlighted, and the debate is repeated, albeit on a higher plane.

In this chapter, we address two areas of disagreement among researchers, involving the two most widely discussed areas of expert testimony in child sexual abuse cases: behavioral symptoms and the suggestibility of children. In each case, subjective differences among researchers in their interpretation of the research lead to differences of opinion regarding what an expert may appropriately testify to in court. There are several questions about which reasonable researchers disagree. How does one weigh false-positive results against false-negative results? How should methodological limitations be weighed? How closely must the characteristics of a study match those of a given situation for the results to apply? How many studies must support a proposition before one should accept the proposition as true? The questions are not new, but their persistence bears repeating in the light of strong claims regarding the ethics and admissibility of various types of expert testimony.

In the case of behavioral symptoms, observational research documenting symptoms in some nonabused children leads different researchers to different conclusions. Some believe that this renders symptoms irrelevant as evidence of abuse; others believe that symptoms may serve as evidence (but not conclusive evidence) that abuse occurred. We argue that a few symptoms are relevant evidence of abuse and the proper subject of expert testimony but that experts should acknowledge the methodological shortcomings of the observational research. In the case of suggestibility, laboratory research demonstrating that some children can be led to make false claims also leads researchers to disagree. Some believe this justifies concerns that a nontrivial number of sexual abuse allegations are the product of coercive interviewing techniques, whereas others question the applicability of the research to most sexual abuse investigations. We believe that laboratory research is often relevant but that experts must acknowledge the potential differences between the research and the nature of interviewing and the dynamics of sexual abuse.

BEHAVIORAL SYMPTOMS OF ABUSE

Several contributors to this volume discuss the admissibility of expert testimony that behavioral symptoms are diagnostic of sexual abuse (Berliner, chapter 1; Fisher & Whiting, chapter 8; Kovera & Borgida, chapter 9; Lawlor, chapter 5; Mason, chapter 10). The consensus is that such testimony should not be admitted, although the chapters by Berliner and Kovera and Borgida are more tolerant of such testimony than are the others.

In our view, experts can reasonably testify that some symptoms are relevant for proving that abuse occurred. Disagreements are inevitable, however, because the research fails to provide conclusive answers.

In assessing the arguments, it is important to emphasize a distinction noted by Kovera and Borgida (this volume, chapter 9) between symptoms that increase the likelihood that abuse occurred and symptoms that are dispositive of abuse. If a symptom occurs more frequently in abused children than in nonabused children, then the presence of that symptom in a child increases the likelihood that the child has been abused (Lyon & Koehler, 1996). In legal terms, the symptom is relevant or probative evidence that the child was abused (*Federal Rules of Evidence* Rule 403). However, a symptom may increase the likelihood of abuse without justifying the ultimate judgment that the child was abused. One can conclude that a symptom is dispositive of abuse only if the symptom occurs in some abused children and is nonexistent in nonabused children. If the symptom appears in some abused children and some smaller number of nonabused children, the symptom is relevant but not definitive evidence of abuse. Whether one can conclude that abuse occurred depends on the strength of the other evidence in the case and on one's standard regarding how sure one must be to diagnose abuse.

If there are symptoms that are relevant but not conclusive evidence of abuse, then such symptoms could properly be the subject of expert testimony that a child exhibited symptoms probative of abuse. The expert could inform the jury that particular symptoms increase the likelihood that abuse occurred but should refrain from expressing an opinion whether the child in question had been abused. An examination of the expert might inquire into the extent to which the symptoms appear in abused and nonabused children and whether the causes of symptomatology in nonabused children can be discerned. As Mason (this volume, chapter 10) points out, such testimony would be consistent with legal proscriptions against testimony in which an expert testifies as to the ultimate judgment whether abuse occurred.

Reviews of the research on the sequelae of sexual abuse tend to find that many symptoms are in fact more common in abused children than in nonabused children (Kendall-Tackett, Williams, & Finkelhor, 1993). Because of their existence in nonabused children, however, reviewers have concluded that such symptoms are insufficient standing alone to prove conclusively that abuse occurred. Kendall-Tackett et al. (1993) concluded that "symptoms cannot be easily used, without other evidence, to confirm the presence of sexual abuse" (p. 175). Berliner and Conte (1993) found that "the qualities or characteristics of children will not be, in themselves, determinative of sexual abuse" (p. 116).

In this volume, Fisher and Whiting (chapter 8) refer to Kendall-Tackett et al.'s (1993) review for the proposition that "practitioners cannot *rely* on the presence or absence of symptom patterns to validate sexual abuse" (italics added, Fisher & Whiting, this volume, p. 168). If one reads "rely" as referring to sole reliance, then the statement captures the position taken by Kendall-Tackett et al. However, Fisher and Whiting's position is different, as revealed in their next paragraph, which concludes that "there is no empirical evidence that such [sexual and other] behaviors can *serve as evidence* that a child has been sexually abused" (italics added, p. 168).

Why is there this difference of opinion? In part, we believe it arises from disagreements among researchers regarding the emphasis that one should place on the probability of false-positive errors—in this case, false allegations of abuse. Symptoms are relevant but not conclusive when they occur in some nonabused children. Their presence in nonabused children raises the potential for false allegations because nonabused children with symptoms may be misdiagnosed as abused. If one has no tolerance for false allegations, then one would require symptoms to be conclusive to be admissible. Fisher and Whiting might have argued that many symptoms do not merely occur in some nonabused children but in fact are quite common, thus increasing the risk of false positives. Yet, the point at which the risk of false positives is so high that testimony regarding symptoms should be inadmissible is a subjective judgment, about which ethical experts may disagree.

A second reason researchers might disagree over the relevance of symptoms of abuse stems from a misunderstanding about the significance of the fact that most abused children do not exhibit any particular symptom. It is neither necessary nor sufficient for a symptom to appear in a majority of sexually abused children to increase the likelihood that abuse occurred. The symptom may appear in a minority of abused children but also be relevant because it appears in a smaller minority of nonabused children. The symptom may appear in a majority of abused children but be irrelevant because it is as common in nonabused children. It is therefore of limited significance that "no one symptom characterize[s] a majority of sexually abused children" (Fisher & Whiting, this volume, chapter 8, p. 168); that "children who have been sexually abused can exhibit widely varying emotional reactions and behaviors, including showing no overt emotional disturbance" (Lawlor, this volume, chapter 5, p. 110); or that "the many studies that have been performed on the indicators of sexual abuse fail to reveal any consistent pattern of behavior that can be identified in the majority of sexually abused children" (Mason, this volume, chapter 10, p. 232).

Consider physical evidence of sexual abuse. No consistent pattern of physical signs can be identified in a majority of sexually abused children because approximately half of sexually abused children appear normal on examination (Bays & Chadwick, 1993). Erythema is the most common physical sign, but it is irrelevant because it appears in the same proportion of nonabused children as abused children (Emans, Woods, Flagg, & Freeman, 1987). Gonorrhea is a rare sign, appearing in fewer than 5% of abused children, but it is highly suggestive of abuse because it is virtually nonexistent in nonabused children (Bays & Chadwick, 1993). In short, the frequency with which a sign appears is a poor proxy for its relevance. Some signs that occur frequently are irrelevant; some signs that occur infrequently are quite relevant.

Lawlor (this volume, chapter 5) notes that whereas 10% of sexually abused children depict genitalia in their drawings only 2% of nonabused children do so. He concludes that because "the numbers are extremely low in each case[,] . . . there is not much predictive value from genitalia in drawings of young children" (p. 116). Yet if the numbers are reliable—that is, if research were to consistently find a 5:1 ratio of abused to nonabused children whose drawings show genitalia—then drawings of genitalia would be probative evidence that abuse occurred.

The fact that many abused children do not exhibit symptoms of abuse is important information but not because it demonstrates the irrelevance of such symptoms. Rather, it raises the potential that clinicians might erroneously conclude that a child has not been abused because that child failed to exhibit the appropriate symptoms. Fisher and Whiting (this volume, chapter 8) cite Finkelhor (1987) to support their position that symptoms of posttraumatic stress disorder (PTSD) should not be interpreted as evidence of sexual abuse. Finkelhor (1987) was indeed critical of the PTSD model:

> First, [the PTSD model] does not adequately account for all the symptoms. Second, it accurately applies only to some of the victims. Finally, and most seriously, it does not truly present a theory that explains how the dynamics of sexual abuse lead to the symptoms noted. (p. 350)

A moment's reflection shows that although these objections undermine PTSD's utility as an explanatory model for understanding the effects of sexual abuse, they are consistent with the possibility that PTSD symptoms are much more common in abused children than nonabused children. Indeed, Finkelhor (1987) never argued that PTSD is not evidence of abuse. Rather, he warned that because many abused children do not exhibit PTSD, it would be an error for experts to "testify in court cases that alleged victims probably were not abused because they do not manifest PTSD" (p. 352).

In summary, symptoms are relevant for proving that abuse occurred if they are more common in abused children than nonabused children. Having said that, we hasten to add that methodological concerns lead us to adopt a conservative criterion for determining when a symptom is indeed more common in abused children. We believe that unless symptoms are more common in abused children than nonabused children in treatment, prudent experts ought to avoid labeling such symptoms as relevant for proving that abuse occurred. Because most of the research selects sexually abused children from sexual abuse evaluations or treatment programs (Kendall-Tackett et al., 1993), the extent to which abused children are symptomatic may be exaggerated (Friedrich, Urquiza, & Beilke, 1986). Unless nonabused children are drawn from clinical populations, differences between abused and nonabused children may be attributable to selection bias rather than to real differences in symptom prevalence.

Our position reflects the possibility that selection biases artificially inflate the apparent relevance of abuse symptoms, but the extent to which they do is unknown. Moreover, we recognize that requiring that symptoms occur in a higher percentage of abused children than clinical nonabused children may lead one to understate true differences in symptoms between abused and nonabused children, in part because asymptomatic abused children are more likely than asymptomatic nonabused children to be referred to treatment simply "because of something done to them (i.e., abuse)" (Kendall-Tackett et al., 1993, p. 165). We prefer to risk understating rather than overstating the relevance of symptoms and, therefore, prefer to rely on comparisons between abused children and nonabused children in treatment.

If our criterion is accepted, then which symptoms are relevant? According to Kendall-Tackett et al. (1993), "sexually abused children showed only two symptoms consistently more often than non-abused clinical children: PTSD (just one study) and sexualized behavior (six of eight studies)" (p. 165). Given Fisher and Whiting's (this volume, chapter 8) extensive critique of PTSD and sexualized behavior, this conclusion may be surprising. The differences of opinion are attributable to disagreements about how the research ought to be interpreted.

Fisher and Whiting (this volume, chapter 8) note that "only" 48–55% of abused children meet the criteria for PTSD. But this figure, standing alone, says little about PTSD's potential as a relevant indicator of abuse. Deblinger, McLeer, Atkins, Ralphe, and Foa (1989) appear to be the only researchers who have examined differences between abused and nonabused children. Fisher and Whiting report that Deblinger et al. (1989) found "no significant group differences . . . when a PTSD symptom checklist was used to compare sexually abused psychiatric patients with physically abused and nonabused patients" (Fisher & Whiting, this volume, chapter 8, p. 166). Strikingly, Deblinger et al.'s is the one study Kendall-Tackett et al. (1993) believe supports the proposition that PTSD is more common in abused children than nonabused clinical children.

Who is right? According to Deblinger et al. (1989), the differences among the percentages of sexually abused children (20.9%), physically abused children (6.9%), and nonabused children (10.3%) who met the diagnostic criteria for PTSD were not statistically significant. However, they also reported that "significant differences were found across groups on specific PTSD categories" (p. 405), namely reexperiencing phenomena and autonomic hyperarousal. Hence, depending on the level of analysis used to examine the Deblinger et al. data, one may conclude that the researchers either did or did not find significant differences among the groups.

One might conclude that because differences in PTSD symptoms between abused and nonabused children have been examined in only one study, it is premature to conclude that PTSD is relevant for proving abuse. Still, one finding reported by Deblinger et al. (1989) is consistent with a substantial amount of other research: Sexually abused children exhibited more sexually inappropriate behaviors than either physically abused or nonabused children (Gale, Thompson, Moran, & Sack, 1988; Goldston, Turnquist, & Knutson, 1989; Hibbard & Hartman, 1992; Kolko, Moser, & Weldy, 1988; White, Halpin, Strom, & Santilli, 1988). Fisher and Whiting (this volume, chapter 8) acknowledge that the rates of sexualized behavior are higher among abused children. In addition, they note that in several well-controlled studies, "Friedrich and his colleagues have demonstrated that sexually abused children exhibit more sexual behavior problems than either nonabused clinical samples or nonreferred children" (p. 169; also see Einbender & Friedrich, 1989; Friedrich, 1995; Friedrich et al., 1986, 1992). Friedrich (1993) himself has reviewed the literature and concluded that "a growing body of increasingly sophisticated empirical research has demonstrated that sexual abuse is related to increased sexual behavior following the abuse" (p. 64).

Why, then, do Fisher and Whiting (this volume, chapter 8) conclude that there is "no empirical evidence that such behaviors can serve as evidence that a child has been sexually abused" (p. 168)? They note that some nonabused children exhibit sexualized behavior but that no more than 42% of abused children do so. As we have discussed, such data indicate that sexualized behavior is not conclusive evidence of abuse but do not undercut its utility as relevant evidence. Indeed, Friedrich et al.'s (1992) position, as cited by Fisher and Whiting (this volume, chapter 8), is that sexualized behavior ought "not be relied on in isolation as the primary indicator of sexual abuse" (p. 169). Kendall-Tackett et al. (1993) similarly concluded that sexualized behavior may "indicate sexual abuse but is not completely diagnostic because children can apparently appear to be sexualized for other reasons" (p. 173).

Fisher and Whiting (this volume, chapter 8) also argue that sexualized behavior may discriminate less well for girls than boys, that patterns of specific behaviors vary across different studies, and that variables other than sexual abuse have been linked to sexual behavior. Whether these are damning criticisms is a question about which ethical experts might disagree.

What appears to be the most serious criticism—the existence of alternative causes for sexualized behavior—is troubling only so long as a testifying expert ignores those causes. The very process by which abuse is diagnosed involves consideration of alternative explanations for a child's statements and behavior. Consider physical abuse. Subdural hematomas are much more common in abused children than in nonabused children. However, subdural hematomas are also associated with nonabusive causes, such as blood disorders, meningitis, blood vessel abnormalities, neurodegenerative disease, birth trauma, and accidental trauma (Lyon, Gilles, & Cory, 1996). An awareness of alternative explanations, far from rendering subdural hematomas irrelevant for proving that abuse occurred, allows for a differential diagnosis that increases the physician's confidence that a particular child's injury is attributable to abuse. Therefore, if a previously healthy infant without a history of major trauma presents with a subdural hematoma, physicians consider it highly suggestive of physical abuse (Case, 1994). Similarly, if alternative explanations for a child's sexualized behavior can be considered and eliminated (e.g., Is the child regularly exposed to nudity in the home?), then the probative value of such behavior increases.

Both Lawlor (this volume, chapter 5) and Fisher and Whiting (this volume, chapter 8) assert that behaviors attributed to sexual abuse may actually be the effects of abuse investigation and therapy, what one might call *iatrogenic effects*. Certainly, the investigation and prosecution of child sexual abuse are stressful for any child and will, in many cases, lead to stress reactions (Goodman et al., 1992). With respect to sexualized behavior, however, there is little evidence for iatrogenesis. Friedrich and Reams (1987) observed that sexual problems emerged during therapy for some of their patients, but Hewitt and Friedrich (1991) and Friedrich, Luecke, Beilke, and Place (1992, as cited in Friedrich, 1995) found decreases in sexual behavior over time. Gomes-Schwartz, Horowitz, and Cardarelli (1990) found little change in inappropriate sex play (a slight decrease) or sexual preoccupation (a slight increase) in their 18-month follow-up of sexually abused children 12 years old and younger. Even if sexual behaviors were to increase over time in therapy, it would be unclear whether therapy played a causal role, just as it would be difficult to credit therapy with reducing such behaviors over time.

The use of anatomically correct dolls has evoked some concern that they might elicit sexualized play. The evidence on this point is mixed. Bruck, Ceci, Francouer, and Renick (1995) interviewed parents of 3-year-olds who had been interviewed with anatomically correct dolls about a pediatric examination. The authors concluded that "parents did not feel that the dolls or the session with the dolls provoked any unusual sexualized behavior in their children" (p. 103). However, Boat, Everson, and Holland (1990) found that following exposure to anatomically correct dolls, many 3- to 4-year-olds were more interested in sexuality and their behaviors became more sexually focused.

We are less skeptical than Fisher and Whiting (this volume, chapter 8) regarding the potential relevance of sexualized behavior in diagnosing sexual abuse, but we do have several concerns. First, we believe that for diagnosis, the multi-item Child Sexual Behavior Inventory may be less useful than a focus on rare but highly probative behaviors. Although the inventory produces a true-positive rate of 70–92%, it produces a false-positive rate of 45–65% (Friedrich et al., 1992). Consequently, a high score on the inventory is only moderately probative of abuse. In contrast, some types of sexualized behavior are infrequent in abused children but so much more infrequent in nonabused children that they are highly probative of sexual abuse. For example, masturbation with an object occurs in more than 10% of abused children but less than 1% of nonabused children (Friedrich et al., 1992).

Several methodological concerns with the research on sexualized behavior in abused children must also be addressed. Sackett (1979) has identified a number of potential biases in case-control research—two of which are particularly important to consider in reviewing research on the behavioral consequences of sexual abuse. First, *exposure suspicion bias* occurs when the awareness of an individual's symptoms (sexualized behavior) increases the intensity of the search for and recognition of a putative cause (sexual abuse). Children who behave sexually are more likely to be questioned by their parents and professionals regarding possible sexual abuse (Friedrich & Reams, 1987; Sorensen & Snow, 1991). If sexualized behavior increases the likelihood that abuse will be discovered, children known to have been abused would exhibit more sexualized behaviors than children not believed to have been abused, even if abused children in general were no more likely than nonabused children to behave sexually. Exposure suspicion bias is minimized to the extent that samples of sexually abused children were originally detected and ultimately diagnosed as abused without reference to suspicious behaviors.

Second, *diagnostic suspicion bias* occurs when the awareness of an individual's exposure to a putative cause (sexual abuse) increases the intensity of the search for and recognition of symptoms (sexualized behavior). Sexual abuse, once discovered, may lead parents and professionals to watch more carefully for sexualized behaviors. Behaviors that might be interpreted as innocent play or natural curiosity in a child not suspected of being abused may be reinterpreted as sexual (Friedrich et al., 1992). Moreover, parents may be more likely to recall sexualized behavior once they believe their child has been abused. Diagnostic suspicion bias is minimized to the extent that sexualized behaviors can be objectively observed and recorded. Both exposure suspicion bias and diagnostic suspicion bias may exaggerate the probative value of some sexualized symptoms, but it would be difficult to measure these effects.

In summary, we believe that expert witnesses can point to research supporting the claim that sexualized behavior and some components of PTSD are probative of sexual abuse. Symptoms need not appear in a majority of sexually abused children or be nonexistent in nonabused children to be relevant. We regard this as a matter of logic, not opinion. Other issues are more subjective. How much more common must symptoms be in abused children than nonabused children before the symptom has practical significance as a symptom of child abuse? How many studies must indicate that a symptom is relevant before one should conclude that it is? How should one weigh methodological objections—should one presume that their existence explains the observed result or should one require evidence that they are operating? Disagreements over these issues do not separate the ethical from the unethical. Instead, they reflect justifiable differences of opinion regarding how certain one must be before giving testimony that a symptom is relevant for proving that abuse occurred.

THE SUGGESTIBILITY OF CHILDREN

Experts in sexual abuse cases frequently spend a lot of time discussing the suggestibility of children. However, we were surprised to find that suggestibility received little attention in most of this volume's chapters. Perhaps this is because the topic fails to evoke skepticism. Testimony on suggestibility is usually based on laboratory research, much of which would seem to satisfy the U.S. Supreme Court's requirement that such testimony "must be derived by the scientific method" (*Daubert v. Merrell Dow Pharmaceuticals, Inc.*, 1993, p. 590; see also Kovera & Borgida, this volume, chapter 9). Furthermore, most suggestibility experts avoid direct comments on the credibility of any particular child witness. For example, in describing her own experience as an expert witness, Bruck (this volume, chapter 4) emphasized that she avoided making statements "explicitly tied to the facts at bar" (p. 89). Thus, suggestibility testimony avoids the infirmities of clinical opinion, which is often based on unsystematic observation and is often case specific.

However, the strengths of such testimony are also its vulnerabilities. There is substantial disagreement among researchers about the applicability of laboratory research on suggestibility to children who actually appear in court (Ceci, 1991). The problem concerns ecological validity. Are the techniques used to interview children in the laboratory sufficiently similar to those used to interview an allegedly abused child in a particular case? Are the events about which children are interviewed in the laboratory comparable with a sexually abusive event? If not, how significant are the differences? In answering such questions, testifying experts are often forced to rely on their subjective judgments and personal experience.

Bruck (this volume, chapter 4) provides illustrative examples of cases in which suggestibility research was discussed, describing her expert testimony in two cases: the Martensville trials (*The Queen v. Ronald Sterling, Linda Sterling, and Travis Sterling*, 1994) and the Little Rascals case (*State v. Robert Fulton Kelly, Jr.*, 1992). In both cases, issues of ecological validity were raised. In *The Queen v. Linda Sterling*, the prosecutor questioned how well the research matched the interviewing actually conducted in the case at bar. In *State v. Kelly*, the prosecutor challenged assumptions that the research applied to allegations of sexual abuse that the child witnesses appeared to find embarrassing, aversive, and painful.

It is often impossible for an expert to know how a child has been interviewed in a particular case, even when the available reports relate what appear to be convincing narratives of abuse: As Bruck notes (this volume, chapter 4),

> I learned that just because a professional concluded in a report that the child was abused, it did not necessarily mean that the child had reported abuse in the manner contained in the report or that the child had spontaneously reported the abuse. I learned that these reports could reflect situations in which the child was repeatedly questioned and finally assented to abuse in response to an interviewer's leading questions. (p. 88)

Verbatim records of interviews are frequently unavailable, particularly those documenting the initial allegation, which is typically made before a formal investigation begins.

Without a verbatim record, a testifying expert can only speculate about whether suggestive methods were used. The expert might assume that interviews were suggestive on the basis of a review of transcripts from other cases, but doing so risks a generalization from a potentially unrepresentative sample (Ceci & Bruck, 1995). Systematic research on suggestive practices in actual interviews is in its infancy (Lamb et al., 1996; McGough & Warren, 1994). Consequently, we know little about the ecological validity of findings from the suggestibility literature. These include conclusions about the impact of such coercive techniques as stereotype induction (Lepore & Sesco, 1994; Leichtman & Ceci, 1995) and questioning in which the child is told (rather than asked) whether the events occurred (Ceci, Loftus, Leichtman, & Bruck, 1994; Leichtman & Ceci, 1995).

For ethical reasons, research on children's suggestibility cannot directly test the proposition that children can be manipulated to recall abusive experiences that never occurred. To the extent that abusive experiences are different than experiences that can be tested, the applicability of suggestibility research to sexual abuse allegations is open to question (Ceci, Bruck, & Rosenthal, 1995; Lyon, 1995). Moreover, even assuming agreement that differences exist, the practical significance of such differences is a matter of subjective opinion.

In legal terms, these issues address what the U.S. Supreme Court in *Daubert* (1993) called *fit*. *Fit* refers to the extent to which the expert's testimony is "tied to the facts of the case" (p. 591). A lack of fit renders an expert's testimony inadmissible under the *Federal Rules of Evidence* (Rule 702). A less than perfect fit raises issues of prejudicial impact (Rule 403) and can lead to the exclusion of expert testimony because juries are often deferential to expert opinion, even when the expert's testimony is of questionable relevance (Kovera & Borgida, this volume, chapter 9). Given the tendency of juries to defer decision making to experts (Miller & Allen, this volume, chapter 7), courts can use issues of fit and prejudice to weed out expert testimony when its persuasiveness exceeds its probative value.

One might argue that because scientific data on interview practices are limited, researchers should be barred from testifying about the suggestibility of children unless they have seen videotapes of the interviews or have at least reviewed transcripts of the interviews in a particular case. However, because documentation is frequently unavailable, this would dramatically limit the ability of experts to warn jurors about potentially suggestive interviewing techniques. Similarly, one might argue that the differences between the events examined by suggestibility researchers and actual sexual abuse justify exclusion of all expert testimony on suggestibility research. However, because it would be unethical for researchers to use coercive techniques to convince nonabused children that they were, in fact, abused, this argument would permanently foreclose all expert testimony on suggestibility. We believe that although expert testimony on suggestibility necessarily goes beyond what has been (or can be) scientifically proven, it should not be treated as inadmissible per se. If jurors are relatively uninformed about the suggestibility of children (or if they harbor misconceptions), expert testimony may be helpful.

At the same time, we agree with several of the contributors to this volume (Lavin & Sales, chapter 3; Pruett & Solnit, chapter 6) that experts are obligated to be candid about the limits of their knowledge: "When research is not available to address the question, they [experts] should present their testimony hemmed with disclaimers alerting the jury that it is not scientifically based and as yet unproven or unprovable" (Lavin & Sales, p. 79). Given Bruck's (this volume, chapter 4) warning that attorneys are often untrained in scientific methods and Kovera and Borgida's (this volume, chapter 9) discovery that cross-examination may fail to alter the jury's initial impressions of an expert's testimony, we would add that the expert should initiate a discussion of such limits in his or her direct testimony rather than wait for cross-examination.

CONCLUSION

Interpretive differences among researchers in child sexual abuse cases reveal the limitations of scientific knowledge. Those who study the behavior of sexually abused children in the real world are unable to subject randomly selected participants to abuse and observe the effects. Consequently, their conclusions may be influenced by illusory correlations born of selection and diagnostic biases. Those who study the suggestibility of children in a laboratory setting are typically unable to recreate the multitude of factors that influence a child's report in the field. Both types of researchers make inferential leaps and judgment calls in court when they attempt to translate their research into case-relevant knowledge. Disagreements are inevitable, not because some researchers are ethical and others are not, but because all researchers are human.

REFERENCES

Bays, J., & Chadwick, D. (1993). Medical diagnosis of the sexually abused child. *Child Abuse & Neglect, 17*, 91–110.

Berliner, L., & Conte, J. R. (1993). Sexual abuse evaluations: Conceptual and empirical obstacles. *Child Abuse & Neglect, 17*, 111–125.

Boat, B., Everson, M., & Holland, J. (1990). Maternal perceptions of non-abused young children's behaviors after the children's exposure to anatomical dolls. *Child Welfare, 64*, 389–399.

Bruck, M., Ceci, S. J., Francouer, E., & Renick, A. (1995). Anatomically detailed dolls do not facilitate preschoolers' reports of a pediatric examination involving genital touching. *Journal of Experimental Psychology: Applied, 1*, 95–109.

Case, M. E. S. (1994). Head injury in child abuse. In J. A. Monteleone & A. E. Brodeur (Eds.), *Child maltreatment: A clinical guide and reference* (pp. 75–87). St. Louis, MO: G. W. Medical.

Ceci, S. J. (1991). Some overarching issues in the children's suggestibility debate. In J. Doris (Ed.), *The suggestibility of children's recollections: Implications for eyewitness testimony* (pp. 1–9). Washington, DC: American Psychological Association.

Ceci, S. J., & Bruck, M. (1995). *Jeopardy in the courtroom: A scientific analysis of children's testimony.* Washington, DC: American Psychological Association.

Ceci, S. J., Bruck, M., & Rosenthal, R. (1995). Children's allegations of sexual abuse: Forensic and scientific issues: A reply to commentators. *Psychology, Public Policy, and Law, 1*, 494–520.

Ceci, S. J., Loftus, E. F., Leichtman, M. D., & Bruck, M. (1994). The possible role of source misattribution in the creation of false beliefs among preschoolers. *International Journal of Clinical and Experimental Hypnosis, 42*, 304–320.

Daubert v. Merrell Dow Pharmaceuticals, Inc., 509 U.S., 113 S. Ct. 2786 (1993).

Deblinger, E., McLeer, S. V., Atkins, M. S., Ralphe, D., & Foa, E. (1989). Post-traumatic stress in sexually abused, physically abused, and non-abused children. *Child Abuse & Neglect, 13*, 403–408.

Einbender, A. J., & Friedrich, W. N. (1989). Psychological functioning and behavior of sexually abused girls. *Journal of Consulting and Clinical Psychology, 57*, 155–157.

Emans, S. J., Woods, E. R., Flagg, N. T., & Freeman, A. (1987). Genital findings in sexually abused, symptomatic and asymptomatic girls. *Pediatrics, 79*, 778–785.

Federal rules of evidence, 28 U.S.C. (West 1994).

Finkelhor, D. (1987). The trauma of child sexual abuse: Two models. *Journal of Interpersonal Violence, 2*, 348–366.

Friedrich, W. N. (1993). Sexual victimization and sexual behavior in children: A review of recent literature. *Child Abuse & Neglect, 17*, 59–66.

Friedrich, W. N. (1995, Spring). The clinical use of the Child Sexual Behavior Inventory: Commonly asked questions. *American Professional Society on the Abuse of Children Advisor, 1*, 17–20.

Friedrich, W. N., Grambsch, P., Damon, L, Hewitt, S., Koverola, C., Lang, R., Wolfe, V., & Broughton, D. (1992). The Child Sexual Behavior Inventory: Normative and clinical findings. *Psychological Assessment, 4*, 303–311.

Friedrich, W. N., & Reams, R. A. (1987). Course of psychological symptoms in sexually abused young children. *Psychotherapy, 24*, 160–170.

Friedrich, W. N., Urquiza, A. J., & Beilke, R. L. (1986). Behavior problems in sexually abused young children. *Journal of Pediatric Psychology, 11*, 47–57.

Gale, J., Thompson, R. J., Moran, T., & Sack, W. H. (1988). Sexual abuse in young children: Its clinical presentation and characteristic patterns. *Child Abuse & Neglect, 12*, 163–170.

Goldston, D. B., Turnquist, D. C., & Knutson, J. F. (1989). Presenting problems of sexually abused girls receiving psychiatric services. *Journal of Abnormal Psychology, 98*, 314–317.

Gomes-Schwartz, B., Horowitz, J. M., & Cardarelli, A. P. (1990). *Child sexual abuse: The initial effects*. Newbury Park, CA: Sage.

Goodman, G. S., Taub, E. P., Jones, D. P. H., England, P., Port, L. K., Rudy, L., & Prado, L. (1992). Testifying in criminal court. *Monographs of the Society for Research in Child Development, 57*(Serial No. 229).

Hewitt, S. K., & Friedrich, W. N. (1991). Effects of probable sexual abuse on preschool children. In M. Q. Patton (Ed.), *Family sexual abuse* (pp. 57–74). Newbury Park, CA: Sage.

Hibbard, R. A., & Hartman, G. L. (1992). Behavioral problems in alleged sexual abuse victims. *Child Abuse & Neglect, 16*, 755–762.

Kendall-Tackett, K. A., Williams, L. M., & Finkelhor, D. (1993). Impact of sexual abuse on children: A review and synthesis of recent empirical studies. *Psychological Bulletin, 113*, 164–180.

Kolko, D. J., Moser, J. T., & Weldy, S. R. (1988). Behavioral/emotional indicators of sexual abuse in child psychiatric inpatients: A controlled comparison with physical abuse. *Child Abuse & Neglect, 12,* 529–541.

Lamb, M. E., Hershkowitz, I., Sternberg, K. J., Esplin, P. W., Hovav, M., Manor, T., & Yudilevitch, L. (1996). Effects of investigative utterance types on Israeli children's responses. *International Journal of Behavioral Development, 19,* 627–637.

Leichtman, M. D., & Ceci, S. J. (1995). The effects of stereotypes and suggestions on preschoolers' reports. *Developmental Psychology, 31,* 568–578.

Lepore, S. J., & Sesco, B. (1994). Distorting children's reports and interpretations of events through suggestion. *Journal of Applied Psychology, 79,* 108–120.

Lyon, T. D. (1995). False allegations and false denial in child sexual abuse. *Psychology, Public Policy, and Law, 1,* 429–437.

Lyon, T. D., Gilles, E. E., & Cory, L. (1996). Medical evidence of physical abuse in infants and young children. *Pacific Law Journal, 28,* 93–167.

Lyon, T. D., & Koehler, J. J. (1996). The relevance ratio: Evaluating the probative value of experts' testimony in child sexual abuse cases. *Cornell Law Review, 82,* 43–78.

McGough, L. S., & Warren, A. R. (1994). The all-important investigative interview. *Juvenile & Family Court Journal, 45,* 13–29.

The Queen v. Ronald Sterling, Linda Sterling, and Travis Sterling, Jud. Centre of Saskatoon, Sask., Q.B.J. No. 74 (1994).

Sackett, D. L. (1979). Bias in analytic research. *Journal of Chronic Disease, 32,* 51–63.

Sorensen, T., & Snow, B. (1991). How children tell: The process of disclosure in child sexual abuse. *Child Welfare, 70,* 3–15.

State v. Robert Fulton Kelly, Jr., Superior Criminal Court, Pitt County, NC, #91-CRS-4250–4363 (1991–1992).

White, S., Halpin, B. M, Strom, G. A., & Santilli, G. (1988). Behavioral comparisons of young sexually abused, neglected, and nonreferred children. *Journal of Clinical Child Psychology, 17,* 53–61.

13

A LEGAL COMMENTARY: THE IMPACT OF *DAUBERT* ON 21ST-CENTURY CHILD SEXUAL ABUSE PROSECUTIONS

LUCY McGOUGH

The ascertainment of truth, the purpose of a trial, is a very complex enterprise. This volume's collection of chapters reflects that complexity and is a very ambitious undertaking, probing the murky epistemological issues of truth finding: "reality," perceptions of reality, memory of reality perceptions, and the probabilities for reliability. Consider the following: An event occurs (reality); remembering the event, the child testifies (the child's present perception of past reality). The task of the trial fact finder is to decide whether the child witness is believable. This credibility judgment creates another reality dimension because it draws on the perceptions of another actor in assessing the believability of the rememberer. A typical child sexual abuse prosecution encompasses all of these abstractions. Weighing the probabilities for reliability, the fact finder (judge or jury) perceives the child as credible or not credible, depending on his or her own knowledge, experiences, and prejudices, and makes a decision about the truth of the past reality.

If these issues have confounded philosophers through the ages, it is little wonder that their contemplation is dizzying. What is the reliability of the fact finder's perception of the witness's perception? Even the question is mind-boggling, echoing Platonic forms and Philosophy 201. Such contemplations make the ancient truth-seeking mode of trial by ordeal and torturing the defendant until he or she confesses seem wonderfully simple, efficient, and appealing by contrast (Spencer, this volume, chapter 2).

Moreover, that description depicts only a skeletal trial with a single prosecution witness. These chapters explicitly address the complicating factor of when the trial court hears an offer of expert testimony. The same process occurs with these differences. From the words of Miller and Allen (this volume, chapter 7), the court must first make a decision on the expert's "authenticity" as an expert by hearing evidence of that expert's purported expertise. If the court agrees that expertise has been demonstrated—as it usually does because very little is required by way of a demonstration—it then receives the expert's testimony. The court hears an expert's perception of the matter at hand and must decide whether the expert's perception (basis of knowledge and opinion) is sufficiently reliable to be helpful and whether the expert is also credible. If these conditions are met, then the court must decide what effect the expert's contribution has on the penultimate assessment of the accuracy of the child's perception of past reality.

I do not belabor the potential metaphysical issues inherent in any trial process. Miller and Allen (this volume, chapter 7) have contributed a clear exposition of the aspirations of the Anglo-American legal system and the rationales underpinning the rules of evidence, including those that govern the receipt of expert testimony. The global companion piece is Spencer's (this volume) chapter, which reminds the English-speaking reader that there is another competing worldview, the civil law system of truth finding. Although as he notes, the "adversarial" and "inquisitorial" systems have far more in common than usually imagined, where there are differences in approach to resolving factual disputes, those differences are quite provocative.[1]

Because these chapters contribute to an appreciation of the complexity of any choice of rules governing the appearance of expert witnesses, they are a helpful antidote to hubris, which is a thread that runs through each of these chapters. As Professor Henry Higgins (in My Fair Lady) once lamented, "Why can't a woman be more like a man?" Similar interprofessional hubris can cause a social scientist to wonder "Why can't a lawyer

---

[1]As Miller and Allen note, "the decline in accuracy that may result from increased deference to expert opinions [the civil law approach to expert witnesses] cannot easily be assessed, which is in itself cause for concern" (p. 139). Empirical study comparing the judgments of American and civilian fact finders on identical hypothetical disputes would be a fascinating and helpful contribution to this debate.

be more like me?," "Why don't judges defer to scientists?," or even "Why are trials so unscientific (or antiscientific)?" Lawyers and judges express similar impatience and occasional exasperation with social scientists. There is also intraprofessional hubris, often inviting condescension from empiricists to clinicians (and vice versa), legal academics to trial lawyers (and vice versa), and well-heeled corporate attorneys to impoverished public defenders (and vice versa). In several of these chapters, the authors acknowledge this expert—this human—tendency by counseling awareness of the limits of one's expertise. Pruett and Solnit (this volume, chapter 6) go the distance by noting that often it is "impossible to know . . . what a child has experienced" (p. 130) and impossible to know whether the "correct" judgment has been reached in any trial.

Taking heed of the need for humility, especially when making projections into the future, in the remainder of this commentary I focus primarily on the application of the guidelines for the admissibility of expert testimony to the types of evidence most frequently offered in child sexual abuse prosecution. The authors of four of this volume's chapters—Berliner (chapter 1), Mason (chapter 10), Fisher and Whiting (chapter 8), and Kovera and Borgida (chapter 9)—explicitly apply the new admissibility calculus of *Daubert v. Merrell Dow Pharmaceuticals, Inc.* (1993) to a consideration of current social science research. The remaining chapters' authors significantly but more indirectly contribute to an understanding of the complexity of expertise.

THE BRAVE NEW WORLD OF *DAUBERT*

Three years ago the U.S. Supreme Court decided *Daubert* (1993). That decision confirmed that in enacting the *Federal Rules of Evidence* in 1975, Congress had intended for federal trial courts to use a very broad and flexible test in deciding whether to admit expert testimony.[2]

Thus, *Daubert* buried the "*Frye* restriction"; that is, expert testimony asserting a scientific principle must demonstrate that the principle has "gained general acceptance in the particular field in which it belongs" (*Frye v. United States*, 1923, p. 1014). Instead, the extent of scientific

---

[2]It is important to recognize that in the *Daubert* opinion, the court was not announcing a policy that would govern all American trials, that is, proceedings in both the federal and state trial systems. Strictly speaking, *Daubert* applies only to the receipt of expert testimony in federal trials. In an exercise of its supervisory authority over the lower federal courts, the court was elaborating only the guidelines for their receipt of expert testimony pursuant to Rules 702 and 403 of the *Federal Rules of Evidence* (1978). However, although technically accurate, such an observation risks being misleading. The *Federal Rules of Evidence* (and their interpretations by the U.S. Supreme Court) have greatly influenced the shape of the states' rules of evidence to the extent that nearly three quarters of the states have enacted or adopted substantially similar rules.

consensus becomes only one of four factors used by a trial court in determining the trustworthiness of an expert's proposed testimony. The other factors weighed by the court are whether the theory or technique has been or can be tested and validated; whether supporting research findings have been published and subjected to peer review; and whether in the case of a particular technique there is a known potential rate of error.

With the demise of the *Frye* restriction, only the vague and admittedly unsettling principles of the *Federal Rules of Evidence* (1978) Rules 702 and 403 remain as guidelines. Rule 702 permits an expert with "scientific, technical, or other specialized knowledge" (which the fact finder lacks because otherwise such testimony would be "common" knowledge) to testify about matters that will "assist" the fact finder "to understand the evidence or to determine a fact in issue." In offering testimony, the expert is not required by the *Federal Rules of Evidence* to volunteer contrary research nor to offer weaknesses in the underlying science, unless questioned by the judge or adverse counsel on cross-examination.[3]

Nevertheless, the expert cannot and does not assist the trial court, unless he or she is willing to take on the educational role described by Miller and Allen (this volume, chapter 7). Thus, there is an embedded expectation that any expert will illumine not only the issues in dispute but also the scientific issues, if any, that are relevant to an assessment of his or her own exposition of opinion. Even within an adversarial system, some overarching and unarticulated ethical constraints limit the role of each player in a trial's pursuit of justice. Elsewhere, Melton (1994) has called this professional constraint the expert's "duty to disclose uncertainty" (p. 69). Thus, the subject of this volume encompasses not only what an expert can say—the minimalist requirements of legal rules and doctrines—but also what an expert should say—the larger professional ethos that guides behavior.

All legal scholars agree that *Daubert* increases the likelihood that an expert will be permitted to give testimony, although in the exceptional case, the trial court may ultimately reject it as useless or counterproductive. The court may determine that the scientific validity of the evidence is so weak that it and the expert's opinion should be rejected. *Federal Rules of Evidence* (1978) Rule 403 authorizes this rejection if the "probative value is substantially outweighed by the danger of unfair prejudice, confusion of

---

[3]The *Federal Rules of Evidence* do not require that an expert first state his or her reasons or scientific premises before offering an opinion. Rule 705 requires such disclosure only if requested by the court or by adverse counsel on cross-examination. As a matter of custom and practice, however, during direct examination the expert's counsel usually asks for the facts or data on which the opinion is based to underscore its significance. As a matter of trial tactics to minimize the sting of anticipated cross-examination, the expert's counsel often will also prompt the expert to admit but explain any apparent weaknesses in the knowledge base.

the issues or misleading the jury" or delay. As Justice Blackmun explained in *Daubert* (1993),

> critics suggest that recognition of a screening role for the judge that allows for the exclusion of "invalid" evidence will sanction a stifling and repressive scientific orthodoxy and will be inimical to the search for truth. . . . The scientific project is advanced by broad and wide-ranging consideration of a multitude of hypotheses, for those that are incorrect will eventually be shown to be so, and that in itself is an advance. Conjectures that are probably wrong are of little use, however, in the project of reaching a quick, final, and binding legal judgment—often of great consequence—about a particular set of events in the past. (pp. 2798–2799)

For trial courts to perform their new and critical "gatekeeping" role, they must be educated by the thorough and candid testimony of the experts, who, in turn, must be educated by empiricists about the validity of current research. In the garden-variety child sexual abuse prosecution, the trial expert is a social worker with a clinical practice, as Mason's (this volume, chapter 10) data indicate (34% of testifying experts were social workers). Only in the most highly publicized cases do empiricists appear in court to present complete "social framework" or global testimony about the reliability risks of children's memories, such as that offered by Maggie Bruck in the Little Rascals Daycare Center case in North Carolina (*State v. Robert Fulton Kelly, Jr.,* 1991–1992). Indeed, many trial courts strongly prefer psychological evidence that is coupled with a personal assessment of the particular child witness.

Lawlor (this volume, chapter 5) describes the ideal clinician–expert witness:

> A competent forensic evaluator needs to maintain a neutral stance, a stance of objectivity, and to engage in as thorough and complete a forensic evaluation as is possible under the circumstances of the particular case. Particularly during the interview of a young child, this approach means that the forensic evaluator has to have a grasp of the developmental literature, which alerts the evaluator to the capacities of children of various ages; a knowledge of the suggestibility and lying behavior literatures, which warn of the many pitfalls to be avoided in these cases; and a thorough grounding in research methodology, which allows the evaluator to read the literature with some degree of sophistication. This latter point is particularly important, in that not all studies or articles that exist in this area are of equal weight or validity. (p. 107)

Although many well-meaning clinicians face considerable pressures,[4]

---

[4]Clinicians are often caught in the crosswinds of professional role conflict: Am I a forensic evaluator or therapeutic caregiver? The court's expert or the prosecutor's principal investigator? A scientist or child's advocate? The chapters (in this volume) by Lawlor and by Pruett and Solnit are especially valuable in exploring these issues.

there is a significant gap between the typical and the ideal expert witness (Mason, this volume, chapter 10). Clearly, there is a "trickle-down" effect in scientific knowledge as well as in macroeconomics. Perhaps the most important contribution empiricists can make is to educate the clinical community through articles in professional magazines rather than scholarly research journals about the lack of validation for commonly used diagnostic tools: anatomically detailed dolls and syndromal checklists.

THE DIAGNOSTIC USE OF ANATOMICALLY DETAILED DOLLS

If 92% of mental health professionals use anatomically detailed dolls in conducting child abuse evaluations (Fisher & Whiting, this volume, chapter 8) and if such evaluators are the most likely professionals to appear in court as expert witnesses, then the diagnostic use of doll-play behavior may be the most important type of evidence to analyze for admissibility. After reviewing the empirical studies, Fisher and Whiting conclude that "at present, there is no evidence that their use constitutes a valid assessment of whether an individual child has been sexually abused" (p. 173). Kovera and Borgida (this volume, chapter 9) are somewhat more equivocal: They conclude that there is "scant empirical evidence to support the discriminative validity of AD [anatomically detailed] doll interviews" (p. 199). Expert testimony that there is scant but some empirical research, although no professional consensus, may be enough to preclude the trial's rejecting purportedly diagnostic testimony out of hand.

Furthermore, the American Psychological Association's (1991) official position statement, although equivocal, certainly implies a professional approval of this methodology: "Doll-centered assessment of children when used as part of a psychological evaluation and interpreted by experienced and competent examiners, may be the best available practical solution" for the investigation of child sexual abuse. In sum, applying *Daubert*'s initial test for reliability, a trial court could reasonably conclude that a clinician could offer observations of a child's doll play in support of a child sexual abuse diagnosis.

Under *Daubert*, the only remaining barrier to the admissibility of such evidence arises if the court is made aware of the weakness of the claim for diagnostic validity and, on balance, finds the evidence to be misleading. On this point, counsel through cross-examination or through a rebuttal expert witness has much potential ammunition to present to the court: the lack of diagnostic validation for the presence of individual forms of behavior and the findings of significant error rates, including false positives, among raters observing doll play. Perhaps the most important point of any rebuttal evidence is the volume of expert opinion voiced against the reliability of using doll play for a definitive diagnosis. Clearly, doll play has failed "to have gained general acceptance in the particular field in which it belongs" (Frye, 1923, p. 1014). Trial judges tend to be conservative by nature and so may well continue to defer to the scientific majority and reject any attempted diagnoses based on doll-play observation. In other words, they may informally continue to use the Frye rule, despite their greater authority under Daubert. Even without rejection of such evidence, the court or jury may well accord little, if any, probative weight to purported expert diagnoses.

THE DIAGNOSTIC USE OF SYNDROME EVIDENCE

Many expert witnesses have been quite willing to testify about clinically derived syndromes, most frequently Sgroi's (1982) child sexual abuse syndrome and Summit's (1992) child sexual abuse accommodation syndrome but also posttraumatic stress disorder and the traumagenic dynamics model. Mason (this volume, chapter 10) states that such testimony may be as common or more common than testimony about a child's play with anatomically detailed dolls and suggests that "clinicians are generally more confident about the reliability of behavioral indicators of abuse" (p. 229) than are empiricists. The ubiquitous 2-day child sexual abuse evaluation workshops and behavior checklists have emboldened some clinicians to claim scientific support for their diagnoses.

Is it enough to meet the Daubert test that some clinicians believe they can discern patterns that empiricists are unable to validate? As Berliner (this volume, chapter 1) notes, "there is agreement among professionals about the criteria they weigh. . . . In spite of this, there is currently no empirical evidence that clinicians reliably arrive at the same conclusions with comparable clinical information" (p. 14–15). Recall that in Daubert, the majority emphasized that the court was to assess the validity of scientific claims, including whether the ideas had been derived and tested by the scientific method, peer review and publication, and known potential rates of error. Those criteria imply that more is required than personal experience or anecdotal confirmation by one or more clinicians.[5]

Mason (this volume, chapter 10) as well as Fisher and Whiting (this volume, chapter 8) point out that two recent surveys of the empirical

[5]There is some doubt about whether Daubert's restrictions apply to a clinician's opinion—that is, is a clinical judgment "scientific" evidence, the subject of Daubert, or (merely) "technical or other specialized knowledge" (Melton, 1994, p. 78)? Certainly a great deal depends on the asserted basis for the opinion and the language used by the expert. Phrasing borrowed from validated research, such as "syndrome," "diagnosis," "finding," "indicative of," or "consistent with" certainly implies that the expert is making a scientific claim for the opinion; thus, the boast ought to be subjected to Daubert's scrutiny. Sales and VandenBos (1995) noted the irony that arises if the court rejects scientific testimony due to its lack of validity but accepts similar testimony based on the "professional experience" (or simply the personal values) of a psychologist.

literature concluded that although known sexually abused children displayed more cited behaviors contained in a lengthy array of behaviors, there is no distinct behavior or pattern of behaviors that could constitute a definitive symptomatology for sexual abuse. Furthermore, many of the same behaviors are displayed by nonabused children. Thus, an expert's conclusion of sexual abuse on the basis of any cluster of behaviors exhibited by a particular child is a "false premise," which should lead to its rejection under *Daubert*. As Miller and Allen (this volume, chapter 7) point out, in such a case the expert has exceeded the scope of the underlying scientific research. In sum, a clinician should not assert that her or his conclusion that a child has been sexually abused is based on validated empirical research. Such an assertion would surely be misleading and might even constitute perjury if the witness know or should know that it is hyperbole.[6]

Aware of the shakiness of the empirical support for any true diagnostic value of various behaviors, some experts attempt to temper their conclusions by offering more ambiguous conclusions, such as that the child's behavior is "indicative of" or "consistent with" child sexual abuse. Consider the testimony of a Wisconsin school guidance counselor who testified that he had suspected sexual abuse of an 11-year-old female student because of

> marked changes in the girl's behavior at school: acting out in class, some on compliance as far as doing homework, standards [*sic*] up to the teachers, being a little bit disrespectful and quite a bit of writing notes to boys, and boys writing notes to her. . . . [She] had been wearing tight jeans and v-necked sweaters without an undershirt; had written "I love ___ " (her boyfriend's name) on the back pocket of her pants.

On direct examination, he also testified

> Q. [the prosecutor]: In your opinion based on your experience, and based upon your training, are the kinds of acting out behavior that the teachers described to you that they were seeing in [this girl] consistent with children who were victims of abuse?
> A. Yes.
> Q. The answer is yes?

[6]In contrast, for reasons that are not entirely clear, Kovera and Borgida (this volume, chapter 9) assert that "research conducted on the behavioral correlates of sexual victimization would survive a *Daubert* hearing" (p. 192). Their syllogism—"the fact that a child exhibits some of the symptoms associated with sexual abuse, although not dispositive, increases the likelihood that the child is an abuse victim" (p. 192)—is faulty logic, although it is a conclusion often made by trial courts. As both Fisher and Whiting (this volume, chapter 8) and Mason (this volume, chapter 10) note, unless the "symptoms" or, more precisely, the "behaviors" accurately discriminate between abused and nonabused children, no reasoned conclusion can be drawn about the status of a particular child. This is the "fallacy of the undistributed middle" in symbolic logic: "Some (many) liars have beards. This man has a beard. Therefore, this man is (is likely to be) a liar" (Beardsley, 1950, pp. 213–215).

A. Yes. One of the, we call them in the workshops that I have attended, in the seminars that I have attended we call them, red flags, they are indicators.

Q. Of a problem?

A. Of a problem, dealing with sexuality . . . sexual abuse. (McGough, 1995, p. 257, quoting from *State v. Jensen*, 1988)

This expert witness certainly suggests in his testimony that there was a consensus within the scientific community that particular behaviors were "red flags" and, furthermore, that these disrespectful and flirtatious behaviors constituted recognized symptomatology. The use of phrases such as "indicative of" or "consistent with," as Lawlor (this volume, chapter 5) observes in his chapter, "is an attempt to do through connotation what cannot be done through denotation. It is a statement designed to leave an impression that is clearly not warranted by the underlying facts" (p. 110). Even under the minimal requirements of the *Daubert* rule, an expert must demonstrate reliable and validated criteria as justification for the probability that a child has been sexually abused.

In sum, any testimony based on claims of a behavior-based diagnosis of child abuse—whether due to syndromes, checklists, or years of clinical practice—should not be admitted under the *Daubert* criteria for reliability. The gloss of purported expertise contributes little and offers a considerable opportunity for predisposing the fact finder toward believing the expert's personal opinion as scientifically probable, if not infallible.

THE (THEORETICALLY) LIMITED REBUTTAL USE OF SYNDROME EVIDENCE

Before leaving syndromal testimony, a note should be made of the legal exception that has developed approving its use as rebuttal evidence.[7] As originally conceived, the prosecution was permitted to present expert testimony about syndromes that helped to explain a child's reactions that a fact finder might otherwise misinterpret as evidence of a child's unreliability.

On cross-examination, the defense counsel will typically try to attack the credibility of the child witness by highlighting inconsistencies in the child's reports of his or her experience or if a fact in the case, then that the child had delayed reporting or even recanted an accusation. Extrapolating from adult behaviors, laypersons, including judges and jurors, are likely to assume that truthful child sexual abuse victims do not typically

---

[7]This exception was nourished by a pair of very influential articles by Professor David McCord (1986, 1987). Like Summit (1992), McCord might now rue some of the current judicial misconstructions of his finely tuned doctrinal exception.

recount inconsistent stories, delay outcry, or recant. To rebut this potential for misinterpretation, many courts have permitted prosecution experts to testify that keeping sexual behavior a secret, displaying ambivalence about an accusation, and even trying to withdraw charges are typical (but not invariable) behaviors of many (but not all) sexually abused children (McGough, 1995). There are two critical limitations governing this exceptional use of syndrome testimony. First, note that the prejudice justifying any rebuttal is that there must be a pervasive lay misconception about child sexual abuse victims' reactions; therefore, to level the playing field, rebuttal should be limited to general evidence of typical reactions of child victims as a group. The second limitation is that the expert's testimony on rebuttal cannot go beyond the generally applicable reliability requirements established by *Daubert*.

The first premise for permitting this testimony is that a layperson, judge, or juror brings to the courtroom misperceptions about the behaviors of abuse victimized children. A very subtle insight offered by Berliner (this volume, chapter 1) is that public perceptions are constantly changing and that media presentations of social science research can and do correct such misconceptions. Periodic sampling of jury attitudes and perceptions about children's reactions would be important information for courts to consider in determining whether there is a continuing need for curative expert testimony. If not, appellate courts might be persuaded to abandon the special exception for rebuttal syndrome evidence, especially because it may be more problematic than helpful.[8]

If syndrome evidence is inadmissible on direct examination because it has not been validated for proving child sexual abuse, it does not magically become valid or more valid simply because it is offered in rebuttal. Although attacking the credibility of the child by cross-examination opens the door to larger issues of the child's credibility and reputation for truthfulness, it does not authorize the receipt of unreliable and prejudicial evidence (McGough, 1995). Mason's (this volume, chapter 10) study makes a significant contribution by documenting the abuses in courts' receipt of rebuttal syndrome evidence. She suggests that some rebuttal experts may be improperly commenting on whether the particular child fits the "profile" of a sexually abused child. She found evidence that rebuttal experts were improperly linking behaviors as "characteristics"

---

[8]A very tantalizing possibility arises from Berliner's (this volume, chapter 1) comment that the jury *voir dire* can serve an educational purpose. Suppose during the questioning of potential jurors, the defense counsel asks whether the jurors were aware that some child sexual abuse victims exhibit behaviors that were different from adults and, through similar questions, disabuses the jurors of possible misconceptions about child abuse victimization. Thereafter, when the prosecution seeks to offer expert testimony about "typical" behaviors of child abuse victims, can the defense counsel object on grounds that any child sexual abuse accommodation syndrome evidence or the like is unnecessary because all jurors had already been educated during the *voir dire*?

(alias "red flags" or "indicators") of child sexual abuse victims—that as discussed above, are assertions that would violate *Daubert*. Mason's preliminary findings are very interesting and should be pursued and expanded. Unless trial courts become more vigilant in hewing the proper boundaries of the exceptions, permitting the use of syndrome testimony on rebuttal has the potential for being an exception that can swallow the rule. Or recalling the old joke about the practices of small town saloons, "the front door closes at midnight, but the back door opens at 12:05."

THE FORM OF REBUTTAL EXPERT TESTIMONY

Kovera and colleagues have sought to study a very important issue for the legal system: Is expert testimony on behavioral reactions to child sexual abuse more probative than prejudicial? (see, e.g., Kovera & Borgida, this volume, chapter 9). Furthermore, their variance of the form of expert testimony is quite ingenious. Lawyers do have options for how they present an expert's testimony. In the first form, counsel can offer an expert to give general background information on the typical reactions of child sexual abuse victims as a group (Kovera's "standard" testimony; see Kovera & Borgida, this volume). As noted above, at the present time, most courts permit such rebuttal testimony. In the second form, the expert witness might testify that the behaviors of a particular child in this case indicate that he or she is abused. Again, as noted above, such testimony should be rejected because there are no validated, discriminating criteria for such an individualized diagnosis.

The response of an expert to a hypothetical set of variables (Kovera's "concrete" testimony; see Kovera & Borgida, this volume, chapter 9) is a third form of expert testimony that falls in between those alternatives. An expert witness may be asked a question based on a hypothetical set of facts, provided that the hypothetical facts accurately mirror the facts of the dispute and only those facts are submitted as premises. Prosecutors prefer to submit hypothetical questions because they believe that this is a more powerful, more persuasive way to present the expert's evidence. A hypothetical question can come very close, as close as is legally permissible, to a pivotal issue of the dispute without explicitly attempting to have the expert witness offer his or her opinion on how the issue should be properly resolved.

Future studies that vary the forms of rebuttal expert testimony about typical reactions of child sexual abuse victims—inconsistent accounts, delays in reporting, and recantations—would be very helpful in determining the accuracy of the lawyers' assumption that the use of hypothetical questions is a more powerful form of expert testimony than any dose of background information.[9]

DIAGNOSIS OF TRUTHFULNESS

As Spencer's (this volume) chapter details, experts routinely testify in trial courts of countries within the civil law system about the credibility of an accusation made by an alleged child sexual abuse victim. Just as routinely, such testimony has traditionally been rejected in Great Britain, Canada, Australia, New Zealand, the United States, and other countries in the common law system. In the American legal system, courts have often relied on the erstwhile *Frye* restriction to reject such testimony because of the lack of scientific consensus about the validity of any truth test. Fisher and Whiting (this volume, chapter 8) detail the continuing search among American social scientists for psychometrically sound instruments capable of discerning reliable child sexual abuse accusations. Among other methodologies, they note the statement validity analysis (SVA), which has evolved from the research of German social scientists (see Raskin & Yuille's, 1989, description of the development of SVA). On the basis of the hypothesis that the account of a child victim of sexual abuse differs qualitatively and quantitatively from a fabricated account, both German (Steller & Kohnken, 1989) and American researchers (Esplin, Boychuk, & Raskin, 1988) have claimed reliability and validation for the criteria that SVA uses to identify the truthful accusation. Testimony based on a trained expert's use of SVA methodology is widely received and relied on by trial courts in France and Germany in deciding whether a child is truthful in claiming sexual victimization.

Obviously the scientific method knows no national boundaries. Absent salient cultural variables, German empirical validation should be as persuasive to an American court as research of the homegrown variety.[10]

---

[9]Kovera et al. (1995) did not precisely isolate this question. If what the jury has seen (a confident child) is incongruent with the expert's testimony ("you should expect a hesitant child when assessing whether child sexual abuse has occurred"), then one would reasonably expect the jury to be confused by this dissonance. In this condition, the expert's global testimony does not assist the jury in resolving this dissonance. That a hypothetical question highlighting the dissonance produces a greater degree of juror skepticism about the prosecution's case is interesting information for prosecutors, should any be inept enough to produce the dissonance in the first place. In addition, note that any hypothetical question must be based exclusively on the facts of the dispute, facts presented by other testimony in the case. If a child has testified confidently, then expert testimony based on a hypothetical situation that child abuse victims often become confused and hesitant properly ought to be rejected as irrelevant to the facts of this case (although no smart defense counsel would object to such a helpful confusion). A study that compares the effects of standard testimony with concrete testimony with congruent child witness behavior would be more useful to the bench and bar.

[10]There have been several international conferences convened for the purpose of sharing social science research relevant to the investigation of child sexual abuse. There are also promising signs of international consensus (Lamb, 1994).

Although the lack of international consensus may have heretofore posed an insurmountable barrier under the *Frye* rule, *Daubert* has lowered that barrier. SVA remains controversial among many of the American scientific community (Fisher & Whiting, this volume, chapter 8), but nonetheless the extant European research would appear to meet the reliability criteria of the new standard. The inference (the truthfulness of the child's statement) has been "derived by the scientific method [and] [p]roposed testimony [is] supported by at least some appropriate validation—i.e., 'good grounds,' based on what is known" (*Daubert*, 1993, p. 2795).

Consequently, if reliability were the exclusive or even the paramount concern of the Anglo-American legal system, it might seem that of all the commonly offered types of expert opinion in child sexual abuse prosecutions, an expert's opinion using SVA is the type of testimony most likely to be welcomed under the *Daubert* rule. Paradoxically, however, the truth-telling assessment of any other witness is the most unlikely type of expert evidence to be received by American courts. Even though such a stance is antiscientific insofar as expert credibility opinion is concerned, this bias is embedded in the American adversarial system and the U.S. Constitution. Several of the amendments contained in the Bill of Rights extend guarantees to an accused individual that were clearly held more dear than merely the reliability of evidence used by the prosecution. Even though utterly reliable, a police-coerced confession is inadmissible against an accused individual (*Colorado v. Connelly*, 1986; *Rogers v. Richmond*, 1961; U.S. Constitution, Amendments V and XIV). Even though utterly reliable, evidence seized in violation of a citizen's rights to be free of unreasonable searches and seizures is inadmissible in a criminal prosecution (*Mapp v. Ohio*, 1961; U.S. Constitution, Amendments IV and XIV). Furthermore, the right to trial by jury guaranteed by the sixth and seventh amendments includes the right to insist that other citizen neighbors make critical factual determinations of witness credibility as well as the ultimate decision of guilt or innocence. Even though the American democratic ideal is hard to encapsulate, one legal scholar has referred to the cluster of constitutionally protected trial rights of an accused as the right to "dignity" (Massaro, 1988). The amendments, individually and collectively, reflect a fundamental and abiding faith in community participation in trials, the integrity of citizen judgment, and a fear of unchecked official power, including the government's relatively greater resources to summon influential truth experts.[11] As a result, despite the siren's song of reliable truth assays, expert testimony concerning the credibility of a child witness is an unlikely development in American law, despite *Daubert*.

---

[11]For further discussion of these very complex issues of constitutional law, see McGough (1995, pp. 233–263).

THE ADEQUACY OF CURRENT PROCEDURE TO EXPOSE "SHAKY BUT ADMISSIBLE DATA"

Daubert relies on the trial judge to make the determination whether expert testimony is relevant and sufficiently reliable to warrant consideration.[12] As previously noted, the trial court must weigh the probative value of relevant, scientifically grounded expert testimony against its potential to distract or mislead the jury.[13] When does expertise cease to be helpful and become so prejudicial (or inefficient) that the jury should not be permitted to hear it? In *Daubert* (1993), the U.S. Supreme Court expressed confidence in the effectiveness of "vigorous" cross-examination, rebuttal experts or documentary evidence, and careful jury instructions to expose any "shaky but admissible data" (p. 2798), that is, an expert's overreaching or offer of pseudoscience.

In the latter part of their chapter, Kovera and Borgida (this volume) challenge the court's assumption of the effectiveness of those safeguards. Their recitation of current empirical research seems to indicate that jurors do not understand jury instructions and that cross-examination, whether or not "vigorous," and rebuttal experts may not overcome the damage done by an ersatz expert once jurors have reached premature conclusions ("belief perseverance"). These lines of research clearly need to be expanded and have forensic significance well beyond their application to the proper evaluation of expert testimony. The presumption of the effectiveness of cross-examination and rebuttal (and surrebuttal) evidence is central to the adversarial system and the structure of American trials. Consequently, this cherished presumption will not be lightly cast aside.

A more productive line of empirical inquiry is to study trial judges who are entrusted with the primary responsibility for discriminating between helpful and prejudicial expert testimony. Although Kovera and her colleagues (see, e.g., Kovera & Borgida, this volume, chapter 9) have studied jury perceptions and decision making, trial judges are a long neglected group, although infinitely more important figures in the Anglo-American

---

[12]Ordinarily, the trial court must hear the expert and any cross-examination or rebuttal expert testimony to make a ruling on admissibility. If the court decides as a matter of law that the testimony is inadmissible, then it orders the court reporter to strike the testimony from the record. Ideally, to avoid any potential prejudicial effect, counsel challenging the admissibility of the testimony will seek to exclude the jury until the issue of admissibility is resolved, that is, during the expert's testimony, the cross-examination, and any rebuttal evidence. However, quite often in the name of efficiency—to avoid making the expert and the judge go twice over the same ground—the jury remains present in the courtroom and hears the proposed expert testimony. As a general rule, the law assumes that even though jurors have heard testimony, they can purge any thought of it in their deliberations when instructed by the court to disregard it as inadmissible. The validity of this assumption also invites empirical inquiry.
[13]Rule 403 of the *Federal Rules of Evidence* (1978) directs the trial court to deny the receipt of any evidence, although relevant, "if its probative value is substantially outweighed by the danger of unfair prejudice, confusion of the issues, or misleading the jury, or by considerations of undue delay, waste of time, or needless presentation or cumulative evidence."

legal system. The trial court, without a jury, decides the majority of criminal cases tried in state courts. Thus, a trial judge makes critical evidentiary rulings in a jury trial, but she or he makes all determinations, including reliability and witness credibility, and reaches the verdict in most criminal trials.[14]

CONCLUSION

Daubert is an attempt to achieve more accurate fact finding in trials. But it is and can only be an attempt to facilitate accuracy. As Spencer (this volume, chapter 2) observes, "there is no such thing as a legal procedure that works perfectly. The best system lawyers can ever aspire to is one that is least bad" (p. 47). An appreciation of the complexity of that aspiration must attend any evaluation of the wisdom of *Daubert* and its impact on expert testimony in child sexual abuse prosecutions for the foreseeable future. In fashioning the new, broader standard for the receipt of expert testimony, the U.S. Supreme Court acknowledged the shifting, constantly evolving state of scientific knowledge. The trial and conviction of Galileo serves as a stern reminder that a scholarly community can misconceive whether a particular scientific theory constitutes a brilliant reconceptualization or heresy. The supreme court was also concerned with the here and now of trial determinations. It can take years for a scientific theory to be replicated and experimentally confirmed, refined, or rejected. In the meantime, what does one make of cold fusion, the orbits of asteroids, or the reliability of child sexual abuse accusations? As Sarason and Doris (1969) have counseled, "we must go by the best light possible" (p. 320, paraphrasing M. Arnold, 1869/1957).

The state of knowledge about the complexity and interaction of the testimonial reliability of children has exponentially advanced and changed over the past decade. If we believe in the infinite possibilities for scientific advancement, experts will be better court advisers in the decades of the next century.

---

[14]In felony prosecutions for serious offenses, only 7% are contested by trial; in the remainder, there is a guily plea. Nearly half a half of trial convictions (3.5%) are the product of a bench trial (no jury); the percentage of convictions by guilty plea (and by bench trial) are even higher in state misdemeanor cases (Alschuler & Deiss, 1994). Furthermore, in most states, judges resolve child custody disputes in the civil courts and dependency hearings in the juvenile courts. As Berliner (this volume, chapter 1) properly points out, the evidentiary barriers to the receipt of expert testimony were designed to insulate juries when sitting as the triers of fact. When the fact finder is a judge, "the risk of the fact finder being overawed by expert testimony or ceding the legal determination is reduced" (p. 15). Note that this is also an assumption that the law has traditionally made, although it has not been subjected to rigorous scientific scrutiny.

REFERENCES

Alschuler, A. W., & Deiss, A. G. (1994). A brief history of criminal jury in the United States. *University of Chicago Law Review, 61,* 867–928.

American Psychological Association. (1991, February 8). *Statement on the use of anatomically detailed dolls in forensic evaluations* (as adopted by the APA Council of Representatives). Washington, DC: Author. (Available from Governance Affairs)

Beardsley, M. C. (1950). *Thinking straight: A guide for readers and writers.* New York: Prentice Hall.

Colorado v. Connelly, 479 U.S. 157 (1986).

Daubert v. Merrell Dow Pharmaceuticals, Inc., 509 U.S., 113 S. Ct. 2786 (1993).

Esplin, P. W., Boychuk, T., & Raskin, D. C. (1988, June). *A field validity study of criteria-based content analysis of children's statements in sexual abuse cases.* Paper presented at the North Atlantic Treaty Organization's Advanced Study Institute on Credibility Assessment, Maratea, Italy.

Federal rules of evidence, 28 U.S.C. (West 1978).

Frye v. United States, 293 F. 1013 (D.C. Cir. 1923).

Lamb, M. E. (1994). The investigation of child sexual abuse: An international interdisciplinary consensus statement. *Family Law Quarterly, 28,* 151–162.

Mapp v. Ohio, 367 U.S. 643 (1961).

Massaro, T. M. (1988). The dignity value of face-to-face confrontations. *University of Florida Law Review, 40,* 863–918.

McCord, D. (1986). Expert psychological testimony about child complainants in sexual abuse prosecutions: A foray into the admissibility of novel psychological evidence. *Journal of Criminal Law & Criminology, 77,* 1–68.

McCord, D. (1987). Syndromes, profiles and other mental exotica: A new approach to the admissibility of nontraditional psychological evidence in criminal cases. *Oregon Law Review, 66,* 19–108.

McGough, L. S. (1995). *Child witnesses: Fragile voices in the American legal system.* New Haven, CT: Yale University Press.

Melton, G. B. (1994). Expert opinions: "Not for cosmic understanding." In B. D. Sales & G. R. VandenBos (Eds.), *Psychology in litigation and legislation* (pp. 59–99). Washington, DC: American Psychological Association.

Raskin, D. C., & Yuille, J. C. (1989). Problems in evaluating interviews of children in sexual abuse cases. In S. J. Ceci, D. F. Ross, & M. P. Toglia (Eds.), *Perspectives on children's testimony* (pp. 184–207). New York: Springer.

Rogers v. Richmond, 365 U.S. 534 (1961).

Sales, B. D., & VandenBos, G. R. (1995). Preface: The value of psychology to the law and law to psychology. In B. D. Sales & G. R. VandenBos (Eds.), *Psychology in litigation and legislation* (pp.1–9). Washington, DC: American Psychological Association.

Sarason, S. B., & Doris, J. (1969). *Psychological problems in mental deficiency*. New York: Harper & Row.

Sgroi, S. M. (1982). *Handbook of clinical intervention in child sexual abuse*. Lexington, MA: Lexington Books.

State v. Robert Fulton Kelly, Jr., Superior Criminal Court, Pitt County, NC, #91-CRS-4250–4363 (1991–1992).

Steller, M., & Kohnken, G. (1989). Criteria-based statement analysis. In D. C. Raskin (Ed.), *Psychological methods in criminal investigation and evidence* (pp. 217–245). New York: Springer.

Summit, R. C. (1992). Abuse of the child sexual abuse accommodation syndrome. *Journal of Child Sexual Abuse, 1*(4), 147–151.

AUTHOR INDEX

Numbers that are in italic indicate names that appear in the reference list.

283

Kohnken, G., *54*, 176, *183*, 276, *281*
Kolko, D. J., 169, *181*, 255, *263*
Koocher, G. P., 198, 199, *212*
Koppitz, E. M., 171, *181*
Kovera, M. B., 193–196, 198–202, 207, 209, *212*, 276n
Koverola, C., *25*, 180, *262*
Krantz, D. H., 205, *211*, *212*
Kravitz, D. A., 203, *214*
Kuhns, R. B., 138n, 138–140, 140n, 143, *154*
Kuiper, J., 169, *180*
Kwak, N., *51*, *54*
Kwon, P., 190, *213*

Ladd, M., 142, 146, *154*
Lamb, M. E., 176, *181*, 259, *263*, 276n, *280*
Landers, S., 173, *181*
Lang, R., *25*, 180, *262*
Langbein, J. H., 49, 50, *51*
Larus, D. M., 244, *247*
Laufer, W. S., *81*
Laws, D. R., *27*
Lawson, L., 17, *25*
Leeper, R. W., 108, *122*
Lehman, D. R., 205, 206, 209, *212*, *213*
Leichtman, M., 101, *103*, 245, 246, 259, *261*, *263*
Leippe, M. R., 192, *212*
Lempert, R. O., 205, *212*
Lepore, S. J., 259, *263*
Levasseur, G., *54*, *57*
Levine, M., 193, 210, 211, *214*
Levy, E. S., 49, *57*
Levy, R., 188, 198, 199, *212*, 226, *234*
Lewis, I. A., 17, *25*, 170, *180*, 245, *246*
Limber, S., 14, *26*, 177, *182*, 198, 207, *213*
Lindsay, D. S., 190, *213*
List, J. A., 190, *213*
Loftus, E., 76, *80*, 176, *183*
Loftus, E. F., 101, *103*, 240, 245, 246, *247*, 259, *261*
Lord, R., 134, *135*
Lozoff, B., 115, *122*
Lyon, T. D., 251, 256, 259, *263*

Maan, C., 199, *213*

MacFarlane, K., 219, 230, *234*
MacIntyre, A., 69, *80*
Maguire et al., *54*, *55*, *57*
Maitland, F. W., 49
Manor, T., *263*
Mansfield, M., *51*
Mant, K., *55*
Mapp v. Ohio, 277, *280*
Marcus, M., *51*
Markesinis, B. S., *51*
Marxsen, D., 241, *247*
Marshall, W. L., *27*
Mason, M. A., 2, 8, 14, *26*, 198, *213*, 220, 221, 224, 231, *234*
Massaro, T. M., 277, *280*
Matter of E. M., 223, *234*
May Committee, *57*
McAnulty, R. D., 15, *26*
McAuliff, B. D., 207, *212*
McCausland, M. P., 170, *179*
McColgan, E., *181*
McCord, D., 188, 192, *213*, 273n, *280*
McCord, J., 239, *246*
McCormick, C. T., 138, 141–143, *154*
McGough, L. S., 259, *263*, 273, 274, 277n, *280*
McGovern, K. B., 161, *182*
McGraw, J., 17, *25*, 177, *181*, 241, *246*
McIlkenny et al., *54*, *57*
McIver, W., 172, *182*
McKenney, 53
McLeer, S., 165, 166, *179*, *182*, 254, *262*
McNally, R. J., 22, *26*
Melton, G., 11, 14, 16, *26*, 130n, *135*, 177, *182*, 198, 207, *213*, 268, 271n, *280*
Merle, R., *52*
Michienzi, T., 166, *184*
Milchman, M., 160, 177, *179*, *182*
Mill, J. S., 59, *80*
Miller, A. G., 185, 204, *212*
Miller, J. S., 142, 143, *154*
Miller, P. S., *213*
Miller, T. W., 170, 175, *182*
Milsom, S. F. C., 49
Monahan, J., 13, *27*, 185, 209, *213*, *215*
Monteleone, J. A., *261*
Moran, T., 169, *180*, 255, *262*
Morgan, M. K., 172, *180*
Morison, S., 13, *26*
Mosek, M. D., 170, *184*
Moser, J. T., 255, *263*

SUBJECT INDEX

ABOUT THE EDITORS

Stephen J. Ceci holds a lifetime-endowed chair at Cornell University. His numerous awards include a Senior Fulbright-Hayes fellowship and a Research Career Science Award from the National Institutes of Health. He is a past president of Division 1 of APA and the author of several hundred articles, chapters, and books, including *Jeopardy in the Courtroom: A Scientific Analysis of Children's Testimony*.

Helene Hembrooke received her PhD in psychology from Binghamton University and is presently a postdoctoral fellow at Cornell University.